VANGUARD REVOLUTIONARIES IN LATIN AMERICA

D0964447

VANGUARD REVOLUTIONARIES IN LATIN AMERICA

Peru, Colombia, Mexico

JAMES F. ROCHLIN

LYNNE
RIENNER
PUBLISHERS

BOULDER
LONDON

Published in the United States of America in 2003 by
Lynne Rienner Publishers, Inc.
1800 30th Street, Boulder, Colorado 80301
www.rienner.com

and in the United Kingdom by
Lynne Rienner Publishers, Inc.
3 Henrietta Street, Covent Garden, London WC2E 8LU

Library of Congress Cataloging-in-Publication Data
Rochlin, James Francis, 1956–
Vanguard revolutionaries in Latin America : Peru, Colombia, Mexico /
  James F. Rochlin.
    p. cm.
  Includes bibliographical references and index.
  ISBN 1-55587-984-5 (hc. : alk. paper) — ISBN 1-58826-106-9 (pbk.)
    1. Latin America—Politics and government—20th century. 2. Insurgency—
Latin America—History—20th century. 3. Sendero Luminoso (Guerrilla group)
4. Fuerzas Armadas Revolucionarias de Colombia. 5. Ejército de Liberación
(Colombia) 6. Ejército Zapatista de Liberación Nacional (Mexico) I. Title.
F1414/2 .R55   2002
980.3'3—dc21   2002075198

British Cataloguing in Publication Data
A Cataloguing in Publication record for this book
is available from the British Library.

Printed and bound in the United States of America

      The paper used in this publication meets the requirements
 ∞   of the American National Standard for Permanence of
      Paper for Printed Library Materials Z39.48-1984.

    5 4 3 2 1

Contents

v

Acknowledgments

I especially want to thank Mark Kerpel for his superb research assistance. I am also deeply grateful to William Ramírez for helping so much during my sabbatical at the Instituto de Estudios Políticos y Relaciones Internacionales at the Universidad Nacional, Bogotá, Colombia. I owe a special thanks for the stellar work of the library staff at Okanagan University College. The inspiration from my students and my family was enormously beneficial. Ruth Rochlin, as always, was a constant source of encouragement and illumination. This project was funded by the Social Sciences and Humanities Research Council of Canada and by various grants from Okanagan University College. Special thanks to the staff at Lynne Rienner Publishers and to two anonymous reviewers whose comments were enlightening.

1

Introduction

The demise of international communism together with the "Revolution in Military Affairs" (RMA) ushered in a dramatically new landscape for Latin American guerrilla movements since the last decade of the twentieth century. The Soviet-Cuban models of development imploded and traditional ideologies lost relevance. A plethora of strategic uncertainties flowed from galloping transnational capitalism and from revolutionary technological developments in the realms of surveillance and communication. Complementing these transformations has been the privatization of warfare, leaving Latin American subversive groups to pursue largely independent sources of financing. Winds of profound change left existing guerrillas to rethink in a sweeping way the nature of their struggle, while emerging rebel groups faced the task of charting an entirely new course. The strategic successes and failures of these guerrilla movements, as well as of those of the state in its attempt to quell them, are related to how effectively each actor has reinterpreted classic strategic themes within a fresh system of knowledge.

The four most powerful Latin American guerrilla movements to operate against this shifting backdrop have been Peru's Sendero Luminoso (SL), Colombia's duo of the Fuerzas Armadas Revolucionarias de Colombia (FARC) and the Ejército de Liberación Nacional (ELN), and Mexico's Zapatistas. Each of these cases is fascinating in its own right. At its peak from 1989 to 1992, Sendero was clearly the most powerful and brutal guerrilla movement in Latin America, but it was snuffed out almost overnight as a result of the Peruvian government's newfangled approach to security. Colombia's FARC was clearly the most militarily powerful subversive movement in Latin America by the beginning of the twenty-first century. Despite the group's Marxist rhetoric, it seems to have more in common with Al Capone and the darker aspects of Clausewitz than with any leftist hero. Together with the somewhat kinder and gentler ELN, it has exacerbated the chaos and mayhem in Colombia to the point that it represents the Americas' most significant strategic crisis at the beginning of the twenty-first century. Mexico's Zapatistas, having begun as a traditional guerrilla group, brilliantly adapted to a shifting strategic context and have earned the title of the world's quintessential postmodern rebels. Beyond the importance of each of these cases individually, a comparative consideration of all four groups points to the transformations and continuities apparent in Latin American guerrilla struggles and the state's strategic attempt to cope with them.

There exists a considerable literature regarding the root causes of rebellion in Latin America and other third world countries, some unique to particular cases and others applicable in a more general fashion.[1] In the economic realm, such factors include poverty and profound economic inequity, unemployment and underemployment, the failure of a country to adapt to dominant economic trends, and the onset of general economic crisis. Common political themes include a lack of adequate representation, rising expectations, exclusion, and the failure of the state to act in tune with dominant international factors. Issues associated with identity politics have also emerged as highly prominent factors over the last decade, especially regarding ethnicity in relation to rebellion. Beyond the important work that has already been done in this regard, it will be suggested here that epistemological factors or systems of thought also can assist in probing the formation and durability of guerrilla movements. While the various causes behind the formation of subversive groups are open to debate, what seems constant is an utter hopelessness regarding the existing system by a considerable portion of the population, who feel compelled to risk everything including their lives in the name of rebellion.

Although the question of why people rebel is significant enough, the chief focus here will be *how* people rebel. Once the decision for rebellion is made, what accounts for the successes, failures, and longevity of these guerrilla groups? What can these cases tell us, individually and comparatively, about guerrilla strategy, power, and warfare in the twenty-first century? Also probed will be the meaning of these cases for conflict resolution and peace studies. Overall, this endeavor represents the concentric area between the fields of security studies, international relations theory, and the study of international political economy. After a brief overview of the cases under consideration, a subsequent section will present a conceptual framework for assessing the various guerrilla groups regarding their grasp of classic strategic themes. Following this will be a discussion of the revolution in military affairs, particularly how developments in the strategic realm rhyme with those in other academic fields of study. A final section will discuss the organization of the book.

The Cases

Peru's Sendero Luminoso formed in 1980 and reached a crescendo of power in 1989–1992, just following the end of the Cold War. The group made a serious bid for power against the Peruvian state and at times looked as if it might prevail in its struggle. Beyond its strength, SL was remarkable in its rigid neo-Maoist ideological platform, its astonishing deployment of horrific violence, its sometimes brilliant organizational and recruitment features, as well as its unique pyramid structure. Incredibly, the group's power base went from maximum to zero virtually overnight following the 1992 capture of its charismatic and dictatorial leader, Abimael Guzmán. The case also sheds light on the strategic successes and weakness of the Peruvian government, which blundered badly during the first ten years of its war with SL before turning to the use of intelligence services to obliterate the rebels. While scattered and insignificant remnants of Sendero linger into the twenty-first century, this rebel group may be finished politically. Hence one can examine SL in a postmortem sense, while the FARC and ELN were works in progress at the time of this writing.

In contrast to the return of relative peace and stability in Peru, the guerrilla struggle in Colombia has raged into the twenty-first century. The FARC represented Latin America's oldest and most militarily potent guerrilla group at the dawn of the millennium. The less powerful but still significant ELN also has deep roots, dating to the 1960s. Both these rebel movements grew more potent in the 1990s than they did during the three previous decades put together. The FARC presided over a special zone the size of Switzerland between 1998 and early 2002, and resorted to a policy of urban terror once it lost that land at the hands of the military. While subversive groups together control about 50 percent of Colombian territory, what is truly remarkable is the horrific degree of carnage that has pervaded the country, rendering it a chief contender for the dubious title of the most violent place on the planet at various points in the 1990s. Excepting the first few decades of the twentieth century, Colombia has been mired in almost nonstop warfare since independence in the 1820s. The Colombian case emerged as the hemisphere's most important strategic crisis in 2000, as evidenced by the implementation of Washington's $1.3 billion Plan Colombia, through which the United States essentially declared war on the FARC. This package boosted the country to the position of the third largest recipient of U.S. military aid in the world by 2002. The case stands as a showpiece for new features of strategy on the part of both the guerrillas and the U.S. government.

The shrewdly postmodern Zapatistas are perhaps the world's most mellow guerrillas, lacking military force but deriving considerable power by surfing a rising tide of both local and transnational social movements. The fact that they have existed within the bounds of the North American Free Trade Agreement (NAFTA) has made them a subject of both regional and national security. Also important in this case has been the strategy of both the U.S. and Mexican governments, which have had to learn the meaning of regional security extemporaneously, given that the Ejército Zapatista de Liberación Nacional (EZLN) emerged on NAFTA's inauguration day. Within the context of Latin America and perhaps the world, the Zapatistas are truly unique. The group's strategic context places it on a frontier of security studies.

While each of the cases is important in its own right, their collective similarities and differences are also worth considering. Common factors affecting the power and strategy of these guerrillas at some point in their struggles have been the context of poverty and maldistribution, crippling political errors on the part of the state, the exacerbation of social and economic tensions at least in the short term through neoliberal restructuring and erratic or inappropriate strategic attention on the part of the United States. Further, unlike the Nicaraguan case from 1979 to 1989, none of the groups considered here have been dependent upon the Soviet-Cuban alliance. Instead these guerrilla movements have been self-sufficient economically, which has permitted them a free and unfettered hand in their political endeavors.

The significant distinctions between the cases are also helpful analytically, since they can provide a wider scope for considering the continuities and alterations in hemispheric strategic affairs. Further, because guerrilla groups reflect widespread social discontent, these cases can also be of utility in a preventative sense since they point precisely to the variety of social vulnerabilities that can descend into the chaos of warfare. The strategic implications of the Zapatistas' nonviolent struggle through social movements, and their manipulation of the new technology of the Internet, are hugely important in defining emerging frontiers for guerrilla groups. A very different and highly violent struggle in Colombia poses some distinct strategic considerations, not the least of which is the enormous and alarming extent to which narcotrafficking and other crime can finance a formidable military machine for subversive movements. In Peru, Sendero's unique deployment of urban terrorism, its pyramid structure and cult of leadership, as well as the failure of the state's massive project of land reform to quell the development of subversive movements, suggest yet another set of strategic lessons. Taken together, these important and interesting cases provide a panorama of the emerging contours of Latin America's strategic terrain in the twenty-first century.

Classic Strategy and Systems of Knowledge

The guerrilla groups' catalog of strengths and successes, their litany of weaknesses and failures, are closely related to their grasp of classic themes of strategy. While these cases point to much that is fresh in the strategic realm, what is indeed new tends not to be the strategic theme itself but rather how a classic theme is filtered and interpreted through a particular epistemology or system of knowledge.[2] For example, while cyberspace is relatively novel within the fabric of strategic thinking, essentially it entails knowing traditional themes—strategic space, time, organization, and so on—in a new fashion. Hence, what tends to change is how those themes are known and interpreted, not the themes per se.

At times of great flux, rather than turning away from the various master strategists who have spanned the ages, a revisit to their masterpieces provides a clear point of reference to gauge strategic transformation and continuity. Further, a reread of the classic texts can assume a more exploratory and exciting ambience during epochs of great change and uncertainty. The texts can be untied from the intellectual constraints associated with relatively static periods such as the Cold War, when Western consultations with the classics were often reduced to the unifocus of fighting Soviet communism. This endeavor shall focus on security themes that appear in the works of various strategic thinkers writing in particular times, spaces, and epistemological epochs. Such thinkers include Thucydides, Sun Tzu I and Sun Tzu II, Machiavelli, Hobbes, and Clausewitz. Just as one could arrange a series of spheres such that they all share a concentric space while at the same time remaining distinct entities, these diverse strategic thinkers remain highly unique but at the same time have much in common with one another.

Many of these classic strategists authored their works on the cusp of major transformations in the history of ideas. Indeed, the chief intellectual gift of many of them is that they were among the first to interpret abrupt changes associated with systems of thought, and they applied these to the realm of strategic affairs. Thucydides, for example, is credited with providing the first "objective" view of history, viewing the Peloponnesian War through an epistemology that focused on facts, sequence, and spatial arrangement. While such an approach now seems commonplace, it was revolutionary at the time. It stood in contrast to the fashion in which the story of politics was typically told in ancient Greece, as evidenced by the works of Homer. His epic poems, *The Iliad* and *The Odyssey,* emphasized divine intervention, analogy, and how it felt to engage in warfare, rather than the factual account of political struggle in war as recorded by Thucydides. Another example of a brilliant strategist writing at the dawn of a fresh epistemological epoch is Machiavelli. He authored his classic works just prior to the emergence of the modern nation-state, early capitalism, and a host of other related changes in an emerging system of thought. As such, he is regarded as the quintessential pioneer in the art of statecraft.

Perhaps the bridge between the twentieth and twenty-first centuries represents another such chasm in terms of how the world is known in a strategic sense. One reflection of this is what some have deemed to be the revolution in military affairs.[3] Here we confront the mix of the old and the new: while certain security themes may appear to be universal or at least very enduring over time and space, they must be reinterpreted for new and particular circumstances. Part of this entails an epistemological shift. That is, universal security themes begin to fall within a new system of knowledge and need to be known or interpreted differently than in the past. These enduring strategic themes include space, time, intelligence/espionage, organization/leadership, coercion, consent, good government, and the perils of severe economic inequity.

Strategic Space

The politics of space represents a favorite theme for the strategic masters. Thucydides, for example, refers to the spatial frontiers of the oceans, the dangers of fighting in uncharted territory, and the importance of spatial defenses such as massive walls designed to seal off and protect cities.[4] Sun Tzu devotes a chapter of *The Art of War* to the topic of terrain, and frequently employs the analogy of water to demonstrate the strategic significance of formlessness and instantly perfect adaptability to given spaces.[5] Sun Tzu II warns that "terrain is what causes militias trouble."[6] It is a sentiment shared by many other strategists, such as Machiavelli, who underscores how significant it is to "learn the nature of the land, how steep the mountains are, how the valleys debouch, where the plains lie, and understand the nature of rivers and swamps."[7]

With even more gusto than the others, Clausewitz analyzed the various relations of space and warfare. He was perhaps the first to note the strategic significance of the spatial transformation of warfare precipitated by technological developments.[8]

If our conception of space "is fundamental in any exercise of power," how has this strategic theme transformed through differing epochs and systems of thought?[9] The twentieth century witnessed an alteration of combat that initially took place on the surface of the earth and then moved toward the air as well as beneath the surface.[10] At the start of the twenty-first century, political space has been compressed and in some respects virtually eliminated by the proliferation of surveillance and communication technology such as satellites and the Internet. In relation to the sudden appearance of cyberspace, the director of the U.S. National Security Agency in 1999 urged the public to "think of it as a physical domain, like land, sea and air."[11] The development of satellites and instruments of surveillance means that it is increasingly difficult to find a space to hide. This panopticon affects strategy and warfare in ways we are still discovering.[12] We shall explore in the case studies here the manner in which strategy is affected when the world becomes such a real-time cinema.[13] Beyond those issues, there are also strategic implications emanating from the political redrawing of spatial boundaries, as exemplified by the creation of NAFTA. Space is a fundamental feature of strategy, and the time frame for the guerrilla groups analyzed in this study has witnessed a great transformation regarding how strategic space is known. As we shall see, being on the cutting edge of appreciating such changes has translated into strategic success.

Temporal Politics

Time represents another standard theme for classic strategists. Sun Tzu, for example, is renowned for his observation that "the condition of a military force is that its essential factor is speed."[14] He also frequently refers to the weather and seasons in a fashion that suggests both the importance of mastering change and the value of strategic timing.[15] Machiavelli offers much advice on timing throughout *The Prince,* and in that work as well as *The Discourses* emphasizes the strategic significance of grasping the meaning of changing times.[16] Clausewitz, too, focuses on a variety of strategic dimensions of time, especially the element of duration vis-à-vis warfare.[17]

How is time known differently within the context of the RMA? As Alvin Toffler and Heidi Toffler have noted, "for only within recent decades have some of the key parameters of warfare hit their final limit.

These parameters are range, lethality, and speed."[18] A related idea concerns the realm of chronopolitics, whereby space is linked to time and both are compressed.[19] That is, surveillance and other electronic communication devices provide strategic information virtually instantaneously, sharply reducing time lapses to almost nothing while bringing the spatially far away up close instantly. Speed has become glorified in Western culture, and this is reflected in many dimensions of warfare.[20] But simpler and traditional dimensions of time still remain relevant in many ways. Strategically, then, time must be known both as instantaneous and according to traditional temporal relations. Thus the spectrum of this analysis ranges from an appreciation of the traditional temporal politics of Sendero's indigenous supporters, to the real-time surveillance images produced by Plan Colombia.

Intelligence

Nearly 2,000 years ago Sun Tzu observed that "only a brilliant ruler or a wise general who can use the highly intelligent for espionage is sure of great success."[21] A similar message is sent by Sun Tzu II.[22] It is also echoed by Machiavelli in *The Prince,* where he writes, "for being foreseen they can easily be remedied . . . for knowing afar off the evils that are brewing, they are easily cured."[23] But the strategic celebration of espionage hit a dead end of sorts with Clausewitz, who lamented:

> By "intelligence" we mean every sort of information about the enemy and his country—the basis, in short, of our own plans and operations. If we consider the actual basis of this information, how unreliable and transient it is, we soon realize that war is a flimsy structure that can easily collapse and bury us in ruins.[24]

Hence for Clausewitz a system of intelligence was viewed as a major contributor to the fog of warfare.

But enthusiasm for intelligence operations returned in spades once technology developed sufficiently to render information more reliable and less transient. By the end of the twentieth century, vital and accurate information could be provided virtually instantaneously, continuously, and globally, essentially erasing many Clausewitzean doubts regarding the value of intelligence. The significance afforded to intelligence and espionage has risen steadily, especially since World War I, and boomed with the revolution in military affairs at the start of the twenty-first century.[25] The RMA has placed information front and center in the realm of strategy. Terms such as *infowar* and *information dominance* are connotative of such alterations.[26] Some strategic futurists have argued, from what appears to be the perspective of economic determinism, that since knowledge has become the basis of economics, it is natural that this should be expressed in warfare, because both domains have common organizational principles.[27]

Thus intelligence and espionage are still important in the traditional sense of spying on an adversary to discover weaknesses or strategic opportunities. But these features are known in new ways in an information or knowledge war. Recent surveillance devices and communication breakthroughs such as the Internet, have provided nonstate actors and guerrilla groups such as the Zapatistas with the capacity to launch an information war that can debilitate government forces. Intelligence can be gathered by new actors and can be distributed in novel fashions to the new audience of global civil society. The most salient change in this regard is that significant information is available that does not have to pass through the ideological and political filters of the major news media, governments, and so forth. Further, as far as the state is concerned in its struggle with guerrilla movements, the RMA has meant a reliance on what the U.S. Department of Defense has referred to as C[4]ISR, or command, control, communication, computers, intelligence, surveillance, and reconnaissance.[28] We shall see that this has been a central feature in all the cases under consideration here.

Organization and Leadership

Sun Tzu argues that good leaders are humane, fair, and trustworthy and actively combat corruption.[29] Similar features are noted by Sun Tzu II in *The Lost Art of War*. Their spiritual mentor, Lao Tzu, observes that good leaders must above all provide social order.[30] These themes are echoed by Thucydides, who emphasizes the various political pitfalls that visit leaders who are tyrannical, selfish, and uncaring.[31] Hence there are a number of features of good leadership that classic strategists identify as necessary to promote political stability. Conversely, if classic lessons regarding good leadership go unheeded or are not interpreted properly within rapidly changing contexts, then subversive tendencies can mount. The increasingly hegemonic notion of democracy throughout Latin America has introduced a frontier such that leadership must be approached in a new fashion by aspiring politicians. This challenge has proven to be a formidable one, and if not handled properly it can contribute to profound strategic problems—as demonstrated by the Colombian case, for example.

The relation between power and good organization represents another common theme among the strategic masters.[32] A chief component of the

RMA entails a major transformation regarding who can be organized, how they can be organized, as well as the spatial location of members. For example, since the mid-1990s there has emerged what some have deemed to be a "social netwar," a phenomenon most apparent in the Mexican case.[33] It involves information warfare on the part of transnational civil society, with the Internet representing the primary and relatively inexpensive tool of organization and dissemination. Other novel forms of political organization concern transnational protest movements, such as those that orchestrate attention-grabbing political demonstrations at world meetings of global economic leaders. In this case, too, the Internet has served as a cheap, quick, and effective method of political organization. The Internet has thus created the possibility of spatially dispersed organizational membership through the instantaneous and continuous connectivity that flows through personal computers. This revolutionary change entails a fundamentally different system of thought regarding time, space, and political organization, and has been embraced in a pioneering way by both guerrilla groups and opposing government forces.

Coercion, Consent, and Good Government

Perhaps the single biggest contributor to the central strategic dimension of the modern nation-state was Thomas Hobbes. He argued that "men have no pleasure (but on the contrary a great deale of griefe) in keeping company, where there is no power able to over-awe them all."[34] Hence, a Leviathan in the form of a state would essentially monopolize armed force to ensure an atmosphere of peace and order rather than warfare and chaos—an idea upon which Max Weber would later build.[35] While achieving the status of Leviathan was never easy, the challenges have become geometrically more difficult for developing countries.

It has become more difficult for the state to monopolize armed force for a number of reasons. The neoliberal era, for example, has been accompanied by the astonishing ascent of the illicit narcotics industry. In both the Colombian and Peruvian cases, narcotrafficking has bankrolled an enormous and sophisticated arms cache for guerrilla movements, and has corrupted the armed forces. Beyond this, even for those groups that lack the lavish finances afforded by the global drug trade, weapons capable of mass destruction are now relatively cheaply made and readily available (e.g., biological weapons, chemical weapons, cylinder bombs). Further, the Leviathan's general objective of "over-awing" subversive tendencies now means far more than the huge task of controlling weapons. It also necessitates, for example, coping with infowar or social netwar. The notion of a Leviathan thus requires transformation to keep pace with alterations in the nature of the state, as well as with respect to vast shifts in the realms of economy, military technology, communications technology, identity politics, and the like.

Closely related to this is the enduring strategic duality concerning the use of force on the one hand, and the power of consent on the other. Coercion—the trinity of warfare, murder, and destruction—is an age-old theme.[36] Perhaps the most unabashed justification for strategic violence comes from Clausewitz, who argues that war is simply "part of man's social existence" and that it is "resolved by bloodshed."[37] Further, he observes that "the maximum use of force is in no way incompatible with the simultaneous use of the intellect."[38] By contrast, while both Sun Tzu I and Sun Tzu II wrote extensively regarding the mechanics of warfare and combat, prominent in their works are clear warnings regarding the limits associated with the use of political violence. Sun Tzu, for example, wrote that "those who render others' armies helpless without fighting are the best of all," and that "those who are not thoroughly aware of the disadvantages in the use of arms cannot be thoroughly aware of the advantages in the use of arms."[39] In a similar vein, Sun Tzu II warns that "those who enjoy militarism, however, will perish" and that "those who despise violence are warriors fit for kings."[40] Hence violence and political murder were to be taken with the utmost seriousness and to be used as sparingly as possible. Both Sun Tzu I and Sun Tzu II were expounding on the chief objective of how to prevail in conflict, the strategic goal being not violent warfare but how to get the upper hand. While Mexico's Zapatistas in particular have largely avoided the use of force, generally a reliance on military might has been a definitive feature of guerrilla warfare and remains so. Certainly Sendero and the FARC have relied heavily on the power of destruction and coercion.

This debate regarding the political utility of force has been revisited in the literature regarding the RMA. The concept of "demassification" of destruction, for example, has been referred to as an emerging third wave of warfare involving more frequent cases where massive death and destruction are absent from conflict.[41] This is because political control increasingly can be achieved through nonviolent maneuvers, such as economic pressure, information warfare, and the use of intelligence rather than force to limit the power of enemy forces. For these same reasons, physical occupation of territory is unnecessary in many cases.[42] The United States, for example, since the closing decades of the twentieth century generally has not relied on military occupation by its own forces to combat guerrilla movements in Latin America. This study will explore the extent to which traditional force remains relevant for new-fangled guerrilla warfare.

The concept of power derived from consent has been a central feature of the neo-Gramscian, or critical realist, school of global politics since the late 1980s.[43] It builds on Gramsci's famous pronouncement that "if the ruling class has lost its consensus, i.e. no longer 'leading' but only 'dominant,' exercising coercive force alone, this means precisely that the great masses have become detached from their traditional ideologies, and no longer believe what they used to believe previously, etc."[44] But this same general idea has been prominent in the works of the strategic masters over the last 2,400 years. Thucydides notes, for example, that Athens's ultimate loss of the Peloponnesian War was due in part to its enslavement of colonies, which turned on the Athenians as soon as the first opportunity presented itself. Having failed to cultivate consent, Athens saw its power debilitated.[45] Similarly, a central component of "the Way"—the dominant concept for both Sun Tzu I and Sun Tzu II—concerns "winning the hearts of the people."[46]

Further, while the idea of societal consent to strengthen leadership is not often associated with the works of Machiavelli, this nevertheless is a prominent theme especially in *The Discourses*. He argues that

> When a prince or a republic is afraid of its subjects and fears they may rebel, the root cause for this fear must lie in the hatred which such subjects have for their rulers: a hatred which is due to their misbehavior; and a misbehavior which is due to their fancying they can hold them by force, or to their foolish way of governing them.[47]

A very similar idea regarding the power of consent is Arab philosopher Ibn Khaldun's concept of "asabia," or social solidarity.[48] Thus there exists considerable agreement among prominent strategists and political thinkers, writing in different times and spaces, that power derived from consent rather than coercion can be more potent and enduring. It is a lesson from which both the state and subversive forces can benefit. To derive consent, it is also necessary to master the related themes mentioned above regarding organization, leadership, and so on, and come to grips with the enormous transformations in those arenas. The failure to muster consent, on the part of both the state and guerrilla movements, has proven to be a major strategic calamity for many of the political actors considered in this study. The Colombian case represents the most extreme example of this.

Inequity and Political Economy

One obvious reason that there are strong guerrilla movements in Latin America concerns general poverty combined with an increasingly inequitable distribution of income in the region. Class consciousness is a significant political factor in Peru, Mexico, and Colombia, and affects the strategies and objectives of both guerrillas and the state.[49] While class as such did not become an analytical category until Marx, classic strategists have noted the dangers of inequity and poverty over the millennia. Earlier we observed Thucydides' suggestion that part of the reason for Athens's ultimate loss in its war with Sparta concerned its enslavement of colonies, a situation that benefited Athens in the short run but that eventually contributed to the downfall of its empire. In a similar fashion, Sun Tzu II suggests that "to accumulate wealth for the people is the means whereby you may accumulate wealth yourself; this is how warriors last."[50] Echoing this general sentiment, Machiavelli warns of the perils associated with leadership that has "injured many and benefited but few."[51]

The point is that issues concerning material well-being, gross inequity, and a rigid and nonfluid class system can result in grave strategic crises by provoking subversive dissent. Such themes must be addressed within the context of the massive shifts that have occurred in the global political economy during the transition from national capitalism in a bipolar world to transnational capitalism in a unipolar world. This is twinned by a new system of thought that reflects the increasing power of finance capital and speculation, the role of knowledge as a basis of economy, the implications of transnational production, and so on—points to which we shall return. Such shifts have drastically altered state structures and social arrangements in the countries under consideration here, and have helped set the stage for subversive movements.

Security, Synergy, and Systems of Thought

Clearly there have been profound changes within the realms of classic strategic themes such as time, space, leadership, organization, consent, coercion, intelligence, political economy, and so on. Although each of these is important in its own right, taken together they signal a rupture in strategic affairs. As one student of strategy observed, "it is the synergy of all these individual effects that create the potential to revolutionize warfare."[52] This synergy is a reflection of widespread changes within a larger system of thought that is analogous in some ways to raspberry cane.[53] While various canes appear in a number of distinct sites that are sometimes quite distant from one another, and may also appear to be unique in many ways, beneath the surface they are linked by a common root system. Further, at certain points in the history of thought there are "sudden take-offs," or what might be referred to as discontinuity—"the fact that within the space of a few years a culture sometimes ceases to think as it had been thinking up till then and begins to think other things in a new way."[54] Hence the cacophony of strategic changes suggested above, taken together, constitute a discontinuity of security that is reflected in a wider transformation of a system of knowledge.

There have been vast and obvious alterations in the realms of science, economy, political identity, and philosophy, as well as spatial and temporal relations. While each of these subjects merits its own volume, let us consider briefly some of the prominent dimensions of such changes in relation to strategic affairs. Much can be said, for example, about shifts in science vis-à-vis security. Technological developments—those that gird alterations in the fields of economy, weaponry, space, and time—are perhaps the most obvious. Beyond this, the modern era—which began around the end of the eighteenth century and ended in the second half of the twentieth—was characterized by a scientific focus on function in relation to the field of biology: biologists probed the functions of plants, animals, and humans.[55] Recently, however, there has been a greater focus on the biosphere, a new and more complex field of study. Rather than focusing on function per se, it emphasizes the transforming and complex relationships among all life forms. With regard to strategic studies, we are concerned not only with the security effects of environmental change, but also with the effects of warfare on the environment. With regard to the specific cases under study here, we shall see that both the Colombian and Mexican situations clearly demonstrate the relation between warfare and ecocide, and between strategy and the biosphere.

Also within the rubric of science, chaos theory, as manifested in the theoretical pursuits of physics and math, has been gaining ground on modern approaches that focused on equilibrium and balance.[56] Strategic studies, reflecting the same epistemological shift, has seen balance of power theory placed on the defensive against a proliferation of rivals who emphasize mounting chaos, disorder, and instability.[57] This development was presaged by some postmodern theorists.[58] Terrorism, the proliferation of increasingly inexpensive but highly potent weapons, widening economic strife, the ultradissemination of information, and threats to the spatial politics of the nation-state, are among the innumerable perils that threaten global stability. Many of those factors, which together breed political chaos, have been present in the guerrilla struggles of Peru, Colombia, and Mexico. If the modern concepts of balance and equilibrium are on the ropes in the world of mathematics and physics, that goes double for security studies, and it is reflected in the cases under consideration here.

During the epoch of modernity, the discipline of economics focused on national production and on industrialization.[59] But increasing attention rightly has been directed toward speculation. The reason is clear: by the late 1990s about 90 percent of all global economic transactions comprised speculative and finance capital, with the production of goods and services representing the remaining 10 percent. These figures represent the reverse of the situation in 1973, following the breakdown of the Bretton Woods system and the subsequent dismantling of fixed exchange rates.[60] There are strategic implications associated with this reversal. We shall see, for example, that chaotic shifts of speculative and finance capital have had punishing effects on Mexico, Colombia, and Peru at precisely the times that subversive activity was gaining ground.

A second and related shift lies in the astounding political role performed by the finance of official government debt. The manipulation of debt can be employed as the ultimate political tool, with its capacity to reshape in the most sweeping way a country's system of economics, government, and culture. As recently as a few of decades ago, military interventions and coups, sometimes supported by the United States, figured prominently in Latin American politics. To some extent this has been displaced by the power of debt manipulation. The post-1982 era of almost perpetual debt crisis has provided the United States with the most complete form of power it has possessed since it formally announced plans to dominate the hemisphere in the 1823 Monroe Doctrine. The politics of debt has meant considerable adjustment pain for the countries examined here, and as a result has exacerbated social tension and stimulated subversion.

A third shift within the field of economics concerns changing patterns of production. Here the term *globalization* is a misnomer in the sense that while finance capital is pervasive globally, production has become increasingly regional. NAFTA is an obvious example of this. To the degree that production has shifted from the national to the regional level, what is required within the realm of strategic studies is a correlative metamorphosis from national to regional security.[61] Not only has this rendered the Mexican situation a case of regional security under NAFTA, it has also created a starker two-tiered system of strategic and economic importance for Washington: the exalted position of Mexico versus the rest of Latin America. Hence, because of vastly shifting production arrangements, Mexico is far more important to the United States than it has ever been, while other cases examined here indicate an uneven and erratic interest by Washington.

The swelling of the informal economy represents another major transformation that affects the realms of both economics and strategic studies. While it has always existed, the informal economy has been particularly powerful in the recent era in the form of narcotrafficking and associated criminal activity. In Latin America, it is directly correlated to the debt crisis and the subsequent neoliberal restructuring, since the trafficking of illicit drugs has provided dollars badly needed by banks and government coffers. It has also supplied jobs and even social welfare programs. Yet it is hidden from official figures regarding gross domestic product (GDP), employment, social services, and the like. Beyond this, it has provided enormous financial resources to powerful guerrilla groups in Colombia and Peru, which have not had to rely on foreign sources of funding as some guerrillas in the Cold War relied on the Soviet Union. It has corrupted governments as well, as in the Mexican case, where guerrillas have bolstered their strength by criticizing obvious government narco-corruption. Overall, enormous shifts in the economic realm have spelled equally significant challenges for security studies.

Considerable change has also occurred within the wide arena of Western philosophy. Modernity was characterized by philosophies that emphasized objectivity, binary thought, origins, human nature, linear progress, and so on. Many of these features persist, but important alterations are apparent with regard to security issues. First, the dispersion of "truth" and the waning of binary thought have not escaped notice by the U.S. government and its leading organic intellectuals. One prominent thinker emphasized the likelihood during the post–Cold War era of a "clash of civilizations," such that Islamic and Confucian-Chinese truths increasingly may be at odds with a U.S.-led Western epistemology.[62] A related phenomenon has been the ascent of identity politics, which entails a political regrouping based on identity categories such as gender and ethnicity. Occasionally falling by the wayside have been clear and binary categories of right/wrong. We shall see that a clash of knowledge structures has been a serious problem faced by governments and guerrilla groups alike in relation to all the cases considered here. The Zapatistas, for example, seized upon an emerging postmodern knowledge structure to assert power, while Sendero Luminoso clashed with the knowledge structure of its own indigenous supporters.

Beyond the wide issue of how one knows the world, epistemology also concerns how one knows something to be true. How is the notion of truth changing, and how is this reflected in the revolution in military affairs? Objective or quantifiable truth still matters. No one will quarrel with the proposition that two plus two equals four. Yet in many ways the concept of political truth has altered vastly. Prior to the revolution in communications technology and surveillance devices, the state and the large media corporations were largely able to manufacture unchallenged political truth. Bolstering this was the political space of the nation-state and the related power of patriotism. But with devices such as the Internet, the state has had a much more difficult time cornering the market on political truth. Information dissemination from such nonstate sources as Internet discussion and news groups as well as nongovernmental organizations (NGOs) means that there is a proliferation of political information that does not have to pass through the confining ideological filters of the state and elite media. Political truth can now be shaped by new actors with new information, sometimes in a fashion that is subversive to state interests.

There are other challenges to what counted as political truth during the epoch of modernity. For example, there is perhaps a more noticeable relationship emerging between spirituality and political truth, as evidenced in some Islamic countries and in Latin America through liberation theology. As well, identity politics—in terms of ethnicity, gender, sexuality, and so on—sometimes entails the shaping of a political truth that does not conform to that of the state or to the spatial boundaries of the nation-state as reflected in national patriotism. The new truths of liberation theology and identity politics have been profoundly important to the Zapatistas' struggle.

Not only do transformations occur within specific fields of study, but they tend to be underpinned by common epistemological links. When one speaks of modernity, reference is made to a number of prominent and interrelated themes within a single system of thought. These are expressed within various fields including strategic studies. For example, modernity entails an emphasis on ideas such as progress, objectivity, binary thought, centrality, balance and equilibrium, production, patriotism, and the political space of the nation-state. But some of those notions appear to be the subject of significant alteration. There appear to be louder doubts about progress, or at least how progress is defined. Rather than centrality, there is a growing focus upon the dispersion of power. Instead of a preoccupation with balance and equilibrium, there is a more pronounced concern with chaos and disorder. There is increasing acknowledgment of differences and multiple truths, rather than a focus on objective truth and binary thought. In contrast to the nation-state and state-based patriotism, political space is more influenced by global and regional boundaries and by ethnic and other identity politics. The examples continue, since such changes are apparent not only in academic fields, but also within many aspects of life in general.

Jean-Francois Lyotard suggested that the term *postmodern* could "describe the condition of knowledge in the most highly developed societies."[63] Hence the dominance of a single system of thought may be a component of some definitions of development. By contrast, developing countries may sometimes host an odd mixture of various epistemological approaches. In Colombia, for example, a patchwork is discernible that entails elements of premodern, modern, and postmodern systems of thought, with none of these apparently dominant. Further, one proposition worthy of further study is that the dominance of a particular epistemological system may also be linked to stability, while admixtures may correlate with instability, or in extreme cases, chaos. With regard to the countries under consideration here, we shall see that Mexico most fully hosts a dominant system of thought, while the less stable cases of Peru and especially Colombia are characterized by the absence of a dominant epistemological approach.

Finally, transformations and continuities in systems of thought are naturally reflected in conceptions of power. The postmodern Zapatistas, for example, have claimed that they do not seek "to take power over" the state, which has been precisely the aim of the more traditional guerrillas such as the FARC and Sendero Luminoso. Conceptions of power affect objectives as well as strategies. The Zapatistas, for instance, have organized a constituency based on identity politics of gender, ethnicity, ecology, and so on, while the FARC and Sendero have relied on the modern Marxist schemes of class politics to achieve their goals. The same general argument applies to the state in its attempt to stem the tide of subversion. A state that is out of synch with fundamental ruptures in an epistemology of security is likely to be doomed in its efforts, as was the case with the Peruvian government until about 1989 and with the Mexican government until about 1995. Both of those states met considerably greater success when they adjusted their strategies to fit a new system of thought emerging in the security arena.

Organization of the Book

The Peruvian case will be the first to be examined. Although Sendero Luminoso reached its apex of power in the post–Cold War era, it is largely a spent force that can be analyzed through the rearview mirror. It had its roots in developments of the 1960s and is clearly the most traditional of the groups analyzed here. Thus it provides a point of contrast from which to consider the other two cases. Following this will be an examination of the Colombian guerrillas. At the time of this writing, the struggle in Colombia represented a work in progress, one that embodied the most serious revolutionary struggle in the Americas. Another continuing saga involves the situation of the Zapatistas in Mexico, where the actions of both the rebels and the state represent the most positive scenario of the cases under consideration. Two chapters each are devoted to the situations in Peru, Colombia, and Mexico. The first of these analyzes the guerrillas' origins, ideology, and support base, while the second examines the rebels in relation to power, strategy, and security. A final chapter offers comparative analytical conclusions.

Notes

1. A short list of excellent contributions in this regard includes Blasier, "Social Revolution"; Booth and Walker, *Understanding Central America;* Castañeda, *Utopia Unarmed;* Collier and Collier, *Shaping the Political Arena;* Dix, "Varieties of Revolution"; Goodwin and Skocpol, "Explaining Revolutions"; Gurr, *Why Men Rebel;* McClintock, *Revolutionary Movements in Latin America;* Moore, *Social Origins of Dictatorship and Democracy;* Skocpol, *States and Revolutions;* Tilly, "War Making and State Making"; and Wickham-Crowley, *Guerrillas and Revolution in Latin America.*

2. The definition of *epistemology* used in this work is found in *The Oxford Dictionary of Philosophy* and begins as follows: "The theory of knowledge. Its central questions include the origin of knowledge; the place of experience in generating knowledge, and the place of reason in doing so; the relationship between knowledge and certainty, and between knowledge and the impossibility of error; the possibility of universal scepticism; and the changing forms of knowledge that arise from new conceptualizations of the world." See Simon Blackburn, *The Oxford Dictionary of Philosophy* (Toronto: Oxford University Press, 1994), p. 123.

3. For a discussion of the revolution in military affairs (RMA), see Owens, "Technology, the RMA, and Future War."

4. In this case of fighting in uncharted territory, Thucydides was referring to Sicily. See Thucydides, *History of the Peloponnesian War,* bks. 6–7. On spatial defenses, see p. 51.

5. On terrain, see Sun Tzu, *Art of War,* chap. 10, pp. 143–148. On the analogy of water, see pp. 92, 96, 112.

6. Sun Tzu II, *Lost Art of War,* p. 31.

7. See Machiavelli, *Prince,* p. 82. See also Machiavelli, *Discourses,* p. 501.

8. See Clausewitz, *On War,* p. 134. See also pp. 543–545, 348–352.

9. Foucault, "Space, Knowledge, and Power," p. 360.

10. Virilio and Lotringer, *Pure War,* p. 177.

11. Comment by Lt. Gen. Michael V. Hayden, *Los Angeles Times,* 31 October 1999.

12. See Foucault, *Discipline and Punish.* Regarding the panopticon, see especially pp. 200–216. Regarding surveillance, see pp. 148, 170, 176.

13. See Virilio and Lotringer, *Pure War,* p. 85.

14. Sun Tzu, *Art of War,* p. 152.

15. Ibid. See, for example, pp. 42, 44.

16. Machiavelli, *Discourses,* p. 430.

17. Clausewitz, *War,* pp. 143, 205–209.

18. See Toffler and Toffler, *War and Anti-War,* p. 30.

19. See Virilio and Lotringer, *Pure War,* p. 13. See also Virilio, *Speed and Politics.*

20. The celebration of speed is apparent in so many aspects of daily Western life, such as the craving for ever faster computers as well as the pandering of sports cars with maximum velocities that vastly exceed normal roadway speed limits.

21. See Sun Tzu, *Art of War,* p. 172. See also pp. 2, 82, 116.

22. Sun Tzu II, *Lost Art of War,* p. 40.

23. Machiavelli, *Prince,* p. 39.

24. Clausewitz, *War,* p. 117.

25. On the rise on intelligence/espionage since World War I, see Ferris and Handel, "Clausewitz, Intelligence, Uncertainty, and the Art of Command," esp. p. 46.

26. See, for example, Brown, "Revolution in Military Affairs"; and Arquilla and Ronfeldt, "Cyberwar Is Coming!"

27. Toffler and Toffler, *War and Anti-War,* p. 71.

28. U.S. Department of Defense, *C4, Intelligence, Surveillance, and Reconnaissance,* p. 1, www.dtic.mil/execsec/adr96/chapt_27.html.

29. Sun Tzu, *Art of War,* pp. 43, 45, 91.

30. Lao Tzu, *Tao te Ching,* p. 12.

31. Thucydides, *History of the Peloponnesian War,* pp. 13, 113, 163.

32. See, for example, Sun Tzu, *Art of War,* pp. 84–93; Sun Tzu II, *Lost Art of War,* pp. 51–53; and Clausewitz, *War,* esp. bk. 5, pp. 279–356.

33. See Ronfeldt et al., *Zapatista Social Netwar in Mexico.*

34. Hobbes, *Leviathan,* p. 185.

35. Max Weber argued that the modern state is a "human community which within a given territory claims for itself the monopoly of legitimate physical coercion." See Weber, *Economía y sociedad,* vol. 2, p. 1056.

36. Thucydides, *History of the Peloponnesian War,* p. 200.

37. Clausewitz, *War,* p. 149.

38. Ibid., p. 75.

39. Sun Tzu, *Art of War,* pp. 67, 59.

40. Sun Tzu II, *Lost Art of War,* pp. 21, 42.

41. Toffler and Toffler, *War and Anti-War,* p. 72.

42. See Szafranski, "Theory of Information Warfare"; Arquilla, "Strategic Implications of Information Dominance"; and Der Derian, "Interview with Paul Virilio."

43. See, for example, Cox, *Production, Power, and World Order;* and Gill, *Gramsci, Historical Materialism, and International Relations.*

44. Gramsci, *Selections from the Prison Notebooks,* pp. 275–276.

45. Thucydides, *History of the Peloponnesian War,* pp. 163–164.

46. Sun Tzu II, *Lost Art of War,* p. 51.

47. Machiavelli, *Discourses,* p. 353.

48. Issawi, *Arab Philosophy of History,* pp. 101, 109, 129.

49. The strong class consciousness in many Latin American countries stands in contrast to the situation in the United States and Canada, for example.

50. Sun Tzu II, *Lost Art of War,* p. 67.

51. Machiavelli, *Prince,* p. 86.

52. Brown, "Revolution in Military Affairs," p. 39.

53. For a broader discussion of episteme and systems of thought, see Foucault, "Will to Knowledge," p. 11. Foucault's best work on the topic of changing epistemes is *The Order of Things: An Archaeology of the Human Sciences,* where he traces the changing system of thought from modernity to postmodernity.

54. Foucault, *Power/Knowledge,* p. 112; and Foucault, *Order of Things,* p. 50.

55. Foucault, *Order of Things.* See esp. chap. 7, pp. 226–232, and chap. 8, pp. 263–279, 289–294.

56. See, for example, Gleick, *Chaos;* Hall, *Exploring Chaos;* and Ruelle, *Chance and Chaos.* See also Kiel, *Chaos Theory in the Social Sciences.* Within the realm of postmodern thought, there is an emphasis on discontinuity and dispersion, which can sometimes rhyme with chaos. See Foucault, *Order of Things;* and Foucault, *Archaeology of Knowledge.* See also Harvey, *Condition of Postmodernity.*

57. Kaplan, "Coming Anarchy"; and Kaplan, *Ends of the Earth.*

58. In *Archaeology of Knowledge,* Michel Foucault argues that "we must accept the introduction of chance as a category in the production of events" (p. 230), which suggests that his central concept of discontinuity is in some respects coterminous with "great accidents" (p. 28). See also Virilio *Speed and Politics;* and Virilio and Lotringer, *Pure War.* More recently, Jean Baudrillard observes that "speculation and chain reactions [are] spinning off towards the extremes of a facticity with which interpretation can no longer keep place." See Baudrillard, *Illusion of the End,* p. 15.

59. Foucault, *Order of Things,* chap. 8; Cox, *Production, Power, and World Order.*

60. A good discussion of this is found in Wriston, "Twilight of Sovereignty."

61. Rochlin, *Redefining Mexican Security.*

62. Huntington, "Clash of Civilizations?"

63. Jean-Francois Lyotard, "The Postmodern Condition: A Report on Knowledge," in Lawrence Cahoone, ed., *From Modernism to Postmodernism: An Anthology* (Cambridge, Mass.: Blackwell, 1996), p. 481. By contrast, Michel Foucault argues that "in any given culture and at any given moment, there is always only one episteme that defines the conditions of all possible knowledge." See Foucault, *Order of Things,* p. 168.

PERU

- National capital
- Department capital
- Town
- Airport
- International boundary
- Department boundary
- Railroad

Callao has the status of a Department.

The boundaries and names shown and the designations used on this map do not imply official endorsement or acceptance by the United Nations.

0   100   200   300 km
0   100   200 mi

Map No. 3838 Rev. 1   UNITED NATIONS
September 2000

Department of Public Information
Cartographic Section

PERU

2

Peru:
The Origins, Ideology, and
Support Base of Sendero Luminoso

Sendero Luminoso emerged in 1980 as one of Latin America's most potent and ferocious guerrilla movements of the twentieth century. At its peak, between 1989 and 1992, it was able to launch an astonishing and credible bid for power against the Peruvian state. Sendero derived much of its power by relying on ethnic factors, and by resurrecting the memory of historical greatness associated with the Inca civilization. The leadership of SL successfully harnessed this through the false promise of restoring grandeur and power to Peru's majority indigenous population. Sendero also flourished through an ideology of violence that unleashed centuries of latent indigenous resentment over their physical punishment, subjugation, and exploitation at the hands of various masters.

SL attempted to employ a neo-Maoist framework to transform Peru into a modern nation-state from its existing predicament, which was marked by premodern elements. Ultimately SL's approach collided with the system of thought predominant among much of Peru's indigenous population, who represented an important pillar of support. It was one factor among others that contributed to the movement's demise. Sendero's most fatal vulnerability, however, proved to be its pyramid framework coupled with the deified status of its leader, without whom the group was unable to survive.

SL's rigidly neo-Maoist perspective was extrapolated to Peru by the movement's charismatic president, Abimael Guzmán. Among Sendero members, but generally not others, he was worshipped as the fourth sword of Marxism after Marx himself, Lenin, and Mao. Guzmán presided in a dictatorial fashion through a notorious cult of leadership. Remarkably, students composed the group's largest sector of membership, a reflection of the leadership's brilliant organizational strategy of tapping

23

into the existing state-organized network of education to recruit Sendero devotees.

In relation to SL, at least two major streams of Peruvian history are worthy of consideration. The first concerns the great Inca civilization, which has continued to represent a focal point for recent indigenous struggle. Although Peru has been unable to achieve a modern sense of nation and internal political hegemony, a social unity of roughly that kind prevailed during the reign of the Incas. This is crucial because the story of Inca greatness and unity clearly has suggested to Peru's indigenous population the possibility of achieving solidarity and grandeur in the future. In particular, this has represented a catalyst of sorts for Sendero's political action. A second and related strain of Peruvian history since the Spanish Conquest of the early 1500s concerns the effects of the country's subjugation first to Spain, then to England, and most recently to the United States. A legacy of exploitation, debt, and general maldevelopment provided ready-made fodder for SL to create a radical and isolationist ideology.

The first part of this chapter explores the tapestry of historical and contextual elements that set the stage for the emergence of Sendero Luminoso. Next the focus will be upon the ideological underpinning of the rebels, based largely on an analysis of the group's original documents. The intriguing nature of Sendero's support base is addressed in a subsequent section. We shall also briefly consider the group's rivals, the much less powerful but still important Peruvian guerrilla organization Movimiento Revolucionario Túpac Amaru (MRTA). This will serve as a point of contrast from which to consider the origins, ideology, and support base of Sendero.

Historical Greatness: The Inca Civilization and Peru's Indigenous Population

Among its roster of extraordinary features, the Inca Empire was orderly, efficient, and centralized. Geographically, it included what is today Peru, Bolivia, Ecuador, and parts of Chile and Argentina, and was connected by a vast network of some 14,000 miles of paved roads. The official Inca language was Quechua, which is still spoken by many in the mountainous regions of southern Peru. The empire had a rich spiritual dimension, and the pantheistic Incas considered all matter to be divine.[1] Economically, they were highly efficient and relied on an essentially communal system of production, especially with regard to farming.

Much of the land was richly endowed with natural treasures—such as gold, silver, and other metals—and yielded fine agricultural produce. Hence, given its beauty, its great natural resources, and its orderly nature, it is easy to understand why Peru became the jewel of Spain's colonial empire in the Americas. The indigenous population made an easy target for Spanish domination, as the majority fell prey to European diseases.[2]

First by the Spanish and then by national feudal lords, the indigenous people would succumb to economic and political subjugation, cultural destruction, and so on. Thus, the stage was set for a charismatic political leader to appear among the destitute indigenous population with the message that it was not always like this, that the splendor and pride of the Inca Empire could be restored. That was a fundamental tenet of Túpac Amaru II, a revered Indian rebel who led an uprising during the late eighteenth century against Spanish colonial arrangements.[3] One of his most famous rallying calls was: "Campesino! Your property shall no longer feed the masters."[4] Although the rebellion ultimately was suppressed, it remained a symbol of ethnic-political unity and hinted at prospects for successful uprisings in the future. This would prove to be a fundamental ingredient of Abimael Guzmán's fiery rhetoric. The greatness of the Inca Empire has remained alive in the hearts of many of Peru's indigenous population. Among a complicated assortment of other variables, it was one important element that contributed to the revolutionary spark of Sendero Luminoso.

A striking feature in much of the literature regarding Peru is that over the last century or so the country has accumulated three distinct systems of knowledge and production. Mariátegui, whose contributions we shall discuss more fully below, observed the coexistence of three types of production systems: Indian communal, feudal, and bourgeois.[5] While Marxist writers emphasize ruptures in economic arrangements, there have also been equally important shifts in the realm of epistemology. These have been reflected in attitudes toward time and space, the role of spiritual knowledge, of conceptions of truth, of proper political structure, and of progress, among other elements. Two important points can be made about this odd mixture of production and knowledge systems. First, it has been related to a pronounced social fragmentation that has impeded the formation of a "hegemonic class."[6] Second, as various episodes have demonstrated, the great art of Peruvian politics would be how to manipulate these three concurrent realities.

This fragmentation of productive structures and of epistemology is related to the trilogy of geography, race, and class.[7] The poverty-stricken indigenous population of Inca ancestry has been concentrated in Peru's mountainous Andean region. It was the location of the Spanish extraction of gold, silver, and other precious metals, and has also been the site of a pronounced clash between feudal and Inca-communal systems of knowledge and production. A world away is the coast, and especially the political giant of Lima, which claimed about a third of the country's 25 million inhabitants by the late twentieth century. Beyond the obvious importance of ports, the coast was the site of the boom in extraction of guano (fertilizer from bird droppings) during the middle to late nineteenth century. As the hub of a centralized country, Lima has been the primary domain of modernity, and also has been home to most of the country's elite, white population. By the beginning of the twentieth century, the ideas and ideals of industrial capitalism, of a solid nation-state, of progress and democracy, emanated primarily from this region of the country.

A series of indigenous "awakenings" was spawned by a collision between traditional indigenous, feudal, and modern approaches. One reflection of this growing awareness was the work of Manuel González Prada, deemed the "father of indigenismo," whose writings gained popularity in the 1890s. He observed that the indigenous population of the sierra region generally suffered a "violation of all rights under a truly feudal regime."[8] Along with Túpac Amaru and González Prada, the third member of a renowned trilogy of heroes for the Peruvian indigenous population is José Carlos Mariátegui. Although his works, especially the famous *Seven Interpretive Essays of Peruvian Reality,* were not read widely until the 1950s, Mariátegui did most of his writing during the 1920s.[9] He is credited with being the first truly Latin American Marxist, in that he extrapolated the historical materialist approach to the Peruvian reality—especially with regard to its agrarian and ethnic dimensions. Through a thoughtful and complex analysis, he argued that liberation from the shackles of feudalism and premodernity could only come by way of a communist revolution combined with a decentralized political arrangement for the indigenous, who were concentrated in remote mountainous regions.[10]

In addition to the empirical elements associated with his analysis of the indigenous predicament, arguably the most compelling analysis until his time, Mariátegui's theoretical framework itself is extraordinarily interesting and represents the foundation of homegrown Latin American Marxism. Beyond the dominant presence of economic factors, Mariátegui also stressed the power of art, particularly of language. He probed, for example, the power relations imbued in words, thought, and syntax.[11] He also highlighted the power of spirituality, as well as mentalities or systems of thought. In this sense his work presages elements of what would become postmodern thinking. Indeed, Mariátegui quotes Nietzche, the godfather of postmodernism, in his introduction to his most famous work, *Seven Essays*.[12]

A rival of Mariátequi was Victor Raul Haya de la Torre, who formed in 1924 what proved to be Peru's most enduring political party, the left-leaning Alianza Popular Revolucionaria Americana (APRA). Haya de la Torre was more moderate than Mariátegui and criticized the latter's affinity with international communism. In his populist manifesto, which includes themes such as land reform, redistribution, and indigenous rights, Haya de la Torre claimed that "only APRA can save Peru." He led a series of political crusades from the 1920s through the early Cold War period. Ironically, the APRA did not reach power until 1985, well after the heyday of Haya de la Torre, and was credited with one of Peru's most calamitous periods of civilian rule.

Peruvian Subjugation and the Rise and Fall of Great Powers

With the fall of the Inca Empire, Peru was successively dominated by Spain, England, and finally the United States. The Spanish Conquest lasted from the mid-sixteenth century through the 1821–1824 period of the fight for independence, when the country was liberated with the help of Simón Bolívar of Venezuela. Peru's commercial relations with Spain were all but terminated by 1840. During this period, Spanish feudal lords were replaced by members of the Peruvian elite, who perpetuated essentially the same political and economic structures in the hacienda system. Globally, Peru established relations in diverse corners of the world. With its location on the Pacific Coast, Peru was naturally influenced by the Orient, especially prior to the construction of the Panama Canal. The country became home to a sizable Japanese population, from which President Alberto Fujimori (1990–2000) emerged. A significant Chinese community also formed in Peru during the nineteenth century. A crucial Chinese influence would later be expressed with the hero status afforded by Sendero to Mao Tse-tung.

But the biggest foreign influence over Peru during the middle to late 1800s was Britain. The boom in guano coincided with the increasing economic dominance of Britain during the heyday of that country's hegemonic position. Guano, which was harvested from coastal rocks, also increased the economic and political dominance of coastal Peru vis-à-vis the mountains and jungle. The height of the guano trade lasted from 1841 until about 1867, providing as much as 80 percent of Peru's revenue in the early 1860s. But the boom turned to bust by the 1880s.

During the peak of the guano era, Peru borrowed heavily from England, largely to finance the construction a railway system. In addition to providing the country with a greater sense of integration, it was hoped that the railway would permit a more efficient movement of its variety of products, therefore diversifying Peru's roster of exports. That did not occur, for a number of reasons, and the country found itself mired in a considerable debt crisis by the 1890s. As a result, Peru was forced to cede control to Britain of the country's railways for a period of sixty-six years, and was also obliged to provide England with all guano not utilized for local consumption. This disastrous debt crisis presaged others that would appear the following century.

As Britain's global power declined and the prospects of the United States grew in strides, the Americans began to play an increasingly dominant role in the Peruvian economy near the turn of the century. Part of this was the result of a rupture in the spatial politics of the Americas created with the construction of the Panama Canal. For Peru, it facilitated even greater ties with the United States by permitting easy shipping access to both the Atlantic and Pacific U.S. coasts. The United States was particularly interested in investing in Peruvian copper and petroleum, and exports of these products skyrocketed in the early 1900s. This era also witnessed the beginning of industrialization, especially in Lima. U.S. capital and political ideals fueled the project of modernity for Peru, and fomented aspirations for insertion into global capitalism. It also promoted the celebration of notions such as the nation-state, progress, and scientific power. All this was especially true under the reigns of President Augusto Leguía, who was in power from 1908 to 1912 and from 1919 to 1930.[13]

Labor became more organized and militant during the Great Depression, against the backdrop of an employment rate of 25 percent. As the plight of the indigenous people became more celebrated, U.S. imperialism increasingly became the target of popular political wrath. Despite the nationalism of the period as expressed through the indigenous movement and APRA, beginning in the 1930s the Peruvian government shunned the nationalist economic path of import substitution industrialization (ISI) that was popular in Mexico, Brazil, and Argentina. Instead, exports of primarily staple products were favored. This meant the perpetuation of a predominantly premodern economy, with its dependence on the extractive industries and upon an agrarian sector that still witnessed the dominance of the feudal hacienda system.

Since the Spanish Conquest social fragmentation has been prominent in Peru for a variety of reasons. Barriers of ethnicity, geography, and production, as well as of systems of knowledge continued to haunt the country through the twentieth century, the negative effects of foreign domination. For instance, the strength of foreign capital overshadowed the formation of strong national capital, diminishing the prospects for hegemony in the country. Local fragmentation combined with foreign domination meant an unstable political situation. Compounding this problem, although political power was highly centralized in Lima, messages emanating from the capital lacked legitimacy in vast regions of the country. In the absence of hegemony, the coercive apparatus of the armed forces was prominent, as often the military was either directly in power or held the reins of politics from just beneath the surface. However, the Peruvian military is quite distinct in the Latin American context, and beginning in the 1960s it implemented one of the most radical economic projects in the region's history.

The Cold War and the Radical Peruvian Military

The pattern of unstable and sometimes chaotic electoral politics continued into the Cold War, amid an absence of hegemony. An APRA-supported candidate, José Luis Bustamante y Rivero, prevailed in the 1945 elections. But he was ousted in 1948 through a military coup led by General Manuel Odría, who also "won" an uncontested election in 1950. Two civilian candidates, Manuel Prado and Fernando Belaúnde Terry, governed from 1956 to 1968 but presided over festering problems that eventually evolved into a dramatic political watershed. The most serious of these difficulties were widespread peasant uprisings and land invasions, involving up to 300,000 peasants and representing one of the largest such movements in modern Latin American history.[14] One influence that helped ignite this powderkeg was the 1959 Cuban Revolution, which sent radical shock waves throughout Latin America. But protracted domestic problems were of course at the root of the crisis, especially the perpetuation of the feudal hacienda system and the highly exploitative social relations associated with it.

Some guerrilla groups also formed during this era, most notably the Movimiento de Izquierda Revolucionario (MIR), which was the precursor of the subversive Movimiento Revolucionario Túpac Amaru, which emerged in the 1980s. The MIR was constructed mainly by disaffected members of the APRA party, and some supporters had received military training in Cuba, North Korea, and China.[15] In contrast to SL and its Maoist roots, the MIR was more mainstream and was influenced, for example, by Castro's Cuba.[16] The Peruvian military, in a drastic attempt to contain these peasant movements and guerrillas, responded with open warfare that by the beginning of 1966 had left 8,000 dead and 19,000 homeless.

The Peruvian case stood in sharp contrast to the more developed countries of Argentina, Brazil, and Chile. As Alfred Stepan observes, in those countries, "with their advanced import substitution economies, conflict centered in the modern industrial sectors and the structural tensions manifested themselves through such 'stress indicators' as high strike and inflation levels and growing external indebtedness."[17] In Peru, by contrast, political problems were concentrated in the agrarian sector, since the country had not yet embarked on a process of significant industrialization. During the 1960s, chronic problems became magnified, including the vast inequity of wealth, issues of land tenure and of indigenous rights, the persistence of feudal haciendas in a country hoping to modernize, and the dubious legitimacy of electoral politics.

With pandemonium and repression dotting the countryside, and with the economy suffering from a nearly 44 percent devaluation of the Peruvian sol, by 1967 the armed forces had grown increasingly restless. Ideologically, Peru's populist military was in a class of its own. Embracing the ideas of the leftist dependency school, which gained popularity during the late 1960s, the Peruvian military essentially implemented a redistributive revolution.[18] Like any large institution, the military should not be viewed as a monolith. But the dominant faction of the armed forces viewed Peruvian civilian politicians as too feeble and too dependent on foreign economic interests to act at the behest of the majority of Peruvians. The military concluded that if fundamental problems remained uncorrected, potent guerrilla movements would appear that would likely be even more threatening than the uprisings that already had occurred. Hence the armed forces propounded the necessity of land reform, income redistribution, and the nationalization of strategic industries in order to promote a stable and modern economy. The military viewed itself as the only Peruvian political actor capable of diagnosing the problem and powerful enough to resolve it.[19]

A military government led by General Juan Velasco seized power from 1968 until 1975. As the leader of the president's advisory committee observed, it was the guerrillas of the early 1960s that "awakened the military to the reality of the country."[20] This prompted the regime to implement one of the quickest and most thorough processes of land reform in Latin American history. By the end of the experiment there were 429,384 beneficiaries, who received 9,762,017 hectares of land (out of a total of 23 million hectares).[21] About three-quarters of all agriculturally usable land was under some type of cooperative ownership. Feudal haciendas were disbanded and the government nationalized major foreign-owned corporations in the areas of banking, petroleum, mining, as well as other strategic sectors.

At first glance, one might think these measures would have been sufficient to stem any imminent revolutionary activity. After all, the military government had essentially implemented a populist revolution whereby the chief beneficiaries were elements of the masses who had been repressed and ignored by previous regimes. Perhaps the biggest lesson to emerge from the Velasco experiment is that land reform must be devised and implemented with extraordinary care and political finesse in order to stem subversive movements. In the Peruvian case, there were a number of flies in the ointment. Near the end of the military regime in 1975, many loud complaints were voiced against the land reform process and the government itself. Peasants resented the top-down and centralized command structure under which the reform was implemented, which had denied them meaningful input into the process. Political tension arose between groups of peasants who had prospered under the former hacienda system versus those who stood to gain by the reform. Corruption among administrators, misuse of funds, and rage by those left out of the process were other sore spots. Further, the reform rendered the agricultural sector less efficient than previously, with a marked decrease in the level of production and exports. The reform process also created rising expectations among the masses that were not realized, precipitating a highly dangerous political situation.[22]

Perhaps the most prominent blemish of the reform process was its uneven geographic application. In the south-central highlands, particularly in places such as Ayacucho, where Sendero Luminoso had germinated, land reform was far from successful. As Cynthia McClintock notes, the effects of reform in Ayacucho were more limited than in almost any other part of the country, partly because there were very few prime targets. That is, there was a dearth of prosperous haciendas in this region, which is famous for its rocky and agriculturally forbidding terrain.[23] Only about 11 percent of Ayacucho's residents benefited from agrarian redistribution, compared to about 54 percent on Peru's north coast, where the presence of Sendero was minimal.[24] Bad weather during these years coupled with inadequate agricultural support from the government in terms of insufficient infrastructure and credits, exacerbated the situation in Ayacucho. Per capita income actually declined in the region during this period, from about U.S.$100 annually in 1961 to under U.S.$70 in 1979.[25] The government considered other parts of the country to be more important, apparently unaware that the Ayacucho area was the hotbed of Sendero's formative years.[26] Further, to the extent that agrarian reform was indeed implemented in the region, the political result was that feudal power brokers were banished, leaving Sendero with a freer hand to operate.[27]

The Emergence of Sendero

Abimael Guzmán sat at the helm of Sendero's pyramid structure. Born in 1934, Guzmán was appointed in 1962 as a professor of philosophy at the Universidad Nacional de San Cristóbal de Huamanga in Ayacucho. The university had just reopened in 1958, having been closed down near the turn of the century. Guzmán was openly teaching Maoist thought beginning in 1963, and made at least two excursions to China in 1965–1966. At a university that was located in one of the poorest and most remote indigenous communities in Peru, Guzmán's worldliness, his command of communist philosophy, and his notorious intensity and charisma combined to make him a highly influential and respected figure on campus.[28] He was promoted to the position of dean of the Faculty of Letters.

Guzmán's reverence for Mao had certain political implications domestically. By 1964 his strong influence among would-be revolutionaries culminated in a pronounced split between pro-Soviet and pro-Chinese supporters in Peru. This occurred within the larger global context of the historic Sino-Soviet split. During the late 1960s and early 1970s, the closeness of the Velasco military government to the Soviet Union became the object of severe criticism by pro-Chinese subversives such as Guzmán. The Peruvian government had purchased a substantial portion of its military hardware from the Soviets, and also received military advice from them. More generally, Sendero's leader argued that the Velasco experiment was too superficial and reformist to deal with the underlying problems of Peru and could only be resolved through an application of Guzmán's neo-Maoist ideology.

By the mid-1970s the outline of SL was becoming clearer. In 1974 a group of revolutionaries called their organization "By the Shining

Path of Mariátegui" (Por el Sendero Luminoso de Mariátegui). During the same period revolutionary student fronts (Frente Estudiantil Revolucionaria), which would evolve into Sendero Luminoso, took form especially in the sierra region of the country, and to a lesser extent in Lima.[29] SL opened its first cell in the capital city in 1976, and its first military school *(escuela militar)* in April 1980, shortly before the group emerged publicly.

Ideology

One of the great distinctions of SL is its infamous ideological framework, sometimes deemed by its followers as "Gonzalo Thought" after Abimael Guzmán's nickname. According to SL documents, "Gonzalo Thought has been forged through long years of intense, tenacious, and incessant struggle to uphold, defend and apply Marxism-Leninism-Maoism, and to retake Mariátegui's path and to develop it, to reconstitute the Party and, principally, to initiate, maintain and develop the People's War in Peru serving world revolution."[30] Other pronouncements by the group indicate that SL members did not view Guzmán as taking a back seat to the other Marxist luminaries. One example was the frequently chanted slogan "Uphold, defend and apply Marxism-Leninism-Maoism, Gonzalo Thought, Mainly Gonzalo Thought!"[31] As the Communist Party of Peru, SL viewed itself as making a highly original and important contribution to revolutionary thought in the Marxist tradition.

The ideology of SL blended many elements of the Marxist tradition. It relied on a rigid and perhaps vulgar view of Marx's historical materialist framework, as we shall see. And despite its rejection of the Soviets, SL incorporated Lenin's notion of the vanguard party and clung to his claim that, even at the end of the twentieth century, "we are in [capitalism's] final and highest phase, imperialism."[32] The ideological dimension of Sendero was entirely geared to the conception of praxis, such that ideas were linked to practical revolutionary action. As Guzmán put it shortly after his capture in 1992, "We are here as the sons and daughters of the people and we are fighting in these trenches, this is also part of the combat, and we do this because we are Communists!"[33]

It was the thinking of Mao that was the most glaring element in Sendero's ideological perspective, especially given the agrarian nature of Peru. That is, the focus by both Marx and Lenin on the proletariat seemed misplaced in a country such as Peru, where agriculture, the extractive industries, and staple products still dominated the economy. SL praised Maoist thought for "taking agriculture as the base, and industry as the leading economic force."[34] Beyond the centrality of agrarian forces in any upcoming revolution, SL revered Mao for darker elements of his philosophy, not the least of which was the important role he afforded to violence within the context of revolutionary struggles. "In scientific socialism, Chairman Mao . . . upheld revolutionary violence as a universal law without any exception whatsoever, revolution as a violent displacement of one class by another, thus establishing the great thesis that 'political power grows out of the barrel of a gun.'"[35] SL's embracement of Maoism resulted in political feuds with both local and global forces. Within Peru, by the mid-1960s Guzmán's Maoist faction of the Communist Party prevailed over the Soviet-Cuban tendency in what amounted to a bitter struggle. Regarding the global context, in 1988 SL proclaimed that "Maoism confronts the triple attack of Soviet, Chinese and Albanian revisionism."[36] With Maoism abandoned even in its founding country of China during the era of SL, Guzmán and his followers were prepared to carry the torch themselves.

While prohibiting the recognition of Christmas and indigenous holidays, SL celebrated the Chinese Revolution and the birthdays of both Guzmán and Mariátegui. The legendary Peruvian Marxist had a deep influence on Sendero. Mariátegui was the founder of the Socialist Party, which transformed into the Communist Party in 1930 and then metamorphosed once again into SL by 1980. Celebrating him as a Marxist to the bone, and one who had the gift of extrapolating revolutionary analysis to the Peruvian landscape, Sendero considered itself to be "the legitimate heirs of Mariátegui."[37] But despite its professed reverence for this hero, much of Sendero's literature curiously minimizes the centerpiece of Mariátegui's analysis—the role of the indigenous population. Instead SL subsumed ethnicity, gender, and other elements under the broad rubric of class struggle. Further, while there is virtually no mention of violence in Mariátegui's most famous work, *Seven Essays of Interpretation of the Peruvian Reality,* it is precisely this theme that SL seems to focus upon in its analysis of Mariátegui's writing. The rebels observed, for example, that "Mariátegui outlined fundamental ideas on revolutionary violence. He said: 'Power is conquered through violence . . . it is preserved only through dictatorship.'"[38] In context, those views probably have more in common with Lenin, Stalin, or Mao than with the overall body of Mariátegui's own work.

Epistemologically, there is no doubt that Sendero's ideology falls solidly within modernity. SL emphasized linear progress toward an ultimate Communist revolution. It saw the world through binary lenses and viewed progress as a consequence of dialectical contradictions. Its

literature emphasized moral dualities, dividing the world into rigid realities of good and bad. Further, the ideology of Sendero was extraordinarily absolutist. It claimed to be based on "the scientific ideology of
the proletariat, all powerful because it is true."[39] The rebels marched to
the beat of "the universal truth of Marxism-Leninism" and "laws of history."[40] The group insisted that "being communists, we fear nothing."[41]
Sendero utterly rejected alternative ideologies and perspectives, coun-
tering them with slogans such as "If we do not understand Maoism correctly as the new, third and higher stage of Marxism, it is impossible to
understand anything."[42] Similarly, SL argued that "society is governed
by laws, but those who do not follow Marxism cannot understand those
laws."[43] Thus SL's modern and communist ideology was exclusive,
rigid, and dogmatic.

SL viewed Peruvian history since the late nineteenth century as
constituting three waves. The first began in 1895, when "industrialization took place in a semi-feudal society whose economy was increasingly subjected to North American imperialism, which displaced English domination."[44] The second wave, from 1945 to 1980, was bisected
into two periods: 1945 to 1963 witnessed the "beginnings of the struggle against revisionism," or Soviet influence; and 1963 to 1980 marked
the "establishment of the general political line and the reconstitution of
the Party." The third wave, from 1980 to 1993, when an incarcerated
Guzmán pleaded for peace from his jail cell, featured the "development
of the guerrilla war."[45]

Sendero found great fault with Peruvian governments and political
parties, even those with redistributionist policies. Despite the wide-
ranging if flawed program of agrarian reform conducted during the
1968–1975 Velasco regime, which disbanded haciendas and left the
great majority of land in cooperative arrangements, SL still considered
that "feudalism or semi-feudalism survives in the structure of our economy . . . with its two elements: Latifundia and servitude."[46] What is
striking is that Sendero failed to appreciate the demise of that system of
production in the wake of Velasco's sweeping agrarian reform, and
through the lens of its vulgar Marxist perspective continued to see a
mirage of feudalism.

Beyond the issue of what it saw as the persistence of feudalism, SL
was critical of the Velasco government on other grounds as well. It chastised "Velasquism and its so-called revolution, the contention and collusion between the comprador bourgeoisie and the bureaucratic bourgeoisie, and opportunism and mainly revisionism by their supporters."[47]
Despite the redistributionist policies of the Velasco government, Sendero

felt that it was not sufficiently radical, that it represented state capitalism rather than socialism, and that the regime employed a top-down
approach that aimed "to organize the producers and all members of
society along corporativist lines."[48] Similarly, Sendero attacked the leftist APRA party for its "fascism and corporativism," with its critique
leaning much more heavily on name calling than on analysis.[49]

Although SL noticed the element of ethnicity and praised the work
of Mariátegui, who placed the indigenous question at the center of his
analysis, the group essentially reduced ethnicity to class politics. It did
so through a rather convoluted process that argued that the Indian problem is fundamentally a land problem, and land problems are a reflection
of class struggle. "Mariátegui set forth that the Indian problem is the
problem of the land; consequently, the national question is based on the
land question and . . . the class struggle of our own masses."[50] SL minimized indigenous culture and tradition in other ways. Sendero's rigid
neo-Maoist ideology forbade traditional indigenous holidays, and in
communities it controlled SL typically replaced traditional indigenous
elders who led the community with younger Sendero leaders.

SL also interfered with indigenous conceptions of space and time.[51]
Sendero Luminoso encircled and contained communities it controlled
rather than permitting Indians to pursue traditional commerce in cities
and in diverse locations throughout the country. Further, Sendero's
modern ideology and especially its linear view of progress, which for
rebel leaders meant protracted and seemingly interminable war, clashed
with indigenous conceptions of time. For some indigenous people, one
dimension of the temporal world is viewed as cyclical. For example,
many complained that their family life cycle was falling prey to SL's
staunch dedication to incessant warfare until revolution was achieved.[52]
In contrast to SL's ideology of linear progress through dialectics, a
major strain of indigenous epistemology views political change as
occurring through a radical reversal of position:

> The Incas believed that history was a succession of ages divided one
> from another by a cataclysmic epoch—a pachakuti—an "overturning
> of the world." . . . The solar power of the Incas, radiating from their
> mountain capital, had been eclipsed by the oceanic power of the
> Christians at Lima on the coast. Upper and lower had reversed . . .
> [but] the past order is not irrevocable; it remains latent in the under-
> world, awaiting a return. . . . Nearly five centuries later, Andeans still
> expect a righting of their world.[53]

Thus for Indians of the Inca tradition, revolution meant revolving
180 degrees to a position opposite the one previously occupied. For SL,

on the other hand, revolution meant a modern dialectical synthesis or leap forward.

Sendero also attempted to smother Indian spiritual values by arguing firmly that "Marx taught us that 'religion is the opiate of the people.' This is a Marxist thesis which is completely valid today, and in the future."[54] Similarly, Guzmán considered the pope to be an agent of U.S. imperialism.[55] Ironically, Guzmán elevated himself to a godlike status, instructing traditional Inca sun worshippers to call him Puka Inti, or Red Sun. Beyond this, the mix of elements in indigenous spirituality from the Christian religion and from Inca pantheism suggests the historical tendency for many Peruvian Indians to accept multiple truths rather the absolutist and rigidly binary dogma of Sendero.

The larger point is that SL clashed epistemologically with much of the indigenous population, who composed the majority of its supporters—especially those who resided in the central and southern highlands. While the indigenous people should not be viewed as a monolithic community, there have been some common views prevalent among Peruvian Indians in the Inca tradition, particularly those who live outside the modernizing influence of Lima. Not content to allow the Peruvian Indians to think freely, or to know the world through their own system of knowledge, Sendero contradicted the indigenous peasants' conceptions of time, space, and spirituality. The rebels attempted to impose upon the indigenous peasant population a modern and communist ideology that left no space for other perspectives, a grave contradiction that served to erode a significant portion of the subversives' support base.

In addition to paraphrasing Mao's dictum of power radiating from a barrel of a gun as ideological support for its extensive and notorious use of violence, Sendero also borrowed heavily from Clausewitz. It bluntly argued that "revolutionary violence is, therefore, the very essence of our historical process. . . . First comes the military deed and later political change. This shows once again that war is the continuation of politics by other means."[56] Hence for SL the struggle to achieve revolutionary nirvana justified any violent measure necessary to attain that objective. Violence was not considered to be in any way immoral, but instead was seen as an indispensable tool that would permit Sendero to impose its own moral code once in power.

Its steady, indiscriminate, and remarkably brutal use of violence earned Sendero many critics, both local and foreign. Students interviewed at the Universidad Nacional de San Cristóbal de Huamanga, where Sendero was essentially formed in the 1960s and 1970s, criticized the group's extreme use of violence and argued that this represented Sendero's most prominent strategic-ideological failure.[57] At the dawn of the twenty-first century, children of former SL members vehemently reject the group's record of carnage, having suffered through its traumatic consequences during their childhood.[58] Further, despite the inclusion of many women into all ranks of SL, the dominance of masculine principles such as a disproportionate reliance on violence led observers to suggest that Sendero's ideological platform was steeped in machismo.[59]

Sendero urged Peruvians to refrain from providing any support, tacit or otherwise, to government structures or other non-Sendero forces. For example, SL instructed Peruvians to boycott government elections. With particular regard to the 1985 presidential elections, whereby Alan García's APRA party ultimately prevailed, Sendero argued that "to vote is to endorse the social system and elect another government, which will bring about more hunger and genocide."[60] SL even admonished the general population not to join nongovernmental organizations that implemented welfare projects, since this too was viewed as an obstacle to revolutionary progress.

With regard to the rival guerrillas, the MRTA, Sendero found fault with the group for lacking "a definite Marxist conception. Thus, they march to serve imperialism."[61] Further, SL balked at the MRTA's support for Soviet ally countries such as Cuba and Nicaragua. For Sendero, the Cuban model demonstrated an important lesson: "Cuba changed hands, from one master to another." For similar reasons, it criticized Nicaragua's dependence on the Soviets.[62] The rebels insisted that foreign domination of any kind was to be shunned, and appreciated no essential difference between U.S. or Soviet imperialism. In justifying its highly isolationist stance, SL argued that because Peru had achieved greatness during the ascendancy of the Inca Empire while avoiding foreign influence, the country should retract from foreign ties and obligations altogether on the road back to greatness.

Beyond these specific features of Sendero ideology, there are some general themes worth considering. SL's ideology was geared to the objective of taking power over the state, a stance of reassertion and vengeance that afforded no room for peace negotiations. The indigenous population wanted to reclaim the greatness of the Inca civilization and to shed the miserable yoke of a half millennium of social subjugation. Thus the exorbitant degree of violence employed by SL suggests that its members sought to convert the memory of centuries of violence suffered at the hands of both local and foreign oppressors into a decade or so of brutal retaliation.

SL's ideology embodied unrefined authoritarianism and hierarchy. The hero worship associated with Gonzalo Thought is indicative of this.

The ideology of SL was not about self-empowerment or free thinking, and it did not embrace the notion of local or autonomous power for indigenous communities. Power was centralized for Sendero, which ultimately frustrated those communities who wished to gain more local control and autonomy. A principal complaint by Sendero supporters against the Velasco military "revolution" (1968–1975) was that it did not provide local communities with the local power they craved. But neither did Sendero.

In sum, Sendero constructed a clearly modern ideology to achieve the goal of a communist revolution within the structure of a nation-state. Modern to the core were its embrace of linear progress, of absolute truth, of binary thought, of dialectical change, and of taking power over a nation state. This modern ideology, in Guzmán's scheme, would constitute the intellectual basis to exorcise from the Peruvian economy what SL saw as the remaining features of feudalism. Yet Sendero never took into account the epistemological dimensions of its ideology, which ultimately clashed with that of many of its indigenous peasant supporters. The SL ideology contradicted an indigenous knowledge system as manifested through attitudes toward time, space, spirituality, and the nature of truth and of change. This represented one significant factor that contributed to Sendero's demise.

Support Base

Abimael Guzmán convincingly estimated that at the height of Sendero's power in 1990 it had 23,430 armed members and the political support of an additional 50,000 to 100,000 unarmed Peruvians. About 86 percent of its armed troops were located in Ayacucho, Huancavelico, Apurímac, Junín, and Pasco.[63] These supporters were typically young people from indigenous peasant families who had been indoctrinated by SL through secondary schools or rural universities. A second set of supporters resided in Lima and were recruited from shanty towns that surround the city and from the alienated middle-class student populations at major urban universities. A final group of Sendero compatriots included those engaged in the narcotrafficking industry, principally in the jungles of the Huallaga Valley.

Sendero profited from the widespread failure of the Velasco military regime, despite its well-intentioned if poorly implemented land reform and at least partial nationalization of strategic industries such as the petroleum, cement, paper, and copper sectors. A prominent failure was that land reform, while thorough, was implemented in a top-down fashion that limited local empowerment and that only served to increase political expectations. It also resulted in less efficient production. More broadly, as Guillermo Rochabrun Silva argues, Velasco's military government "depleted the ideas" of Peru's legitimate left, such that many viewed both the Peruvian left and the Peruvian right as devoid of workable policies.[64] Further, the popularity of the military itself, having accumulated massive debt under the tarnished policies of Velasco, withered in the public eye. Beyond economic mismanagement, the military's deployment of indiscriminate terror in the early 1980s to combat Sendero alienated the public even further, and in some cases pushed populations into the arms of SL.

Even democratically elected governments proved to be a disappointing for many Peruvians. At a time when the notion of democracy was becoming practically hegemonic throughout the Americas, Peru's dubious record of fifty-one of its seventy-one presidents having been military officers seemed out of step with emerging trends. So the transition toward democratic rule following the collapse of the Velasco experiment in 1975 was greeted with considerable enthusiasm and high expectations. But in the end this transition resulted in disillusionment as well. For example, while claiming to represent the interests of the masses and the poor for almost six decades, the APRA party reached power for the first time in 1985. But rather than a better socioeconomic situation for the majority population through the center-left doctrine it preached, APRA's defiant policy toward transnational finance capital spelled a punishing and even calamitous economic and political predicament. Such episodes may have tarnished the ideal of democracy to some extent, fortifying the prospects for Sendero's growing support base.

Pronounced economic stagnation or recession coincided with the formation and reign of Sendero Luminoso. Growth of gross national product (GNP), for example, was 0.3 percent from 1976 to 1977, 1.3 percent from 1980 to 1982, –2.3 percent from 1983 to 1985, –8.2 percent in 1988, –11.8 percent in 1989, and –4.0 percent in 1990.[65] Real minimum wages fell almost steadily from 1979 through the early 1990s.[66] The economy entered horrific straits in 1986, with President García's defiant declaration of paying no more than 10 percent of the country's export earnings to finance foreign debt. The result was that the International Monetary Fund (IMF) blacklisted Peru as an "ineligible borrower," a move that triggered huge disinvestment and capital flight. Poverty jumped from 17 to 44 percent during 1985–1990, while inflation reached astronomical figures such as 2,775 percent in 1989.[67]

In response, President Alberto Fujimori implemented his neoliberal "Fujishock" beginning in 1990. This drastic IMF-sponsored austerity plan meant that prices of basic necessities such as food climbed almost 400 percent, pushing between 20 and 50 percent of Lima residents into soup kitchens by the early 1990s.[68] By 1993, three-quarters of Peruvians were undernourished and were classified as unemployed or underemployed.[69] Hence Sendero benefited from the disastrous financial predicament in Peru because government authorities were blamed for the crisis.

Guzmán had imagined that SL would comprise a mix of campesinos (agrarian peasants), the proletariat (e.g., Lima's industrial workers), and the petite bourgeoisie (e.g., owners of small businesses, teachers, bureaucrats, etc.). Teachers and professors dominated the group's upper ranks and were crucial agents of recruitment. All of this initially emanated from the Andean town of Ayacucho, where Abimael Guzmán's worldliness, charisma, and rigor earned him the great respect of colleagues and students at the newly reopened Universidad Nacional de San Cristóbal de Huamanga.[70] By 1980, with the exception of Guzmán, most SL leaders were from the Ayacucho area. Professors and teachers trained by SL, many of whom were transferred throughout Peru by the government, recruited students as Sendero members.[71] Indeed, students were the largest single group of supporters among the rebels.

Why would teachers and students be so vulnerable to the ideas of Sendero and Guzmán? In addition to the contextual elements noted above, the monthly salary Sendero paid to many of its members, U.S.$250–$500, was three to eight times the normal salary of a teacher.[72] Thus, beyond any ideological sympathy among professors and teachers for Sendero, often the pay was good. With regard to university students, between 1960 and 1980 their numbers swelled twentyfold in the Ayacucho region, and eightfold nationwide.[73] Yet the troubled economy was unable to keep pace and absorb these new job seekers. This was true for both the university students of the central and southern highlands, many of whom were from indigenous peasant families, and the university students in major centers such as Lima, who often had a middle-class background. Sendero provided identity to its young student members, and its ideology of dialectical progress offered a sense of hope in an otherwise difficult context.[74] Materially, university students benefited from a Sendero paycheck as well.

Other elements of Peruvian society also lent their support to Sendero. A recruitment target for all radical groups were the *pueblos jovenes,* the ultra-poor shantytowns that surrounded Lima and were home to about half of the city's population. Many of the inhabitants of *pueblos jovenes* were campesinos who had migrated to Lima in the hope of finding work. These shantytowns were a venue where Sendero competed for support among other groups beginning in 1977.

Further, a significant portion of those engaged in the illicit drug trade, particularly in the Upper Huallaga Valley region of Peru, worked with or supported Sendero. The arrangement was based less on ideological affinity than on pragmatic economic concerns. SL worked to obtain the best price for Peruvian coca from Colombian traffickers and processors, and also fought attempts by the U.S. and Peruvian governments to eradicate coca growth through the use of herbicides.[75] SL obtained an estimated U.S.$20 million to $30 million annually from the illicit drug trade, which financed the purchase of arms by the rebels and helped pay members' salaries.[76] Those engaged in narcotrafficking were not the only "pragmatic" supporters of Sendero. According to an analyst in Ayacucho, many locals viewed SL as the lesser evil in a context of economic despair and political disillusionment.[77] Hence, rather than through the lure of ideological motivations, these supporters were drawn to Sendero by material and practical benefits.

There were other drawing cards for Sendero Luminoso's recruitment campaign. One of these was the group's status as the only powerful nonstate organization in the country dedicated to mobilizing primarily on behalf of the interests of the poor and the indigenous. Civil society during this period was relatively weak. Mature NGOs with a national reach that focused on poverty and ethnicity had not yet developed.[78] Hence Sendero faced scant competition in its endeavor to mobilize and represent this immense but marginalized population.[79] As a result of SL's messianic ideology, its escalating power during the 1980s, as well as its material provisions, Sendero sympathizers were generally divided into two groups: SL supporters who had pragmatic motivations but who lacked loyalty to the rebels, and a sizable population for whom Sendero was able to provide a strong sense of identity.

Women and children played an important role in Sendero as well. Although women were present in the top ranks of SL and represented between one-third and one-half of its members at various times, the group did not have a feminist appeal.[80] There was a single cult of leadership under the helm of one man, Guzmán. SL heavily relied on masculine principles of politics and security, such as violence and domination.[81] Some prominent feminists have criticized Sendero as patriarchal, and for subverting women's issues to those of class. Further, SL spoke harshly of international women's NGOs, deeming them to be agents of imperialism. Indeed, Sendero issued death threats against leaders of both domestic and international women's movements, and provoked widespread condemnation in 1992 when it publicly and brutally assassinated Maria Elena Moyano, former president of the Federation of Women, who had organized the poor to form self-defense units against SL in one of Lima's *pueblos jovenes*.[82] Sendero readily inducted children into its ranks, militarily training them beginning at age eight in many SL communities. Young children were also taught by rebel leaders to commit brutal acts, in the context of a strategy that leaned heavily on terrorism. Women and children, however, were the first to revolt against Sendero, partly because male members of SL were threatened with the harm of their families if they defected.

Finally, there is considerable evidence that a significant proportion of those Sendero counted as supporters may have been intimidated into acquiescence by the rebels' brutal tactics. The formation and widespread popularity of *rondas*—localized anti-Sendero self-defense units equipped by the military—suggested that many were eager to protect themselves from the imposition of Sendero's power. Hence, while it is undeniable that SL had constructed a massive and well-organized support base, not all of its official recruits appear to have been willing participants.

Movimiento Revolucionario Túpac Amaru

While not nearly as powerful and as politically important as Sendero Luminoso, the MRTA nevertheless represented a significant guerrilla presence in Peru during the late 1980s and early 1990s. The group also offers a point of contrast from which to consider SL. Ironically, the MRTA achieved its greatest notoriety from its 1996 seizure of the Japanese embassy in Lima, even though this occurred when the group was severely debilitated in relation to its height of power a few years earlier. In 1991 MRTA activity accounted for 14 percent of all terrorist attacks in Peru and 5 percent of political deaths. By comparison, in the late 1980s Sendero was held responsible for 75 percent of all terrorist attacks and about 50 percent of political deaths.[83] The core of the MRTA originated from a rebel group that formed during the period 1958–1964, the Movimiento de Izquierda Revolucionaria. Many of its members were disaffected supporters of the APRA party and were inspired by the revolutionary success of Cuba. According to MRTA documents, a second wave of this group emerged in the wake of the success enjoyed by Nicaragua's Sandinistas. The essence of the MRTA had formed by 1980 under the command of Victor Polay Campos, or Comandante

Rolando.[84] From the beginning, this group rejected the Maoism that was at the foundation of Sendero's ideological platform, and instead opted for pro-Soviet revolutionary models.

The MRTA established its name in 1982, inspired by the indigenous struggle of Túpac Amaru centuries earlier.[85] Although officially inaugurated in 1984, the group did not launch significant armed struggle until 1986–1987. With 1,000–1,500 guerrilla members, it was concentrated in Lima, Huancayo, and Peru's northern Amazonian region, an area instrumental to the illicit drug trade.[86] Its relatively small membership included a mix of intellectuals, marginalized workers, and a portion of those engaged in narcotrafficking.

What were the ideological motivations of the MRTA? First, it argued that the antifeudal position of the APRA and Sendero was misplaced, since Peru superseded feudalism in the wake of Velasco's land reform and was now in a state of "dependent capitalism." From the vantage point of the MRTA, Peru was characterized by "an industrialization dependent on North American capital under the conception of a process called import substitution industrialization."[87] Neoliberalism had been on the ascendant in the country since the late 1970s, according to the group, and so it was committed to struggling against the likes of the IMF, the World Bank, and other agents of transnational capital.[88] The MRTA argued that revolutionary groups such as itself attracted supporters because democracy in general had failed in Peru, while the legitimate left, such as the APRA, had become institutionalized and had lost direction. The rebels observed that democracy had been reduced "to a simple act of electing every five years a state administrator."[89]

The MRTA was never shy about its view that Sendero Luminoso had given revolutionaries a bad name. According to the MRTA's Comandante Andrés:

> Sendero is characterized by its negative image. They don't seek to win hearts and minds, but imposed their direction on the people. . . . Sendero is also characterized by its cruelty, which is strongly repudiated. I would hesitate to describe Sendero as a revolutionary group because their Pol Pot concept of life and revolution is a long way from what we think of as revolution. . . . We do things like expropriate food from the big supermarket chains and hand it out to the people.[90]

In other writings, the MRTA described SL as a disgrace to the revolutionary cause and chastised it for being Stalinist and dogmatic.[91] Hence, the MRTA was proud of an image it perceived as markedly kinder and gentler than Sendero's.

Conclusion

Sendero Luminoso came close to toppling the Peruvian government in part due to its ability to harness a latent desire among the masses for a reassertion of power, harkening back to the greatness of the Inca civilization almost a half millennium ago. An almost deified Abimael Guzmán led the charge by relying on a modern brand of authoritarian communist ideology that was quite easily propagated through a virtually ready-made network of professors, teachers, and students. Several elements contributed to Sendero's success. In the local context, Peru had a rich history of revolutionary treatises and subversive action. Túpac Amaru, González Prada, and Mariátegui are among the country's roster of indigenous revolutionary stars. The guerrilla groups and land invasions of 1958–1964 sowed the seeds for subsequent revolutionary action by Sendero and others almost a generation later. Thus, while SL was original in many ways, the success of the group rested on a solid foundation of Peruvian revolutionary thought.

Within the global context, the growth of Sendero from 1980 until 1992 coincided with the last hurrah of international communism and the end of the Cold War. The fall of the Soviets and of the Sandinistas by 1990 suggested to others that the curtain was closing on leftist revolutionary organizations. But SL's isolationist posture and its self-reliant financial situation rendered the group relatively immune to such developments. Indeed, Sendero was arguably at the peak of its power in the early 1990s, an era President George Bush had deemed to be "the new world order." Yet in what seemed like the product of a time warp, Sendero gleefully insisted that the "highest stage" of imperialism had been reached.

The economic difficulties suffered by ordinary Peruvians added to Sendero's good fortune. Precipitous economic contraction in the mid-1980s to early 1990s, the proliferation of huge corps of unemployed and underemployed, plus a glut of educated youth combined to set the stage for an economic and political crisis in Peru not seen since the Great Depression. For many, it seemed that various models of capitalism were a failure. From the statism and reformism of Velasco to the neoliberalism and privatizations of Fujimori, nothing seemed to work particularly well. Sendero seized on that sense of hopelessness.

A crucial lesson to emerge from the Peruvian experience is that economic nationalization and even a revolutionary degree of land reform were insufficient by themselves to stem revolutionary sentiment. About three-quarters of the land was under some sort of cooperative arrangement by the time Sendero commenced its activities. But the reform was least effective in precisely the areas in which Sendero predominated. Some of this was due to natural factors, such as a limited number of prosperous haciendas that could be targeted in the Ayacucho region as a result of unfavorable agricultural conditions. In the main, however, mistakes were political in nature. Reform in the south-central highlands arrived tardily, and was not accompanied by substantial agricultural credits and programs until the García government post-1985. Beyond those factors, even in regions where a significant amount of agricultural parcels had been redivided, the grass roots—the indigenous that compose the overwhelming majority of the country's population— still felt that they lacked power vis-à-vis land-related decisionmaking. Hence, land reform did not work in the absence of a corresponding political empowerment of the beneficiaries. Further, the redistribution process raised expectations enormously. The grass roots craved real political power that would be visible in their daily life. This is exactly what Sendero promised to deliver, despite its fatal contradictions.

Peru's historic struggle to evolve into a modern nation-state represents an important backdrop for the Sendero experience. This preoccupation with achieving the project of modernity has been very apparent since the Leguía regime near the beginning of the twentieth century. But various attempts at this objective have not yielded full success. For example, the radical military government of Velasco tried to achieve the nationalism and industrialization associated with modernity through a project of agrarian reform and ISI. While the Velasco regime was indeed successful at abolishing the feudal production system of the hacienda, it did little to empower the masses or to affect the premodern system of thought still apparent among much of the country's indigenous peasant population.

Two points flow from this. First, premodernity is associated with far more than just the means and relations of production, though these are important. Premodernity, in the Peruvian case, also means a system of thought prevalent among Indigenous peasants that is manifested through the power of spirituality, art, and culture, and in conceptions of time and space, the nature of political change, and so on. Second, by the late twentieth century Peru was a patchwork of modern and premodern elements. There is nothing particularly postmodern regarding Peru's experience with SL—no considerable involvement of NGOs, of space-shrinking technology such as the Internet, of speculation, or even of identity politics, since SL subsumed themes such as ethnicity and gender to modern class struggle. Like the Velasco project, Sendero's failure to achieve a neo-Maoist nirvana represents a failed bid at modernity.

In the Peruvian mosaic, what elements of modernity have been apparent and relevant throughout the experience of Sendero? While Peru is a notoriously centralized country, the periphery (especially the noncoastal regions) has been largely disconnected from the core. The "spokes" have been few and inefficient, and there has been no strong sense of nationalism in Peru. While there has been a sentiment of unity among many of the indigenous, this has had more to do with their common ancestry of the great Inca civilization than with any sense of patriotism to the nation-state. Moreover, the notion of a Leviathan, which entails a government monopoly on the use of armed force, had always been a basic presumption in Peru until the Sendero experience. The military was among the most important power brokers in the country, and comprised most of the governments in Peruvian history. Further, the armed forces easily suppressed rebellions in the early 1960s. Yet Sendero in the early 1990s posed such a credible challenge to the Peruvian armed forces that it seemed the military did not in fact have a monopoly on the use of force, and that the state could in fact be toppled.

Peru lacked other elements associated with modernity. There has been no hegemony in the country's political landscape. Sometimes this has meant the emergence of military governments devoted to achieving a semblance of stability. Other times this has meant a failed democratic process mired in chaos and divisiveness. In the absence of hegemony, brutal force has been employed by both the state and subversive groups. Related to this nonhegemonic context, civil society was notoriously weak throughout the reign of Sendero, which was able to gain popular strength in part because it faced no real competition from other significantly powerful organizations aimed at representing the interests of the majority population of the country, the indigenous poor. Finally, despite the presence of some industrialization characteristic of modernity, overall Peru remained a staple economy with a premodern reliance on the agrarian and extractive sectors. It was a patchwork of modern and premodern features that set the stage for Sendero's struggle.

Which elements of Sendero's ideology and support base contributed to the group's success, and which were associated with its demise in the early 1990s? Sendero's resurrection of the image of historical Inca grandeur provided a sense of unity among Sendero's predominantly indigenous supporters. It was a key ingredient in SL's claim that it could lead the way toward restoring past glory to a population that suffered intensely under political subjugation for almost 500 years. Sendero was further able to harness the latent violence among the indigenous, accumulated over centuries of brutality at the hands of their oppressors. Guzmán summoned from the Inca legacy a passionate vengeance aimed at correcting past wrongs, which became a central pillar·of the group's strategic success.

The cult of leadership surrounding Guzmán was tied to his godlike stature of representing the fourth sword of Marxism. Thus, part of the power of Sendero's ideology lay in the presumption that its source was a living philosophical legend in the form of Guzmán. Beyond the specifics of his ideological platform, Guzmán was able to cultivate a remarkable degree of devotion among Sendero followers. His was a philosophy of praxis, whereby he designed ideas to motivate concrete revolutionary actions among his followers. The tight catechism of Sendero's ideology provided focus and direction to members, and equipped them with a perspective aimed at explaining the roots of their exploitation and subjugation.

What better vehicle for ideological dissemination than professors, teachers, and students—who dominated the ranks of Sendero? Through established schools, the state had essentially provided SL with an organized network for political indoctrination. Grossly underpaid and overworked teachers, many located in the periphery and disconnected from any sense of power, made for a natural base of recruits. Another easy target was the gargantuan surplus army of students, who were susceptible to radical explanations for the lack of adequate political representation and for the absence of suitable work. Here the role of language is crucial in relation to power. Many indigenous people in the Andean highlands spoke little or no Spanish, and many Lima-based government officials did not speak the native language of Quechua, creating a sense of alienation. Sendero teachers and professors reached students in their native tongue, while in many cases the state could not. There have been systems of power associated with language—Spanish as the language of Peru's coastal modern elite, and Quechua as the language of the indigenous poor in the highlands.

While Sendero had much in its favor with respect to both ideology and support base, it also possessed crucial weaknesses. Perhaps chief among these was Sendero's attempt to smother elements of the indigenous epistemology. Sendero's prohibition of indigenous holidays; its suppression of indigenous spirituality; and its contradictions to indigenous conceptions of time, space, family, and the nature of truth and political change spawned considerable resentment. Particularly repugnant for many was Sendero's ideological justification for extraordinary degrees of violence. These features became more unpopular as the war dragged on. Many indigenous people did not wish Sendero to impose upon them its modern communist ideology, and this is most evidenced by the huge popularity during the early 1990s of anti-Sendero self-defense groups. Hence this clash of epistemology, of systems of thought, represents an important piece of the puzzle concerning the demise of Sendero Luminoso.

Further, Guzmán's dictatorial role over a pyramid-structured organization spelled fatal vulnerabilities. Sendero Luminoso fell apart when Guzmán was captured. This godlike figurehead was instantly demoted to the position of incarcerated thug. Sendero's support base, having been the subject of dictation, did not know how to act when its dictator was jailed. Thus the combination of dictatorship and commensurate lack of autonomous power among members represented a crucial weakness for Sendero. It would render the group particularly vulnerable to government intelligence operations aimed at decapitating and thus dissolving the group.

Notes

1. For a discussion of Inca spirituality, see Owens, *Peru*, pp. 20–22.
2. An excellent discussion of cultural and other aspects of the Inca civilization can be found in Wright, *Stolen Continents*.
3. For a discussion of Amaru II, see Cotler, *Estado y nación en el Perú*, pp. 57–58.
4. Vásquez, "Peruvian Radicalism and the Sendero Luminoso," p. 198.
5. Mariátegui, *Seven ensayos*, p. 28.
6. Cotler, *Estado y nación en el Perú*, pp. 145–146.
7. This idea was apparent throughout the work of Mariátegui, for example. See *Seven ensayos*, pp. 20, 43.
8. González Prada, *Horas de luchas*, p. 185.
9. For an excellent overview of Mariátegui's work, see Vanden, *National Marxism in Latin America*.
10. See, for example, Mariátegui, *Seven ensayos*, pp. 43, 51–53, 201.
11. Mariátegui offers a complex analysis of the power of literature and words in *Seven ensayos*, pp. 239–350, esp. p. 235.
12. Ibid., p. 11.
13. Gamarra, "Estado, modernidad, y sociedad regional."
14. For a good discussion of this, see Stepan, *State and Society*, pp. 123–124.

15. Tapia, *Las fuerzas armadas y Sendero Luminoso,* pp. 23–25.

16. Movimiento Revolucionario Túpac Amaru (MRTA), "La historia del Movimiento Revolucionario Túpac Amaru," 9 June 1990.

17. Stepan, *State and Society,* pp. 124–125.

18. Dependency theory advocates the position that too close an economic relationship with northern powers such as the United States would likely result in maldevelopment. This school recommends a nonaligned political path combined with nationalist economics and redistribution of wealth and land. See, for example, dos Santos, "Structure of Dependence"; and Gunder Frank, *Latin America.*

19. Stepan, *State and Society,* pp. 127–136.

20. General José Graham Hurtado, leader of the president's advisory committee, quoted in Liisa North, "Ideological Orientation of Peru's Military Leaders," in Cynthia McClintock and Abraham Lowenthal, eds., *The Peruvian Experiment Reconsidered* (Princeton: Princeton University Press, 1983), p. 250.

21. Regarding land issues, see the superb work Hunefeldt, "Rural Landscape and Changing Political Awareness." Statistic from p. 110.

22. For the classic work on the theory of rising expectations, see Gurr, *Why Men Rebel.*

23. Cynthia McClintock, "Peru's Sendero Luminoso Rebellion: Origins and Trajectory," in Susan Eckstein, ed., *Power and Popular Protest: Latin American Social Movements* (Los Angeles: University of California Press, 2001), p. 73.

24. Ibid., p. 74.

25. Ibid., p. 68.

26. Tom Marks, "Making Revolution with Shining Path," in David Scott Palmer, ed., *Shining Path of Peru* (New York: St. Martin's Press, 1994), p. 213.

27. See Degregori, "Cosechando tempestades," p. 144. See also McClintock, "Peru's Sendero Luminoso Rebellion," p. 73.

28. Author interview with Jefrey Gamara, professor, Departamento de Antropología y Historia, Universidad Nacional de San Cristóbal de Huamanga, Ayacucho, Peru, 19 April 2001. Professor Gamara's uncle had worked at the university when Guzmán was there.

29. Jiménez Bacca, *Inicio, desarrollo, y ocaso del terrorismo,* p. 27.

30. Sendero Luminoso, "Documentos fundamentales y programa," 1988 (no specific date), translation by author.

31. Sendero Luminoso, "Línea internacional del PCP," no date, translation by author.

32. Ibid.

33. Sendero Luminoso, "Historic Speech from the Dungeons of the Enemy," 24 September 1992.

34. Sendero Luminoso, "Documentos fundamentales y programa."

35. Ibid.

36. Ibid.

37. Sendero Luminoso, "Para entender Mariátegui," 1969 (no specific date), translation by author.

38. Sendero Luminoso, "Línea militar," 1988 (no specific date), translation by author.

39. Sendero Luminoso, "Documentos fundamentales y programa."

40. Ibid., and Sendero Luminoso, "Somos los iniciadores," 19 April 1980.

41. Sendero Luminoso, "Entrevista al Presidente Gonzalo," July 1988 (no specific date).

42. Sendero Luminoso, "Sobre la campaña de rectificación con elecciones," August 1991 (no specific date), translation by author.

43. Sendero Luminoso, "Para entender Mariátegui."

44. Sendero Luminoso, "Retomemos a Mariátegui y reconstituyamos su partido," October 1975 (no specific date), translation by author.

45. Sendero Luminoso, "Línea militar."

46. Sendero Luminoso, "Retomemos a Mariátegui y reconstituyamos su partido."

47. Sendero Luminoso, "Documentos fundamentales y programa."

48. Sendero Luminoso, "Entrevista al Presidente Gonzalo," translation by author.

49. Sendero Luminoso, "Línea militar."

50. Sendero Luminoso, "Retomemos a Mariátegui y reconstituyamos su partido."

51. Peruvian indigenous culture in the Inca tradition is not a monolithic, institution, but there are many important commonalities, and these shall be the focus of the following discussion.

52. Author interviews with Jefrey Gamarra, 19 April 2001; and José Coronel Aguirre, manager, Ministerio de Promoción de la Mujer y del Desarrollo Humano, Ayacucho, Peru, 20 April 2001. See also the excellent piece Degregori, "Cosechando tempestades," esp. pp. 139–155.

53. Wright, *Stolen Continents*, pp. 180–181.

54. Sendero Luminoso, "Entrevista al Presidente Gonzalo."

55. Ibid.

56. Sendero Luminoso, "Línea militar."

57. Author interviews with various students at the Universidad Nacional de San Cristóbal de Huamanga, Ayacucho, Peru, 16–20 April 2001. For security reasons, students wished to remain anonymous.

58. Author interview with Jefrey Gamarra, 19 April 2001.

59. See, for example, del Pino, "Familia, cultura, y 'revolución,'" p. 180.

60. Sendero Luminoso, "No votar," February 1985 (no specific date).

61. Sendero Luminoso, "Línea militar."

62. Sendero Luminoso, "Entrevista al Presidente Gonzalo."

63. For a good contextual discussion of this, see Tapia, *Las fuerzas armadas y Sendero Luminoso,* esp. pp. 86–89.

64. Author interview with Guillermo Rochabrun Silva, professor, Departamento de Sociología, Pontificia Universidad Católica del Perú, Lima, 17 August 1999. See also Silva's excellent article "Crisis, Democracy, and the Left in Peru," *Latin American Perspectives* 15, no. 3 (1998): 79.

65. See Wise, "State Policy and Social Conflict in Peru," p. 72.

66. See McClintock, *Revolutionary Movements in Latin America,* p. 165.

67. For a broader discussion of this, see Rochlin, *Discovering the Americas,* pp. 211–213.

68. See McClintock, *Revolutionary Movements in Latin America,* p. 166.

69. Rochlin, *Discovering the Americas,* p. 211.

70. Author interview with Jefrey Gamarra, 19 April 2001.

71. For a good discussion of this, see Gorriti Ellenbogen, *Sendero,* p. 46.

72. See McClintock, *Revolutionary Movements in Latin America,* p. 292.

73. Ibid.

74. Degregori, "Cosechando tempestades," p. 134.

75. I interviewed peasants in the Huallaga Valley who were engaged in coca cultivation. See Rochlin, *Discovering the Americas,* pp. 210–213.

76. *El Comercio* (Lima), 28 July 1990.

77. Degregori, "Cosechando tempestades," p. 148.

78. Author interview with Carlos Reyna, investigator, DESCO, Centro de Estudios y Promoción del Desarrollo, Lima, 17 August 1999.

79. An obvious exception is the MRTA. But since the MRTA possessed far less power and far fewer supporters than Sendero Luminoso, it did not represent significant competition for SL.

80. For a good discussion of the role of women during the reign of Sendero, see Coral Cordero, "Las mujeres en la guerra"; Blondet, *La situación de la mujer en el Perú;* de la Cadena, "Las mujeres son mas indias"; and Kirk, *Grabado en pierda.*

81. See Spike Peterson, "Security and Sovereign States: What Is at Stake in Taking Feminism Seriously," in Spike Peterson, ed., *Gendered States: Feminist (Re)Visions of International Relations Theory* (Boulder: Lynne Rienner, 1992), pp. 31–64.

82. For an excellent discussion of the relation between women's movements and Sendero Luminoso, see Coral Cordero, "Las mujeres en las guerra," esp. pp. 337–357.

83. See P. B. Sinha, "Shining Path and the Problem of Subversion and Terrorism in Peru," *Strategic Analysis* 15, no. 16 (January 1993): 927. See also McClintock, *Revolutionary Movements in Latin America,* p. 47.

84. MRTA, "La historia del Movimiento Revolucionario Túpac Amaru," translation by author.

85. MRTA, "Las resoluciones de 1 Marzo 1982."

86. *Taz* (Germany), 6 May 1990, interview with Victor Polay Campos, leader of the MRTA, translation by author.

87. MRTA, "La historia del Movimiento Revolucionario Túpac Amaru," translation by author.

88. MRTA, "Neoliberalism and Globalization," no date; and MRTA, "Nota de prensa," 13 March 2001, translation by author.

89. MRTA, "Comunicado del MRTA," January 2001 (no specific date), translation by author.

90. Barricada International, "Light at the End of the Tunnel: Interview with an MRTA Leader (Comandante Andres)," 19 January 1991, http://burn/ucsd.edu/~ats/mrta/mrta-91.htm.

91. MRTA, "Mensaje a la nación," 19 April 2000, translation by author; and *Taz,* 6 May 1990, interview with Victor Polay, translation by author.

3

Sendero Luminoso: Concepts of Strategy, Security, and Power

Sendero Luminoso devised a daring and ultraviolent strategy that threatened to catapult the rebels into state power between 1989 and 1992. Sendero's most successful endeavors occurred against the backdrop of prevailing chaos and dysfunction in the "legitimate" political arena. Abruptly, the group crashed and burned almost immediately after the capture in 1992 of its deified leader. Supporters reached the end of the line with no remnants of tangible success and looked back at a horrific trail of carnage and destruction that SL leader Abimael Guzmán had insisted was necessary to restore the grandeur of the Inca Empire. In contrast to the assortment of cheerleaders behind the Mexican and even the Colombian guerrillas, it is striking that one is hard-pressed to find anyone with something positive to say about the legacy of Sendero Luminoso.[1]

Within the realm of strategy, Sendero Luminoso displayed particularly clever organizational skills. But most important, the Peruvian rebels clearly demonstrated that traditional force still matters, especially when combined with a steely resolve to do whatever is takes to reach power. The Sendero experience is also the story of the strategic lessons learned by a government that fared badly during the first ten years of its twelve-year war with the group. Such lessons concerned the power of consent, the importance of intelligence, the dangers of abusive violence, and the significance of localized power to Peru's predominantly indigenous population.

This chapter begins with a consideration of some broad strategic themes inherent in the actions of SL, before turning to an examination of the group's organizational structure and an analysis of particular phases of SL strategy based largely on original Sendero documents. A variety of implications surrounding state strategy during the crucial

1980–1992 period are also addressed. The chapter concludes with a theoretical analysis that draws from the classic strategic literature, and that
also probes the role of epistemology vis-à-vis the themes of power and
strategy. A brief analysis of the rather obscure guerrilla group the MRTA
is presented as a point of comparison from which to view Sendero.

Sendero and Broad Strategic Themes

Sendero Luminoso's central objective was to take power over the state
through the vehicle of a violent revolution. The group was not satisfied
with obtaining only a quotient of power, or with becoming an important
voice among others in political debates. SL strove for absolute and dictatorial power through state control. More specifically, according to a
Sendero document, the chief goals of the rebels were the

> demolition of the Peruvian State . . . to sweep away all imperialist
> oppression, mainly Yankee, and that of Soviet social-imperialism . . .
> to destroy bureaucratic capitalism . . . the liquidation of semi-feudal
> property . . . to respect the property and rights of the national bour-
> geoisie, or middle bourgeoisie, in the country as well as the city . . .
> develop the People's War . . . through a revolutionary army of a new
> type under the absolute control of the Party . . . and to complete the
> formation of the Peruvian nation.[2]

While there may be doubts surrounding some of Sendero's policies, its
objectives were simple and clear.

What were the strategies and tactics employed by Sendero to attain
its goals? First, timing is an important ingredient in any strategic affair.
In the group's attempt to read the pulse of change, in the spring of 1980
Sendero leaders declared, "It is time for a rupture."[3] This statement was
made in the context of Velasco's failed agrarian project, and more generally in the context of a nonhegemonic environment that precipitated
chaos and instability in "legitimate" politics. Hence, in a cacophony of
competing voices Sendero Luminoso viewed 1980 as the perfect time to
assert itself as *the* political voice.

SL devised a national military plan that was "strategically centralized and tactically decentralized."[4] In broad strokes the rebels' strategy
was rather basic. At the appropriate time, they would mobilize guerrilla
troops, assemble an arms cache, and obtain independent sources of
funding to initiate a guerrilla war that would gain momentum, eventually reach equilibrium with the state, and then overthrow it. It was a

strategy that rested heavily on violence and terror, transnational crime, and Maoist and other styles of guerrilla warfare. There were three general periods of struggle. The first involved a defensive strategy of guerrilla warfare whereby Sendero, initially weaker than the state, would build its forces and seek funding. After protracted struggle, SL planned to reach a phase of strategic equilibrium with the government whereupon the rebels would prepare the population for an imminent revolutionary takeover. A third period, the final offensive, would install Sendero as the sole state authority.[5]

Central to the group's strategy was the theory of terror and extraordinary use of violence. SL relied on classic terrorism to achieve power by instilling intense fear among the population through the awesome use of force. The state, from SL's perspective, would look increasingly powerless and ineffectual as Sendero's attacks grew more dramatic in the face of the government's inability to contain the situation.[6] According to the classic terrorist theory upon which Sendero relied, the government would attempt to restore its power through extreme emergency measures that inconvenienced, and in some cases brutalized, the general population in a desperate attempt to find and contain the guerrillas. It was during this process that Sendero planned to reach equilibrium with and then overthrow the state.

Violence for Sendero was not simply a tactic that served strategic ends; it represented a vital element of strategy itself. According to the group's documents, "Revolutionary violence is, therefore, the very essence of our historical process."[7] Much of this was justified with reference to Maoism. Sendero argued that "with regard to violence we start from the principle established by Chairman Mao Tse-tung: violence, that is the need for revolutionary violence, is a universal law with no exception."[8] Further, SL insisted that

> the party cannot be developed more but through the use of arms, through armed struggle. That is the hard lesson we have learned in 50 years, a great lesson that we should never forget: We have no power because we have no guns. Like Chairman Mao has written, whoever has more guns has more power.[9]

SL also leaned on homegrown heroes such as Mariátegui for ideological justification vis-à-vis the carnage committed by the rebels. The group did so by ignoring the bulk of the Peruvian thinker's literature and by focusing instead on quotes from his work such as "power is conquered through violence."[10] For Guzmán, human life was cheap, as evidenced by his assertion that the "triumph of the revolution will cost one million deaths."[11]

According to Guzmán, "war has two aspects, destructive and constructive."[12] Horrific violence and destruction, from Sendero's perspective, would permit the construction of a nirvana based on Gonzalo Thought. In order to deploy such violence, SL had to inculcate followers with the idea that revolutionary ends justified ultraviolent means. It also meant that Sendero had to devote considerable ideological work toward encouraging supporters to accept the notion of self-sacrifice.[13]

Organization

SL benefited from a sophisticated and effective organization (see Figure 3.1). Centralized under the command of Guzmán, the group's pyramid structure featured a variety of specialized and efficient departments. Sendero's cell structure also afforded a relatively high degree of security. SL had two major organizational structures, one primarily political and the other military. They were both under the authoritarian command of Guzmán, who acted as president of Sendero. At his right hand was the Central Committee, whose membership, which varied from nineteen to twenty-five persons at various times of SL's incarnation, represented the core of the party. There was a roughly equal division of men and women. In conjunction with Guzmán and his close aides ("Feliciano" and "Miriam"), this committee was responsible for developing and administrating political directives as well as strategic and tactical elements of military policy. Under the Central Committee were a Military Commission, national conference bodies, as well as the party congress. The presidency was also connected to a Political Bureau. These structures together composed the group's upper echelon, which presided over an assortment of specialized units. Below the major organizational structures was a hierarchy of cells. These generally included between five and nine members each, only one of whom was in contact with the immediately superior cell.[14]

Central military decisions rested with the president and his Central Committee. The Military Commission was divided into two separate departments, devoted to the countryside and to the cities (primarily Lima). Beyond this, the Sendero army was divided into the geographic regions. Each regional army consisted of battalions (composed of three companies), companies (composed of three platoons), and platoons (composed of nine to twelve combatants). These units were responsible

Figure 3.1   Organization of Sendero Luminoso

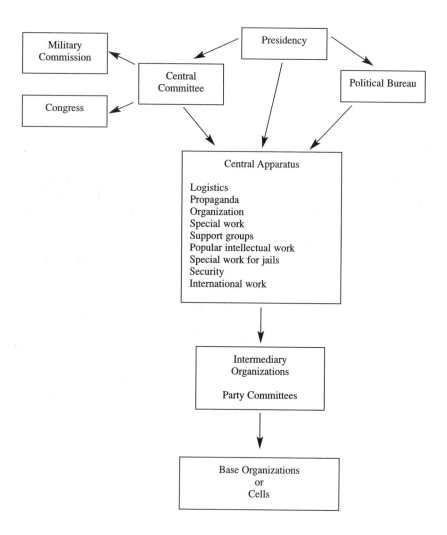

Source: Various SL documents and Jiménez Bacca, *Inicio, desarrollo, y ocaso del terrorismo.*

for committing the majority of SL's military and terrorist activities. Under these fell *fuerzas locales* (local forces) and *fuerzas bases* (base forces), which provided general support to the military and included a popular militia of permanent and part-time fighters.[15]

How did the organizational structure of the group affect its power? The reverence afforded to Guzmán by Sendero supporters meant that his ideas on strategy and politics were executed in a thorough and unchallenged fashion by devotees. The clearly dictatorial hierarchy was effective in ideological inculcation and in the execution of political and military directives emanating from Guzmán's inner circle. The extreme centralization of power in Gonzalo also meant that SL was virtually free of the divisive tendencies that have torn apart and thus debilitated the power of other Latin American guerrilla groups. Further, the sophisticated vertical hierarchy, and especially the cell structure, provided SL with clarity, efficiency, and a considerable degree of security. SL was not an easy group for intelligence forces to penetrate.

The strengths of Sendero also represented fatal weaknesses. The group was organized such that it could not survive the absence of Abimael Guzmán.[16] Further, the top-down, authoritarian nature of SL's structure increasingly alienated existing and potential supporters. As we saw, the failure of Velasco's aggressive land reform experiment was due in large part to the government's authoritarian directives and its antipathy toward localized and grassroots power. That popular craving for autonomous and localized power was also frustrated by Sendero's vertical and dictatorial framework. It is ironic that Sendero criticized the Velasco government for its centralized power structures, since the rebels were guilty of essentially the same grave error.

Phases of Strategy, Tactics, and Power

Beginning with its initiation of guerrilla warfare on 17 May 1980, Sendero Luminoso viewed itself as evolving through five phases of strategic development. The first phase, the "Initiation Plan," began in May 1980 and lasted through December of that year. It represented SL's commencement of armed struggle, with the rebels calculating that they committed 1,342 actions during their eight-month debut.[17] According to Sendero's own assessment of this period, "The beginnings were modest, almost without modern weapons."[18] Although the rebels were indeed weak at this incipient phase, the Peruvian government had misunderstood the nature of Sendero Luminoso, and had grossly underestimated its potential power—blunders that helped bolster the group's fortunes.

The second phase, the "Deployment Plan," lasted from January 1981 to January 1983 and included 5,350 armed actions by Sendero's count. The chief strategic goal during this period was to establish guerrilla zones by seizing control of specific territories and communities. An intensive campaign to obtain weapons was launched from May through September 1981, with the bulk of active guerrilla tactics conducted after that time. A chief objective, in the group's own words, was to "rock the countryside with guerrilla actions."[19] Particularly, this meant dominating the Ayacucho region, a goal that the group successfully accomplished during this period.

Classic tactical elements employed by Sendero during this phase were significant and continued through subsequent phases. SL implemented Mao's "basic tactics: when the enemy advances, we retreat; when the enemy is stalled, we harass him; when the enemy is tired, we attack him; when the enemy withdraws, we pursue him."[20] During this phase of Sendero's trajectory, the rebels explored the notion of moving toward the central and northern interior of the country, as the Peruvian military grew more cognizant of the group's activities in Ayacucho and surrounding regions. Sendero's fondness for the tactic of sabotage also became obvious during this phase, and became increasingly visible as the group evolved. Leaders argued that "sabotage weakens and undermines the social and economic system of the ruling exploiters, as in demolishing electrical towers and producing blackouts in wide areas of the center and north of the country."[21] Related attacks against the U.S. and Chinese embassies, as well as other symbolic sites, were contemplated during this period.

The third phase, the "Plan to Conquer Bases," lasted from May 1983 until September 1986 and featured an alarming escalation of armed attacks—28,621 by SL's count. This phase was highlighted by the migration of Sendero into various regions of the country, as it had contemplated earlier. To a significant extent the migration was a reaction to government advances in areas previously dominated by SL, but this shift of territorial position was also aimed at employing the Maoist tactic of "surrounding the cities from the countryside."[22] The rebels sought to arrive at a position whereby SL could starve Lima by choking it from food, fuel, and other necessities normally transported from rural areas. This move clashed with the spatial politics of the indigenous population, who traditionally had conducted busy commerce with Peru's urban centers. It represented one factor among others that would lead to escalating alienation among the indigenous from SL policies.[23]

Sendero supporters occasionally had been noticed since 1977 in the Huallaga Valley region, which is renowned as a chief site of narcotrafficking. Conclusive evidence of the group's presence in the area appeared in 1984–1985.[24] There are many strategic implications of Sendero's apparent role in this illicit trade. SL defended the financial interests of Peruvian coca growers and processors vis-à-vis higher-level Colombian traffickers, and also protested against the use of anticoca herbicides on the part of the U.S. and Peruvian governments. It is estimated that SL received U.S.$20 million to $30 million annually from its involvement in the trade.[25] Perhaps the illicit narcotics trade ranks with other economic booms witnessed by Peru over the ages, such as those associated with precious metals, guano, and the like. In some ways it was strategically wise for SL to take advantage of narcotrafficking, as it provided the guerrillas with economic self-sufficiency and helped finance arms purchases as well as relatively good salaries for many of Sendero's soldiers. All this contributed to Sendero's objective of constructing a bigger guerrilla army and creating the physical capacity to unleash horrific violence in a crusade to take power over the state.

But involvement in narcotrafficking was a double-edged sword and weakened Sendero's ideological credibility. Given that narcotrafficking represents unbridled neoliberalism, SL actively benefited from the very system it criticized and was attempting to overthrow. Sendero's legitimacy was also eroded by its participation in what amounted to international crime. Vulnerable to charges of terrorism, ideological hypocrisy, and crime, Sendero would be unable to claim the moral high ground that Mexico's Zapatistas later achieved.

Sendero's involvement in narcotrafficking intensified during the group's fourth strategic phase, the "Plan to Develop Bases," which lasted from December 1986 through May 1989. The group dominated the Uchiza region of the Huallaga Valley by 1987 and apparently deepened its involvement in the illicit trade. Guzmán became more adamant in his attempt to ward off anticoca herbicides in the area. He argued, for instance, that "we also denounce APRA's plans in the Alto Huallaga, where, under the pretext of fighting drug trafficking, they permit the use of the deadly pesticide 'Spike,' which the Yankee monopolies themselves say is like a series of small atomic bombs."[26] SL's role in this lucrative crime helped finance the astonishing 63,052 armed actions the group claimed to have committed during this twenty-nine-month period.

The rebels also took control of key areas of the country's central highlands, which supplied much of Lima's food, electricity, and water.[27] Not only was Sendero solidly entrenched in its tactic of choking the city by dominating the countryside, but it also began making significant inroads into Lima itself, which Sendero referred to as the "macrocephalic capital of an oppressed and backward nation."[28] Sendero Luminoso was approaching the peak of its power.

The final and most eventful phase of Sendero's reign of power, the "Great Plan to Develop Bases and to Serve the Conquest of Power," lasted from August 1989 until the capture of Guzmán in September

1992. It was during this phase that the group reached its apex, with armed membership swelling to over 23,000 soldiers. In 1990 alone, SL committed 23,090 armed actions.[29] And by late 1991 and early 1992, SL controlled about 40 percent of Peruvian territory.[30] Moreover, not only had the group consolidated power in key strategic areas of the countryside—its home base in the southern Andes, the narco-jungles of the Huallaga Valley, and the indigenous hinterland of the central and southern highlands—but Sendero was now deep into its scheme of conquering the urban terrain of Lima as well.[31]

With strong support from students and from residents of *pueblos jovenes,* by 1991 it looked as if SL might succeed in its goal of taking the capital and thus Peru. In May of that year a jubilant Guzmán declared that the rebels had finally achieved their long-established objective of strategic equilibrium with the state. The group was now ready to embark upon a final offensive to take control of the country, once Lima had been conquered.[32] Sendero's strategy during this period, which rested on a massive campaign of violence, is a textbook case of terrorist theory. The style of violence was typically gory and attention-grabbing. It went beyond SL's earlier antics such as hanging cats and dogs coupled with routine murders, and now graduated to an extraordinary brutality that at times appeared sadistic. Daily life in Lima during this period included profuse and random car bombings in conjunction with the placement of deadly explosives in scores of popular sites such as supermarkets. Political assassinations occurred regularly, while Sendero simultaneously succeeded in creating widespread power outages and severe shortages of water and other necessities. Further, some analysts note that residents of Lima, who had experienced a relatively peaceful history, were not as accustomed to violent injustice as the indigenous populations of the mountains, who had endured centuries of abuse at the hands of feudal masters. Hence, the real and horrific violence perhaps made a greater impact in Lima than in the Andes, where locals were more accustomed to such violence.[33]

The population grew increasingly terrorized as SL increased its bombing of Lima and cut off the bulk of the city's electricity and water. About 83 percent of Sendero's victims were unarmed civilians, compounding the sense of insecurity to the point of horror. Total political deaths, half of which were attributed to Sendero, jumped from 1,511 in 1988 to 2,877 in 1989; 3,734 in 1991; 3,044 in 1991; and 2,683 in 1992.[34] The state, unable to stem the rising tide of violence, appeared to much of the population as simultaneously inept and oppressive.

As Sendero's power escalated, it attempted to annihilate perceived threats to its authority. Perhaps the most notorious case was SL's 1992 assassination of Maria Elena Moyano as family members looked on. She was a famous Peruvian women's rights leader and an organizer of anti-Sendero self-defense groups in the *pueblos jovenes*. The assassination backfired, galvanizing public opinion to an even harsher view of the rebels and providing a focal point of public outrage over the carnage that had already been unleashed throughout Lima.[35] Sendero had also vehemently criticized the work of other humanist NGOs, such as the "glass of milk program," which the rebels chastised as being "mortgaged" to a dominant capitalist system. Beyond this, SL attacked the legal left in Peru as ineffectual and also launched armed struggle against its rival guerrillas, the MRTA. Overall, then, a central element of Sendero's strategy at this point was to decimate rivals on its violent path to take power over the state.

Sendero's involvement in narcotrafficking escalated during this period and helped finance its increasingly frequent armed offensives as well as its swelling roster of soldiers. In reaction to the charge that it received U.S.$30 million–$500 million annually in profit from the illicit trade, Sendero argued that

> drug trafficking is a "weapon to recover the moral superiority" of Yankee imperialism, providing it with a "moral position for a coordinated offensive" and with "hemispheric vision." . . . We see very clearly how sinister is the plan to slander the People's War as a "narco-terrorism" whose interests it serves.[37]

Branded as narco-terrorists, the rebels obviously were threatened by the U.S. Andean drug war of 1989–1990 (the Bush administration's Andean Initiative), which had the dual purpose of stemming drug flows and diminishing the power of local guerrillas.

Despite its steady acceleration of power and credible takeover bid against the state, Sendero began to suffer serious strategic losses in 1991 and 1992. Following a refashioned security approach by the new Fujimori government in conjunction with escalated U.S. military assistance under President Bush's Andean drug war, SL abruptly collapsed with the September 1992 capture of Guzmán by Peruvian security police.

Sendero Luminoso and Government Strategy

Sendero's successes and ultimate failure were considerably linked to security policies pursued by the state, particularly by the Peruvian armed forces. Prior to any knowledge of SL's existence, the military, before ceding power in 1980 to the civilian government of Fernando Belaúnde Terry, had entrenched a mobilization law that permitted it to intervene independently if security was threatened.[38] Despite this measure, however, the military would find itself ill-prepared to confront Sendero.

State policy evolved through five phases. The first period, 1980–1983, was characterized by a refusal to acknowledge Sendero's existence and significance. Although the intelligence agency of the Peruvian air force observed in February 1980 the existence of a guerrilla group preparing for war "under a Maoist conception," it erroneously likened the group to Nicaragua's Sandinistas and both the government and armed forces failed to act.[39] In fact, Sendero was all but ignored until about 1983. In the interim, despite the SL's escalating if still subdued public attacks, the government minimized the significance of the group by dismissing the subversives as cattle thieves and delinquents.[40] Still mired in a swamp of misconceptions regarding Sendero, President Belaúnde implied in 1981 that SL was directed by Colombian guerrillas who themselves had been under the tutelage of Cuba and the Soviet Union.[41] As the state fumbled, Sendero's forces flourished.

Policy shifted from the sheer denial that characterized the period 1980–1983 to the disastrous deployment of what amounted to state terror between 1983 and early 1986. The Peruvian military belatedly became convinced that its chief security threats were no longer located on the traditional terrain of the country's borders, but instead were internal. President Belaúnde, seemingly lacking a strategy of his own, yielded to policy established by the military.[42] Once the armed forces finally appreciated the threat posed by SL, they concocted a policy of indiscriminate terror designed to intimidate the rebels into submission, and to horrify the population into believing that joining the subversives was the wrong thing to do. It was a strategy similar in tone to the notorious "Dirty War" deployed by the Argentine government in the 1970s. Yet there was clear dissent regarding this policy from within sectors of the armed forces. Military police chief Adrián Huamán, who was stationed at the heart of Sendero's base in Ayacucho, urged leaders to promote developmental assistance rather than a campaign of terror. He was removed from office in 1984.[43]

The Peruvian scheme failed badly. Rather than selecting specific targets, the state alienated the masses by imposing a blanket of violence that resulted in the death, injury, and terrorization of thousands of innocent civilians. Deaths from presumed state violence reached a horrific peak of 4,319 in 1984, before falling to 1,359 in 1985 and 1,268 in 1986.

By comparison, murders on the part of SL rose from 1,760 in 1984 to 2,050 in 1985 and 2,549 in 1986.[44] The government and armed forces became even more unpopular against the backdrop of the military's previous loss of face during the Velasco regime. This amplified the sense of chaos emanating from the lack of political hegemony in the country. Ultimately, the unleashing of state terror played into the hands of Sendero. It swelled the group's membership and fanned the flames of further subversive activity, while the government looked worse daily.

The grim Peruvian "Dirty War" of 1983–1986 ended with the arrival of President Alan García of the APRA party, the first APRA candidate to reach the presidency. Haya de la Torre's old slogan that "only APRA can save Peru" became a sour joke during the incredibly chaotic García administration. Amid the failure were significant bright spots, however. Strategically, the high point of García's first two years of government (1986–1988) was the termination of the military's wall of violence. To his credit, the new president insisted that the armed forces show much more respect for human rights. He also directed considerable development assistance, particularly the provision of ample agrarian loans at a zero interest rate, to the Ayacucho region as well as to the southern highlands in general, which had been the heartland of Sendero influence. Public investment in Ayacucho increased some 400 percent between 1985 and 1986. In addition, public works projects employing nearly 100,000 people in the southern highlands were implemented in 1987.[45] Combined with other policies, the development effort helped to reduce Sendero's support base in this crucial strategic region.

But there were immense problems. Tension and suspicion between the military and the García government grew increasingly fierce. The president was rightly nervous about the prospects of a coup, as he alienated both local and global capital, the economy fell apart, and SL grew stronger. While García demonstrated the gumption to reduce sharply human rights abuses on the part of the military, he failed to grasp the importance of respecting the armed forces at the crucial time when the country was at war with potent subversives. For example, salaries at all ranks of the military were dismal, and up to 70 percent of military helicopters were inoperable due to a lack of fuel and spare parts.[46] Morale was at an all-time low for the Peruvian military during the late 1980s.

The last two years of the García presidency (1988–1990) witnessed an important shift in strategy that would not yield concrete effects until a few years later, when President Alberto Fujimori would take credit for them. Perhaps the most important development during this period was the establishment of the Dirección Nacional Contra el Terrorismo (DIN-COTE), an offshoot of which would be largely responsible for the capture of Abimael Guzmán in 1992. The creation of DINCOTE represented a key strategic shift toward a reliance on intelligence rather than force to topple Sendero, a strategy that ultimately proved quite successful.

The focus on intelligence was the highlight of a major strategic rethinking featured in a 1989 armed forces manual.[47] Given the pyramid structure of Sendero, it was now appreciated that an intelligence operation that succeeded in capturing Guzmán would decapitate and presumably destroy the rebel group. This refashioning of strategy included an appreciation of the perils associated with indiscriminate military violence. It also recognized the significance of improving the economic well-being of a population desperate enough to look to Sendero for leadership. While this rethinking of strategy was indeed crucial during the 1988–1990 era, concrete action by the government and armed forces vis-à-vis Sendero was minimal. To the Peruvian public, it looked as if the government was doing nothing while SL's power grew in leaps and bounds.

A vastly different political landscape appeared with the government of Alberto Fujimori. Despite vehement campaign promises to the contrary, he enacted one of Latin America's harshest IMF austerity packages almost immediately after assuming power in 1990. Military tanks prowled the streets of Lima to quell public protest over the removal of subsidies from basic items such as food and gasoline, and the majority of Lima's population was pushed into soup kitchens. Despite the draconian features of the austerity measures and the intense hardship they initially caused, the economic program eventually contributed to the return of stability in Peru by increasing the confidence of both domestic and global capital. Inflation, for example, fell drastically from over 7,000 percent in 1990 to double-digit figures in 1992. As the economic situation moved from the sheer chaos of the García government to the more orderly and stable ambience of the Fujimori presidency, the Peruvian public very slowly began to place more faith in the state.

Even Fujimori's move toward authoritarian political structures was greeted with widespread public support. This was the case with respect to his April 1992 *autogolpe* (self-coup), which empowered the executive at the same time that it obliterated both the Congress and the country's constitution. This move was seen by many as erasing a dysfunctional and divisive legislative system that produced scandals and infighting, but that could not manufacture clear and effective policy. It is remarkable that Fujimori's popularity rating swelled above 80 percent just after the *autogolpe*—a period that marked the peak of his checkered political career.[48] With his combination of economic and political "reforms," most Peruvians apparently viewed Fujimori as a firm and visionary politician. This served to stem the tide of support for subversive groups such as SL and the MRTA. More particularly, the theory of terrorism pursued by Sendero—which depended on a dithering state apparatus incapable of achieving public order—was neutralized by the strong policies of Fujimori, which contributed to the return of order in the country.

Beyond the sense of greater social order generated by the first Fujimori administration, two specific policies were most significant in leading to the decimation of Sendero by September 1992: the state's increasing reliance on intelligence, and the extraordinary promotion of self-defense units, or rondas, in the countryside.[49] With respect to intelligence, DINCOTE's leader, Antonio Ketín Vidal Herrera, indicated that his job was "to know everything about the adversary."[50] This data included not only addresses and phone numbers, but also personality traits, communication systems and codes, security systems, and so on. He used the analogy of the human body to explain that "to operate effectively, you have to know just where to go and how the system works."[51] Within DINCOTE a special intelligence subagency had been created by the García government in March 1990, the Grupo Especial de Inteligencia Nacional (GEIN), which would eventually capture Guzmán. By June 1990 the GEIN had raided an important SL safehouse.

Substantially increased state intelligence operations yielded the capture in January 1991 of Nelly Evans, a former nun and aunt of a dancer whose house was Guzmán's Lima hideout. Once President Fujimori's power became concentrated following his successful *autogolpe* of April 1992, he ordered thorough intelligence operations to be conducted throughout Lima, especially at universities, in an effort to gather information concerning the subversives. In contrast to the benign intelligence gathering by DINCOTE and GEIN, brutal antisubversive activities that occurred during this period may have been masterminded by the state's coordinating intelligence body, the Servicio de Inteligencia Nacional (SIN), which was headed by Vladimiro Montesinos.[52] These activities included the assassination of a professor and nine students at the Universidad de la Cantuta in Lima and the disappearance of over thirty-six students from the Universidad del Central in Huancayo. Thus, one component of Peruvian intelligence was directed solely at tracking key SL leaders, while other streams of covert activity had a more repressive tone.

Undercover operations were also established to infiltrate the narco-trafficking business in relation to Sendero. Leads established from the Evans arrest and other intelligence projects, plus valuable assistance from the U.S. Central Intelligence Agency (CIA), led to the pivotal arrest in September 1992 of Guzmán and other key Sendero leaders. This essentially decapitated the leadership of Sendero's extremely authoritarian structure. According to Colonel Benedicto Jiménez Bacca, who led the team that arrested the rebel leader, the CIA provided his group with equipment, counterinsurgency training, surveillance devices, transportation, and U.S.$5,000 a month for additional expenses.[53]

The second crucial strategic element pursued by the state that helped bring an end to Sendero Luminoso was the heavy reliance under the Fujimori government on rondas, especially in the countryside. Just as the apparatus of state intelligence systems existed but were underused in the 1980s, so too was the case with rondas, which had been used as early as the late 1970s in Peru to combat cattle thieves (whom, ironically, the state blamed for SL's actions during 1980–1982). The first strictly military rondas appeared in Ayacucho in 1982 and expanded in 1984, when they numbered approximately 200.[54] The idea behind these self-defense units was to arm peasants heavily enough that they could protect themselves from incursions by Sendero. Thus an underlying premise was that SL had bullied its way into controlling Peruvian territory and that many peasants did not wish to succumb to the imposition of SL control.

The idea of converting rondas into a centerpiece of government strategy emerged during the 1988–1989 rethinking of Peruvian security, which also bolstered the role of intelligence.[55] While the rondas would expand enormously under the Fujimori administration, the idea behind them had been hatched during the previous García government. Rondas repelled Sendero incursions in a variety of venues, including Ayacucho, Apurímac, Junín, Huancavelica, Pasco, and elsewhere. They provided formidable combat potential to formerly defenseless communities. The number of these self-defense units jumped dramatically from 200 in 1984 to 1,400 in 1991, when 10,000 guns in that year alone were distributed by the state to Andean peasants.[56] The use of rondas rose geometrically once again after Fujimori's *autogolpe*. By 1994, there were an estimated 232,668 ronderos, which essentially represented an immense localized army almost ten times the size of Sendero's militia at its peak.[57]

Rondas worked well primarily because the state strategically and cleverly chose to take advantage of the fact that the majority of Peruvians did not want Sendero to assume power in their communities, or in Peru more generally.[58] Second, the establishment of these self-defense units channeled autonomous and localized power to peasant communities. While the state provided guns and minimal training, real control was afforded at the local level to peasants themselves, who warded off Sendero based largely on their own strategies and tactics. The absence of localized power had been a chronic political problem in Peru. It was a major factor behind the failure of Velasco's agrarian reform policy, and also proved to be a fatal weakness in Sendero's strategy of imposition. In this sense, the establishment of rondas may have strengthened the weak fabric of Peruvian civil society. Further, rather than contributing to violence, the massive expansion of rondas during 1991 actually reduced politically related deaths by deterring Sendero attacks.[59] In addition, fewer human rights abuses were committed by the armed forces in these years—535 cases in 1991, 239 in 1992, and 105 in 1993.[60]

Although the strategic situation for the Peruvian state improved decisively during the first years of the Fujimori government, this period was not without blemish. While rondas were strategically effective and empowered local communities, the Peruvian armed forces continued to face a strong language barrier vis-à-vis many Andean peasants, since the majority of the military could not communicate in the indigenous language of Quechua. Beyond this, military morale remained notoriously low. Salaries for officers were desperately inadequate—a Peruvian general in 1991 received a paycheck of only U.S.$210 monthly, compared to U.S.$558 in Ecuador and U.S.$1,115 in Chile.[61] This set the stage for widespread political corruption among the Peruvian armed forces. While human rights abuses declined on the part of the military, other horrific aspects of warfare accelerated. Political deaths rose from 2,877 in 1989 to a peak of 3,745 in 1990, fell to 3,044 in 1991, and fell again to 2,683 in 1992.[62] Out of 7,383 "disappearances" (murders) estimated to have been perpetrated by the state, 27.6 percent are attributed to the 1990–1996 period of the Fujimori government.[63] President Alejandro Toledo, elected in 2001, estimated that at least 10,000 Peruvians disappeared at the hands of state forces in the struggle against Sendero and the MRTA.[64]

There were other problems. A popular target of criticism during this era was a "faceless judge" system implemented between 1992 and October 1997. Detractors viewed it as undemocratic and unfair, while supporters argued that system was necessary to confront death threats and intimidation vis-à-vis judges who tried suspected subversives.[65] Convincing arguments have been made that the judicial system may have been highly overzealous in its attempt to imprison Sendero suspects. Peru's national coordinator of human rights indicated that by 1996 about 30 percent of 5,000 jailed "terrorists" were probably innocent.[66] In addition, although economic order did indeed visit Peru in the early years of the Fujimori government, it came at the cost of vast impoverishment. Finally, a host of "dirty deals" fomented by Fujimori and his spy chief, Vladimiro Montesinos, occurred during this period, but would not become obvious to the public until the twilight of the Fujimori presidency.

Following the decisive September 1992 arrest in Lima of Guzmán, his close aide "Miriam," and the near entirety of SL's Political Bureau, President Fujimori opportunistically framed the capture into a sensational media spectacle.[67] Steeped in a carnival ambience, the highlight of this extravaganza was the unveiling of the SL leader in a circus-style animal cage. Guzmán, dressed in a stereotypical black-striped prison outfit, was ordered to remove his shirt, revealing his obesity and a range of skin ailments. The Fujimori public relations team worked diligently to present Guzmán as a monster who had committed the worst terrorism in the country's tortured history, rather than the "Last Inca," as his supporters had thought of him.

From his prison cell on a remote coastal island, Abimael Guzmán in 1993 ordered SL supporters still at large to engage in a peace process with the Fujimori government. Outraged at his concessions, hardcore SL Political Bureau member Alberto Ramírez Durand ("Feliciano"), still at large, created a new organization called Sendero Rojo. This splinter group, which rejected Guzmán's desperate plea for peace, vowed to perpetuate the armed struggle. But Sendero Rojo floundered and bore little resemblance the thriving revolutionary movement of Sendero Luminoso. With just a few hundred supporters compared to the 23,000 armed members of Sendero at its peak in 1991, the offshoot withered in the absence of its small, charismatic cadre of original leaders, who had dictated policy to supporters in a highly authoritarian manner. The Rojo rebels spent much of their time hiding in the country's northern jungle, the heart of Peru's narcotrafficking sector, until Ramírez Durand and his chief associates were captured on 14 July 1999. President Fujimori unsuccessfully attempted to manipulate this event in a desperate move to boost his doomed political career, which imploded in late 2000 when he was literally fired from his position as head of state.

Thus without any significant measure of decentralized power and decisionmaking apparatus, SL dissolved almost instantly after the capture of its leader and his close circle of comrades. Thousands of former SL supporters accepted various rounds of amnesty offered by the Fujimori government. At present a few hundred Sendero supporters led by Eulogio Cerdón Cardozo ("Artemio") are presumed to persist near Ayacucho and in the Huallaga Valley region of Peru.[68] In what appeared to be an isolated incident, SL was blamed by Peruvian authorities for detonating a car bomb in March 2002 near the U.S. embassy in Lima, just days before the official visit of President Bush.

The MRTA: Power and Strategy

With only about 1,500 combatants, the MRTA never approached the power wielded by Sendero. Yet this guerrilla group made its mark on Peruvian politics, the highlight of which was its seizure of the Japanese embassy in Lima between December 1996 and April 1997. Like Sendero, the MRTA found the Peruvian political system to be unworkable. According to Victor Polay Campos, the group's leader, "the goal of the MRTA is to replace the so-called representative democracy with the power of the people."[69] This would entail a revolutionary "seizure of power" to create a socialist political economy.[70] The group's documents stress that "the economic vision of the MRTA is a mixed economy based on communal planning. This would allow for limited private ownership, but an emphasis would be placed upon communal ownership."[71] This objective was similar to the kind of political economy imagined by the Sandinstas in Nicaragua, for whom the MRTA had a great deal of respect. The MRTA's goal of establishing a Cuban-Nicaraguan model differed substantially from the closed, Maoist economy vaguely imagined by Sendero.

Although the MRTA did indeed utilize force in a vain attempt to achieve its goals, it did not deploy the sort of indiscriminate violence that resulted in the carnage created by Sendero. The MRTA relied on a strategy that involved specific targets, and that tended to avoid innocent civilians. It was an approach calculated to avoid the public outrage evoked by SL's path of destruction. The MRTA strategically presented itself as a much kinder and gentler subversive movement than Sendero, in the hope of attracting huge numbers of supporters, who ultimately never materialized. Demonstrative of this strategic style was the MRTA's occupation of seven radio stations in Lima in 1988, its kidnapping of a prominent air force general and businessperson that same year, and its seizure and redistribution to striking miners of a truckload of chickens in October 1988. In January 1990 the group assassinated former defense minister E. López Albujar in what the rebels claimed was retaliation for the minister's hard-line policy toward the group. Thus, the MRTA did indeed commit assassinations, kidnappings, and the like, but in general its targets were more specific than Sendero's.

The MRTA had a three-tiered revolutionary strategy. The first stage was defensive and aimed at ensuring the survival of a core group of revolutionaries. The second step entailed an accumulation of supporters through "education, organization and revolutionary mobilization." The great majority of MRTA members were students, especially near the beginning of its struggle. A final stage involved the creation of a revolutionary army that would "capture power" and destroy the "repressive apparatus of class domination."[72] This revolutionary army was structured through a loose, three-level organization that included the army itself, a part-time militia, and communities that served as a support base.

Organizationally, the MRTA was headed by its National Executive Committee, which was directed by Campos until his final arrest in 1992. Because the MRTA was not directed by a cult of personality and did not adopt the pyramid structure that characterized Sendero, it was able to survive despite the periodic capture by Peruvian authorities of leading members. Under the executive level fell commissions dedicated to organization, security, recruitment, public relations, and community work. The group was also divided politically into various regions and zones.

Although at times it succeeded at making its voice heard, the group was never relatively powerful. Geographically, the MRTA established a presence in Huancayo (the heartland of its precursor group, the MIR), in the capital of Lima, and in the department of San Martín. Since San Martín has been a bastion of narcotrafficking, part of the MRTA's strategy apparently involved the financial support derived from its participation in the illicit drug trade, which has been documented by authorities.[73] In 1987 the group briefly occupied the town of Juanjui in the Huallaga Valley, where it captured an arms cache. Yet overall the MRTA lacked the lavish finances of Sendero, and paled in most other respects as well. It had less than 10 percent of SL's membership base, and was responsible for less than 10 percent of the number of violent deaths attributed to Sendero Luminoso.

While Peruvians had been familiar with the MRTA and its activities since the mid-1980s, the rebel group did not receive international renown until its seizure of the Japanese embassy in Lima. According to MRTA documents, the seizure occurred about a year after the government foiled a plot by the rebels, known as Operación Edgar Sanchez, to attract widespread attention by "occupying" the Peruvian Congress.[74] Fourteen MRTA members disguised as food servers entered a lavish party held at the Japanese embassy on 17 December 1996 and seized control through what amounted to a mass kidnapping. Within days the rebels freed many hostages, but continued to hold seventy-two people, including the brother of President Alberto Fujimori. According the MRTA documents, "The operation has been conducted to protest the imposition of the Japanese Government in the political life of our country with its violation of human rights applied by the government of Alberto Fujimori." MRTA demands included a "change in the political economy," the liberation of all MRTA members held captive by government forces, and payment by the government to the MRTA of a so-called war tax.[75]

The seizure of the embassy by the MRTA proved to be a strategic disaster that ultimately eroded any credibility the group had hoped to establish. Its demands appeared as foolish to most Peruvians, and it seemed likely from the beginning that the episode would end badly. After four months of unfruitful negotiations, the Peruvian government finally ordered U.S.-trained special forces to storm the embassy. All fourteen MRTA members were executed in what the rebels complained was "unequal combat" launched by the "dictator Fujimori" and the "Montecinista mafia" (a reference to Vladimiro Montecinos).[76] Evidence later emerged suggesting that at least some of the MRTA militants were needlessly executed by the government's special forces. Japanese embassy workers who witnessed the episode eventually testified that certain MRTA members had clearly asked to surrender peacefully, and that at least three MRTA rebels had been tied up and interrogated by state forces before later turning up dead with bullet wounds to the head.[77]

While the MRTA purported to be a kinder and gentler rebel movement than Sendero and tended to avoid episodes that resulted in the deaths of innocent civilians, its support base and power never approached that of Sendero. And although it relied upon specific assassinations, targeted kidnappings, and selective bombings rather than the more random violence associated with Sendero, some of the MRTA's demands and objectives appeared nevertheless unachievable. For example, the group's goal of constructing a Cuban-Nicaraguan styled revolutionary army to take power over the state seemed unworkable and outdated in the 1990s. Thus without a charismatic leader, a brilliant organizational machine, a feasible ideology, or a willingness to employ extraordinary degrees of force, the MRTA never appeared as a serious contender to either Sendero or to the state. While scant remains of the MRTA persist at the dawn of a new millennium, experts concur that especially since the Japanese embassy incident the group is finished politically.[78]

Security, Strategy, Power: Theory and Analysis

"Presidente Gonzalo" was revered by his followers as the fourth sword of Marxism and held a deep ideological devotion to Mao Tse-tung. But how closely did Guzmán follow his Asian hero? Guzmán's view of Peru rhymed with Mao's 1937 assessment of China as being "half colonial and half feudal; it is a country that is politically, militarily, and economically backward."[79] There are some other similarities in terms of the strong indoctrination process present in both cases, as well as the reverence afforded by supporters to the supreme leadership. In terms of military structure, there is some resemblance between Sendero's model and that described by Mao in his tract *On Guerrilla Warfare,* particularly in regard to the organization of combat units and the nature of background support.[80]

But there are probably more distinctions than similarities between the strategies of Mao and those of the less successful Guzmán. In contradistinction to the rigid, top-down control imposed by Sendero, which usurped autonomous or community-based power, Mao writes that those higher on the military hierarchy "suggest the nature of the action to be taken but cannot define it" so that subordinate groups "have more or less complete local control."[81] There are other contrasts. Sendero's brilliant recruitment policies, particularly the use of teachers and schools, as well as its horrific deployment of violence, more closely resembled the tactics of the Khmer Rouge than Maoist thought.[82] And while SL claimed to mimic Mao's strategy of "surrounding the cities from the countryside," the group took a fundamentally different fork in the road. "Going further, President Gonzalo specifies that in the cities armed actions should be carried forward as a complement, since international experience, as well as our own, demonstrates that this is feasible."[83] Yet another distinction is that while Mao demonstrated a profound grasp of the historical dimensions of strategy and of the strategic classics, Sendero displayed little evidence of such familiarity.[84]

Mao and Guzmán also differed on the supremely important issue of force. Mao accepted the role of violence in warfare and argued that "guerrilla activities are the university of war."[85] But he also warned against the strategic dangers associated with the abuse of violence, especially in relation to the necessity of cultivating consent from the masses. Moreover, he argued that a cardinal rule for guerrillas is to "be neither selfish nor unjust" and to "be courteous" to the general population.[86] Mao noted that "because guerrilla warfare basically derives from the masses and is supported by them, it can neither exist nor flourish if it separates itself from their sympathies and cooperation."[87] In sharp contradiction to this strategic maxim was Sendero's heavy reliance on outrageous violence and indiscriminate terror, which predictably served to erode mass support for the rebels. Further, since SL did not come close to generating the consent of most Peruvians, it presumably would have relied on a continued reign of terror had it actually succeeded at its goal of usurping the state.

Although Sendero documents in general do not refer to the classic strategic literature outside the traditions of Lenin and Mao, there are some elements of the group's strategy that are commensurate with the classics. Perhaps chief among these are the grim features of warfare underscored by Clausewitz.[88] Relevant to the SL experience are his dictums that "war is an act of force, and there is no logical limit to that force," and that the fundamental trinity of war includes "primordial violence, hatred, and enmity."[89] Sendero also seemed to follow Clausewitz's advice "to bring about a gradual exhaustion of his [the enemy's] physical and moral resistance."[90] Beyond Clausewitz, the story of Sendero is also reminiscent of Thucydides' contention that war is motivated by a lust for power and by fear.[91]

Given Guzmán's devotion to an Asian revolutionary such as Mao, he might have paid more attention to the classic Chinese strategists Sun Tzu I and Sun Tzu II. Some of Sendero's successful strategic features had been propounded upon by that duo many centuries earlier. These include Sun Tzu II's contention that meaning is important for battle, as was manifested in SL's masterful indoctrination process for the purpose of warfare.[92] Yet Sendero veered from the central concept in the works of both Sun Tzu I and Sun Tzu II—"the Way," which entails the notions of humaneness and consent and also includes a repugnance for violence.

All the classic strategic masters emphasized the importance of terrain in warfare.[93] What is interesting about Sendero is not so much its maneuvers in the mountains or jungles, since guerrilla warfare in such environments has been commonplace throughout Latin America. Rather, a distinguishing feature is Sendero's attempt to take Lima—one of Latin America's largest cities, with 7 million people—and therefore to deliver guerrilla warfare to urban terrain. It accomplished this principally through the use of terror and sabotage. Although SL can be distinguished from other post–Cold War guerrilla groups as introducing the urban landscape as a fresh terrain of guerrilla warfare in the Americas, strategic blunders on this uncharted site contributed to the group's demise.

The element of organization represents another classic feature of strategic thinking—one especially emphasized by Clausewitz, Sun Tzu I, and Sun Tzu II. SL's strategic framework was simultaneously a strength and a liability. Although Sendero expressed brilliant qualities in its organizational framework—especially with regard to the use of teachers and schools as recruitment camps, and to the security afforded by the group's cell structure—a gaping failure was its extreme concentration of power at the top of the hierarchy, especially in the figure of Guzmán. Ultimately, Sendero rested on a wobbly structure of megalomania.

Beyond the points of strategy associated with the classic literature, the issue regarding systems of thought is also germane to the Sendero experience.[94] SL clashed with the epistemology of many of its indigenous supporters, which served to limit the tenure of existing members and to repel potential candidates. Its modern and traditionally communist ideology collided with the indigenous sense of time, space, family cycle, and spirituality. Further, as a relic of a previous epoch, Sendero Luminoso's commitment to pseudo-Maoism would not have been an easy fit with the global environment of transnational capitalism had the group actually succeeded at usurping the Peruvian state. Except for its involvement in the realm of global crime, Sendero did not at all conform to postmodern developments in terms of economy, politics, culture, ethnicity, and the like. Ultimately, Sendero represented a failed bid at modernity.

Finally, what is particularly striking about Sendero is the extraordinarily negative public image it managed to generate. Praise for the group has been almost nonexistent since it fell apart in 1992. This is especially obvious in the substantial body of literature that has been published on this important subversive movement. It stands in contrast to the situation of other guerrilla organizations, which despite the presence of animosity toward them have cultivated some identifiable degree of public respect and admiration. Sendero's penchant for terror and violence, its view of power over society and of taking power over the state, among other factors, led many to concur that it was a "total failure, ideologically, militarily, in every way."[95] Yet the Sendero experience brought into focus serious problems in the Peruvian political landscape that require attention at the beginning of the new millennium, including social fragmentation, problems associated with ethnicity and class, and the perils of the country's overcentralized political system.

How does the government fare with regard to the quality of strategy it pursued during the reign of SL? It got off to a poor start, to say the least. Many classic strategists, such as Lao Tzu, suggest that it is important to detect problems early and to deal effectively with them at an incipient phase.[96] Yet the Peruvian government under Belaúnde floundered badly, ignoring existing information from intelligence services that indicated the creation and advance of a significant revolutionary movement. Root causes of revolutionary sentiment went undiagnosed and untreated, allowing Sendero to flourish from 1980 to mid-1983.

Disastrously, the military chose to unleash a reign of indiscriminate terror between 1983 and 1986. While *terrorism* is a term usually reserved for nonstate actors, the state's campaign of violence during this grim period had objectives similar to those of Sendero: to terrorize the masses into fearful submission. The result is reminiscent of a negative lesson emphasized by Sun Tzu: "To be violent at first and wind up fearing one's people is the epitome of ineptitude."[97] A basic strategic point, one not appreciated by the state during this period, is that the government must avoid indiscriminate and unnecessary force.

There were other weaknesses. First, because the state did not appreciate the organizational structure of Sendero, especially its pyramid framework and its cult of leadership, it did not at first formulate the correct strategy to combat the group. The strategy that eventually proved successful at destroying SL—the capture of Guzmán through the use of intelligence and surveillance—presumably could have been effective near the beginning of the struggle had the government appreciated the structure of the rebel movement. Second, and perhaps even more serious, the state did not appear to understand such basic concepts as good government, the cultivation of societal consent, and the attempt to consolidate hegemony.[98] If it had, it never would have embarked upon its failed strategy of indiscriminate terror in the countryside, which served to push much of the neutral population into the arms of Sendero.

The García government (1985–1990) badly exacerbated the already woeful predicament in Peru. The policies of President García that contributed most to Sendero's surge of power during this pivotal period were in the realm of international finance. Foremost, the García government failed to appreciate a fundamental rupture in global politics. Transnational capital was now largely calling the shots, not nationalistic third world governments, as may have occurred to varying extents in Latin America from the 1930s to the 1970s. Thus the García government failed to take heed of Machiavelli's basic assertion that "it behoves one to adapt oneself to the times if one wants to enjoy continued good fortune."[99] Beyond the state's failure to read the pulse of change, much of the blame should also be placed on the IMF and international finance, whose tough unifocus on imposing neoliberalism to cure the ills of the Peruvian economy ignored its effect of promoting the strength of Sendero Luminoso. Some sort of economic restructuring was required, but such projects cannot be anything near successful if they worsen existing strategic problems.

President Alberto Fujimori got off to a rough start. His administration's first few years in office were blighted by public outrage over the "Fujishock," by the escalation of Sendero's power, and by widespread desertion among the nation's armed forces. But the tables turned by 1992, when most Peruvians grew wildly enthusiastic about their bold leader. He understood Lao Tzu's cardinal rule that "in government it is order that matters."[100] The president restored order by implementing ideas established during the García administration. Principally this meant a reliance upon intelligence and surveillance, an approach celebrated by strategists over the millennia, as a means of decapitating the top of Sendero's pyramid.[101] It also entailed a strategy of limiting the bottom of that pyramid by proliferating rondas, whereby state-armed peasants were afforded with rare localized power. Rather than clashing with the indigenous epistemology as SL had, the state now placed power in the hands of indigenous Peruvians. Still, the government itself in many ways failed to understand the indigenous culture, as exemplified by a language barrier that has blocked communication between the state and much of the Andean population.

Conclusion

The rise and fall of Sendero Luminoso suggests important lessons regarding strategy and security. Many such lessons, both positive and negative, come into clearer focus through a consultation with the classic strategic literature. In broad strokes, Sendero owed much its success to classic themes relating to political organization, leadership, the role of indoctrination, the use of force, and the manipulation of grave errors on the part of the enemy. The saga of the Peruvian government is related to strategic themes such as timing, knowing the enemy, as well as the utility of intelligence and surveillance. Although the issue of consent was relevant to the struggles of both parties, their grasp of basic strategic principals was decidedly incomplete.

The analysis of systems of thought can also be helpful in considering the successes, failures, and strategic lessons of the Sendero experience. SL's modern system of thought clashed with its dominant support base of indigenous members. This entailed dispositions toward such concepts as time, space, spirituality, family cycle, authority structure, and commerce. It was one important factor among others that weakened the group, by slowly alienating its membership and by repelling potential supporters. Further, almost the entirety of Sendero's project was out of step with what could be viewed as an epistemological rupture in global power relations. SL's Maoist and xenophobic political-economic model, especially after the fall of the Soviet Union in 1990, did not flow with broad global trends. Neither did its grim reliance on violence, its failure to cultivate social consent, its shunning of national and international NGOs, its secrecy, its fanaticism and absolutism, its unifocus on class, and its binary analysis. Thus, even if Sendero had succeeded in usurping the state, it would not likely have held power for long.

Similar criticisms can be made regarding the Peruvian state. Certainly the García administration was out of synch with major transformations in global political economy, forcing ordinary Peruvians to pay an exorbitant price for their government's myopia. This also played directly into the hands of Sendero, which took advantage of weak and blundering politicians. Despite their profound differences, both Sendero and the pre-Fujimori state represented failed attempts at a modern project. Order did not return to Peru until after 1990, when the country adopted economic and security policies commensurate with the post–Cold War era, including a more workable relationship with transnational capital and a strategic focus upon intelligence, surveillance, and reconnaissance (ISR). The readjustment of Peru's economy to synchronize with transnational capitalism promoted order to the extent that local and global capital were no longer fiercely hostile to the country's economy, as they had been from 1986 to 1990. But if such policies exacerbate the division of wealth and fail to redress endemic poverty, the seeds will be sown for future guerrilla movements. And it is unlikely that ISR alone can erase the strategic effects of such fundamental problems.

Another striking element of the Sendero experience is the politics of ethnicity. Sendero Luminoso channeled centuries of indigenous hostilities and resentments into an angry rebel movement. Remarkably, through ideological smoke and mirrors, it did so by subsuming the crucial element of ethnicity to that of class. It seems entirely possible that an uprising could occur in Peru once again with the issue of ethnicity much more in the forefront than was the case in the Sendero struggle. That is, there will likely be other attempts at restoring the greatness of the Inca Empire. This would be especially probable if persistent problems that contributed to the rise of SL remain unaddressed, such as extreme poverty and unemployment, the lack of localized power, and the persistence of racism and language barriers. President Alejandro Toledo (2001–), emphasizing his own indigenous background, has pledged to fight these chronic problems. But a host of security woes could easily reemerge if President Toledo succeeds at raising political expectations with false promises. A hint of this appeared with the sudden emergence of a network of paralyzing and violent strikes throughout Peru in June 2002, when the populace rebuked President Toledo's aggressive scheme of privatization of state industries in contradiction to his earlier campaign promises.

Notes

1. This is obvious after a rather thorough inspection of the literature on Sendero. More subjectively, even among discussions with dozens of students I interviewed at the Universidad Nacional de San Cristóbal de Huamanga in Ayacucho, where Sendero formed, any commentary concerning Sendero was negative.

2. Sendero Luminoso, "Documentos fundamentales y programa," 1988 (no specific date), translation by author.

3. Sendero Luminoso, "Somos los iniciadores," 19 April 1980, translation by author.

4. Sendero Luminoso, "Línea militar," 1988 (no specific date), translation by author.

5. For a discussion of this, see Jiménez Bacca, *Inicio, desarrollo, y ocaso del terrorismo,* pp. 80–81.

6. For a discussion of this, see Manrique, "La guerra en la region central," p. 197.

7. Sendero Luminoso, "Línea militar," translation by author.

8. Sendero Luminoso, "Entrevista al Presidente Gonzalo," July 1988 (no specific date), translation by author.

9. Sendero Luminoso, "Somos los iniciadores," translation by author.

10. Sendero Luminoso, "Retomemos a Mariátegui y reconstituyamos su partido," October 1975 (no specific date), translation by author.

11. Quoted in Degregori, "Cosechando tempestades," p. 149.

12. Sendero Luminoso, "Entrevista al Presidente Gonzalo," translation by author.

13. See Gorriti Ellenbogen, *Sendero,* p. 171.

14. Under the upper-echelon nexus formed by the presidency, the Central Committee, and the Political Bureau fell the Central Apparatus. These were essentially administrative agencies enacting policies formulated by the president and his Central Committee. These nine departments were devoted to logistics, propaganda, organization, special work, support groups, popular intellectual work, special work for jails, security, and international work. Under that centralized bureaucracy were geographically divided grassroots organizations. The intermediary organizations and party committees included eight regional

committees. The principal committee, which directed the others, was located in the Sendero heartland of Ayacucho-Apurímac-Huancavelica. The other regional committees were devoted to the south, north, center, metropolitan, mid-north, and mid-south areas of the country. Also under the principal regional committee were various grassroots structures including zonal committees, subzonal committees, cell committees, and cells.

15. For a detailed description of the structure of Sendero Luminoso, see Jiménez Bacca, *Inicio, desarrollo, y ocaso del terrorismo,* pp. 269–536.

16. Author interview with General Hector Jhon Caro, dean, Universidad Nacional Federico Villareal, Lima, 17 August 1999.

17. Sendero Luminoso, "Plan of Strategic Development," 1990 (no specific date).

18. Sendero Luminoso, "Línea militar," translation by author.

19. Sendero Luminoso, "Plan of Strategic Development," translation by author.

20. Sendero Luminoso, "Línea militar," translation by author.

21. Sendero Luminoso, "Desarrollar la guerra," 1981 (no specific date), translation by author.

22. Sendero Luminoso, "Línea militar," translation by author.

23. Author interview with José Coronel Aguirre, manager, Ministerio de Promoción de la Mujer y del Desarrollo Humano, Ayacucho, Peru, 20 April 2001.

24. See, for example, Gorriti Ellenbogen, *Sendero,* pp. 81, 169. See also Jiménez Bacca, *Inicio, desarrollo, y ocaso del terrorismo,* pp. 387–389.

25. See Jiménez Bacca, *Inicio, desarrollo, y ocaso del terrorismo,* p. 389.

26. Sendero Luminoso, "Entrevista al Presidente Gonzalo," translation by author.

27. McClintock, *Revolutionary Movements in Latin America,* p. 86.

28. Author interview with General Hector Jhon Caro, 17 August 1999, who estimated that SL penetrated Lima beginning in 1987.

29. Sendero Luminoso, "Plan of Strategic Development."

30. See McClintock, *Revolutionary Movements in Latin America,* p. 81.

31. See Burt, "Sendero Luminoso y la 'batalla decisiva,'" p. 265.

32. Sendero Luminoso, "Historic Speech from the Dungeons of the Enemy: Speech from the Tiger Cage," 24 September 1992. See also Burt, "Sendero Luminoso y la 'batalla decisiva,'" p. 284.

33. Author interview with Jefrey Gamarra, professor, Departamento de Antropología y Historia, Universidad Nacional de San Cristóbal de Huamanga, 16 April 2001.

34. McClintock, *Revolutionary Movements in Latin America,* p. 117.

35. See, for example, Tapia, *Las fuerzas armadas y Sendero Luminoso,* p. 133.

36. See Manrique, "La guerra en la region central"; and Burt, "Sendero Luminoso y la 'batalla decisiva,'" pp. 202–211, 272.

37. Sendero Luminoso, "Plan of Strategic Development."

38. For a broader discussion of this, see George Vásquez, "The Peruvian Army in War and Peace: 1980–1992," *Journal of Third World Studies* 11, no. 2 (fall 1994): 102.

39. Gorriti Ellenbogen, *Sendero,* p. 91.

40. See Mauceri, "Military Politics and Counter-Insurgency in Peru," p. 90.

41. See Gorriti Ellenbogen, *Sendero,* pp. 175–176.

42. See Enrique Obando, "Las relaciones civiles-militares en el Perú, 1980–1990," in Stern, ed., *Los Senderos Insólitos del Perú,* pp. 177–379.

43. Ibid., p. 378.

44. See Tapia, *Las fuerzas armadas y Sendero Luminoso,* p. 40.

45. See Cynthia McClintock, "The Decimation of Peru's Sendero Luminoso," in Cynthia Arnson, ed., *Comparative Peace Processes in Latin America* (Washington, D.C.: Woodrow Wilson Center Press, 1999), p. 227.

46. See Mauceri, "Military Politics and Counter-Insurgency in Peru," p. 101.

47. Ejército Peruano, *Guerra no convencional.*

48. See Roberts and Arce, "Neoliberalism and Lower-Class Voting Behavior."

49. Author interviews with Antonio Ketín Vidal Herrera, former head of DINCOTE, Lima, 18 August 1999; and Carlos Ivan Degregori, Sendero specialist and investigator, Instituto de Estudios Peruanos, Lima, 25 August 1999.

50. Vidal Herrera's tenure began in November 1991. By this time, both the DINCOTE and the GEIN were subsumed under a larger intelligence agency headed by Vladimiro Montesinos, the Servicio de Inteligencia Nacional (SIN).

51. Author interview Antonio Ketín Vidal Herrera, 18 August 1999.

52. McClintock, "Decimation of Peru's Sendero Luminoso," p. 229.

53. *New York Times,* 8 December 2000; Jiménez Bacca, *Inicio, desarrollo, y ocaso del terrorismo.*

54. Masterson, "In the Shining Path of Mariátegui," p. 168; Mauceri, "Military Politics and Counter-Insurgency in Peru," p. 101.

55. See Tapia, *Las fuerzas armadas y Sendero Luminoso,* p. 27.

56. See Masterson, "In the Shining Path of Mariátegui"; and Starn, "Sendero inesperados," p. 232.

57. See Reyna and Toche, *La inseguridad en el Perú,* p. 40.

58. While the use of rondas represented good strategy overall, this practice was not without its blemishes. There have been frequent reports of forced membership in ronda units, and of the presumption by the armed forces that failure to join rondas was equivalent to admitting support for Sendero.

59. See Starn, "Sendero inesperados," p. 246.

60. See Tapia, *Las fuerzas armadas y Sendero Luminoso,* p. 80.

61. See Mauceri, "Military Politics and Counter-Insurgency in Peru," p. 100.

62. See McClintock, *Revolutionary Movements in Latin America,* p. 117.

63. *La Jornada* (Mexico City), 14 March 2001. Of the disappearances, 41.8 percent were estimated to have occurred during the García government, and 30.6 percent under the Belaúnde administration.

64. *La Jornada,* 7 December 2000.

65. Author interview with Daniel Espichan, congressman, president of the Comisión de Acusaciones Constitutionales, and former faceless judge *(jucio sin rostro),* Lima, 23 August 1999.

66. See McClintock, "Decimation of Peru's Sendero Luminoso," p. 240.

67. An excellent firsthand account of the capture of Guzmán and other Senderistas is found in Jiménez Bacca, *Inicio, desarrollo, y ocaso del terrorismo,* vol. 2, pp. 740–773.

68. Author interview with Medardo Purizaga, dean, Ciencias Sociales, Universidad Nacional de San Cristóbal de Huamanga, Ayacucho, Peru, 16 April 2001.

69. *Taz* (Germany), 6 May 1990, interview with Victor Polay Campos, leader of the MRTA.

70. Movimiento Revolucionario Túpac Amaru (MRTA), "Goal of the Revolutionary Strategy of the MRTA," no date.

71. MRTA, *Brief History of the MRTA*, no date.

72. MRTA, "La historia del Movimiento Revolucionario Túpac Amaru," 9 June 1990, translation by author.

73. See Jiménez Bacca, *Inicio, desarrollo, y ocaso del terrorismo*, pp. 842–843.

74. MRTA, *Brief History of the MRTA*.

75. MRTA, "Comunicado 1," 17 December 1996, translation by author.

76. MRTA, "Nota de prensa," 13 March 2001, translation by author.

77. For a larger discussion of this, see *New York Times*, 12 March 2001.

78. Author interviews with General Hector Jhon Caro, 17 August 1999; and Antonio Ketín Vidal Herrera, 18 August 1999.

79. Mao Tse-tung, *Guerrilla Warfare*, p. 11.

80. See ibid., esp. the appendix "Organization of an Independent Guerrilla Company," pp. 29–31.

81. Ibid., p. 29.

82. The link between Sendero and the Khmer Rouge is noticed in McClintock, *Revolutionary Movements in Latin America*, p. 63.

83. Sendero Luminoso, "Línea militar," translation by author.

84. Mao demonstrated considerable command of classic strategic literature, as evidenced in *On Guerrilla Warfare* in the sections "What Is Guerrilla Warfare" (pp. 1–4) and "Guerrilla Warfare in History" (pp. 7–10).

85. Mao Tse-tung, *Guerrilla Warfare*, p. 20.

86. Ibid.

87. Ibid., p. 2.

88. In fact, Sendero mentions ideas of Clausewitz without direct attribution. For example, one document states: "This shows once again that war is the continuation of politics by other means" Sendero Luminoso, "Línea militar."

89. Clausewitz, *War*, pp. 77, 89.

90. Ibid., p. 93.

91. See Thucydides, *History of the Peloponnesian War*, pp. 199, 408, and bks. 7–8, pp. 425–548.

92. Sun Tzu II, *Lost Art of War*, p. 22.

93. In addition to various discussions of terrain throughout *On War* (e.g., p. 141), Clausewitz devotes chap. 17 of bk. 5 to this topic (pp. 348–352). Sun Tzu emphasizes the importance of mastering terrain throughout *The Art of War* (e.g., pp. 83, 93, 143); mastery of terrain is also identified as one of the five central strategic elements of warfare (p. 42). Sun Tzu II also refers to the significance of terrain in *The Lost Art of War* (e.g., p. 31).

94. Foucault's work centered on what he called "systems of thought." See Foucault, "Will to Knowledge," p. 11. His most solid work on this topic, in which premodern and modern epistemes are discussed, is *The Order of Things*.

95. Author interview with a student who wishes to retain anonymity, Universidad Nacional de San Cristóbal de Huamanga, Ayucucho, Peru, 19 April 2001. This view is common and is evidenced throughout the literature on Sendero. Indeed, careful readers will have difficulty finding any praise regarding any element of Sendero in the academic literature on the topic, much of which is listed in the endnotes of this and the previous chapter.

96. See Lao Tzu, *Tao te Ching*, p. 71: "It is easy to maintain a situation while it is still secure."

97. Sun Tzu, *Art of War*, p. 139.

98. These basic themes are found throughout the strategic classics. Machiavelli notes in *The Prince* the importance of cultivating the favor of the inhabitants (p. 35) and notes in *The Discourses* that social consent for government policies reduces the potential for violence (pp. 425–426). Hobbes stresses in *Leviathan* the importance of establishing a tight social contract to reduce chaos and violence (p. 192). A central core of Gramsci's thought is that hegemony is based more on consent than coercion, and that consent and coercion are generally inversely related (*Selections from the Prison Notebooks*, pp. 275–276).

99. Machiavelli, *Discourses*, p. 430. The identical point is made by many other strategists, such as Sun Tzu I and Sun Tzu II, in regard to understanding what those Chinese thinkers call "seasons," or times of change.

100. Lao Tzu, *Tao te Ching*, p. 12.

101. On the strategic approach of intelligence and surveillance, see, for example, Sun Tzu, *Art of War*, pp. 168–172; and Sun Tzu II, *Lost Art of War*, p. 40.

COLOMBIA

4

Colombia:
The Origins, Ideology, and
Support Base of the FARC and the ELN

The conflagration in Colombia is of interest not only to students of Latin American politics but also to a broader array of academics and practitioners whose interests focus upon the causes of human violence. The country represents a laboratory to assist in explaining the social and political structures that contribute to exorbitant levels of brutality. The situation supersedes modern debates within the field of political science that have focused on the conception of human nature as conflictive and barbarous.[1] That is, if a "human nature" does indeed exist, it is by definition the same everywhere. How have Colombian social structures accentuated violence to the point that it has become a way of life?[2]

Over the last two centuries Colombia has hosted virtually continuous warfare. The country has been characterized by a pronounced dispersion of power, manifested through extreme levels of localism and regionalism. Related to this is Colombia's unique, premodern sense of political space as comprising parcels rather than the grand spaces typically associated with modern nation-states. The degree of this prominent feature has distinguished the country from others in the Americas. Beyond the absence of a Leviathan and of nationalism, there has existed a plethora of dispersed political identities and political truths. All this is related to the disproportionately high levels of violence in Colombia.

As with the other countries examined here, the Colombian case is analyzed in the space of two chapters. This chapter traces the origins of Colombia's rebel movements, as well as the historical context of the country's imbroglio. As we shall see, persistent problems have been apparent for nearly two centuries. The focus here is also upon the ideology and support base of Colombia's two largest leftist guerrilla groups, the Fuerzas Armadas Revolucionarias de Colombia (FARC) and the

Ejército de Liberación Nacional (ELN). Right-wing paramilitary forces are also discussed, but they will be dealt with in greater depth in the subsequent chapter. This chapter analyzes developments occurring through the end of the 1980s, at which time a rupture of sorts took place. A distinguishing feature of that crucial turning point is that the military capacity of the rebels and the paramilitaries increased more during the 1990s than during the three previous decades put together. The next chapter focuses on the Colombian guerrillas post-1990 and also considers U.S. interests, including Plan Colombia.

1819–1902:
From Independence to the War of 1,000 Days

During colonial rule, Nueva Granada, the site of latter-day Colombia, was ruled by a strong if decentralized state. Periods of extreme political violence were limited to the implementation and termination of colonial rule.[3] These two key features, a strong state and the absence of high levels of violence, distinguished the colonial period from that of postliberation. The struggle for independence from Spanish colonialism in Colombia began in the early part of the nineteenth century. One of the country's principal cities, Cartagena, declared its independence in 1810. Struggles for independence existed elsewhere in Colombia, but in a piecemeal fashion. Significant parts of the country never declared their independence, and among those that were engaged in the struggle, there was typically little cooperation or coordination. Hence, under rather chaotic circumstances the Spanish were able to reassert control over Colombia in 1815–1816.

Decisive independence for Colombia came by way of a foreigner, Simón Bolívar of Venezuela, in the battle of Boyaca. In 1821, Bolívar's dream of Gran Colombia—which was to include most of modern-day Venezuela, Colombia, Ecuador, Bolivia, and Peru—was manifested through the constitution of Cucuta.[4] The central government for this grand region was to be located in Colombia. Indeed, Bolívar's vice president, Francisco Santander, was a Colombian who remained in the country while Bolívar ventured to other regional states to liberate them from Spanish colonial rule. When Bolívar returned to Colombia—after having departed in 1822 to struggle for independence in Ecuador, Bolivia, and Peru—he was greeted with an immense disappointment. The prevailing factions of the Colombian political elite had decided they no longer wished to be a component of Gran Colombia. They preferred to maintain their control over fragmented portions of Colombia rather than becoming a part of a larger and centralized unit.[5] Indeed, the most powerful landowners and entrepreneurs deeply resented the centralized control associated with colonialism, and welcomed the opportunity for localized and dispersed political power.[6]

Some crucial points flow from this. First, from the very beginning, dominant political and economic elites in Colombia could not relate to centralized power arrangements. They were more comfortable with power being dispersed among regions and localities. Part of this may be due to the strong geographic obstacles in Colombia that isolated various regions of the country. But this is not an altogether sufficient explanation of the extraordinarily dispersed and decentered constellation of power. Other countries in the Americas were able to form strong federations despite prominent geographic obstacles, as demonstrated by the case of Mexico, for example. Further, other Latin American countries also shared a colonial past whereby power was centralized, but did not view centralization per se in a negative light. A more significant explanation may be found in the realm of epistemology.[7] In Colombia, political elites have been influenced by a premodern system of thought that strongly favored a more or less feudal arrangement of city-states, rather than the modern nation-state with its centralized power and promotion of nationalism.

In the first century following independence, Colombia endured civil wars between the Liberals and the Conservatives in 1830–1831, 1839–1842, 1851, 1854, 1860–1862, 1876–1877, 1885, and 1895, culminating in the absolutely devastating War of 1,000 Days in 1899–1902. The Conservatives favored the interests of landed aristocrats who ruled under the encomiendas system—a Latin American version of feudalism. They strongly supported the Catholic Church, and were committed to blurring distinctions between state politics and church power. Hence, the Conservatives reflected a largely premodern epistemology that was manifested through a reliance on feudal agrarian production, economic protectionism, and an emphasis on divinity as a key source of knowledge and power. This stood in contrast to the modern epistemology, which celebrated industrial production and knowledge based on reason, science, objectivity, and so on.

The Liberals, on the other hand, favored many elements of modernity as well as the political systems that were popular in Europe at the time. They were supporters of free trade, mercantile capital, a secular state, and federalism. However, despite the Liberals' commitment to secularism, the country as a whole was deeply committed to Catholicism, which until the end of the twentieth century remained one of the two principal anchors of identity for Colombians. The other source of identity, until the 1970s, was a loyalty to one of the two feuding parties.

The violent and interminable contests between the Liberals and Conservatives involved primarily private armies, set against the backdrop of a poorly conceived constitutional arrangement and fragmented political identities. The Colombian constitutions of 1853, 1858, and 1863 were borrowed from relatively developed European countries, and have been considered to be among the most decentralized federal arrangements on the planet.[8] Political identities were localized to the extreme. This is epitomized by the writings of José María Samper, a Colombian historian who wrote in the 1860s. His work attempted to define the divisive identities and characteristics of various regions in the country. He portrayed residents of Antioquia, for example, as "interesting, the most beautiful in the country . . . energetic . . . diligent . . . intelligent . . . frugal, etc."[9] His accounts of the inhabitants of other regions were often considerably less flattering.

These fragmented regions and identities did not coexist peacefully, and were prone to violent confrontation. Indeed, each Colombian department had its own army, among a vast assortment of private armies. These private militias largely consisted of men working on the encomiendas. Hence, male bodies were exploited both as soldiers and as agricultural producers in a clientelistic system headed by the encomiendas' patrons. Private armies often comprised a pooling of soldiers from various encomiendas. Overall, the country more closely resembled a loosely knit and conflictive array of geographically isolated city-states than a coherent, centralized, and modern nation-state.

The frequency and intensity of civil wars in Colombia suggests two significant points. First, violence in Colombia historically has represented a more or less legitimate and accepted avenue through which political disputes have been settled. The federal state has been too weak to provide a forum for peaceful conflict resolution. Second, the notion of balance or equilibrium—a centerpiece of modern epistemology—has been noticeably absent in Colombia. A political balance has never been struck between competing forces in any sense, and no actor has achieved hegemony or even the preponderant force required to deter another from attacking.[10]

Colombian production of coffee after the 1870s represented the ticket to the country's first major international commercial contact since colonialism. Coffee production boomed in Colombia beginning in 1880. But it was set against the backdrop of a global economic depression and restructuring. The coffee boom ended in 1898, largely due to international economic circumstances. This set the stage for the War of 1,000 Days, one of the most important turning points in the history of the country.

The war began in July 1899 and ended in June 1902. It was the familiar refrain of brutal armed conflict between the Liberals and the Conservatives. What was new was the extraordinary fervor of the war, which left 100,000 dead and demolished much of the country's economic capacity. The War of 1,000 Days commenced with an attempt by the Liberals to overthrow the Conservative government. Since the Conservatives held the reins of the state, they also had control of the country's relatively weak federal army. In their efforts to topple the Conservatives, the Liberals formed a number of guerrilla armies throughout the country, but especially in the departments of Tolima, Cundinamarca, and Santander, and in the Cauca region. Liberal guerrilla fighters represented the poorest social sectors of Colombia, which included landless peasants, Indians, and poverty-stricken urban dwellers.[11]

Four important points flow from the War of 1,000 Days. First, the formation of guerrilla groups by components of the Liberal Party foreshadowed the birth of the FARC in the late 1940s and early 1950s, which also began as a radical splinter group of the Liberals. Second, as a consequence of the war the country lacked the wherewithal to resist the U.S.-directed separation of Panama from Colombia in 1903. Third, the aftermath of the war prompted the formation in 1907 of the country's first significant national military force.[12] But the use of force continued to be largely privatized and regionalized in the hands of competing local elites. Hence, the historical absence of a forceful and centered federal power—a Leviathan—may be regarded as one important piece of the puzzle that explains the prevalence of violence in the country. Finally, the profundity of the war politically exhausted Colombia to the extent that violence and armed conflict remained relatively minimal for almost half a century, until the emergence of La Violencia in the late 1940s. Thus the War of 1,000 Days can be viewed as the crescendo of a period of violence that began some seventy years earlier. Perhaps at the beginning of the twenty-first century Colombia has once again reached such a crescendo.

1902–1946: A Unique Period of Peace

The termination of the War of 1,000 Days ushered in the longest period of relative peace in the country's history.[13] To the extent that significant episodes of violence occurred between the turn of the century and the mid-1940s, these were concentrated in the departments of Boyaca, Santander, and Norte de Santander.[14] Perhaps Colombians were simply too exhausted and too preoccupied by the enormous task of reconstruction to engage in the carnage that was characteristic of the periods both before and after this era. But seeds were sown during these four decades that would culminate in yet another intense maelstrom of bloodshed in the late 1940s—the notorious La Violencia. An important backdrop to this era was a process of economic modernization characterized by increased U.S. investment and a booming export market for coffee. Also significant was a process of politicization and radicalization of components of both the agricultural and the industrial workforces, in the context of accentuated economic inequity and obvious political fraud. Tension between the Liberals and Conservatives resurfaced, resulting in sporadic and localized violence. This period also witnessed the development of a credible and professional army.

U.S. investment and hence U.S. political interests in Colombia increased substantially from about 1915 until the beginning of the Great Depression in 1929. Much of this was concentrated in the petroleum and mining sectors. A celebrated feature of Colombia's history is the so-called Dance of the Millions, an episode during which the U.S. government paid Bogotá $25 million for the loss of Panama as Colombian territory and also loaned Colombia another $173 million. It is widely understood that this U.S. largesse had less to do with compensating Colombia for the loss of Panama than with allowing U.S. oil companies to buy a piece of Colombia's strategic resources.[15] U.S. political interests in the country grew in step with economic interests, and toward the end of the twentieth century these would be exploited by leftist guerrilla groups.

Colombia also witnessed a relatively rapid phase of industrialization during this period, and became substantially integrated into the global economy through another boom in the coffee export market. This was a reflection of a remarkable sense of entrepreneurial dynamism in Colombia that is unique in the Latin American context, with the possible exception of Chile. This same capitalist spirit would come to underlie Colombia's role as kingpin of the global illicit drug market beginning in the 1970s.

But the benefits of this economic expansion were distributed in a highly inequitable fashion, a fact that did not go unrecognized by the Colombian population. In the context of the successful Bolshevik Revolution in the Soviet Union, various unions as well as a Socialist Party were formed in Colombia during the 1920s. These would serve as the precursors for radical movements that would blossom in the late 1940s and 1950s during the Cold War.

Tension between the Liberals and Conservatives, which had been responsible for the series of wars throughout the nineteenth century and which culminated in the War of 1,000 Days, materialized once again in a rather ominous fashion beginning in the 1930s. Although the background to this was the economic downturn associated with the Great Depression, its effects for Colombia were not as severe as they were for many of its Latin American cohorts, since the country was largely self-sufficient in the 1920s and 1930s. The Liberals rose to power in 1930, but it was the Liberal government of López Pumarejo with its 1934–1938 "Revolution on the March" that drew considerable ire on the part of the Conservatives. The Liberals' attempt at secularization drew the wrath of the Catholic Church, which was among the major pillars of support for the Conservatives. The Liberals also attempted to decentralize the already anemic Colombian state, in contrast to the Conservatives' preference for the fortification of the central government. A radical element of the Liberal Party present during this time touted land reform and workers' rights, further alienating the Conservatives. But despite the sometimes fiery rhetoric of the Liberals, real wages fell for both industrial workers and peasants during their reign. However, while significant elements of labor and peasants maintained their support for the Liberals through the mid-1940s, many became increasingly disillusioned with the party. These were the roots of a faction of the party that would form leftist guerrilla groups beginning in the late 1940s.

A final point concerns the development of a professional and relatively centralized Colombian armed forces during this period. The Colombian military grew substantially during 1932–1933, when it was engaged in a border dispute with Peru, and further fortified itself through World War II. The military underwent a period of professionalization during this period, whereby high-ranking officers were now graduates of military schools. Nevertheless, the class origin of most officers left them in close alignment with the oligarchy, and hence there was a certain degree of mistrust among them vis-à-vis the Liberal Party and its sometimes radical, if empty, rhetoric. This was exemplified by a failed coup attempt by factions of the army in 1944.[16]

Thus 1902–1946 was a significant period. It witnessed a process of industrialization, the refinement a keen entrepreneurial spirit, Colombia's insertion into the world economy, and the development of a professional military. This represented the beginning of the country's metamorphosis toward some of the fundamental components of a modern nation-state.

Further, the presence of relative peace for four and a half decades was a notable rarity in the country's otherwise violent and chaotic history. Yet beneath these positive developments were other features of the political landscape that would help set the stage for Colombia's free fall into the depths of the ensuing period of La Violencia, including mounting hostility between the Liberals and the Conservatives and the continued dispersion and fragmentation of power throughout the country. Also important were the pauperization of the masses and the horrific inequity that existed even during times of rapid economic growth. Finally, the escalating disenchantment among the popular sectors with the two traditional parties helped point the way to the emergence of subversive movements.

1946–1990:
La Violencia and the Birth of Subversive Movements

This period can be divided into two eras. The first, from 1946 until 1958, witnessed the notorious La Violencia, a resurrection of intense combat not seen in the country since the War of 1,000 Days half a century earlier. In an attempt to halt the panoramic bloodbath, the National Front was implemented in 1958 as a power-sharing agreement between the Liberals and the Conservatives—the leading protagonists of brutal conflict in the country since the time of liberation. But a fresh landscape of political exclusion and violence emerged during this period, entailing the germination of leftist guerrillas in the 1950s. Hence the procapitalist forces of the Liberals and the Conservatives would unite in their contest against leftist guerrillas in the global context of the Cold War.

During this period Colombia witnessed the ascendancy of many of the features commonly associated with modernity. Economically, industrial production and global trade accelerated. Politically, the classic modern conflict between left and right took root, and a binary epistemology tended to dominate political contests. For some, this included the Marxist dialectic, with its emphasis on the Hegelian contradiction of thesis versus antithesis. This period also involved the inclusion/exclusion duality that underpinned the Liberal-Conservative attempt to preclude the left from legitimate political life. Secular politics became more accepted, and was no longer a central catalyst of the vicious warfare between the two dominant parties that animated the previous 150 years. All of this occurred against the global backdrop of the conflict between the United States and the Soviet Union.

But despite the emergence of certain elements associated with modernity, Colombia retained many crucial premodern attributes that would distinguish it from the larger developing states of Latin America. Principal among these was the continued dispersion and fragmentation of power throughout the country. A Leviathan still failed to materialize in Colombia. A strong state, and mechanisms for conflict resolution, remained illusive. While the Liberals and Conservatives proved successful in their attempt to act in concert, the left was remarkably fragmented and unfocussed. Violence continued to represent a widespread means of dealing with common conflict. Overall, the country remained as a collection of pseudo-feudal city-states, rather than a modern nation-state.

La Violencia

La Violencia represented the final phase of open warfare between the Liberals and the Conservatives, and occurred between 1946 and the formation of the National Front in 1958. Tension between the two parties had been escalating considerably since the 1930s. The Conservatives took the presidency in 1946 under Mariano Ospina Pérez. Ospina's victory was made possible in large measure by the split within the Liberal Party between a right-wing faction, led by Gabriel Turbay, and an increasingly dominant leftist faction led by the charismatic Jorge Eliécer Gaitán.

Although he was not a communist, Gaitán vehemently criticized the exaggerated maldistribution of wealth in the country as well as the concentration of political power in the hands of a miniscule oligarchy. In fact, about three-quarters of the population at this time were peasants, with 3 percent of landowners controlling more than half of the agricultural territory—and often the best land.[17] Gaitán's message was directed not only to peasants, but to poorly paid industrial workers. Gini coefficients rose from 0.45 in 1938 to 0.53 in 1951, indicating a significant exacerbation in the country's maldistribution of wealth. Incited by the populist rhetoric of Gaitán, which rang true to most of the population, considerable violence erupted throughout much of the countryside and in the principal cities. As one observer notes, since 1946 the severity of violence in Colombia never fell to the normal levels of other Latin American countries.[18]

The assassination of Gaitán on the streets of Bogotá initiated the "Bogotazo," a massive uprising in the capital city culminating in an anarchic orgy of violence. More generally, it initiated the most horrific levels of carnage that occurred during this chaotic era, which lasted through the mid-1950s.[19] It is estimated that some 100,000 to 300,000 political murders were committed throughout the entirety of La Violencia.[20] This was largely an intercapitalist war, a battle between factions of the Liberals and Conservatives, and not yet dominated by the contest between communism and capitalism.[21]

For a generation of Colombians, La Violencia reintroduced violence as a way of life—an orientation to dealing with conflict reminiscent of the previous century. But this orientation had its limits. In the wake of the horrendous levels of bloodshed, negotiations between key members of the Liberal and Conservative parties commenced in Spain in 1956 and resulted in the formation of the National Front in 1958.[22] Lasting until 1974, the front represented a power-sharing agreement between the Liberals and Conservatives within which the presidency alternated every four years between the two major parties, and legislative bodies were divided equally between the Liberals and Conservatives.

The National Front terminated the violent conflicts between the Liberals and Conservatives that blighted the country's history from independence through the middle of the twentieth century. But a new political landscape of conflict emerged, rooted in the old game of political exclusion.[23] For a century and a half, the Liberals and Conservatives tried to exclude each other from political power in Colombia. After the establishment of the National Front, the Liberals and Conservatives jointly attempted to exclude other segments of society from the political arena. Those shut out from legitimate political avenues were the newly emerging middle class, the educated, the poverty-stricken majority population, and the left. A dark example of this was a wave of government repression unleashed in the 1950s and 1960s upon labor unions, student groups, and peasant organizations. It was this situation that helped spawn leftist guerrilla movements.[24]

The FARC

At the beginning of the twenty-first century, the Fuerzas Armadas Revolucionarias de Colombia was militarily the strongest subversive movement in Colombia and in the Americas, and one of the most potent in the world. Its roots can be traced to a radical faction of Liberal guerrillas that emerged during La Violencia in the 1940s. The leader of the FARC at the beginning of the twenty-first century, Manuel Marulanda Vélez (given name Pedro Antonio Marín), began as a Liberal guerrilla member in 1947. A couple years later, what is considered to be the nucleus of the FARC began as roaming Liberal guerrilla units. Their aim was to confront, and to defend against, official government violence. The Liberal guerrilla movement lasted from the 1940s through the mid-1950s. Marulanda's command of the FARC was based in part on his leadership during brutal confrontations with the Colombian military in the early 1950s. By 1955, inspired by leftist thought that dotted Latin America, the Colombian guerrilla movement became dominated by communist guerrillas. This occurred against the backdrop of the heyday of global communism with the emergence of the Chinese Revolution and of Soviet superpowerdom. Armed and mobile guerrilla fronts, which represented the precursor of the FARC, were supported from the beginning by campesinos, and predominated in the regions of Villarrica, Sumapaz, and the south of Tolima.[25]

The formation of these radical guerrilla groups in Colombia was inspired principally by the failure of the Liberal Party, especially the leftist faction of that party, to achieve any significant land reform in the country. This explains in large measure why the guerrillas' original and subsequent support base primarily has been peasants. Beyond their focus on a more equitable redistribution of land, they also called for the nationalization of strategic industries and for breaking the yoke of imperialist domination—all common themes among the left in Latin America during the early Cold War period. According to Marulanda's autobiography, the assassination of Gaitán, and the failure of the Liberals to realize the promises expressed in their populist rhetoric, pushed many campesinos toward the leftist guerrilla movement once they perceived no other credible alternative.[26] Similarly, official documents of the FARC historicize the formative period under consideration here into two distinct eras. The first era comprised the assassination of Gaitán in 1948 as well as the subsequent development of a Liberal guerrilla movement. The second era erupted with the formation of a military government under General Gustavo Rojas Pinilla in 1953, and the outlawing of the Communist Party in 1954.[27] This initiated the government's official exclusion of the left. It was also indicative of a general trend in Latin America whereby the enemy (the left) was considered to be internal, in contrast to the external threats that typically preoccupied the developed countries of the north.

The FARC was essentially formed in 1964, and conducted its first "Guerrilla Conference" in September of that year. From the FARC's perspective, that period was decisive not only because of its formation, but also because the Colombian government commenced an intense military attack against leftist subversives. The Colombian armed forces were increasingly influenced by U.S. national security doctrine, which included training for various Latin American military personnel at the School of the Americas.[28] Washington had pushed the panic button following the successful consolidation of the Cuban Revolution against the backdrop of the Cold War, and it was entirely clear that the United States was not willing to tolerate another Cuba.

The FARC expanded its territorial control considerably between 1964 and 1966, the latter date marking the group's first constitution. Between 25 April and 5 May 1966, the Second Conference of the Guerrilla Block of Southern Colombia was held, at which time the FARC declared its official formation with some 350 recruits.[29] The FARC's documents state that since the date of its creation there has been a steady deterioration of the political situation in Colombia, given what it claims are the country's false democracy, class domination, and maldistribution of wealth.[30]

The Cuban Revolution served as a great inspiration for the FARC, as it did for most other Latin American guerrilla groups.[31] The general message seemed to be that if a small island some ninety miles from the United States could successfully implement a communist revolution, what was to stop other groups throughout the Americas from doing the same? More particularly, according to a former member of the FARC, there were three fundamental lessons espoused by the revolutionary pop stars Che Guevara and Régis Debray. First, popular forces can win a war against national armed forces. Next, one does not have to wait for all conditions for revolution to be met before launching a struggle, since an insurrectional *foco* can create them. Finally, the revolutionary struggle should be launched primarily from the countryside.[32] While the FARC has launched its own struggle from the countryside, since its inception it has ignored the advice of Cuban-based ideologues by focusing almost exclusively upon military rather than political or ideological power.

Land reform and distribution of wealth provided the backdrop to the FARC's struggle from 1964 to 1980. There exists a consensus that attempts at land reform during those years can be viewed as an utter failure. There were a number of reasons for this. At times, the government attempted to implement agrarian reform, but this was resisted and negated by big landowners. For example, President Carlos Lleras Restrepo in 1968 granted rights of landownership to sharecroppers and tenants. But landlords responded vigorously with armed expulsions of would-be property recipients. In the late 1970s and beyond, narcotrafficking and political violence resulted in a further concentration of land. Agricultural land remained extremely concentrated, contributing to extreme poverty in the countryside. While the country's poverty rate has hovered at around 70 percent for the last few decades, 1973 statistics indicate that 59 percent of the urban population remained in poverty, while 88 percent of the rural population was poverty-stricken.[33] Guerrilla groups such as the FARC have been able to make substantial political gains from this.

Regarding the overall distribution of wealth in Colombia during these years, the situation improved from 1964 through 1978. Gini coefficients demonstrate a more equitable division of wealth, improving from 0.55 in 1964 to 0.53 in 1971 to 0.48 in 1978. In other terms, this meant that in 1964, the top 10 percent of the population controlled 45.5 percent of the country's total wealth, falling to 37.6 percent of the total national wealth in 1978. The bottom 50 percent of the population saw their share of national wealth increase from 14.8 percent in 1964 to 18.6 percent in 1978. Overall, although the general trend during these years was in the direction of greater equity, the division of wealth remained highly polarized. This, too, played into the hands of leftist guerrillas.

In 1979, at its ebb, the FARC had only eight fronts, dispersed throughout locations in the departments of Huila, Cauca, Tolima, Putumayo, Caquetá, Antioquia, and Córdoba, and in the Magdalena Medio region.[34] Although its military power was weak during this period, its presence in Putumayo, Caquetá, and Antioquia, in the southern and central regions of the country, would prove to be quite propitious beginning in the early 1980s. These would emerge as the epicenter of Colombia's burgeoning cocaine industry. Its initial dominance in that region in large measure accounts for the group's expansion to thirty-two fronts with 3,200 armed troops by 1985.[35]

The FARC's relationship to narcotrafficking in the 1980s, like most aspects of Colombian politics, is complicated. Components of the FARC essentially provided law, order, and protection to populations and regions involved in coca cultivation, chemical processing of raw coca into cocaine, as well as distribution. The FARC is alleged to have charged a 10 percent tax on the aspects of the industry in which it was involved. As this burgeoning enterprise grew explosively in the 1980s, the FARC expanded its territorial and military influence. By the mid-1980s, according to a former FARC member, it extended its power beyond the areas noted above into the key narco-industry departments of Guaviare and Meta, as well as the key regions of Bota Caucana, Sierra Nevada de Santa Marta, and Serranía de San Lucas.[36] Others have noted the FARC's additional presence in the narcotrafficking areas of the departments of Choco, Bolívar, Vichada, and the two Santanders.[37]

There are complications and caveats associated with the FARC's relationship to the narco-industry. First, not all members or fronts of the FARC have been involved in the illicit drug trade. Second, components of the FARC that participated in this business during the 1980s essentially represented a security apparatus to protect and regulate dimensions of the trade. By the mid-1980s, the kingpins of Colombian narcotrafficking, such as Pablo Escobar and a shifting assortment of other cartel leaders, created their own security forces rather than leasing components of the FARC. This was largely due to ideological motivations. Narcotrafficking kingpins have been renowned for being fiercely capitalistic, and have considered themselves to represent the legitimate bourgeoisie of Colombia. Hence the obvious ideological clash with the socialistic FARC, which, for example, has insisted upon land reform that threatens the huge estates controlled by narcotrafficking executives. Thus the paramilitaries, created in the mid-1980s partially at the behest of narco-kingpins, have largely served the security functions previously performed by the FARC.

The FARC's relation to narcotrafficking made the rebel group self-sufficient economically, so it did not have to rely on outside support from such countries as Soviet Union and China. As with the case of the ELN, this goes a long way toward explaining why guerrilla groups in Colombia have actually gained military power since the 1980s, while other Latin American leftist groups dependent on Soviet-Cuban support were forced to the bargaining table and subsequently withered. Beginning in the 1990s, the FARC would rely increasingly on other forms of private economic support, especially kidnapping and extortion (see Chapter 5).

The FARC's involvement in narcotrafficking is yet another reflection of the broader privatization of Colombia's civil war—that is, the war is financed by private enterprise that is often illicit. There is a profound contradiction here. The FARC has claimed to be ideologically committed to its own brand of socialism, but the group's power is largely military, rather than political or ideological, and its military power is rooted in its participation in the booming capitalist enterprise of narcotrafficking. The rebels' active role in this industry naturally has affected their support base. The FARC's most loyal followers since the 1980s have been peasants who cultivate coca in the south of the country. It is a relationship that has been based largely on the immediate economic interests of poverty-stricken peasants, rather than any ideological devotion. More generally, the FARC's role in narcotrafficking and other illicit businesses has blurred the distinction between war and crime.

* * *

Specific policies advocated by the FARC during the 1980s included land reform, guaranteed base prices for agricultural products, as well as the provision of agrarian credit, health care, and education for peasants. This was reflective of a socialist ideology aimed at a support base composed almost entirely of peasants. Beyond this, the FARC bitterly criticized the human rights abuses entailed in the security policies of the Colombian government. These included kidnapping, torture, and general terror—all of which the FARC viewed as inherent in the doctrine of the "national security state."[38] While the Colombian military's involvement in such atrocities is beyond debate, the country's armed forces remained relatively weak. One comparative measure of this weakness is that while Latin American militaries as a whole had an average of 4.4 soldiers per 1,000 inhabitants in 1981, Colombia had an average of 2.3 soldiers in that year.[39] This contributed to the general growth in power of the FARC vis-à-vis the Colombian government during the 1980s.

While its power escalated during the 1980s, the FARC participated in what were ultimately unsuccessful peace negotiations with the Colombian government. During 1982–1985, Conservative president Belisario Betancur initiated a so-called peace process with Colombia's guerrilla movements, which included an amnesty for guerrilla members as well as a ceasefire agreement. Some 400 guerrilla members accepted the offer of amnesty during the first three months of its availability. But as one astute analyst observed, "tactics of peace" since the 1980s have had a decidedly false ring, since actual war continued apace.[40] For its part, the FARC criticized the Colombian government for peace offensives throughout the 1980s and early 1990s that lacked any resolve to correct the socioeconomic problems that underpinned the country's protracted warfare. The FARC insisted on government action regarding issues such as land reform, the redistribution of wealth, and higher rents from transnational investments.

Despite profound doubts, the FARC accepted the government's gesture of peace. It hoped that the state's offer to reincorporate guerrilla members into "legitimate" politics could provide the group with political benefits. Without disarming, the FARC created a new leftist political party in 1985, the Union Patriótica (UP). Crucially, it represented the first time the group gave serious attention to political as opposed to military struggle. Initially, the results seemed promising. In the national congressional elections of 1986, the UP won a surprising fourteen seats. But ultimately the UP experiment proved to be one of the most dismal chapters in Colombian history. Former guerrilla members who in good faith put down their weapons and who, through the UP, participated in the so-called legitimate political arena became the targets of systematic assassination at the hands of right-wing paramilitary death squads. Some of these had ties with the Colombian state. During the late 1980s and early 1990s, between 2,000 and 4,000 UP leaders and supporters were assassinated by right-wing paramilitary forces that the FARC claimed were often aligned with the government.[41] The FARC learned from the murder of key UP members during 1986–1990 that there was no legitimate political space available for the left in Colombia, and that the familiar game of political exclusion continued unabated in the country.[42]

The FARC also found it difficult to promote fruitful cooperation among the left during the 1980s. The Coordinadora Nacional Guerrillera (CNG), which represented an attempt in 1985 to create a leftist umbrella organization, was viewed by the FARC as fraught with infighting. In an attempt to cultivate a more harmonious institution, the FARC, the ELN and the Ejército Popular de Liberación (EPL) created the Coordinadora Guerrillera Simón Bolívar (CGSB) in 1987. The CGSB remained significant until the early 1990s and as an umbrella group was able to demonstrate significant flashes of coordinated military and political maneuvering in the period 1990–1992. Ultimately, however, the left in Colombia has proven to be as fragmented as the rest of the political actors in the country. Even when they demonstrated an occasional capacity for their members to act in harmony, the FARC and the ELN have always maintained a distance.

The ELN

Until the late 1980s, the Ejército de Liberación Nacional remained a rather obscure guerrilla group. It lacked substantial military and political power, and had difficulty controlling specific territory for any significant period of time. Its small membership was often on the run, and the movement's first two decades were marked by frequent infighting, desertion, and substantial losses at the hands of the Colombian military. Founded by the charismatic Fabio Vásquez in 1964, the ELN made its first public and official appearance on 7 January 1965 by temporarily capturing the small town of Simacota in the department of Santander.[43] These rebels were especially inspired by the Cuban Revolution, and attempted somewhat unsuccessfully to adhere to the *foquista* ideology as propounded in the works of Che Guevara.[44]

But Che Guevara was not the only guiding light for the early ELN. The group, for example, also modeled itself after the "steal from the rich and give to the poor" philosophy of the legendary Robin Hood.[45] More fundamentally, from its inception the ELN has had strong Christian roots. This is due in large measure to the fact that one of its key founding members was the radical priest Camilo Torres, whose 1966 death in combat—just a year after the group's official formation—represented a huge blow to the rebels.[46] The ELN's commitment to Christianity has injected a moral component to many of its actions. One early and important expression of this was the ELN's serious quandary over how to find coherence between the strategic lessons espoused by Clausewitz and Guevara, on the one hand, and the Christian view of murder as the ultimate sin, on the other.[47]

Mixing its unique interpretations of Christianity and political realism, the ELN attempted to win the hearts and minds of campesinos by propounding that the state represented the enemy of common people. The relatively sophisticated intellectual and moral elements of the group's ideology eventually garnered them additional support from middle-class students and professionals alienated by the exclusionary politics of the National Front, which failed to tolerate even moderate leftist thought.

But the ELN's endeavors in the 1960s proved to be less than successful. There were a number of reasons for this. First, the group was plagued by considerable infighting. Sometimes this was expressed through substantial debates over issues such as the role of political murder in guerrilla struggle. Other times, bitter feuds between personalities cast a deep pall over the ELN. There were allegations, for example, that certain key members were simply too proud to admit error.[48] This is significant not only because there has been a historical dispersion of power in Colombia, but also because the left in general has failed to achieve significant unity both between and within guerrilla groups. Second, a strong military campaign launched by the Colombian government considerably weakened the already feeble ELN in the late 1960s. Finally, key members such as Manuel Pérez Martínez were expelled from the country.[49] Although their expulsion weakened the group at the time, their travels to Spain and elsewhere attracted substantial international political support that would come to benefit the ELN in the 1990s and beyond.

The 1970s greeted the ELN with more of the same. In some ways, the beginning of the decade looked bright, with the group making territorial gains between 1970 and 1973 in the departments of Santander, Sur de Bolívar, and Antioquia, and more generally in the region of Magdalena

Medio. Despite this, significant infighting and subsequent desertion continued to debilitate the group. Key leaders considered 1972 to be the rebels' historical ebb, given the detention of 100 of its members by the Colombian military.[50] The ELN leadership would later criticize this period as one marked by an abandonment of the *foquista* philosophy. The rebels focused almost exclusively upon military power (which it was losing at the hands of the Colombian military), with scant attention devoted to political work either in the cities or in the countryside.[51]

The true ebb for the group, however, did not arrive until 1978, when the ELN was all but annihilated.[52] The Colombian military prevailed over the ELN in many battles during 1977 and 1978, erasing much of the rebels' territorial gains achieved earlier in the decade. One of the group's key members, José Manuel Martínez, was killed by the military, and infighting and desertion continued. The ELN estimates that in 1978 it had just thirty armed supporters.[53] This atmosphere of devastation led the movement's remaining members to embark upon a serious rethinking of the group's goals and strategy. This period of reorientation and soul-searching occurred against the backdrop of much needed inspiration drawn from a second generation of Latin American revolutionaries, Nicaragua's Sandinistas, who emerged in 1979.

Despite its virtual annihilation in the late 1970s, the ELN staged a dramatic resurgence in the 1980s, particularly during the period of 1983 to 1986. In terms of support base, the group's strategy was to unite Christians, students, and middle-class professionals who felt excluded from the political class, which was tightly dominated by elite members of the Liberals and Conservatives.[54] Although this was important, the strategy that would ultimately deliver significant power to the ELN vis-à-vis the government and other subversive movements was the ELN's scheme to control key economic regions of the country. According to the movement's leader, Nicólas Rodríguez Bautista ("Gabino"), this plan was devised between 1983 and 1986, and was implemented immediately afterward. These strategic regions were concentrated in the Magdalena Medio area, as well as in the country's frontier with Venezuela. More specifically, the ELN planned to play a dominant role in the oil-producing area of Barrancabermeja, in the coal-producing region of Carmen and San Vicente, as well as in northern Antioquia and southern Cauca, which were the site of strategic highways and important agricultural production. The ELN also established a strong presence in Norte de Santander, near the country's border with Venezuela, as well as in Urabá, the banana-producing region on the Caribbean coast.[55]

Armed dominance of these key strategic areas allowed the ELN to impose *impuestos* (taxes) on large businesses located in the region. Many of these were multinational corporations. The significance of this taxation cannot be underestimated. It provided the group with substantial economic coffers, which would increase throughout the 1990s and into the twenty-first century. This permitted the ELN to be entirely self-sufficient economically. While Soviet-supported leftist groups would begin their swan song in the 1980s, the ELN would ride a wave of increasing power through the dawn of the twenty-first century.

A number of factors, then, served to fortify the power and support base of the ELN in the 1980s. The success of Nicaragua's Sandinistas in the early 1980s provided a badly needed source of inspiration for the group. Indeed, the rebels sent some of their members to Nicaragua in the early part of that decade, and the experiment there served to demonstrate that renewed possibilities of power existed for the Latin American left.[56] The ELN's newfound and brilliant strategy of militarily dominating strategic economic regions of the country—especially the oil-producing areas—provided the group with considerable wealth and economic self-sufficiency. This translated into military power vis-à-vis the government and in relation to other subversive groups in Colombia. This winning strategy, combined with political work that attracted the support of urban students and professionals, meant a substantial increase of the ELN's armed membership. Between 1983 and 1986, the group's armed forces increased fivefold, to between 600 and 800 troops on eleven fronts. Their numbers would increase to 3,000 troops in 1995, and to 4,500 troops by the turn of the century.[57]

There were attempts at unity among the left in the 1980s, as noted in the previous discussion of the FARC. These were inspired largely by the Sandinistas' seizure of power, a feat that relied on leftist unity in Nicaragua. The first important bid at harmony among Colombia's left was the formation of the CNG in 1985. Key members of the left belonged to the group, including the ELN, the M-19, Quintín Lame (QL), and the EPL. Because the FARC had a tenuous ceasefire agreement with the government, it held an arm's-length relationship with the CNG. The ELN as well never felt comfortable within the CNG. From the ELN's perspective, the FARC continued to march to its own drummer with its bilateral relations with the government, and other groups such as the indigenous QL focused narrowly upon specific issues (indigenous rights in QL's case). Division over crucial themes such as disarmament and ceasefire arrangements plagued the umbrella CNG, with the ELN particularly reluctant to give up arms in the face of a government it profoundly mistrusted. Further, the ELN saw no sign that the government was serious about implementing socioeconomic policies aimed at redressing the horrific division of wealth in the country.[58] For those reasons, among others, the CNG dissolved by 1987, and was replaced shortly afterward by another failed attempt at unity, the Coodinadora Guerrillera Simón Bolívar.

* * *

The 1980s witnessed an overall rebirth for the ELN. Rising from the ashes of the late 1970s, when the group was all but annihilated, the rebels revised their strategy between 1983 and 1986. The most important element of this rethinking was the scheme to exert military control over economically strategic areas of the country, particularly the oil-producing zone near the Magdalena Media region. The strategy was put into action after 1986, when the ELN began imposing "taxes" on large corporations involved in resource extraction. Many of these businesses were foreign-owned. The result was considerable wealth and self-sufficiency for the ELN. This was the beginning of a trajectory whereby the ELN would emerge as the country's second-ranking leftist subversive group. While the rebels grew substantially in political and military strength, they failed to unite with other leftist forces in Colombia. This is yet another expression of the dispersion of power and fragmentation of politics that has characterized the country since its inception.

The Radical Right: Paramilitaries in the 1980s

Since the 1980s the radical right in Colombia has emerged as a major political player. This is due to four principal factors. First, Colombian paramilitaries have represented significant political interests, interests that have not been accommodated through legitimate political channels. Related to this, the Colombian state has been so weak that sizable components of the population have sought to defend themselves from a variety of threats through allegiance to right-wing paramilitary forces. There is a significant irony here in that the paramilitaries have formed due to the weakness of the state, but simultaneously have contributed to the state's frailty. Third, in some cases the Colombian military and components of the state have relied on the paramilitaries to do their dirty work, specifically in launching vicious military attacks against the Colombian left—with targets ranging from its "legitimate" components, such as members of Union Patriótica, to full-fledged guerrilla groups. Finally, paramilitary armies have defended the economic interests of

Colombia's large and powerful landowners and narcotraffickers, and therefore have been extremely well funded.

Although signs of paramilitaries were noticed in the late 1970s, their presence became unmistakable in 1981 with the formation of the Muerte a Secuestradores (MAS; Death to Kidnappers). This was in response to an increasing wave of kidnappings committed primarily against the rich by leftist guerrillas such as the FARC and the ELN, which used ransoms from this practice to fund their military activities. In the department of Córdoba, historically one of the strongholds of the paramilitary forces, the level of such kidnappings doubled between 1983 and 1990, adding fuel to the fire of paramilitary development.[59] In this sense and others, MAS and other paramilitary forces have viewed themselves as self-defense groups in the context of a state too weak to protect them.

Other such groups proliferated, with an ideological agenda that included "social cleansing" of such targets as homosexuals, prostitutes, drug addicts, beggars, and the homeless. The paramilitaries also have been fiercely anticommunist, and some important elements have displayed a neofascist agenda. Overall, they have promoted ultra-right-wing social policies against the backdrop of a society beset with a shifting moral code.

More important than the ideological component of the paramilitaries have been the powerful economic interests behind them. These are essentially twofold—big landowners and narcotraffickers. Initially, the paramilitaries had their strongest following in regions dominated by powerful farmers and ranchers, who fiercely resisted giving up their feudal latifundia (estates) to placate cries for equity through land reform. In the early 1980s, the paramilitaries were strongest in Córdoba and the Magdalena Medio region, where agricultural land was among the most concentrated in the country. By the late 1980s, the distinction between big farmers and ranchers on the one hand, and narcotraffickers on the other, became blurred. In fact, during the mid-1980s narcotraffickers invested their illicit wealth through the purchase of 4 to 6 million hectares of land.[60] Hence the premodern agricultural landlords and the postmodern narco-landholders shared an economic interest in resisting land reform. They pooled their finances to create a security regime in the form of the paramilitaries.

Even without their increasingly immense landholdings, however, the narcotraffickers required an apparatus to provide security for their multibillion-dollar enterprise. They originally relied on components of guerrilla groups such as the FARC to provide this service in the late 1970s and early 1980s. But the ideological divide between the narcotraffickers and the guerrillas was too wide for any lasting association.

The first manifestation of the narcotraffickers' own security apparatus appeared in the form of the *sicarios* in Medellín. Many *sicarios* had relatives who had participated in La Violencia and who harbored memories of political scores that they felt still needed to be settled. Many also shared the ultraconservative views of these early paramilitaries.[61] Thus the paramilitaries have had a strong relationship to narcotrafficking from the beginning of their formation in the 1980s. Indeed, the leader of the paramilitaries from the mid-1990s through the early twenty-first century was Carlos Castaño, brother of Antioquia's renowned narcotrafficker, Fidel Castaño.

Beyond providing security for illicit and legitimate economic interests, and for defending components of the population who feared guerrillas tactics such as kidnapping, the paramilitaries have also demonstrated a keen interest in becoming a legitimate political actor. They possessed a clear constituency and ideological agenda. This was obvious since Pablo Escobar's 1989–1991 campaign. It represented an unsuccessful attempt to pressure the Colombian government into recognizing his group as the country's new legitimate bourgeoisie. From Escobar's vantage point, his group was no different than the Kennedy family of the United States, whose initial wealth was derived from bootlegging during the U.S. era of Prohibition. The goal of being recognized as a legitimate political actor would intensify during the late 1990s and into the twenty-first century under the leadership of Carlos Castaño.

Another crucial aspect of the paramilitaries has been the nature of their relationship to the Colombian state. From the beginning there have been clear links between components of the Colombian armed forces and the paramilitaries. A 1983 government report, for example, observed the presence of at least 163 paramilitary members in the Magdalena Medio region, with at least 59 of these being from the Colombian armed forces.[62] A stream of subsequent documentation stretching into the twenty-first century has demonstrated ties between members of the armed forces and the paramilitaries. What is also clear is that the Colombian government, the military, and the paramilitaries have had a common enemy—leftist guerrillas. Brutal paramilitary attacks against the left have had the potential to serve the strategic interests of the Colombian state, leaving the government free to claim it had no knowledge of such attacks. By 1989 the paramilitaries were estimated to have at least 2,000 full-time troops, and as many as 20,000 part-timers.[63]

Because the situation with the paramilitaries has been complicated and characterized by nuance, it is difficult to describe them in absolute terms. For example, while the paramilitaries and the Colombian state have had common objectives, it has never been clear that the paramilitaries have been directed by the federal state. Further, only certain components of the armed forces have shown support for the paramilitaries. Finally, the paramilitaries themselves have been fragmented, mirroring the general pattern of political dispersion in the country.[64] Overall, the right-wing paramilitaries represent a complex conglomerate of forces that began in the 1980s, and have attempted since the 1990s to unify themselves and to be counted as a legitimate political actor in Colombia.

Other Guerrilla Movements in the 1980s

While the focus of this chapter and the next is upon the two largest and most powerful guerrilla groups in Colombia, the FARC and the ELN were not alone in the 1980s. Their compatriots included the M-19, Quintín Lame, and the EPL. The M-19 had a significant presence in the 1980s, before disbanding in 1990. The group represented a second generation of leftist guerrillas in Colombia. Inspired by the 1979 Sandinista Revolution in Nicaragua, the M-19 was primarily an urban guerrilla organization, though it began in the countryside. It was supported by the young, the educated, and the middle class, and was perhaps most potent in the capital city of Bogotá.[65] Its supporters were components of society who were shut out by the exclusionary politics of the Liberal and Conservative parties, and who could not relate to rural-based policies of guerrilla groups such as the FARC.

The M-19 is perhaps most notorious for its horrific November 1985 attack on the Palace of Justice in Bogotá. At least 100 people were killed, including twelve supreme court justices. The attack followed failed peace efforts with the government and allegations that M-19 members were assassinated by paramilitary forces with the complicity of the Colombian state. The group signed a peace agreement with the government in 1989–1990, and metamorphosed into a "legitimate" though ultimately insignificant political party after that time. The broader significance of the M-19 concerns its utilization of terror in the capital city, which brought the civil war to a new phase. The group also demonstrated that dispossessed members of the middle class were prepared to resort to radical politics.

Another group operating in the 1980s was the indigenous guerrilla movement Quintín Lame. Although never strong militarily in comparison to the other rebels discussed above, the group possessed coherent interests and was strong enough to get the government's attention. The indigenous people represent 2–3 percent of Colombia's population.

Their most significant political interests as expressed through Quintín Lame were land reform and preservation of culture through such methods as the development of an indigenous radio station.[66] They were successful at obtaining 74,000 hectares of land through government negotiations, and also received another 18.3 million hectares as indigenous reservations. The government also initiated programs aimed at economic development for indigenous communities. By 2000 the group's leaders observed the irony that while government programs ultimately failed, the entrepreneurial spirit and connections the group obtained during its years as a guerrilla movement helped them to achieve a significant degree of economic development on their own.[67]

Finally, the Ejército Popular de Liberación also made its presence known in the 1980s. The EPL was strongest in certain areas of Antioquia, Urabá, and Córdoba. Politically and military, it was the weakest of the groups examined here. It was especially debilitated by pronounced infighting. The EPL drew support from a rural population, and embraced an ideology heavily influenced by Maoism. By 2000 many of its remaining militants had been absorbed by the FARC and especially by the ELN.[68]

Colombian State and Society in the 1980s

The notion of a partial collapse of the state in the 1980s is a common theme in the political literature regarding Colombia. While there is no debate that the state weakened considerably in that decade, it is important to emphasize that there was not much of a state to collapse in the first place. The Colombian state has been altogether absent in significant regions of the country, such as the *zona de distensión,* or ceasefire zone, which the government gave to the FARC in 1998. Beyond this, it has been held in contempt by much of the population in the areas of the country in which the state has been present, due to intense corruption, the state's role in perpetuating human rights abuses, as well as the extraordinarily exclusionary politics of the government, among other factors. The fact that Colombia by 1990 had the second worst distribution of wealth in Latin America after Brazil did little for the Colombian government in winning the hearts and minds of the population.[69]

Why did subversive movements gain so much strength in Colombia during the 1980s, in a manner that would foreshadow the virtual disintegration of the Colombian state and society by the turn of the century? Certainly poverty and inequity of wealth were important factors. In the absence of those factors, it seems unlikely that leftist guerrillas would enjoy any significant support. However, poverty and inequity have existed throughout Latin America and in much of the developing world, yet most of those countries have not witnessed the potency of subversive movements that Colombia has endured. What, then, are the other contributing factors in the mosaic of Colombian political chaos?

The exclusionary policies of the Colombian government have certainly blighted the political landscape. Important components of Colombian society—such as the young, the educated, and the middle class—could not find a voice in the Liberal or Conservative parties. But even when the government did attempt to incorporate the left, through various peace initiatives and through the legitimization of parties such as the M-19 and the Union Patriótica, the failure was so devastating that chaos became even more exaggerated. So while exclusionary policies of the government represent one contributing factor to the strength of subversive movements in Colombia, the reasons behind the failure of attempts at political inclusion represent a complementary factor. That failure was rooted in the pronounced intolerance for even the peaceful left among sectors of Colombian society, particularly on the part of the economic elite and the paramilitary right.

Another factor concerns the historical tendency of Colombians to settle political differences with violence, to the extent that violence has assumed some measure of legitimacy. Certainly this was the case in the period between liberation and La Violencia. A similar pattern seems to have reemerged with considerable vigor in the 1980s. Related to this is the pronounced lack of legitimacy among key political actors outside their narrow bases of support. The governing parties have been viewed by many with contempt for the reasons mentioned above. The leftist guerrillas have lost legitimacy due to their brutal military and terrorist tactics, as well as their obvious and widespread participation in crimes such as narcotrafficking, kidnapping, and extortion. Right-wing paramilitary forces have invited widespread disgust due to their extraordinary penchant for violence and human rights abuses, and for their strong reliance on narcotrafficking as a source for funding. In short, the lack of legitimacy and esteem associated with political actors in Colombia is perhaps unmatched in the Americas. It has added to the circular landscape of subversion, since no group seems politically sacred in a country historically prone to resort to violence in attempts to settle political scores.

A basic point of modern political philosophy is that when there exists a strong and centralized state that possesses a monopoly on the means of force—a Leviathan, in the words of Thomas Hobbes—there is less of a tendency for subversion and violence. To achieve such a situation, a strong sense of unified national identity must be present. Lacking a national identity and a strong centralized state, Colombia has been a living portrait of the premodern, or pre-Leviathan, dog-eat-dog world of violent chaos. This tendency has been present since the birth of the country. Power has been dispersed to the extreme, and this was further exaggerated in the 1980s due to the proliferation of various subversive forces. Hence the 1980s witnessed the amplification of dark forces present in the country since the early 1800s. The traditional warring factions of the Liberals and Conservatives, which ended their carnage in 1958, gave way to a new menu of belligerents in the 1980s. Foremost among these were the guerrilla left and the paramilitary right.

Adding considerable fuel to the fire was the emergence of narcotrafficking in the 1970s, and its increasing dominance in the 1980s. The country's strong sense of entrepreneurialism and individual gain, which is perhaps unmatched in the Americas, explains in large measure why Colombians have been leading participants in the inter-American drug trade. A crucial point is that while narcotrafficking did not create subversive movements in Colombia, it provided some of them with a virtual blank check to arm themselves to the teeth. This proved to be particularly pernicious in a country characterized by the absence of both a strong state and a national identity, and by the presence of a historical violent streak unmatched in the hemisphere.

Conclusion

The particularly vicious nature of protracted warfare in Colombia appears to have rendered guerrilla groups more interested in military prowess than political or ideological development. That is, Colombian subversive groups have had to construct powerful military machines just to survive, and this has often eclipsed political struggle. The important exception to this occurred during the late 1980s and early 1990s, with the participation of the UP and the M-19 in the so-called legitimate political sector. There was considerable common ground ideologically among those groups, and also with regard to the FARC and the ELN. On the economic front, much of this centered on the need for land reform, agrarian credit, guaranteed prices for crops, a better distribution of wealth, and proper taxation for foreign companies doing business in Colombia. Politically, these groups fought for the notion of inclusion within the existing system, and for a state that possessed the willingness and wherewithal to protect its citizens.

The significant electoral performance of the UP, and to a lesser extent the M-19, temporarily demonstrated a plural support base for the emerging "legitimate" left. This support ranged from traditional members such as peasants who endured the brunt of the nation's poverty, to newcomers in the form of urban and middle-class residents who felt excluded from the elite politics of the Liberals and Conservatives. The disastrous nature of the UP experiment, and especially the state's failure to protect thousands of UP members from assassination, represented a profound turning point for the country. It signaled to the leftist guerrillas such as the FARC and the ELN that there was no space for the left in "legitimate" politics, and that the only way to achieve any sort of power in Colombia was through the use of horrific force. After this point, political and ideological struggle fell by the wayside, while the rebels focused on illicit means to construct the most formidable forces of destruction possible.

The role of epistemology represents an important backdrop from which to consider the Colombian imbroglio. Elements of premodernity, modernity, and postmodernity have been present in the country in a manner such that none has been dominant. It was observed that the twentieth century greeted Colombia with a process of industrialization, participation in the world economy, and other features typically associated with modernity. But stronger elements of premodernity have often prevailed. These include the lack of a Leviathan, a feudal disposition toward political space, a pronounced dispersion and fragmentation of power, the absence of notions such as balance or equilibrium, as well as the utter lack of conflict resolution mechanisms. A few postmodern elements would appear in the 1990s in the realms of speculation and crime, as well as with regard to methods of warfare employed by the United States in Colombia, reflecting the country's lack of a dominant episteme and concomitant legacy of chaos and warfare.

Notes

1. See, for example, Morgenthau, *Politics Among Nations.*
2. For a discussion of this, see Pécaut, "Presente, pasado, y futuro de la violencia."
3. For an excellent and detailed discussion of this, see Orquist, *Violence, Conflict, and Politics in Colombia,* pp. 21–23.
4. For an interesting discussion on the FARC's view of Bolívar and this component of Colombian history, see Fuerzas Armadas Revolucionarias de Colombia (FARC), "La estrategia política del libertador," May 1997 (no specific date), translation by author.

5. For an excellent historical discussion, see, for example, Deas and Gaitán Daza, *Dos ensayos especulativos sobre la violencia;* and Kline, *Colombia,* esp. chap. 2.

6. See Jaramamillo Uribe, "Nación y región en los orígenes del estado nacional," p. 120.

7. The distinctions between modern and premodern epistemologies are brilliantly discussed in Foucault, *Order of Things*.

8. See, for example, Deas and Gaitán Daza, *Dos ensayos especulativos sobre la violencia;* and Kline, *Colombia*.

9. Quoted in Victor Álvarez, "Notas sobre la constitución del estado," pp. 154–157, translation by author. The original text appears in José María Samper, *Ensayo sobre las revoluciones políticos y la condición social de las repúblicas colombianos* (1861; reprint, Bogotá: Universidad Nacional de Colombia, 1969), pp. 83–85.

10. Balance represented a key component of modern epistemology, as exemplified by the popularity of balance of power theory after 1815, as well as by the central place occupied by balance in physics (equilibrium) and other disciplines.

11. For an excellent and critical discussion of Colombian politics and history, see Pearce, *Colombia*. A capsule review of the War of 1,000 Days appears on p. 25.

12. In 1907 the country's first national military school was established, five years after the conclusion of the devastating War of 1,000 Days. See Francisco Leal Buitrago, "Estamos en una carrera contra tiempo," in *La paz: Análisis del proceso y propietas para una nueva sistema político en Colombia* (Bogotá: Ediciones Aurora, 2000), p. 139.

13. Author interview with Alfredro Rangel Suárez, director, Política y Estrategia, Fundación Social, Bogotá, 6 May 1999.

14. See Deas and Gaitán Daza, *Dos ensayos especulativos sobre la violencia,* p. 222.

15. See, for example, Kline, *Colombia,* p. 37.

16. See, for example, Pearce, *Colombia,* pp. 41–42.

17. See Kline, *Colombia,* p. 43.

18. See Gaitán Daza, "Una indignación sobre las causes de la violencia en Colombia," in Deas and Gaitán Daza, *Dos ensayos especulativos sobre la violencia,* p. 396.

19. For an excellent discussion of this, see Pizarro Leongómez, *Las FARC (1949–1966),* pp. 39ff.

20. There are some important empirical problems in measuring with accuracy the number of deaths that can be directly attributed to La Violencia. That is, various body counts may include deaths that are not directly attributable to political violence during this period. An excellent discussion of this appears in Gaitán Daza, "Una indignación sobre las causes de la violencia," pp. 180ff. Violence was not evenly spread throughout the country. The black-populated Atlantic and Pacific Coasts have always tended to be among the most peaceful regions of the country. By contrast, the departments of Antioquia, Santander,

Norte de Santander, and Boyaca, and more generally the coffee cultivation zones, have been among the most violent regions. See Pécaut, "Presente, pasado, y futuro de la violencia," p. 896.

21. See Gaitán Daza, "Una indignación sobre las causes de la violencia," p. 211.

22. Colombians historically have been more comfortable with peace negotiations in Europe than in the United States.

23. Author interview with Padre Gabriel Izquierdo, professor, Instituto Pensar, Pontificia Universidad Javeriana, Bogotá, 7 May 1999.

24. See, for example, Leal Buitrago, "Las utopías de la paz," p. 132.

25. A superb discussion of the history of the FARC has been written by Eduardo Pizarro Leongómez, a former FARC member. Following his participation in that organization, he was director of the Instituto de Estudios Políticos y Relaciones Internacionales at the Universidad Nacional in Bogotá. Following a nearly successful attempt on his life in late 1999 by ultra-right-wing paramilitaries, he left Colombia to seek asylum in Canada. See his book, *Las FARC (1949–1966)*. For the early history of the FARC, see, for example, pp. 18–22.

26. As quoted in ibid., pp. 58–63.

27. See FARC, "Octava conferencia nacional de las FARC-EP: Programa agrario," 2 April 1993, translation by author; and "Octava conferencia nacional de las FARC-EP: 30 años de lucha por la paz, democracia, y soberanía," April 1993 (no specific date), translation by author.

28. See FARC, "Octava conferencia nacional de las FARC-EP: 30 años de lucha por las paz, democracia, y soberanía," translation by author.

29. See Pizarro Leongómez, *Las FARC,* pp. 198–199.

30. FARC, "34th aniversario de las FARC-EP," 27 May 1998, translation by author.

31. Author interview with Padre Gabriel Izquierdo, 7 May 1999.

32. See Pizarro Leongómez, *Insurgencia sin revolución,* pp. 32–33.

33. See, for example, Nazih Richani, "The Political Economy of Violence: The War System in Colombia," *Journal of Interamerican Studies and World Affairs* 39, no. 2 (summer 1997): 3; and Kline, *Colombia,* p. 10.

34. See Pizarro Leongómez, *Insurgencia sin revolución,* p. 99.

35. See Rangel Suárez, *Colombia,* p. 12.

36. See Pizarro Leongómez, *Insurgencia sin revolución,* pp. 126–127.

37. See Pécaut, "Presente, pasado, y futuro de la violencia," p. 897.

38. See FARC, "Acuerdos de la Uribe," 28 May 1984, translation by author; and FARC, "Octava conferencia nacional de las FARC-EP: Programa agrario," translation by author.

39. See Gobierno de Colombia, Departamento Nacional de Planeación, *El gasto militar.*

40. See Zuluaga Nieto, "De guerrillas a movimientos políticos," p. 20.

41. The FARC estimates that 4,000 UP leaders and supports were murdered. See FARC, "Intervención de Alfonso Cano en el Lanzamiento del Movimiento Bolivariano," e-mail redresistencia@freesurf.ch, 29 April 2000 (no

website given). Other estimates place UP assassinations at about 2,000. See Chernick, "La negociación de un paz," p. 35.

42. See FARC, Manuel Marulanda Vélez, "Texto completo del discurso pronunciado," 27 May 1994, translation by author.

43. For an extensive account of the ELN's seizure of Simacota, see Rodríguez Bautista, "Ejército de Liberación Nacional," pp. 59–69.

44. Ibid., p. 27.

45. Ibid., p. 32.

46. Ibid., p. 76.

47. Ibid., pp. 39, 43, 58.

48. See, for example, Pérez Martínez, "Ejército de Liberación Nacional," p. 177.

49. Ibid., p. 169.

50. Ibid., p. 185.

51. Ibid., p. 187.

52. See Pizarro Leongómez, *Insurgencia sin revolución*, p. 99.

53. Rodríguez Bautista, "Ejército de Liberación Nacional," p. 141.

54. See, for example, Pérez Martínez, "Ejército de Liberación Nacional," p. 207.

55. See Rodríguez Bautista, "Ejército de Liberación Nacional," pp. 151–152. See also Pizarro Leongómez, *Insurgencia sin revolución*, pp. 156–157.

56. See Rodríguez Bautista, "Ejército de Liberación Nacional," pp. 150–151.

57. The highly respected strategist Alfredo Rangel Suárez estimates that the ELN had 800 armed supporters in 1995. See his excellent book *Colombia: Guerra en el fin de siglo*, p. 12. The ELN itself estimates it had 600 to 700 armed troops at the time it conducted its first national assembly in 1986. See Pérez Martínez, "Ejército de Liberación Nacional," p. 214.

58. See Rodríguez Bautista, "Ejército de Liberación Nacional," p. 152; and Pérez Martínez, "Ejército de Liberación Nacional," pp. 218–222.

59. See Romero, "Élites regionales, identidades, y paramilitares en el Sinú," p. 196.

60. See Richani, "Political Economy of Violence," p. 17.

61. Author interviews with Mauricio Molina Molina, director, Relaciones Internacionales, and Professor Carlos Patiño Villa, coordinator, Estudios Políticos, Universidad Pontificia Bolivariana, Medellín, 15 May 1999. See also Pécaut, "Presente, pasado, y futuro de la violencia," p. 904.

62. See Marco Palacios, "La Solución Política al Conflicto Armado," in Camacho Guizado and Leal Buitrago, eds., *Armar la paz es desarmar la guerra*, p. 368.

63. See Pearce, *Colombia*, p. 262.

64. Author interviews with Alfredo Rangel Suárez, 6 May 1999; and Rafael Nieto, defense analyst, Bogotá, 5 May 1999.

65. See Zuluaga Nieto, "De guerrillas a movimientos políticos," pp. 11–39.

66. For an excellent discussion of Quintín Lame, see Ricardo Peñarada, "De rebeldes a cuidadanos."

67. *El Tiempo* (Bogotá), 28 May 2000.

68. Author interview with Ernesto Rueda Suárez, director, Escuela de Ciencias Socio-Políticas, Universidad Industrial de Santander, Bucaramanga, 7 June 2000.

69. The figure is from Comisión Económica para América Latina y el Caribe, and is noted in Richani, "Political Economy of Violence," p. 14.

5

The FARC and the ELN: Concepts of Strategy, Security, and Power

Since the 1990s, Colombia's subversive movements have competed viciously to maximize their relative power and have engaged in an increasingly brutal contest with the generally inept Colombian state. This chapter addresses what the Colombian imbroglio can tell us about the strategy, security, and power of leftist guerrilla movements at the dawn of the twenty-first century. It also considers the significance of this situation vis-à-vis the broader issue of continuity and transformation in warfare. Colombia represents a case study of the factors that contribute to human violence and warfare, and offers outstanding negative lessons regarding the importance of good government. In this sense, an examination of Colombia entails a consideration of what may be the most significant themes in politics.

The chapter begins with a contextual sketch of the remarkable background in which the guerrilla groups have operated. The centerpiece will be a post-1990 analysis of the strategies, ideologies, and actions of the country's leftist rebels and, to a lesser extent, the paramilitary forces. Also under analysis here is Plan Colombia, the extravagant U.S. military package designed to weaken the FARC. The strategic successes and failures of the guerrillas, and of the United States through Plan Colombia, are linked to their grasp of classic strategic themes. Also relevant to the warfare in Colombia are systems of thought. The chaotic political nature of the country has been an expression of an odd blend of premodern, modern, and postmodern features.

Contextual Elements

Prior to an analysis of the belligerents themselves, let us consider some of the prominent features that mark the surface of this civil war in terms of violence, crime, migration, and other contextual factors. The level of violence and crime in Colombia is particularly striking. Close to 40,000 people were slain for political motives between 1990 and 2001, with murders of all kinds totaling 25,660 in 2000 alone. Between January 1995 and January 2001, there were 2,027 victims of political massacres, and 3,618 acts of political terrorism—with the vast majority of these occurring in 1999 and 2000.[1] Over 5,400 civilians lost their lives in Colombian warfare during 2001, which represents an increase of about 350 percent since 1998.[2] Colombia was host to over 90 percent of the world's total number of labor activists murdered for political motives in 2001.

Compounding this atmosphere of chaos and carnage has been the booming industry of kidnapping, estimated to be worth at least U.S.$80 million annually. There were 7,748 reported kidnappings between January 1995 and January 2001, and it is acknowledged that most kidnappings go unreported due to fear of reprisal.[3] Another victim of the war has been the environment. Since 1986, for example, eleven times more oil has been spilled in Colombia as a result of guerrilla bombings than was spilled in Alaska's *Exxon Valdez* disaster.[4]

Colombia is also notoriously distinguished as the planet's epicenter of narcotrafficking, and this has figured prominently in the country's civil war.[5] Colombia dominates the global cocaine trade, and since the 1990s it has been bolstering its position as a lead player in the world opiate market. The country's immense illicit narcotics industry, in tandem with the other highly lucrative black markets of kidnapping and extortion, have fueled the civil war by handsomely financing subversive groups and by exacerbating the corruption of a historically feeble state.

This panorama of warfare and crime has contributed to the most severe economic depression ever to strike Colombia, with unemployment hovering over 20 percent during 2000–2001.[6] During 1999, industrial production slid 17 percent. Annual levels of foreign investment declined by 70 percent between 1993 and 1999, as investors fled the country due to security fears and a dwindling local market.[7] Compounding these woes, the country's foreign debt doubled to U.S.$33 billion between 1998 and 1999, while interest payments on the debt soared as a result of Standard and Poor's degradation of Colombia's debt load from "stable" to "negative" in April 2000.[8] An International Monetary Fund (IMF) loan and restructuring package was created in December 1999 and administered in 2000, spelling increased taxes, privatization, and drastic cuts in social welfare—though military spending escalated significantly.[9] By 2002, about 40 percent of government revenues were earmarked for debt payments. Exchange rates roughly doubled from 1,141 pesos in 1997 to over 2,300 through 2002. The profound extent of the depression, worse in Colombian terms than the Great Depression of 1929–1933, came as a brutal shock to the country's population, who had grown accustomed to a booming economy that was immune even to the Latin American debt crisis of the 1980s. Exacerbating the economic catastrophe was a further concentration of wealth in Colombia, which already had hosted one of the three worst distributions of income in Latin America, along with Brazil and Mexico. Indicative of this were Gini coefficients that rose from 0.55 in 1991 to 0.59 in 1999.[10]

Depression, inequity, and warfare have generated intense waves of internal and external migration. By mid-1999, 1,582,683 people had been displaced by Colombia's warfare, with that number escalating to over 2 million by 2002.[11] Within this time frame, the internal refugee population of the country represented the third largest in the world, and the highest in the Americas. Beyond internal refugees, there has been a great hemorrhage from the country, predominantly among the wealthy and privileged. Indeed, there was an exodus of 1,072,449 Colombians between 1997 and 2000, out of total population of about 40 million.[12] An astonishing 41 percent of respondents to a poll conducted in December 2000 indicated that they would leave the country if they could.[13]

Against a backdrop of intensifying warfare and dispersed political power, Colombia's civil society has been notoriously weak.[14] While the country has had among the highest numbers of NGOs per capita in Latin America, these groups often have been uncoordinated in their activities. Fear to speak openly due to death threats and the like has represented an important contributing factor to their general timidity. An individualistic mentality among much of the society, an entrenched system of political clientelism that emphasizes numerous vertical patterns of political power rather than a horizontal communitarian spirit, plus a related dispersion of power in the country, are other factors that explain the frailty of Colombian civil society. Despite the vast unpopularity of the country's belligerent forces, the feeble nature of the country's civil society so far has limited its capacity to stage a united front in opposition to the war, or to create the widespread support that could help establish a strong and legitimate government. Yet there have been more frequent signs of public frustration with escalating warfare, as evidenced by increasing if disparate peace rallies throughout the country in the period 2001–2002.

The ELN

Ideology in the 1990s

Rising from virtual defeat in the 1970s and early 1980s, the ELN during the 1990s emerged as Colombia's second largest leftist guerrilla group.

It has been generally regarded as the most politically developed of Colombia's subversive movements and has relied on a traditional though effective approach.[15] ELN leader Nicholás Rodríguez Bautista ("Gabino") suggests that at the beginning of the 1990s Colombia was a caricature of a Hobbesian dog-eat-dog world in the absence of a Leviathan. For Gabino, the country was characterized by a "violent society, but this is not a natural condition, and within the context of violent institutions, the people must respond equally to defend themselves."[16] Hence the challenge for the ELN became how to maximize its power in Colombia's violent and chaotic atmosphere through the vehicle of its Christian-Marxist ideology.

Not only had the assassination of Union Patriótica (UP) members at the hands of paramilitaries meant that there was no political space for the peaceful participation of leftists, but the ELN argued that to be part of that system would ultimately mean the corruption and ideological sellout of the group. Consider, for example, the observations of the ELN's political commander, Manuel Pérez Martínez, regarding the case of the M-19—a group of former guerrillas who put down their arms to form a political party. From the vantage point of the ELN, through its participation in mainstream politics the M-19 had descended into "practices of clientelism and corruption. . . . They not only lost their weapons . . . they lost their ideals. . . . We find no difference between the political practices of traditional parties and those of the M-19."[17] The ELN, then, was fully prepared for a protracted revolutionary struggle.

Crucial ruptures occurred globally during the early 1990s that demanded the attention of Colombia's subversive movements. The swan song of the Soviet Union, the Sandinistas' electoral loss of power in Nicaragua in 1990, and the virtual collapse of the leftist guerrilla movement in El Salvador did not represent particularly encouraging news for the few remaining leftist revolutionaries around the planet. Although the ELN lamented those events, its lack of financial ties to external parties such as Moscow meant that the group came away from that situation totally unscathed. Indeed, the ELN's Gabino went so far as to put a positive spin on the general context by arguing that "the socialist system is an extremely young project" and that the ELN was bound to be among the successful "pioneers" of this emerging revolutionary scenario.[18] During the early 1990s, then, rather than being discouraged, the ELN rightfully viewed itself as an up-and-coming power.

Yet there was friction on the horizon, in the eyes of the ELN leaders, since formidable ideological enemies appeared to be accumulating power. The principal threat, according to Gabino, appeared in the form of the capitalist restructuring demanded by neoliberalism through global institutions such as the World Bank and the IMF. For his cohort, Manuel Pérez Martínez, neoliberalism would mean violations of human rights, as well as pronounced economic misery associated with a concentration of wealth.[19] These features were part of the centerpiece of the ELN's general ideological platform in the 1990s and into the twenty-first century. Viewing themselves as moral and ethical combatants poised against the threat of creeping neoliberalism, the rebels vowed to fight what they viewed the North American "monocultural parameter" that would be imposed upon Colombia and the entire world through this emerging economic system.[20] In contrast to what they saw as an inherent pattern within neoliberalism to concentrate wealth, they advocated a system of economic redistribution.[21] Indeed, Manuel Pérez Martínez, the ELN's political commander, suggested that "the only reason there is the violence of a revolutionary struggle" in Colombia is due to economic "misery and exploitation."[22]

The ELN during this time frame also presented well-developed if controversial ideas regarding such issues as foreign investment and privatization. Since the early 1990s, despite their opposition to neoliberalism, the rebels have stated staunchly that they do not oppose foreign investment in Colombia, especially in the extractive sector. Instead, they have argued that Colombia requires a better deal from transnational corporations (TNCs) in such industries. This includes a bigger share of the profit, as well as a contribution by TNCs toward Colombia's own "human, material, scientific and technological infrastructure" in order to help the country participate more fully in these areas without such a pronounced dependence upon foreign interests.[23] Although the ELN encouraged its own version of foreign investment, it has adamantly opposed privatization of some of the country's strategic industries, especially the energy sector.[24] Indeed, the rebels' dramatic bombing attacks of energy towers throughout the country during 2000 did little to attract foreign buyers for the energy industries that the government, through IMF pressure, had hoped to privatize.[25]

The ELN and Other Contenders

Like most political actors in Colombia, the ELN has experienced difficulty getting along with other subversive groups and with the state. While the ELN coordinated some its military activities for the first time with the FARC in 1991 and 1992, through the Coordinadora Guerrillera Simón Bolívar (CGSB), this united front was tenuous and dissolved shortly afterward. Ideological differences and turf wars were among the root causes. Further, the FARC's considerably stronger military capacity presumably would have allowed it to dominate when inevitable disputes arose with the ELN regarding any coordinated activities. Generally, each group has been more interested in maximizing its own power and controlling its private territorial enclave than in working together to achieve a common revolutionary objective. Notable animosity between the two leftist rebel groups escalated throughout the 1990s and into the twenty-first century. Early in 2000, for example, the ELN and the FARC engaged in intense hostilities in a contest to control portions of Antioquia, which is rich in strategic resources such as oil. In that bitter dispute, the ELN accused the FARC of executing five of its commanders.[26] Despite the bellicose pitch of such skirmishes, the ELN also has had overlapping interests with the FARC, particularly regarding the establishment of ceasefire zones. That is, despite its general animosity toward the FARC, the ELN has insisted that such zones for both itself and the FARC are necessary as a "space for peace."[27] Further, the ELN joined military forces with the FARC in 2001, at least temporarily, to cope with mounting pressure from paramilitaries and from the U.S.-sponsored Plan Colombia. While the move was strategically wise in the near term, the tortured history between the FARC and the ELN suggests that the duo is not headed for an enduring partnership.

Although its dealings with the FARC have been generally frosty, the ELN's relations with more ideologically distant actors such as the state and the paramilitaries predictably have been even worse. Since the early 1990s the ELN has blamed components of the state for directing a "dirty war" involving paramilitary attacks against it and other leftist groups.[28] In a typical editorial penned by the ELN in October 1999, the rebels accused the government of "deepening social inequities, and strengthening state terrorism, corruption and exclusion." Further, they rebuked Colombia's political class for engaging in an alleged strategy designed to use so-called "processes of peace as an opportunity to wear out and break insurgent groups at the negotiating table."[29]

The ELN's most venomous attacks, however, have been launched against its archenemy, the right-wing paramilitaries—the Autodefensas Unidas de Colombia (AUC). Because the ELN has considered the AUC to be politically influenced or perhaps directed by components of the Colombian state and by sectors of the country's economic elite, the rebels have therefore regarded the AUC as hired mercenaries.[30] The ELN has accused the paramilitaries of waging a murderous campaign of social cleansing aimed principally at intellectuals, and at various members of the left.[31] The bitterest point of ire for the ELN, however, has been the AUC's staunch opposition to the establishment of a *zona de encuentro,* or ceasefire zone, for the rebels. The government appeared to be on the verge of agreement with the ELN for the creation of such a territory in spring of 2000. But when a tentative agreement was announced, a crippling series of roadblocks surprisingly commenced in the south of Bolívar and spread to other parts of the country. Transportation and ground-based commerce came to a halt, spawning a national crisis. A similar but more subdued series of events occurred when the ELN and the government attempted to reach another agreement on a ceasefire zone in 2001. The ELN bitterly blamed the AUC for orchestrating many such popular protests and for doing everything it could to prevent the creation of the ceasefire area that the ELN so obviously cherished.[32]

Political Objectives

The ELN formulated three major goals during the 1990s and into the twenty-first century. The first was to expand its finances as well as the capacity of its military troops in order to achieve the status of a major political actor among Colombia's potent assortment of belligerents. Second, given the predominance in the country of a premodern epistemological approach to space, the ELN has been nothing short of desperate for a piece of territory under its own control. Indeed, at the turn of the century, this became the group's most enunciated objective. Finally, the rebels have been attempting to influence a restructuring of the Colombian political economy consistent with their ideological premises.

The fundamental premise inherent in the ELN's strategic thinking is that "to the disgrace of Colombian society, the governing class will only listen to the voice of dynamite and of guns."[33] Thus, due to the strong exclusionary tendencies that historically have blighted government policy, the principal strategy of the ELN was to get the state's attention through the clever and organized deployment of shocking and often nonmurderous spectacles. But this required substantial funding. Increasingly through the 1990s and into the twenty-first century, the rebels have relied on two main sources of income: what the ELN views as "retentions," which others call kidnappings, and what the ELN says are "taxes," which others refer to as extortion.[34] The group has denied repeated accusations of engagement in narcotrafficking, however.[35] Retentions, or kidnappings, of predominantly foreign executives hired by TNCs in the extractive sector have yielded substantial income for the ELN since the 1990s, and therefore have helped finance the group's political and military endeavors. Further, the rebels have imposed taxes on extortion from such corporations as a guarantee that they will not kidnap company employees or damage infrastructure. To achieve those objectives the ELN has attempted to dominate the resource-rich territory of eastern Colombia—especially southern Bolívar, the Magdalena Medio, Santander, and Norte de Santander, among other areas.

The group's most spectacular retentions/kidnappings have not been for profit, but instead have been largely successful public relations schemes to attract global media coverage. Three such incidents, all since 1999, are particularly noteworthy: the retention/kidnapping of the passengers and crew of an Avianca jetliner in Bucaramanga in April 1999, of an entire church congregation in southern Cali on 30 May 1999, and of more than thirty patrons of a resort just outside Cali in September 2000. Most of the group's victims were detained for months, and some were held for over a year.

Those massive kidnappings were compounded by two other tactics designed to serve the ELN's broad strategy of attracting the attention of the government and the global media through nonmurderous extravaganzas. The first consisted of the bombing of Medellín's power grid in January of 2000, which knocked out the city's electricity for days. Similar attacks on energy towers occurred in Bogotá and elsewhere, earning the rebels a reputation as terrorists. Beyond this, the consistent bombing of oil pipelines by the ELN and other subversive groups is estimated to have cost the Colombian government and private businesses U.S.$32 billion between 1998 and October 2000, exacerbating the already severe depression that gripped the country.[36] The ecological damage from such attacks has been exorbitant. This controversial strategy, which avoided the indiscriminate use of carnage that has characterized the activities of both the FARC and the AUC, ultimately was effective at influencing the state to enter into dialogue with the ELN.

Any achievements the group has accomplished have been with a comparatively small, rather unprofessional, and "privatized" army. Only a few hundred troops in the 1980s, the ELN's ranks rose to 3,000 troops on thirty-two fronts in 1995, and were estimated by the Colombian armed forces to number 4,533 troops at the beginning of 2001.[37] But in contrast to the highly trained, full-time, and professionalized armies of both the FARC and the AUC, many of the ELN's troops have been part-time and have had less rigorous military training.[38] Generally the ELN has been more adept at committing spectacular crime and terrorism than at direct military combat. Further, experts have suggested that the group's military power faded considerably during 2000–2001 due to lost battles with the Colombian armed forces, the FARC, and the AUC.[39]

A central objective of the ELN has been to acquire a ceasefire zone over which it has substantial political control. This goal became especially important after the FARC proved successful at obtaining its *zona de distensión* in November 1998. On 25 April 2000 the Colombian government announced it was prepared to cede to the ELN its own zone. Among spirited political commotion, the country's top peace negotiator resigned in protest. The announcement also sparked a countrywide wave of paralyzing roadblocks, the worst Colombia had ever witnessed. The rebels were devastated, having had their much hoped-for zone waved in front of them, only to have the government dither and finally retract the offer in the context of surprisingly widespread public opposition. Amid the ensuing chaos and uncertainty, the ELN rightfully blamed the bad publicity surrounding the FARC's *zona de distensión* for the public's unwillingness to carve out another piece of the country's territory for the ELN.[40]

Unwilling to accept defeat after coming so close to achieving its goal, the ELN in 2000 launched a fresh wave of sensational sabotage and kidnappings that prompted the government in January 2001 to consider once again a ceasefire zone for the ELN. At that point, in an attempt to avoid repeating what have been widely viewed as big mistakes regarding the government's provision of a *zona* to the FARC, the state reached an agreement with the ELN regarding a series of rules that would be necessary for such a zone to be established. The agreement in principle with the ELN came with eighty-four clearly defined rules attached. Among the most important of these were a nine-month limitation for the zone, respect for existing municipal governments within the territory, no kidnappings or other intimidating acts by the ELN within the area, and the forbiddance of the Colombian military or police to enter the zone. Also included in the deal was a verification commission with an auxiliary force of fifty international members.[41]

Despite this elaborate litany of rules that the ELN and the government agreed upon regarding principles for the establishment of a ceasefire territory, many significant obstacles stand in the way for such a zone to reach fruition. Chief among these is that large numbers of inhabitants in the territory have expressed their adamant opposition to the proposal. Indeed, at least 15,000 residents of the area protested vigorously against the plan in February 2001.[42] This stands in stark contrast to the FARC's *zona,* where residents were generally supportive. Further, the southern Bolívar region represents a crucial piece of real estate for the narcotrafficking interests of the AUC. The paramilitaries do not wish to cede to the ELN what they view as highly strategic space, since it represents a principal venue of the group's funding. Fear of warfare between the AUC and the ELN, should a ceasefire territory be established, is one of the central reasons local inhabitants have opposed the zone's creation.[43]

Although the government earlier had appeared willing to provide the ELN with territory, the United States clearly has been opposed to such an eventuality and presumably conveyed this to the Pastrana administration. Given local protests regarding the creation of an ELN ceasefire zone, combined with U.S. opposition the idea, the ELN's attempts at reaching its preeminent goal seemed destined for failure. Enormously frustrated, and in retaliation for the government's temporary suspension of talks with the rebels, the group launched a series of grizzly attacks beginning in the summer of 2001 in which innocent civilians were killed.[44] In many ways this served to neutralize any moral claim the ELN had been attempting to make. Finally, the nail in the coffin for any hopes the ELN had harbored regarding the establishment of its own *zona* occurred when the government militarily repossessed the FARC's *zona* in early 2002.

In the highly unlikely event that a ceasefire zone is established, the required international verification commission will need to be established. The ELN would likely prefer candidates from Cuba, the source of its founding inspiration, and from European countries such as Germany and Switzerland, where the rebels have established political contacts and where they have conducted peace negotiations with the Colombian government. The ELN has also been friendly with neighboring Venezuela, and surely its presence on any verification commission would represent a thorn in the side of the Colombian government. Bogotá on various occasions has accused Venezuela's Hugo Chávez of engaging in a cozier relationship than it would prefer with both the ELN and the FARC. On this count, there have been numerous instances when the ELN has praised the anti-neoliberal platform of Chávez, as well as the charismatic leader's bravado against an assortment of U.S. policies in the region. Particularly alarming for both the Colombian and U.S. governments has been praise from the ELN for Chávez's conception of "Bolivariana," signifying a regionwide defiance of U.S. political and economic interests.[45]

Regarding the policies of the United States, the ELN has shown a decidedly unfavorable view of Washington's interventions in Colombia and elsewhere in Latin America. It has congratulated both Brazil and especially Venezuela for resisting U.S. pressure, and has bitterly rebuked

Argentina's former president Carlos Menem as well as Peru's former president Alberto Fujimori, characterizing them as U.S. patsies.[46] Further, the ELN has staunchly opposed Plan Colombia. The rebels viewed the U.S. plan as representing a war against both the ELN and the FARC, one that entailed the strategic use of the paramilitary forces of the AUC. The rebels also suggested that Plan Colombia's so-called war against drugs was simply a pretext for U.S. intervention, and that this stance was highly hypocritical since "marijuana is the primary agricultural product" of the United States. The ELN argued that other objectives of the plan included the political isolation of Venezuela's Hugo Chávez, and the imposition of U.S. forces in Ecuador to quell popular indigenous uprisings in that country.[47] When President Bill Clinton traveled to Cartagena in August 2000 to finalize Plan Colombia, the ELN deemed it a *visita no grata* and observed that the event represented a "ceremony of colonial possession."[48]

Analytical Context

The principal means by which the ELN has derived power since the late 1980s has been through control over strategic space. It has successfully dominated areas rich in natural resources in order to impose a tax upon, or extort money from, transnational corporations working in Colombia's extractive and energy sectors. This has provided funding for the group to construct an army, which has been comparatively weak in relation to both the FARC and the paramilitary AUC. But more importantly, it has financed the ELN's capacity to stage massive and newsworthy kidnappings, and has also funded the group's ability to launch spectacular attacks against the country's vital infrastructure such as energy grids. Thus the ELN has not achieved power from winning the hearts and minds of significant portions of the population. Indeed, it is far from clear that the ELN enjoys any measure of substantial political support, even from the inhabitants of the region in which it wishes to establish its own ceasefire zone. Further, it has attracted only miniscule levels of political support in the country's major cities.

The central political problem for the rebels has been to obtain power primarily in order to force the country's weak government to cede the group a section of territory under its dominance. It has also sought power, according to its literature, in order to influence government policy regarding issues such as redistribution of income as well as the alteration of terms under which TNCs operate in the country. Finally, an additional political objective of this group may be to obtain some quota of power in the event that the Colombian government is radically restructured through eventual negotiations with competing belligerents. Clearly, however, the group has been sufficiently realistic in its strategic assessment to appreciate that it sorely lacks the capacity to take power over the country as a whole.

In relation to conceptions of power and strategy, none of this is particularly novel. Certainly the notion of controlling strategic space has been a common topic throughout the classic literature, as demonstrated in the works of Thucydides, Sun Tzu I, Sun Tzu II, and Machiavelli, among others.[49] Given that the country is already a collection of city-states, the territory the rebels wish to dominate is akin to a feudal fiefdom. Further, the ELN's strategy of obtaining power through warfare could not be more commonplace. Of particular relevance to the context of Colombia are Hobbes's Leviathan and Clausewitz's infamous assertions that war equals an instrument of policy as well as a continuation of politics by other means.[50] Finally, the ELN's goals of influencing state policies and of achieving a quota of state power are also quite traditional, and have been apparent in cases throughout the world.

While the ELN's conceptions of power and security have not been especially pathbreaking, they nevertheless have been harnessed with some success by the rebels. In many ways, the ELN has demonstrated a mastery over key aspects found in the classic strategic literature. In the context of the power grab that developed since the 1990s, one could say that the group has embraced Machiavelli's strategic advice of correctly gauging the meaning of changing times.[51] Further, the rebels have appreciated Sun Tzu's maxim of "attacking the empty" to the extent they have exerted power in areas where the state has been either absent or insufficiently powerful.[52] The group also has successfully implemented traditional hit-and-run combat tactics apparent in the texts of both Clausewitz and Che Guevara, works that the ELN admittedly has studied since the 1960s.[53]

Aspects of ELN strategy that may initially appear novel seem more traditional upon closer inspection. Although the group has indeed utilized new communications technology such as the Internet for political communication, it has not done so in a manner that has significantly bolstered its power, or in a way that reflects a fresh means of political organization as demonstrated in the case of the Zapatistas. And while much of the ELN's power has been underpinned by funds derived from the activities of postmodern transnational capitalism—that is, by "taxing" TNCs in Colombia's extractive and energy sectors—there is nothing particularly new about the politics of extortion. Yet if there is something remarkably unique here, at least compared to Cold War guerrillas, it is that the ELN has generated its own source of funding rather than relying on foreign states. This is evidence of the group's pronounced entrepreneurial spirit, which has yielded it a free political rein.

Certainly the ELN has employed a brand of terrorism that destroys power grids and other infrastructure but generally avoids taking human lives. Further, when the ELN has staged dramatic kidnappings—or so-called retentions—it eventually has released virtually all its victims unharmed. Clearly, many of the policies of the ELN have reflected some sort of spiritual sanctity for human life. But this has been inconsistent, since the rebels have indeed launched attacks whereby innocent civilians have been killed. Overall, while the group's occasional reluctance to resort to political murder may be unusual in the context of carnage-ridden Colombia, on a broader scale this does not represent a new feature in the realm of power and strategy. Gandhi's passive resistance comes to mind, for example. So too does the centuries-old advice of Sun Tzu II to employ as much as possible a sense of humaneness in strategic endeavors.[54] Beyond that, the ELN's penchant for the novel use of words—such as the use of "taxes" for extortion, or "retentions" for kidnappings—is indicative of Thucydides' contention more than 2,400 years ago that wordplay represents a common feature of warfare.[55]

In sum, the ELN's policies have met with mixed success, and have largely reflected traditional conceptions of power and strategy. Since the mid-1980s the rebels have succeeded in rising from virtual political oblivion to the position of one of Colombia's key political contenders in the context of pronounced civil war. But by 2001–2002, the group appeared to have reached a dead end of sorts, particularly regarding its failure to achieve its own territory in the form of a ceasefire zone. Reflective of many aspects of Colombian politics, the ELN's conceptions of power and strategy have represented a crazy quilt of epistemological approaches. For example, the group has embraced a premodern attitude toward political space, has adopted the modern ideology of Marxism, and has financed its strategic endeavors by taxing/extorting the postmodern economy of transnational capitalism.

The FARC

At the dawn of the twenty-first century the FARC stood as the largest and the most militarily powerful leftist guerrilla group in the Americas. Like the rest of the warriors in Colombia's imbroglio, the FARC saw its power increase more during the 1990s than during the previous three decades combined. This power surge came as a defiant response to the horrendous experience of the UP. What is remarkable about the FARC has been the group's successful endeavor to marry big profits derived from its deep involvement in narcotrafficking and other crime with a strategic shrewdness that has relied heavily on carnage. Along this rather spectacular trajectory, perhaps the hilt of the FARC's power was the achievement in November 1998 of a *zona de distensión,* a 42,000-square-kilometer ceasefire zone over which it presided. But this achievement came at a high cost, since it represented the proverbial last straw for the United States, which hurried to produce Plan Colombia—a strategic package aimed at debilitating the FARC. Emboldened by its initial success at achieving the *zona,* the FARC as well as its rivals escalated warfare between 1998 and 2002 in the context of what appeared to be an intensified power grab. A decisive watershed in Colombia's civil war occurred in February 2002, when the government militarily invaded the *zona* and seized power over the territory.[56] The FARC responded with a strategy of urban terror.

Power and Objectives

What has been the nature and object of the FARC's power since the 1990s?[57] In the eyes of the rebels, power would have to be achieved outside the official political system. This was a result not only of the FARC's experience with the UP, but also of what the group has referred to as President César Gaviria's planned "operation to exterminate the Secretariat of the FARC" through "Operación Marquetalia" beginning in 1990.[58] This general theme of political exclusion, combined with threats of military annihilation by the government and paramilitaries, has appeared frequently in the FARC's literature. It has been utilized by the rebels to explain their own route of guerrilla warfare, as well as the high abstention rates in Colombian elections throughout the decade.

In terms of clear objectives, the FARC continued to pursue in the 1990s and beyond its traditional goals of altering or overthrowing the government, and of reducing as much as possible U.S. influence in Colombia. In addition, since the early 1990s the FARC had expressed its desire to obtain officially a section of territory in the country's southern region.[59] The rebels had already succeeded at dominating this strategically significant site at the heart of the country's coca and poppy cultivation—an area where the state has been completely absent. Thus the FARC wished to take power over strategic territory. However, the group appears to have had the consent of the majority of the region's inhabitants. The FARC has represented the economic interests of local coca cultivators and also has provided some semblance of law and order by performing functions normally handled by the state. When the Pastrana government in 1998 naively ceded the FARC a *zona de distensión,* with the purpose of creating a ceasefire territory that would contribute to successful peace negotiations, it served to embolden the rebels considerably.

By late 1998, given the mounting strength of the FARC and the concurrent weakness of the government, the option of taking power over the state as a whole appeared as a credible if far from certain possibility. But that notion quickly evaporated. On the one hand, in contrast to the situation in the *zona,* where the inhabitants largely favored the presence of the FARC, it became increasingly clear that the rebels lacked the political support of the vast majority of Colombians, especially urban dwellers. On the other hand, by the dawn of the twenty-first century the rival right-wing paramilitaries had fortified their power immensely and the United States had commenced its formidable intervention through Plan Colombia. As a result, the group's objectives shifted first and foremost to maintaining and perhaps enlarging its control over the its *zona de distensión.*Thus, rather than retaining its original status as a ceasefire zone that would contribute to peace talks with the government, it became clear that the FARC wished to control this territory on a permanent basis. But that endeavor clearly failed when the government repossessed the territory in early 2002, arguing convincingly that the rebels had abused the *zona* by utilizing it as a guerrilla training camp and as a base for narcotrafficking. Regarding its second major objective, the FARC strived to negotiate either a quota of power or a strong political voice in a restructured national political economy.

Ideology in the 1990s

If the FARC's aim has been to take control over strategic territory, and to become a key actor in any negotiations aimed at restructuring the state, what sort of political influence would the group like to have? Here it is worth examining the ideological underpinnings of the FARC in the post–Cold War era. What is striking is that the FARC has demonstrated far greater prowess at maximizing its military power than it has at developing a sophisticated political-ideological package. An analysis of the group's literature reveals four basic categories of ideological points.

First, a disproportionately large amount of the FARC's ideological commentary concerns important and often reasonable criticisms of the state and its allies, rather than the provision of clear models of political and economic alternatives. The FARC has offered stinging and substantiated rebukes of the government's relation to terror, of the state's apparent policy of impunity for human rights abusers, and of the widespread corruption throughout government offices.[60] Similarly, it has criticized the state for representing a false democracy, for highly exclusionary political practices, and for presiding over patterns of economic inequity and class domination that have deteriorated over the years.[61] Further, it has mocked Colombia's two traditional parties for submitting to U.S.-dominated neoliberal economics.[62] The FARC also has opposed Colombian government support for extradition to the United States of presumed narcotraffickers.[63]

Second, because the FARC's supporters overwhelmingly have been poverty-stricken campesinos, the rebels have attempted to construct a political platform that represents the voice of the rural poor.[64] They have demanded a policy of major land reform, and especially a distribution of land away from giant landholders who since the 1990s have increasingly become synonymous with high-level narcotraffickers. Related to this, the rebels have vaguely proposed a system of agrarian credit, a scheme of subsidies and guaranteed basic prices for agricultural products, and the provision of health and education services to a rural population who in many areas of the country lack social services entirely.[65]

Third, the FARC has supported the construction of an active or interventionist state that used to prevail in many areas of the world until about the 1970s. This entails policies such as protectionism and import substitution industrialization, as well as state control over strategic resources such as the energy sector. Related to this, the FARC has suggested that the state renegotiate with TNCs operating in Colombia to obtain a better deal from them.[66] Also on the rebels' wish list was a request to the international community to provide the country with a moratorium on its debt until 2006.[67]

Finally, in an attempt to escape from perceptions that the group advocates what many consider to be outdated conceptions of Marxism, the FARC increasingly has used the nomenclature of "Bolivarian" (Bolivariano) to characterize its ideological platform. An examination of the group's literature reveals that Simón Bolívar has emerged as the group's newfound hero in a manner that was more pronounced as the decade of the 1990s wore on. Bolívar has been idolized by the FARC as a symbol of anti-U.S. imperialism. In an altogether unenergetic endeavor, the FARC created an unpopular political arm in 2000 called the Movimiento Bolivariano.[68] Further, the use of the term "Bolivariano" also suggests an ideological affinity with Venezuela's President Hugo Chávez, who has built a political career around defying U.S. policies and by claiming to represent the interests of the majority population of the poor. The FARC has called for the establishment of "one Bolivarian nation."[69]

There are at least five general strategies that the FARC has pursued to achieve its goals. First, the FARC has sought considerable economic enrichment to permit self-sufficiency. Second, such funding would underwrite costly dimensions of the group's strategy, such as the construction of the biggest and most professionalized guerrilla army in the Americas. Third, a key component of the group's strategy has centered on achieving global recognition as the principal nonstate power in Colombia in efforts to ensure a strong footing in potential peace negotiations. Fourth, the FARC has attempted to reduce U.S. influence over Colombia by bolstering relations with other developed countries. Finally, the FARC has sought to maximize its power through exclusionary policies that have shut out political rivals at the bargaining table. That is, the FARC has insisted on bilateral negotiations with the government that have excluded other guerrilla groups, the paramilitaries, as well as civil society.

The FARC and funding. If one were to take "before-and-after" snapshots of the FARC, one would observe a rather weak guerrilla movement prior to the mid-1980s and a highly potent rebel movement riding a remarkable growth curve after that point. While some of this increase in power can be attributed to the context of a weak and wilting state, among other variables, perhaps the single biggest factor that explains the FARC's military growth after the mid-1980s has been its apparently enormous monetary enrichment. This funding has come almost exclusively from the group's participation in crime—especially global narcotrafficking, but also kidnapping and extortion.

Regarding narcotrafficking, the FARC's dominance of the strategic southern departments of Guaviare, Putumayo, and Caquetá has meant that it has presided over the chief coca and poppy cultivation zones of the country.[70] In fact, this general area is where the FARC's Switzerland-sized *zona de distensión* was located during the period 1998–2002. Although there were some new twists in the 1990s, much of the dynamic for the rebels' participation in this illicit industry was already in place in the previous decade. The FARC has represented the political interests of peasant cultivators who, due to a general agricultural crisis as well as a local ecosystem generally inhospitable to other types of cultivation, perceive they have no other realistic economic alternative. For establishing law and order in the region, and for representing their political interests, the FARC has received a cut of the cultivators' profits. Representing the political interests of campesino cultivators has included such tasks as the FARC's vigorous protest against U.S.-driven attempts to eradicate illicit crops through fumigation and biological warfare.[71] Ironically, there exists considerable evidence that fumigation attempts have actually driven peasants closer politically to the FARC, since the rebels are their principal political ally in the struggle against this rather extreme policy.[72] Further, the FARC has endeavored to obtain for cultivators the highest possible price for the crops from other participants in the global trade who chemically process the raw crops into the finished products of cocaine and heroin.

In November of 2000, substantiated allegations surfaced suggesting that the FARC's role in the illicit drug trade goes far deeper than simply representing the interests of peasant growers. At that time, a member of the FARC—Carlos Ariel Charry Guzmán, a medical doctor—was arrested in Mexico after evidence allegedly was found that he was trading substantial quantities of cocaine to Mexico's notorious Tijuana cartel in exchange for weapons.[73] A major implication flowing from that incident is that the FARC may also have been involved in transnational aspects of the trafficking of illicit drugs, and therefore may represent a self-contained or vertical cartel engaged in all aspects of cultivation, production, and sales.

The FARC's position vis-à-vis the illicit drug industry is complicated. Despite obvious evidence to the contrary, the FARC in the late 1990s denied links to narcotrafficking, though it opposed fumigation and admitted to be working on the behalf of peasant coca cultivators.[74] In the twenty-first century, however, the rebels have been less adamant in their denial of relations to the business of illegal drugs, and have expressed the problem differently. In May 2000, for example, the FARC observed that, in addition to representing a pretext for U.S. military intervention in Colombia, "narcotrafficking is a phenomenon of global capitalism and of the Gringos in the first place. It is not a problem of the FARC. We reject narcotrafficking."[75] At other points the FARC has called for the legalization of illicit drugs, and for rigorous programs of demand reduction in the United States and other northern countries.[76] Further, the rebels have played both sides of the fence on this issue of coca eradication. Despite participation in the illicit drug trade, the group has also participated in alternative development projects involving crop substitution and the like. It has done so under joint projects with the UN

Drug Control Program, and the rebels suggested in 2001 the establishment of additional cooperative programs with a variety of mostly European countries.[77] Hence the FARC pacified a variety of global political interests by cooperating with attempts at coca eradication, but simultaneously enriched itself from the drug trade.

Some important qualifications need to be made on this theme. First, not all fronts of the FARC have been engaged in illicit drug trafficking. The director of the UN Drug Control Program in Colombia, who has worked with the FARC to develop small projects of alternative development, has suggested that factions of the FARC do not support the group's participation in the trade.[78] Further, while the group apparently has received lavish finances from narcotrafficking, the FARC's existence has not been dependent on this. The FARC was around long before narcotrafficking predominated in Colombia, primarily due to a horrendous distribution of wealth in the country in tandem with a highly exclusionary state—factors that have persisted into the twenty-first century. Attempts by the United States and others to label the FARC as narcoguerrillas have indeed represented a pretext for U.S. military intervention through Plan Colombia. Here the leftist and anti-U.S. ideology of the FARC is a factor, since the ultra-right-wing AUC, which admittedly obtains 70 percent of its funding from narcotrafficking, has not been a major target of U.S. military wrath. Finally, narcotrafficking would not be such a lucrative industry if the United States and other northern countries focused more intensely upon demand reduction.

Beyond narcotrafficking, the FARC has required "tributes" of corporations operating in territory influenced by the rebels. This was formalized by the establishment of the FARC's "Ley 02," or Law 2.[79] Beyond enshrining their insistence on taxation/extortion, the rebels through this act were also attempting to present themselves as a governing power implementing legislation. The group is more likely to rely on this method of funding, and others such as kidnapping, if its profits from the drug trade are curtailed by U.S.-led actions.

The FARC as a military power. By the late 1990s, the rebels were organized into over sixty fronts and were present in 622 of Colombia's 1,071 municipalities.[80] The Colombian army estimated that the FARC comprised about 16,500 troops by early 2001, alongside rumors of double that amount.[81] The group constructed a professionalized, full-time army. In many ways, the organization has benefited from almost constant leadership for over three decades, with Manuel Marulanda at the helm. With the nickname of Sure Shot, he has shown himself to be a shrewd military strategist and tough negotiator, but he has lacked charisma and has not been renowned for intellectual depth. Well into his seventies at the turn of the century, Marulanda was accompanied on the FARC national secretariat by six other men, mostly middle-aged and graying.

In sharp contrast to the maturity of the upper-echelon leadership, as showcased by their portraits on the group's web page, is the significant number of children that the FARC has employed as soldiers.[82] This attracted severe public criticism especially in 2000 and beyond, as the use of such youngsters as warriors became more obvious to the public. In response, in May 2000 the FARC announced it would dismiss child soldiers under fifteen years of age.[83] However, since that time child warriors younger than fifteen have continued to be captured by the army or have deserted the rebel group. Strategic experts have observed that the FARC has used children to commit the most brutal acts of combat and terror, since such youngsters may not yet have developed a sense of justice or a strong sense of morality.[84]

The FARC has employed indiscriminate and often brutal acts of violence in its attempt to maximize power. These include attacks against entire villages, bombs placed in public places, and a variety other tactics whereby innocent victims have been killed or severely injured. The global NGO Human Rights Watch severely criticized the FARC for its documented murder of 496 innocent civilians in 2000 through the use of weapons such as cylinder bombs.[85] The FARC's strategy has been to instill fear in the targeted population to either support the group or else suffer horrific consequences. The rebels' participation in gory spectacles also has been designed to attract media attention in an effort to demonstrate their military power to the rest of the country and to the world. The FARC has not been shy about admitting its penchant for carnage, as exemplified by its own documents, which flatly state that violence is justified by guerrillas in revolutionary situations.[86] The group also has relied on this rationale to justify the use of such violence by rebels elsewhere. For example, the FARC defended the MRTA's violent takeover of the Japanese embassy in Lima, Peru, in 1996.[87]

In terms of organization, although the FARC concentrated some of its forces in San Vicente del Caguán in the southern department of Caquetá between 1998 and 2002, many of its troops have been strategically scattered throughout the country. These deployments include sites that have permitted the extortion of money from TNCs engaged in the energy and extractive sectors, and other locations that have served as vital posts for arms transfers and narcotrafficking.[88] For example, FARC documents captured by the Colombian armed forces in December 2000 indicated that the rebels' objective at that time was to achieve increasing military dominance over Medellín and Urubá.[89] The dispersion of its troops beyond their concentration in Caguán meant that the FARC could not be eliminated when the government repossessed the *zona* in 2002.

With respect to the waxing and waning of the FARC's military power, the group's potency may have peaked during the period 1996–1998. During that era the rebels achieved important military victories over the army in Puerres, Nariño (1996); at the army's Las Delicias military base (1996); and at the La Carpa military base in Guaviare (1996). The FARC also prevailed during a confrontation with the armed forces in Meta and Arauca (1997) and during a spectacular attack against the Colombian army in El Billar (1998). Those demonstrations of strategic prowess and of brutal military might, in conjunction with the FARC's achievement of the *zona de distensión* in late 1998, sparked both a major restructuring of the armed forces and the military intervention of the United States through Plan Colombia. Both events halted the escalation of the FARC's military capacity and may have initiated a phase characterized by the relative decline of the rebel army's power.

Appreciating this potential threat, the FARC launched a two-pronged strategy in the summer of 2001. First, it at least temporarily joined forces with the ELN. The move was strategically wise in the sense that the combination of rebel forces totaled over 20,000 troops. But it also signaled desperation on the part of the FARC to align with a group it historically has viewed as a foe. In fact, intense combat had occurred between the FARC and the ELN within the year prior to their cooperative effort. Based on a history of friction and feuds between the groups, the partnership did not appear destined to last very long.

Yet another sign of desperation, and of a stop-at-nothing mentality, was the FARC's threat in June 2001 to take the war from the countryside to Colombia's urban centers, such as Bogotá. The rebels in 2000–2001 expanded their territorial influence from the *zona* northward through the department of Huila as a step toward taking armed action in the country's capital city. Since the FARC's support has been primarily rural and because it has commanded scant support in Colombia's cities, the rebels would not be capable of militarily usurping the urban centers. Rather, they could contemplate the implementation of paralyzing terrorist actions against the city as a bargaining chip in negotiations with the government on a variety of issues.[90] The August 2001 arrest in Colombia of three members of the Provisional Irish Republican Army (IRA), who apparently had been training FARC members in their *zona* for a period of five weeks, further suggests that the group has been plotting a move toward urban terrorism as its traditional military power is threatened. This represents the contemplation by the FARC of a crucial shift in strategy, one that will likely inspire a related rethinking among the group's enemies.

The option of urban terror became increasingly likely after the government militarily invaded the FARC's *zona* in February 2002. The FARC anticipated the state's intervention, given that the *zona* had been surrounded by the government's military forces and had been the object of almost continuous aerial surveillance missions since at least late 2001. This was a reflection of Plan Colombia, which will be analyzed in detail below. Within such a context, the FARC orchestrated high-profile kidnappings and terror tactics in 2002, including a notorious incident in Bogotá in which three bicycle bombs placed around the city killed and injured scores of innocent civilians. This sparked a terror alert on the part of the state in early 2002, whereby the military indicated that it was concentrating surveillance on at least 2,000 sites throughout the country.[91] With the loss of the *zona,* and with the intensification of the war against the FARC in the countryside by government forces and by the paramilitaries, all signs pointed toward urban terror as the principal means by which the FARC would attempt to reassert military power. Its unrelenting style of terror has included high-profile assassinations and kidnappings, the deployment of indiscriminate violence such as the placement of bombs in public sites, and especially the destruction of key city infrastructure such as power plants, bridges, and water storage facilities.

Overall, the FARC has utilized funding provided by its lucrative involvement in narcotrafficking, extortion, and kidnapping to construct the most formidable leftist guerrilla army in the Americas. But money alone is not sufficient for the establishment of such a potent military machine. A strong sense of strategic prowess on the part of the leadership has been the most vital element of the rebels' success. Devising strong sources for funding, knowing where and when to act militarily, convincing many Colombians that a war against the FARC is not winnable, plus innumerable political victories over an inept government, are all testimony to the rebels' strategic strength. To the extent that the FARC has presided over considerably more military and strategic power than ideological or political support, the group's leadership has had far more in common with Clausewitz than with their professed allegiance to socialist heroes or to Bolívar.

Political power and U.S. counterweight. Another dimension of the FARC's strategy has been to achieve international recognition as the

principal belligerent in Colombia and as a political actor that overshad-
ows the Colombian state. This would provide the FARC with significant
clout aimed at reaching some of its objectives in any negotiated settle-
ment, particularly one involving international facilitators of conflict resolution. The central object of the FARC's international endeavors has
been Europe, which the group has attempted to use as a counterweight
to U.S. power. Shrewdly, the rebels played on latent political resentment
among Europeans regarding the enormous U.S. dominance over both
Latin America and the world. Since at least the mid-1990s, the FARC
has suggested that any sort of political legitimacy to be established in
Colombia would necessitate the presence of the Europeans. This was
exemplified when the FARC insisted in September 1997 that elections in
Colombia could only be considered valid if the European Parliament sent
a crew of observers to monitor the process throughout the country.[92]

But the hilt of the FARC's cultivation of Europe as a political ally
did not arrive until the twenty-first century. Along with the government,
components of the FARC leadership embarked on an extensive tour of
Europe in early 2000 under the dubious guise of studying European
political economies as models for Colombia.[93] Leaving aside the ques-
tionable notion of importing Europe's first world structures to the
chaotic and war-torn environment of Colombia, the trip was a huge
strategic success for the FARC and a loss for the inept Pastrana government. By traveling to Europe with the rebels, President Andrés Pastrana
played into the hands of the guerrilla group by essentially presenting
them as a power on par with the government. Beyond that important
coup, the trip was also an enormous political and strategic success for
the FARC, since it curried enough favor to influence the European Parliament in February 2001 to condemn the U.S. plot to confront the
FARC militarily through Plan Colombia.[94] Similarly, the FARC has
insisted that any subsequent process of peace negotiation "must consult
the European Community."[95]

The rebel group also held a conference with the chair of the New
York Stock Exchange in the Colombian jungle in 1999, and has held
meetings with international business leaders there on a number of occasions. This, too, bolstered the image of the FARC not only as a major
belligerent in Colombia, but also as a power capable of conducting
international political and economic diplomacy.

But much of the FARC's successes in international diplomacy were
negated by grave errors on the part of the rebels in 2001. The European
Union (EU) formally threatened to sever any contact with the group
after it committed a wave a kidnappings in that year.[96] One prominent

case concerned the former governor of the department of Meta, who was kidnapped by the group while he was aboard a UN vehicle, leaving the FARC guilty of ignoring diplomatic immunity and of kidnapping. This came against the backdrop of a growing chorus of global criticism regarding the FARC's barbaric tactics, including the aforementioned charges of human rights abuses launched by the NGO Human Rights Watch. Further, the global political climate turned against the FARC following the terrorist attacks on the U.S. World Trade Center in September 2001. The EU, for example, became increasingly critical of the Colombian rebels in early 2002.[97] Overall, the FARC's strategy has proven to be weak in the international arena, with key gains neutralized by the rebels' gravitation toward carnage and crime.

Another case of exclusion. The FARC has embarked on a double campaign of excluding its nonstate political rivals and of delegitimizing the government. Beyond recounting the flaws of the Colombian state, the FARC has also warned the Colombian population not to vote in various elections since the rebels were committed to "totally sabotaging" them through brutal violence at polling sites.[98] Further, throughout the 1990s and into the twenty-first century, the FARC has engaged only in bilateral negotiations with the government. The group has resisted the participation in such negotiations of civil society or of rival guerrilla groups such as the ELN. It has refused even to speak with the paramilitary AUC. All of this is indicative of the FARC's conception of "power over" the population and territory, rather than any consensual or inclusionary sense of power. It is symptomatic of a two-century-old legacy of Colombian politics that has been dominated by a mentality of extreme political exclusion.

Victories and Defeats

Have the FARC's strategies been a success, have the rebels achieved their objectives? By 2002 there was no question that the group had indeed achieved a number of goals. It had financed a huge military machine, had received global recognition as Colombia's leading belligerent force, and had succeeded at excluding rivals in key negotiations with the government. The FARC's crowning achievement, however, was its consolidation of power between November 1998 and February 2002 over the *zona de distensión*. Within its *zona* the FARC established its own system of justice and performed functions that would otherwise be expected of the state.[99] It conducted numerous public *audiencias* there, designed to cement the public perception that this was indeed FARC territory.[100] When so-called peace negotiations were conducted between the government and the FARC, rather than the guerrilla leaders traveling to the country's capital of Bogotá, President Pastrana trekked to the FARC's *zona* at a date specified by the FARC and not the government. Having accomplished its goal of taking power over this strategic space, the FARC made it abundantly clear that it did not wish to return its *zona* to the Colombian government. Indeed, in January 2001 the FARC indicated that it wished to retain its control of the territory for an "indefinite period."[101] By February 2001 the government on six occasions had given into FARC demands that it extend the deadline for return of the *zona*.

But there have been glaring failures that threatened to intensify in coming years. First, the FARC's loss of its *zona* in 2002, and the related military offensives aimed at the rebels, suggest that there is a strong chance its military power could decline. Any plans the group may have had for taking power over the state as a whole had completely vanished. Perhaps the most profound debility of the FARC has been the group's failure to cultivate meaningful popular support outside its enclaves in the countryside. The rebels have not attracted a measurable following in cities, where the vast majority of Colombians reside. The FARC's brutal and indiscriminate use of violence has alienated much of the population. Its shift in 2002 toward a strategy of terror is likely to erode the rebels' already scant popularity by amplifying the tenor of public outrage, which could in turn lend support for ever harsher government policies designed to decimate the rebels militarily. The FARC's legitimacy has also been undermined by its deep involvement in crimes such as narcotrafficking, kidnapping, and extortion. A famous letter written by Colombia's leading intellectuals, including Gabriel García Márquez, condemned the group for such practices, suggesting that the FARC had lost any political legitimacy it had sought to achieve.[102] Further, civil society, including NGOs, has been alienated by the bilateral and exclusionary nature of the FARC's "peace" negotiations with the government.[103] This negative public perception of the group casts it as a military bully and political lightweight. Within such a context, the FARC's attempt in the twenty-first century to establish a political arm, the Movimiento Bolivariano, proved to be an utter failure.[104]

In the international arena, the FARC has not done particularly well. It neutralized key support that it had cultivated in Europe, largely due to the same reasons that earned the group widespread repugnance on the part of Colombians. The FARC also raised the ire of global NGOs such as Human Rights Watch. Further, it has not been capable of generating a global network of support similar to the one the Zapatistas have constructed, precisely because the FARC primarily has been a military machine rather than a credible political crusader. On both the domestic and international fronts, then, the FARC's record of victory has been mixed, and its star may be on the descent.

Analytical Context

If there is a new wrinkle here with regard to power and strategy, it is the degree to which Colombia's war has been privatized. The FARC is a perfect example of this in that it has fed off illicit neoliberalism—the transnational business of drug trafficking, the practice of kidnapping foreign executives of TNCs, and the extortion of "taxes" from corporations and the wealthy. Economic self-sufficiency has yielded political freedom, with no foreign benefactor telling the FARC what to do. The FARC has also cultivated as an ally, if only temporarily, a relatively new political actor on the global scene, the European Parliament. In this sense, one might be tempted to suggest that the FARC's epistemological view is postmodern to the extent that it appreciates the borderless world of transnational capitalism and the new political spaces that have spawned fresh actors such as the European Union.

Despite those new twists, in the main the FARC has been steeped in traditional or even premodern conceptions of strategy and power. The Colombian context itself is premodern in the absence of a Leviathan, or strong state. As the situation of the *zona* demonstrated, the FARC's sense of political space is commensurate with the fiefdoms and city-states of the feudal epoch. Rather than conceiving of a nation in any sense, the FARC pursued a private chunk of territory. Hence, the group's attitude toward political space and its role as one of the chief belligerents in a pre-Leviathan world are suggestive of a premodern disposition toward space and politics.

Strategic ghosts of modernity also haunt the FARC. Rather than evoking the image of a post-Marxist pioneer exploring the frontiers of leftism, the FARC is more illustrative of Mao's grim dictum that power comes from the barrel of a gun. For the FARC, power is imposition through force; it is "power over," or the power of brutality.[105] Such situations fell under the careful study of Clausewitz, many of whose ideas seem to rhyme with the FARC. The notion of war as extreme violence, bloodshed, hatred, and enmity—the traditional view of war—is entirely commensurate with the ideas and actions of the FARC.[106]

Related to the FARC's view of warfare and strategy is its implicit conception of human life. Innocent people become the expendable targets of indiscriminate violence through episodes involving bomb attacks and the like. Children have been admittedly used by the FARC as soldiers and have been employed to commit the most horrific acts of violence due to their lack of moral maturity. Civilians have been kidnapped and exchanged for money. Bodies are the sites of abuse for the illicit drugs the FARC has helped cultivate, process, and traffic. To say the least, the FARC's political power is not based on a sacrosanct view of human life.

Overall, the FARC is characterized by a mix of postmodern, premodern, and modern systems of knowledge, with none of these dominant. Beyond that odd epistemological cocktail, the rebels' political position has also been contradictory in many respects. While the group has displayed a leftist tinge, it would possess no significant military power without the aforementioned relationship to illicit transnational capitalism. Despite its egalitarian rhetoric, the group's actions suggest calculated criminal neoliberalism. More recently, the rebels have taken up Bolívar as the hero of their discourse to escape being associated with old-style Marxism. Yet Bolívar's dream of a Gran Colombia, of a large modern territory with a sense of nation, is light-years from the premodern fiefdom of the FARC's *zona*.

The AUC:
The Right-Wing Paramilitary Response

Although the focus here is on the FARC and the ELN, it is worth discussing briefly their archenemy and the major military actor, the paramilitaries. The paramilitary forces of the 1990s were essentially an outgrowth of groups that emerged in the 1980s largely to act as the security apparatus for narcotraffickers and large landowners—who increasingly were one and the same. In the early 1990s they started to organize in an effort to draw national political attention. Principally from the Córdoba area, they began to mobilize support among those who felt ideologically threatened by the success of the leftist UP in national elections, by some minor land redistribution that had occurred, and by the rising power of the FARC. The paramilitaries are a product of Colombia's violent and chaotic landscape, where pockets of the population have felt defenseless against leftist guerrillas. Adding fuel to the fire, the Colombian state has encouraged rightist political vigilantism by systematically arming

The Autodefensas Unidas de Co ombia is distinguished by the most rapid military growth of any Colombian subversive group in the 1990s. It has also earned a reputation as the most brutal and violent contender for power in the country, and has generated a support base crowded with big landowners and major narcotraffickers, among others. Officially formed in 1994 under its former name of Autodefensas Campesinas de Córdoba y Urubá, the paramilitaries territorially expanded their military alliance under the banner of the AUC. The group is renowned for its compelling and unflattering critiques of the leftist guerrillas and of the state, although group leaders have repeatedly lied regarding dark aspects of their own organization. The AUC has much in common with leftist subversives in Colombia in terms of its financial base, its penchant for carnage and terror as the principal basis for its political power, as well as its general objectives of political recognition and perhaps the acquisition of territory.[108] The paramilitaries differ by their ultra-right-wing ideological stance, and by their parallel strategic objectives with the U.S. and the Colombian governments.

Politically, the AUC has striven for power over selected territories and their inhabitants through the exaggerated use of force and fear. The group has had two principal objectives. The first is to create the "political and military opposition to the subversive armed machine under the same conditions of provocation and aggression established by guerrilla organizations." Second, the AUC pledged an agenda of "strategic political opposition to the State, reclaiming the arms monopoly delegated by the people, and filling in for society the gaps and inconsistencies of the State."[109] Accurately assessing the government's utterly crucial failure to monopolize the use of force in Colombia, the paramilitaries have attempted to present themselves as the would-be Leviathan. But a Leviathan entails a social contract between the population and the state, a contract that requires a considerable degree of consent or at least acquiescence on the part of the populace. No such social contract has materialized. Although the paramilitaries comprised between 8,000 and 11,000 troops by 2002, they clearly lacked the military and political capacity that would be necessary to become the dominant force in the country over the next decade.[110]

While the AUC has correctly observed the absence of a Leviathan, it nevertheless has become part of Colombia's general problem by contributing to mayhem. Indeed, the paramilitaries have been the leading perpetrators of human rights abuses in the country since the mid-1990s.

U.S. statistics report that human rights violations by paramilitaries rose 100 percent between 1995 and 1996. Other data indicate that they committed 69 percent of political assassinations in 1997, and by the turn of the century were responsible for the plight of 35 percent of the country's 2 million internally displaced persons.[111] The AUC committed 70 percent of Colombia's political massacres in 2000.[112] While the group's strategy has been to maximize power through violence and fear, in the end this has curtailed the group's political power by rendering it feared but unpopular. This important contradiction has debilitated the AUC considerably.

A sophisticated and accurate critique of the Colombian state and of the guerrillas, plus the AUC's military power, have provided the group with a voice in the country's political debate. With regard to its trenchant critique of leftist rebels, the AUC has argued, for example, that the guerrillas'

> supreme, sole, and principal political aspiration is a violent take-over. This seems to be the objective pursued by subversive groups not only because, until now, they have used the dialogues of peace as a means of gaining political, economic, and military strength without showing a real will to resolve the conflict, but rather because they have proven that, in occupied territories militarily dominated and conquered by guerilla forces, the latter have never assisted in the economic, social, or land recovery, which would ease the misery brought about by violent occupation of those regions.[113]

Similarly, the AUC has attacked the government and the FARC for lack of meaningful negotiations. In February 2001, the AUC noted that for "more than two years of negotiations the guerrillas have not offered a single gesture of peace to Colombians. Where is the triumph of the government, in defense of national interests?"[114] Also in that month, the AUC blamed widespread roadblocks in much of the country on the government's proposed policy of providing a *zona de distensión* to the ELN.[115]

But despite what may sometimes appear as reasonable critiques of other contenders in Colombia, the AUC has diminished its own political credibility by lying and through participation in crime. Although AUC leader Carlos Castaño admitted during a televised interview that about 70 percent of the group's financing had come from narcotrafficking, previously he had repeatedly denied that the AUC had anything to do with the illicit drug trade.[116] The paramilitaries have sought military dominance over key strategic territory from which they have derived their illicit wealth. Like the guerrillas, the AUC has blurred the distinction between crime, terror, and warfare, and this has served to weaken the group in the public eye. And like the situation of the guerrillas, the situation of the paramilitaries is indicative of the privatized nature of the Colombian civil war.

Many contradictions haunt the paramilitaries. Although the AUC has claimed to be fighting against subversive groups, it is clearly a subversive group itself. The AUC has also declared that its members consider themselves to be "an expression of civil society."[117] Yet it has been more of a threat to, rather than an expression of, an imagined Colombian civil society. For example, it has established a pattern of assassinating outspoken critics of the paramilitaries, compounding a huge fear in Colombian society to speak freely in political terms. Further, although it has clearly acted to the contrary, the AUC has claimed that "we reject the destruction of the nation's public and private infrastructure, as well as kidnapping, extortion, forced disappearances, and all forms of violence used in order to change the country or settle conflicts."[118] Overall, although Carlos Castaño's brother, the late and infamous narcotrafficker Fidel Castaño, had clearly enunciated in 1991 the necessity that the paramilitaries construct a solid and coherent political platform, they have not achieved this goal.[119] Lies, hypocrisy, and misrepresentations, together with a record of brutality surpassing that of its rivals, have neutralized whatever popular political power the AUC had hoped to achieve.

In a surprise move, Carlos Castaño resigned from his longtime position as leader of the AUC on 30 May 2001 and again in 2002. Various reports suggested that this was the product of infighting among the group's comandantes, who each direct distinct territorial regions of the country. The paramilitaries, in a press release, indicated that there had been heated debates among the group's leaders regarding the AUC's strategy for dealing with the government.[120] While the group remained militarily strong, these episodes suggest a pattern of political fragmentation common in Colombian politics, one that could eventually weaken the paramilitary forces.

If the nature, objectives, and instruments of the AUC's power are relatively clear, what may be less obvious is the issue of whose power the paramilitaries represent. What is known is that the group is supported by Colombian narcotraffickers and large landowners, by small businesses that appreciate the AUC's ideology and the security it provides, as well as by local campesinos who share some of the political objectives of the AUC. For example, more than 15,000 campesinos demonstrated in February 2001 against the government's plan to provide the ELN with a *zona de distensión* in the Sur de Bolívar, an episode in which the government claimed the AUC had played an important organizing role.[121] Others have supported the paramilitary group for its highly conservative moral views, which express disdain for prostitutes, drug users, homosexuals, and street people, among others.[122]

What is the relationship between the AUC, on the one hand, and the United States and the Colombian governments on the other? The AUC echoes their military objective of eradicating or at least debilitating the guerrillas. The paramilitary group is on record as supporting Plan Colombia.[123] It also shares with Washington and Bogotá the common enemy of Hugo Chávez, who the AUC suggests has been aligned with leftist guerrillas in Colombia.[124] The United States has been far less critical of the AUC than either the FARC or the ELN. Washington resisted any serious critique of the paramilitaries until 2000–2001, when considerable pressure mounted from assorted NGOs, the UN High Office on Human Rights, and the European Parliament. Further, the AUC has launched brutal attacks aimed at achieving its common objectives with the U.S. and Colombian governments, without those governments being criticized for any direct involvement in such episodes. While there indeed has been evidence that identifies members of localized military installations who are working in collusion with the paramilitary forces, there has been no solid proof linking the Colombian federal government or Washington directly to the paramilitaries.

The Colombian State, the United States, and Plan Colombia

Two major watersheds exaggerated the already violent and politically chaotic tendencies in Colombia during the 1990s and into the twenty-first century. The first was the dreadful failure of the government to provide security for the Union Patriótica in the late 1980s and early 1990s, prompting the left to work outside Colombia's official political system. The second was the maturation of the industries of narcotrafficking and other high-end crime, which would finance profound political corruption and intense subversive activity. This served as the context for the power grab in Colombia during the 1990s.

Colombian subversives ambitiously and successfully attempted to maximize their military power and shunned serious negotiation during that era. The government floundered badly, both politically and militarily. The Gaviria government (1990–1994), faced with the belligerency of the guerrillas after the state's failure to stop right-wing paramilitaries from slaughtering UP candidates and supporters, responded with an ill-fated military escalation aimed at crippling the guerrillas. The corrupt Samper administration (1994–1998), feuding with Washington over the narco-cassettes scandal, which linked Ernesto Samper to the narcotrafficking industry, paid scant attention to the guerrillas or to the political crisis mounting in the country. Occasionally there were some positive rumblings from President Samper, such as the suggestion of establishing dialogue between the government and the rebels during which their safety would be ensured. But in other respects Samper fanned the flames of the country's paramilitary forces by funding "Convivir," a project that armed peasants to fight off leftist guerrillas.[125] Overall, Samper's troubles with Washington represented the central preoccupation of his tenure, and this eclipsed significant attention to the country's mounting civil war. Thus the government's strategy during this period demonstrated an extraordinary lack of vision as well as calamitous strategic ineptitude.

Beginning with the Pastrana Administration of 1998–2002, Colombia entered a decidedly different era, as the nature of the state transformed. The Colombian government became a vehicle for more clearly defined U.S. strategic and economic interests. One of the many factors that explained the context of the intensifying subversive activity prior to this period was the relative absence of Washington in Colombian affairs. But the context changed considerably after 1998. In the economic realm, while Colombia previously seemed to have a Teflon coating that protected it from the Latin American debt crisis and other common economic ailments of the 1980s, the country now found itself mired in a severe depression. Dramatically declining rates of foreign investment, damage to oil pipelines and other industries from warfare, generally low agricultural prices due to global overproduction, plus a brain drain, all added up to the worst economic crisis of the country's history. A booming illicit economy was insufficient to neutralize the effects of disaster in the legitimate sector. The result was greater U.S. influence over the Colombian political economy through an IMF restructuring program at the turn of the century, an experiment aimed at gearing the country more fully to neoliberalism.

The election in 2002 of the hard-line and independent candidate Álvaro Uribe suggested that much of the Colombian population was ready to support a tougher military stance against leftist rebels, given the dreadful failure of so-called peace negotiations during the Pastrana government. However, although Uribe successfully dwarfed his rivals in the presidential election, an abstention rate of over 53 percent cast some doubt over the extent of his support among the population in general. Uribe promised a bolstered and refashioned military and suggested that his government was willing to introduce emergency powers to combat guerrillas, which might entail an erosion of basic political rights enshrined in the constitution. Overall, the election of President Uribe represented a dramatic failure for both the FARC and the ELN, since it clearly suggested that Colombian voters wished to diminish the power of leftist guerrillas through hawkish government policies.

In terms of military affairs and strategy, the United States has assumed an increasingly directorial role over Colombian affairs since the late 1990s. The lavish military funding of Plan Colombia, in tandem with a U.S.-inspired restructuring of the Colombian armed forces, was aimed at seriously debilitating the country's guerrillas, especially the FARC. Hence what is new and interesting about this phase is more reflective of growing U.S. influence than homegrown Colombian government strategy and power.

Before Plan Colombia is addressed in detail, important changes within the Colombian military are worthy of consideration. As the 1990s wore on, given the growing strength of the guerrillas combined with the severe losses incurred by the military, it became clear that a restructuring of the Colombian armed forces was imminent.[126] The military was increasingly assuming a defensive rather than offensive stance, and was an easy target for guerrilla attacks because of its bulkiness, immobility, and weak intelligence structure. The goal became the achievement an offensive posture through the creation of quick, mobile, highly trained, and well-informed units.

Beginning in the late 1990s a special rapid action squad was formed while larger military installations were streamlined. A top-heavy military structure was met with the forced or encouraged retirement of high-level officers.[127] A better capacity for intelligence, communication, and integration came with the technology supplied by Plan Colombia. The country's 150,000 troops began a process of professionalization, whereby more members were encouraged to attend military school. Troops also were educated to respect human rights, and their record of infractions improved significantly in the late 1990s. Prior to the middle of the decade, Colombia's official security forces were often the leading perpetrators of human rights abuses. But between 1995 and 2000, Colombian government statistics indicate that the armed forces and police were accused of 327 violations of human rights, compared with 15,744 for leftist guerrillas and 3,759 for the AUC.[128]

Plan Colombia, which had been devised during the period 1998–2000, was signed into law by President Bill Clinton in July 2000.[129] Of the U.S.$1.139 billion package, about two-thirds—$860 million—was devoted to Colombia, with the rest directed to Peru ($32 million), Bolivia ($110 million), and Ecuador ($20 million), and to a major regional surveillance network ($116.5 million). The breakdown for the aid to Colombia is as follows: $519 million for military assistance, $123 million for police assistance, $68.5 million for alternative development, $51 million to bolster respect for human rights, $45 million for law enforcement, $37.5 million to aid to the displaced, $13 million for judicial reform, and $3 million for peace objectives. Regarding the $519 million in military assistance, about $417 million of this has been channeled toward the strategic southern Colombia region, particularly near the *zona de distensión* where the FARC had concentrated its forces. About $328 million of the total military assistance involved the purchase of helicopters, including sixteen UH-60 Blackhawks ($208 million) and thirty UH-1H-Hueys ($120 million). Plan Colombia also established a cap on U.S. forces in Colombia to a maximum of 500 troops plus 300 private "contractors," except in the case of emergency or intense military hostilities.[130]

What are U.S. strategic interests in Colombia, and how do these relate to the power and strategy of Colombia's subversive movements? The relatively huge sums of U.S. assistance destined for Colombia, as well as the nature of that assistance, suggest that the chief motivation of the United States has been to weaken the FARC significantly. By November of 1998, just when the FARC received its *zona,* Colombia became the world's third largest recipient of annual U.S. aid.[131] U.S. antinarcotics assistance to Colombia, which has been used to fight the guerrilla left in the country, rose from $30 million in 1995, to $83 million in 1998, to $294 million in 1999.[132] With the huge addition of funds from Plan Colombia, the country became the second largest recipient of U.S. military assistance after South Korea, and was virtually guaranteed of occupying a similar rank during the first few years of the twenty-first century. For Washington, the FARC represented the epitome of the post-Soviet guerrilla threat in the Americas, with its strategic prowess, its escalating military power, its penchant for terror, a seemingly bottomless source of illicit funding, and its scalding anti-U.S. rhetoric. While the United States is no fan of the ELN either, the ELN's small power base compared to that of the FARC made it less of a target.

Certainly the FARC appreciated Plan Colombia for the dire threat it represented, responding as it did with an official declaration of war against the United States. The military repossession by the Colombian government of the FARC's *zona* in February 2002 could not have occurred without Plan Colombia. Indeed, given the general strategic ineptitude demonstrated on the part of the Pastrana administration as evidenced by its provision of the *zona* to the FARC in 1998, it is entirely possible that the decision to militarily retake the rebel enclave in 2002 was heavily influenced or perhaps even directed by the United States.

Beyond the perceived threat of the FARC, Plan Colombia represented a response to other strategic worries for Washington in the general region that Bolívar referred to as Gran Colombia. The United States has had strained relations at best with Venezuela's fiery Hugo Chávez. Perhaps most alarming to the United States has been the charismatic leader's keen ability to mobilize the majority poor population of Venezuela, often by utilizing democratic structures such as referendums to enact policies perceived as threatening to the rich or to foreign investors. He frequently has been accused by the Colombian government of sharing strategic interests with the FARC and with the ELN.

Washington faced other regional issues. The loss of official control over the Panama Canal has meant at least mild strategic concern by the United States regarding Colombia's warfare and criminal activities spreading northward to Panama. The most serious possibilities for a regional conflagration involve simultaneous civil wars in Colombia and Venezuela as well as neighboring Ecuador, where massive indigenous uprisings have occurred in protest of political corruption, severe economic depression, and the stresses associated with adopting a restructured and dollarized economy. There exists clear potential for a truly regional crisis to emerge in the short to medium term.

The Colombian imbroglio may also be important to the United States as a strategic laboratory to combat a new and potent form of guerrilla groups—entrepreneurial, self-financed, participants in crime, strategically shrewd, large and well organized, and willing to terrorize with the utmost violence. The central problem for the United States has been how to weaken and perhaps neutralize the FARC. It has sought to do so inexpensively and without attracting much negative attention in the United States. To achieve those objectives, it has launched a strategy that entails aerial surveillance, the use of neomercenaries, and biological warfare.

The United States initiated a sophisticated surveillance system over Colombia in 1999, about the time it opened its Tres Esquinas military base near the FARC's *zona*. By 2000 the U.S. Department of Defense had installed five radar stations in Colombia. These included three ground-based sites located at Marandúa, Vichada; San José del Guaviare,

Guaviare; and Leticia, Amazonas; plus two additional sites that are part of the U.S. Air Force Caribbean Basin Radar Network, in Riohacha and San Andrés.[133] These were complemented by radar sites at forward-operating locations in Manta, Ecuador; Aruba; Curaçao; and Comalapa, El Salvador, and in the Amazonian region of Brazil.[134] Such radar stations have worked in conjunction with special reconnaissance aircraft equipped with forward-looking infrared vision, multispectral cameras, and communications and intelligence-gathering packages.[135] While the surveillance system was officially designated to combat narcotrafficking, the U.S. General Accounting Office indicated in 1999 that since experts at the U.S. embassy in Colombia view narcotraffickers and guerrillas as sometimes indistinguishable, U.S. officials would be allowed to supply Colombian colleagues with intelligence not directly related to narcotrafficking.[136]

Hence the United States and its assistants increasingly relied on the panopticon to contain the guerrillas. Washington was now able to see movements of guerrilla troops, arms, drug shipments, and the like, as well as intercept the guerrillas' communications systems. What was previously hidden was now exposed; the mountains and jungles would no longer provide foolproof camouflage for the FARC. While this alone was insufficient to win the war, it chipped away at the strategic position of the guerrillas and strengthened the hand of the United States. The FARC was destined to be debilitated financially and militarily through the growing transparency of its actions.

Since the Vietnam War, the United States has cherished the strategic lesson of avoiding the provision of numerous ground troops abroad. Whether by training local soldiers, such as the Nicaraguan Contras in the 1980s, or by relying on high-tech carpet bombing from the air, as in the cases of Iraq and post-Yugoslavia in the 1990s, Washington has been creative in its ability to deploy substitutes for large numbers of U.S. troops. Colombia is meant by Washington to be yet another showcase of its great strategic imagination. Evidence suggests that while the United States has maintained its agreed limits on official U.S. troops, so-called contractors, or neo-mercenaries, have exceeded the legally sanctioned number of 300 to 800. A Cable News Network on-site report observed that there were about 1,000 such contractors in February 2000. Private mercenary corporations such as DynCorp Inc. and Military Professional Resources Inc. (MPRI) have specialized in providing the U.S. government with trained experts tailored to strategic needs in terms of language, appearance, and military and technical skills. The contract basis of the agreement means that this kind of arrangement is ultimately cheaper for the United States, since it does not have to provide multi-year care and benefits for the neo-mercenaries as it would for official U.S. forces. Thus this entourage of neo-mercenaries has provided Washington with well-honed expertise at a bargain rate.

MPRI has established a database of 11,000 retired military officers and has a previous record in the Balkans, the Middle East, and Africa. In 2000 it signed a contract for at least U.S.$6 million to assist the Colombian military in terms of intelligence, logistics, and combat techniques. Since almost all of MPRI's work has been clandestine and because it can hire neo-mercenaries with Hispanic features, it is difficult to document exact numbers of its personnel and other data. What has been revealed, by *Jane's Defence Weekly,* is that MPRI exceeded its legal capacity when it officially provided military "writers" to Croatia in 1995, and it clearly had engaged in military training.[137] Such neo-mercenaries, along with the 500 official U.S. specialists, were hired to train many of the officers of the projected 8,000 Colombian troops housed at the Tres Esquinas military base near the FARC's former *zona.*

The use of neo-mercenaries has strengths as well as drawbacks. The arrangement is cheap and effective for the United States. Vietnam-style public relations disasters generated by the use of numerous U.S. troops are avoided. Moreover, the United States has cut about 40 percent of its military personnel since the 1980s and has employed neo-mercenaries to balance part of this loss.[138] But their use raises some important problems, particularly involving accountability. While U.S. military personnel, or any official government troops, can be held accountable to their own citizens and to certain international organizations, what about the actions of neo-mercenaries? The problem is compounded by the clandestine nature of such "contractors" and by the related lack of transparency of their actions. It is another sign of a privatized war, and of the new nonstate actors of post-Soviet warfare.

Beyond the use of a high-tech surveillance system and the employment of neo-mercenary troops, a third dimension of U.S. strategy has been a form of biological warfare designed to eliminate coca growth in an area controlled by the FARC near in its former *zona.* While herbicides had been used previously, Plan Colombia involved the intensive use of glyphosate, which kills all plant growth where it is applied.[139] Compounding its direct effect of killing all vegetation, it subsequently kills or expels related life and hence threatens biodiversity in an area that is a tributary to the Amazon River. The practice has been halted in certain regions due to loud complaints by local farmers regarding ill effects on their legitimate crops, and for causing skin irritations in humans.

Washington employed this strategy to eradicate coca growth in a region that is the stronghold of the FARC in order to weaken its financial base and hence military power. But the strategy may prove to be a failure. Peasants, desperate to eke out a living in dire circumstances, have been cutting down swaths of forests to replant coca.[140] Because the trade is of course driven by northern demand, a balloon effect will likely occur such that other regions and countries pick up the slack created in areas where the United States has conducted fumigation. The practice also has deepened regional peasants' support for the FARC, which they view as protecting their livelihood.[141] In terms of its damage to the environment, its unintended strategic fortification of the FARC, and what is likely a miniscule effect on diminishing the overall trade in drugs, this component of U.S. strategy is likely to be a dreadful failure.

The distressingly profound strategic problems surrounding Colombia's involvement in narcotrafficking would disappear instantly if cocaine and opiates were legalized. Prices for those drugs, and the crops from which they are derived, would plunge rapidly and drastically. Hence a principal source of financing for the FARC and the AUC would disappear almost overnight. This is not to suggest that Colombian guerrillas would not exist without narcotrafficking. But there is no doubt that this and other crime has exacerbated the war by financing the subversives' extravagant military machines. Numerous studies have demonstrated that legalization, or state control of presently illicit drugs, would also be beneficial to users and to society in general.[142] Overall, the point is that legalization of cocaine and opiates would surely diminish the pitch of Colombia's feverish civil war. If Washington is serious in its contention that the FARC and other subversives have derived power from narcotrafficking, legalization represents a far better route than the failed policy of eradication.

Finally, the invasion by the Colombian military of the FARC's *zona* in February 2002 represented a major turning point in the country's civil war. The government's reclamation of this territory was a natural reflection of Plan Colombia, which was foreshadowed in 1999 when the United States opened the Tres Esquinas military base on the outskirts of the rebel enclave. Plan Colombia will likely diminish the traditional military power of the FARC, given the related professionalization of the Colombian military, the provision of new military equipment to the government, and the extensive use of surveillance and biological warfare, among other measures. The FARC is apt to respond by an increasing reliance on urban terror. Thus, Plan Colombia was under pressure to be refashioned to cope with the predominance of terror tactics rather than the conventional guerrilla warfare for which it was originally designed. That objective fits nicely with Washington's general redefinition of global security in the wake of the 2001 attacks on the World Trade Center.

Conclusion

The Colombian case is a truly fascinating one because it touches upon some of the most important questions in politics, such as the role of good government and the causes of war. Beyond this, the experiences of the FARC and the ELN have much to tell us regarding the continuity and transformation of guerrilla warfare in the Americas at the dawn of the twenty-first century. Both groups have relied on a mixture of premodern, modern, and to a more limited extent, postmodern epistemological approaches to power and strategy.

The premodern context in which the rebel groups have operated is analytically significant in many ways. Colombians have never known a strong and legitimate state, a Leviathan that could monopolize the use of force, a sense of nationalism, a developed civil society, or the simple ambience of political equilibrium and tranquility. Given a context featuring premodern elements, the guerrillas' actions and policies naturally have reflected this. For instance, their attitude toward political space has resembled feudal fiefdoms—they have sought small enclaves with a localized constellation of power. While cries for political autonomy and for nations based on ethnic relations have frequently been heard in the postmodern era, the FARC's *zona* had nothing at all to do with ethnicity or even localized political autonomy per se. This site had much more to do with its strategic role vis-à-vis the group's involvement in transnational crime. Further, both the FARC and the ELN have conceived of "power over" strategic space, rather than the cultivation of popular consent and the development of a social contract, which are the chief foundations of modern and postmodern democratic political structures.[143] Another indication of this tendency toward coercion rather than consent was the FARC's apparent strategic shift in 2001 toward adopting IRA-styled urban terrorism, given the context of its weakening performance in the realm of traditional guerrilla warfare. Prospects for the escalation of urban terror were further amplified by the FARC's loss of its cherished *zona* in early 2002. The Colombian guerrillas' reliance on force, especially in the case of the FARC, their restless desire for coercive power, and their provocation of political chaos are reflective of the premodern, pre-Leviathan, dog-eat-dog world grimly envisioned by Hobbes.[144]

Beyond the presence of premodern characteristics, elements of modernity have also figured into the guerrillas' context and actions. The modern ideology of Marxism has been reflected in the policies and rhetoric of both the FARC and the more politically sophisticated ELN. The influence of modern strategists over Colombia's guerrillas has also been apparent, particularly with regard to Lenin and Clausewitz. Further, if a celebrated feature of modernity is a binary approach to knowledge generally, and to politics in particular, certainly this is relevant to the cases of the ELN and the FARC. Related to this, both groups have been enthusiastic participants in the politics of exclusion. Further, in some sense the actors themselves are a familiar refrain from Cold War modernity—a contest between leftist guerrilla groups and a weak, developing state. The Colombian case, then, represents a chaotic mix of both modern and premodern elements.

To the extent that there are postmodern aspects involved, they have more to do with U.S. policy than with the Colombian contenders themselves. Washington's Plan Colombia has featured new ways of knowing combat, in terms of how the war is fought, who fights it, and what kinds of weapons are used. Indicative of this is Plan Colombia's extensive reliance upon surveillance, mercenaries, and biological warfare. It is a style of warfare influenced by the information economy and by neoliberal "just in time" efficiency.[145] It also conforms to the vast redefinition of security spawned by Washington's post–September 11 war on terrorism. The FARC, the ELN, and the AUC subsequently have been blacklisted by the United States as among the thirty-one global terrorist organizations it would like to eliminate.[146]

The revolution in military affairs is reflected in Washington's policy toward Colombia, especially in the implementation of what the Department of Defense has called C^{4}ISR—command, control, communications, computers, intelligence, surveillance, and reconnaissance.[147] Plan Colombia's intensive use of radar, reconnaissance aircraft, and satellites was designed to shine a floodlight on the FARC's spatial movements and communications. Given the FARC's threat in 2001 to mimic IRA-styled urban terrorism, the focus of this surveillance is likely to shift from its initial concentration on the countryside to the dual fronts of urban and rural areas. As Sun Tzu observed, "those skilled in attack maneuver in the highest heights of the sky."[148] While this may not mean the guerrillas' defeat, the power of the panopticon will likely curb the power of the FARC within the space of a few years.[149] Hence, from the perspective of the United States, these features render the Colombian conflict as an information and surveillance war. Also new, or at least a fresh twist on a premodern theme, is the employment of neomercenaries to direct much of the war in Colombia. And while the Colombian case does not represent the first time biological warfare has been utilized, the blatant nature of the U.S. fumigation of southern Colombia with glyphosate is novel in degree.

In terms of epistemological structures, then, the Colombian case represents a crazy quilt of premodern, modern, and postmodern features. The latter are dominated by the United States in its contest with the guerrillas. Perhaps the only postmodern feature of the guerrillas themselves is their reliance on transnational crime, especially the narcotics trade. In contrast to the almost feudal agricultural circumstances of the Colombian peasants whom the FARC claims to represent, the guerrilla leadership itself has exhibited an intimate knowledge of the complexities associated with illicit transnational economics—including the global spaces of the drug and weapons trade, the unwritten rules by which it abides, and the urgent and capital-driven tempo to which it moves. This has enlarged the rebels' coffers and increased their military power, but has cost them dearly in terms of political and ideological legitimacy. In this sense, the war has been more about military contests and dominance of strategic sites of crime than about ideas or competing resolutions to the imbroglio in the country.

It has been observed throughout the discussion that classic security themes are particularly relevant to the Colombian imbroglio. The notion of mastering strategic space and time—a theme emphasized by Sun Tzu I and Sun Tzu II, Thucydides, Machiavelli, Clausewitz, and others—has been particularly prominent here. The politics of space has been manifested in issues ranging from feudal *zonas* to the high-tech panopticon of Plan Colombia. It should be emphasized that conceptions of strategic space have been at the heart of the country's protracted warfare. From the beginning, Colombian leaders backed out of Bolívar's plan for a Gran Colombia, which would have comprised parts of today's Venezuela, Colombia, Bolivia, Ecuador, and Peru. Colombian elites simply could not relate to large political spaces 200 years ago, and still cannot do so at the beginning of the twenty-first century. With multiple belligerents craving their own fiefdoms or unwilling to give up their existing ones, and with none of these contenders capable of neutralizing the power of the others, protracted warfare seems likely.[150]

Temporal politics and strategy, in their variety of dimensions, have been especially relevant. These include issues such as the guerrillas' sense of timing, the quick tempo of the illicit crime that feeds the rebels, and the real-time images conveyed through C^{4}ISR. Related to this, Plan

Colombia has introduced in a major way the theme of intelligence, which may assist in turning the tide of warfare away from the guerrillas. Because the Colombian rebels have not been characterized by a cult of leadership or by a pyramid structure, they cannot be decimated easily by intelligence operations, as was the case for Peru's Sendero Luminoso. Rather, real-time information from the new panopticon is more likely to eat away slowly at the guerrillas' military power by limiting their supply lines and by exposing their battle plans.

The strategic theme of organization has been emphasized by classic thinkers such Clausewitz, Sun Tzu I, and Sun Tzu II. It has proven to be crucial in the Colombian case. The guerrillas would not have emerged in such a strong position at the turn of the century were it not for superb organizational skills. This includes not only the structure of their military machine, but also the role of guerrillas in transnational criminal organizations. Further, the use of neomercenaries on the part of the United States suggests an immensely important revision of military organization that may represent the wave of the future. It also raises serious questions regarding political accountability.

Regarding the pertinence of other classic security themes, the celebrated notion of good government—present in the writings of Thucydides, Sun Tzu I and Sun Tzu II, Machiavelli, and Hobbes—has been sadly absent in Colombia's political history. This goes a long way to explaining the country's legacy of political strife. So, too, do issues concerning political economy. Inequity, premodern economic territoriality, and misguided policies on the part of international financial agencies such as the IMF have all represented important contributing factors in the country's civil war. Beyond this, the classic duality of consent versus coercion—a notion celebrated by neo-Gramscians but present since the writings of Thucydides and Sun Tzu—has also proven to be a prominent negative lesson in Colombia. No political actor in the country has succeeded at generating widespread social consent; all instead have relied on the most brutal forms of coercion. Overall, it is clear that classic strategic themes have been strongly relevant to the successes and failures of those engaged in Colombia's protracted warfare. Their relevance has been manifested in both traditional and novel forms.

A remarkable feature of the Colombian political landscape is that it has been difficult to identify the proverbial good guys. This is especially true of the 1990s and beyond, when the Thucydidean elements of fear and uneven growth of the subversives vis-à-vis the state served to accelerate the war.[151] Each of Colombia's belligerents have used so much horrific force and committed so many political blunders that there has been no clear hero on the scene. In contrast to the dismal record of Colombia's *políticos,* any hero who manages to emerge in the country will likely address classic strategic themes in a positive and creative fashion.

Notes

1. Statistics from the Ejército Nacional de Colombia and the Policía Nacional de Colombia, released in *El Tiempo* (Bogotá), 4 February 2001.
2. See *Los Angeles Times,* 19 February 2002.
3. Statistics from the Ejército Nacional de Colombia and the Policía Nacional de Colombia, released in *El Tiempo* (Bogotá), 4 February 2001.
4. See *New York Times,* 16 August 2001. About 2.6 million barrels of oil have been spilled due to guerrilla bombings since 1986.
5. For a superb discussion of the politics of Colombia's narcotrafficking industry, see Vargas Meza, *Fumigación y conflicto.*
6. An estimated 2,858,000 Colombians were officially unemployed by July 2001. See *El Tiempo,* 31 July 2001.
7. *New York Times,* 26 April 2000.
8. *El Tiempo,* 11 April 2000.
9. For a discussion of terms of the IMF package, see *El Tiempo,* 21 December 1999.
10. For an excellent discussion of Gini coefficients and other social indicators in the 1990s, see Sarmiento Anzola, "Debacle del estado social," pp. 27–39 (p. 31 for data regarding Gini coefficients). See also World Bank, *Distribution of Income and Consumption.*
11. *El Espectador* (Bogotá), 20 May 1999.
12. *El Espectador,* 22 January 2001.
13. *El Espectador,* 11 December 2000.
14. Many Colombians I interviewed noted the weakness of the country's civil society and the various reasons behind this. Author interviews with Padre Gabriel Izquierdo, Instituto Pensar, Pontificia Universidad Javeriana, Bogotá, 7 May 1999; Gabriel Murillo Castaño, professor, Ciencia Política, Universidad de los Andes, Bogotá, 4 May 1999; Jorge Hernández, professor, Departamento de Sociología, Universidad del Valle, Cali, 19 May 1999; Adriana González Gil and Juan Carlos Vélez Rendón, professors, Departamento de Historia, Universidad de Antioquia, Medellín, 27 May 1999; Freddy Salazar, professor, Departamento de Filosofía, Universidad de Santander, Bucaramanga, 8 June 2000; Carlos Franco, Fundación Progresar (an NGO), Bogotá, 30 May 2000; Anna Teresa Bernal, director, Redepaz (an NGO), Bogotá, 15 May 2000; Javier Sanin, dean, Departamento de Ciencias Sociales, Universidad Javeriana, Bogotá, 12 May 2000; Humberto Vélez, professor, Departamento de Historia, Universidad del Valle, Cali, 21 June 2000; and William Ramírez Tobón, director, Instituto de Estudios Políticos y Relaciones Internacionales (IEPRI), Universidad Nacional de Colombia, Bogotá, 26 January 2001.

15. See, for example, Francisco Leal Buitrago, "Estamos en una carrera contra tiempo," in Francisco Leal Buitrago et al., eds., *La paz: Análisis del proceso y propuestas para un nuevo sistema político en Colombia* (Bogotá: Ediciones Aurora, 2000), p. 134. Further, many of the persons I interviewed between 1999 and 2001—academics, government officials, as well as NGO members who wish to remain anonymous for security reasons—viewed the ELN as the most politically developed of the subversive groups in Colombia.

16. See Rodríguez Bautista, "Ejército de Liberación Nacional," p. 159, translation by author.

17. Pérez Martínez, "Ejército de Liberación Nacional," p. 241, translation by author.

18. See Rodríguez Bautista, "Ejército de Liberación Nacional," pp. 163–164, translation by author.

19. Pérez Martínez, "Ejército de Liberación Nacional," pp. 230, 238, translation by author.

20. Ejército de Liberción Nacional (ELN), *Correo del Magdalena*, no. 122 (15 May 2000), translation by author.

21. ELN, Comando Central, *Actualidad: De gira por América el Virrey McCafrey afina la estrategia*, 17 September 1999, caobo23@geneva-link.ch, translation by author.

22. Pérez Martínez, "Ejército de Liberación Nacional," p. 240, translation by author.

23. Ibid., p. 233.

24. ELN, "Entrevista con Nicholás Rodríguez y Antonio García," 1 January 2000. See also, ELN, "Posición del ELN sobre la privatización," March 2000, pamphlet.

25. For a discussion of this, see *El Tiempo*, 30 March 2000.

26. See *El Tiempo*, 9 January 2000.

27. ELN, "Venemos contra la paz," 20 May 2000, translation by author.

28. See Pérez Martínez, "Ejército de Liberación Nacional," p. 235, translation by author.

29. ELN, *Correo del Magdalena*, 18 October 1999, translation by author.

30. ELN, *Correo del Magdalena*, no. 122 (15 May 2000), translation by author.

31. ELN, *Correo del Magdalena*, no. 115 (18 October 1999), translation by author.

32. ELN, *Correo del Magdalena*, no. 122 (15 May 2000), translation by author.

33. That quote was taken from ELN, "Entrevista con Nicolás Rodríguez y Antonio García," translation by author. A variation of this appears as an emblem on many of their hardcopy publications: "The Colombian bourgeoisie only listens to the voice of dynamite and guns." See, for example, ELN, "Posición del ELN sobre la privatización," title page, translation by author.

34. See, for example, Pérez Martínez, "Ejército de Liberación Nacional," p. 225.

35. Ibid.

36. *El Tiempo*, 6 October 2000.

37. See Rangel Suárez, *Colombia*, p. 12; and statistics from Ejército Nacional de Colombia, reported in *El Tiempo*, 4 February 2001. The group may have reached a peak of 5,000–6,000 troops by 1999.

38. Author interview with Armando Borero, professor, Departamento de Derecho, Universidad de los Andes, Bogotá, 16 May 2000.

39. See Alfredo Rangel Suárez, "Dos despejes," an excellent editorial that appeared in *El Tiempo*, 2 February 2001.

40. ELN, "Pastrana le incumple a la paz"; and ELN, "Venemos contra la paz." Also, author interview with Freddy Salazar, professor, Departamento de Filisofia, Universidad Industrial de Santander, Bucaramanga, 8 June 2000.

41. All eighty-four rules of the agreement are available for inspection in *El Tiempo*, 27 January 2001, www.eltiempo.com.co. The agreement is also available by e-mail from caobo23@geneva-link.ch.

42. See, for example, *El Espectador*, 5 February 2001.

43. See, for example, Rangel Suárez, "Dos despejes."

44. See *El Tiempo*, 7 August 2001 and 9 August 2001.

45. See, for example, ELN, *Correo del Magdalena*, no. 113 (21 September 1999), translation by author.

46. See, for example, ibid.; and ELN, *Correo del Magdalena*, no. 115 (18 October 1999), translation by author.

47. See, for example, ELN, "A rechazar el Plan Colombia," 9 December 2000; and ELN, *Correo del Magdalena*, no. 115 (18 October 1999), translation by author.

48. ELN, "Comunicado del ELN," translation by author.

49. On the theme of strategic space, consider the following: In *A History of the Peloponnesian War*, Thucydides referred to strategic space in a number of senses. He noted Athens's dominance over the strategic space of oceans, and Sparta's strategic dominance over land, for example. He emphasized the strategic frontier of the sea (p. 7), in which pirates fed off the resources of unsuspecting ships—a rough analogy to the ELN's dominance over the resources of particular territories. He also underlined the notion of walled cities and enclaves, which may be roughly similar to the ELN's quest for protection within a ceasefire zone; see pp. 50–51, 57, 77, 168, 278. Machiavelli noted the importance of strategic space, in both *The Prince*, p. 82, and *The Discourses*, pp. 100–101, 352. Relevant notions of strategic space are also dealt with by Sun Tzu in *The Art of War*, pp. 42, 44, 119, 143–152, 157; Sun Tzu II in *The Lost Art of War*, pp. 31, 47, 51, 99, 101; and Clausewitz in *On War*, pp. 128–132, 143, 393, 417, 543.

50. This view is expressed throughout Hobbes's *Leviathan*, especially in relation to a "restless desire for power" (p. 161) that has cataclysmic consequences in the absence of a Leviathan (p. 185). On war as an instrument of policy and as a continuation of politics by other means, see Clausewitz, *War*, pp. 605 and 87 respectively.

51. See Machiavelli, *Discourses*, p. 430.

52. Sun Tzu, *Art of War*, p. 112. Sun Tzu refers to "attacking the empty" in the context of the formless and powerful nature of water, a frequent analogy in his work.

53. This point was discussed in the previous chapter. The guerrilla tactics of Che Guevara have had a particularly profound influence upon the ELN. See Guevara, *Guerrilla Warfare*.

54. See Sun Tzu II, *Lost Art of War*, pp. 23, 111–112, for example.

55. See Thucydides, *History of the Peloponnesian War*, p. 199.

56. In May 2000 the Colombian government claimed that the FARC had expanded the *zona* to more than twice the original size, 96,032 square kilometers. See *El Tiempo*, 14 May 2000.

57. Much of the discussion in this section has been influenced by anonymous interviews I conducted throughout Colombia during the period 1999–2001. Such anonymity is necessary due to the sensitive nature of these points, and because many outspoken thinkers in Colombia on both the right and the left have been murdered, confronted with death threats, and/or forced into external exile. These interviews were conducted with former guerrilla members, rival guerrilla members, former officers of the Colombian armed forces, high-placed members of the government, a variety of academics, lawyers, members of private think tanks, and NGO directors, among others.

58. Fuerzas Armadas Revolucionarias de Colombia (FARC), "Octava conferencia nacional de las FARC-EP: Programa agrario de los guerrilleros," 2 April 1993, translation by author.

59. For an excellent discussion of the Colombian guerrillas' desire for a ceasefire zone, as expressed through the Coordinadora Guerrillera Simón Bolívar, see, for example, Chernick, "La negociación de una paz," pp. 41–44.

60. See, for example, the following FARC documents: "Comunicado público," 12 November 2000; "Comunicado," 10 July 2000; letter from the FARC to President Pastrana, printed in *El Tiempo*, 20 January 2001; "Denuncia pública," 5 August 1997; "Comunica a la comunidad internacional," 19 February 1998; "El Gobierno Samper es el culpable," 6 August 1998; and "Comunicado a la opinion pública," 10 September 1998.

61. See, for example, FARC, "Comunicado," 10 July 2000; and FARC, "34th aniversario de las FARC-EP," 27 May 1998.

62. See, for example, FARC, "Clinton Go Home," 23 August 2000; and FARC, "Comunicado público," 12 November 2000.

63. See FARC, "Comunicado de prensa," 8 June 1997, translation by author.

64. See FARC, "Comunicado pública a extranjeros y colombianos," 12 July 1998.

65. See FARC, "Octava conferencia nacional de las FARC-EP: Programa agrario de los guerrilleros," 2 April 1993; and FARC, "Comunicado público," 12 November 2000, translation by author.

66. See FARC, "Plataforma para un gobierno de reconstrucción," 3 April 1993, translation by author.

67. See *El Tiempo*, 9 March 2001.

68. For more information on the FARC's Movimiento Bolivariano, see the group's website, www.farc-ep.org/pleno.html, especially the document "Manifesto de Movimiento Bolivariano por la Nueva Colombia," 25 March 2000.

69. See FARC, "Contra la intervención," 1998 (no specific date). For other discussions by the FARC regarding Bolívar and Bolivariano, see, for example, FARC, "Mensaje de Año Nuevo," 26 December 2000; FARC, "Plataforma para un gobierno de reconstrucción"; and FARC, "Clinton Go Home," translation by author.

70. See Rangel Suárez, *Colombia,* p. 150.

71. The best political and scientific discussion of fumigation of illicit crops in Colombia is Vargas Meza, *Fumigación y conflicto.*

72. This point is well known, and is similar to the circumstances in Peru's Huallaga Valley during the 1980s and early 1990s, when peasant cultivators supported guerrilla groups such as Sendero Luminoso and the MRTA due to economic more than ideological reasons. See, for example, Rochlin, *Redefining Mexican Security,* pp. 101–103. Regarding the Colombian case, there are many discussions of this. Beyond Vargas Meza's *Fumigación y conflicto,* see, for example, Pécaut, "Presente, pasado, y futuro de la violencia," p. 906.

73. See *Revista Cambio,* 3–20 November 2000, www.cambio.com.co/20001113/pais1.html.

74. See FARC, "A la comunidad internacional," April 1998 (no specific date); and FARC, "Carta pública al pueblo," April 1998 (no specific date), translation by author.

75. See FARC, "36 años por la paz," 20 May 2000, translation by author.

76. See *El Tiempo,* 31 March 2000; and FARC, *A la comunidad internacional,* translation by author.

77. See *El Tiempo,* 9 March 2001.

78. Author interview with Klaus Nyholm, representative, UN Drug Control Program, Bogotá, 6 May 1999.

79. FARC, "Ley 02: Sobre la tributación," March 2000.

80. See Romero, "Élite regionales, identidades, y paramilitares en el Sinú," p. 175.

81. The first estimate is from ibid. The second estimate is from the Ejército Nacional de Colombia, statistics released in *El Tiempo,* 4 February 2001.

82. See the FARC's website, www.farc-ep.org/pleno.html.

83. See *El Tiempo,* 12 May 2000.

84. See Rangel Suárez, *Colombia,* pp. 104–105.

85. See *New York Times,* 10 July 2001.

86. See FARC, Manuel Marulanda Vélez, "Texto completo del discurso pronunciado," 27 May 1994.

87. See FARC, "Comunicado," 2 May 1997, translation by author.

88. See *Jane's Security,* "Furezas Armadas Revolucionarias de Colombia," 19 October 2000, www.janes.com/security/terrorism/news/jwit/jwit001019_1_n.shtml.

89. See *El Tiempo,* 3 December 2000.

90. See *El Tiempo,* 6 June 2001 and 3 August 2001.

91. See *El Tiempo,* 26–27 January 2002.

92. FARC, "Comunicado a la opinion pública nacional y internacional," 28 September 1997, translation by author.

93. For a discussion of the tour, see *New York Times,* 9 February 2000.

94. See *El Tiempo,* 2 February 2001.

95. Letter from FARC leader Manuel Marulanda Vélez to Colombian president Andrés Pastrana, printed in *El Tiempo,* 20 January 2001, translation by author.

96. See *El Tiempo,* 31 July 2001.

97. See *New York Times,* 23 February 2002.

98. See FARC, "Las FARC-EP llaman al pueblo colombiano," 8 October 1997. Quote from FARC, "El bloque sur de las FARC-EP," 17 October 1997, translation by author.

99. *El Tiempo,* 2 May 2000.

100. The FARC held its first *audiencia* on 10 April 2000.

101. Letter from FARC leader Manuel Marulanda Vélez to Colombian president Andrés Pastrana, printed in *El Tiempo,* 20 January 2001. In the summer of 2000, the FARC had indicated through its documents that attempts by the government to win back the *zona* would be antithetical to the "process of dialog for peace." See FARC, "Comunicado," 10 July 2000, translation by author.

102. The letter was printed in *Nacia* 27, no. 4 (January–February 1994): 10–11.

103. Author interviews with anonymous directors and representatives of NGOs throughout Colombia, 1999–2001. Anonymity due to security reasons.

104. See the FARC's website, www.farc-ep.org, for a discussion of the Movimiento Bolivariano, especially "Manifesto de Movimiento Bolivariano por la Nueva Colombia," 25 March 2000.

105. See Hobbes, *Leviathan,* p. 161, for his discussion of a restless desire for power, and p. 186, for example, for an analysis of the misery that comes with the absence of a Leviathan.

106. See Clausewitz, *War,* pp. 75–76, 149, concerning the relationship between war and murder, and p. 89, for example, concerning war as violence, hatred, and enmity. Beyond these characteristics of warfare, much of the tactical discussion by Clausewitz concerning organization, terrain, and so on, is also pertinent to the FARC.

107. For a good discussion of the legacy of so-called self-defense groups, see Ramírez Tobón, "Violencia, guerra civil, contrato social," p. 51.

108. The group has always admitted its desire to achieve official recognition as one of Colombia's principal political actors. This was evidenced by Castaño's demand in March 2000 for the AUC to be present at peace negotiations with other belligerents in Colombia. See *El Tiempo,* 2 March 2000. An anonymous expert on the paramilitaries claimed in early 2001 that the group's objective was to control strategic territory partially through the tactic of "cleansing," or murdering, campesinos who are not sympathetic to the paramilitaries. See *El Tiempo,* 28 January 2001.

109. Autodefensas Unidas de Colombia (AUC), "Political-Military Nature of the Movement," May 1998 (no specific date).

110. In March 2000, Castaño said he had 11,200 armed supporters. Reuters News Service, 1 March 2000. Colombia's Ministry of Defense maintained that

the AUC had about 8,000 troops in 2000–2001, as reported in *El Tiempo*, 7 January 2001.

111. On political assassinations, see Rangel Suárez, *Colombia*, pp. 46, 120. The statistic on internally displaced persons is according to Colombia's Ministry of Defense, as reported in *El Tiempo*, 19 December 2000.

112. As reported in *El Tiempo*, 28 January 2001.

113. AUC, "Political-Military Nature of the Movement."

114. AUC, Carlos Castaño, "Entrevista del Comandante Castaño a RCN radio," 18 February 2001, translation by author.

115. AUC, Carlos Castaño, "Carta abierta a Andrés Pastrana Arango," 17 February 2001, translation by author.

116. The television interview, Castaño's first, was also covered by *El Tiempo* and by Reuters News Service on 2 March 2000. On Castaño's previous denial, see AUC, "Letter to Dr. Curtis Kamman, Ambassador of the United States to Colombia," 8 May 1998, www.colombialibre.org.en/curtis.htm.

117. AUC, "Entrevista a los comandantes de Las ACCU," 9–10 September 1998, translation by author.

118. AUC, "Nucleo de Paramillo Acuerdo," 26 July 1998, translation by author.

119. For an excellent discussion of this, see Ramírez Tobón, "Violencia, guerra civil, contrato social," p. 57.

120. See *El Tiempo*, 6 June 2001.

121. AUC, Carlos Castaño, "Carta abierta a Andrés Pastrana Arango."

122. See, for example, Romero, "Élites regionales, identidades y paramilitaries en el Sinú," pp. 177–180.

123. See *New York Times*, 4 December 2000.

124. AUC, "Reportaje del Comandante Castaño al periodico Notitarde," 23 December 2000, translation by author.

125. For a good discussion of this, see Chernick, "La negociación de una paz," p. 47.

126. An excellent work in this regard is Rangel Suárez, *Colombia*.

127. In 1999, for example, 95 officials among the ranks of colonels, lieutenant colonels, and majors were retired, in addition to 30 captains and 120 subofficials. Improved mobility, technology, and financing were part of the larger restructuring package. Author interviews with Eduardo Pizarro Leongómez, director, Instituto de Estudios Políticos y Relaciones Internacionales, Universidad Nacional de Colombia, Bogotá, 13 May 1999; and Alfredo Rangel Suárez, director, Política y Estrategia, Fundación Social, Bogotá, 17 May 2000.

128. Ejército Nacional de Colombia, Policía Nacional de Colombia, *Infracciones al derechos internacional humanitario y violaciones a los derechos humanos 1995 al 2000*, 10 January 2001, released in *El Tiempo*, 4 February 2001.

129. When one observes the official Colombian government version of Plan Colombia, one is struck by the ten strategies it associates with the plan. Only the sixth makes any reference at all to antinarcotics strategies, the fourth makes a vague reference to the modernization of the armed forces, and none directly addresses the war against the FARC and perhaps other subversives.

Despite the fact that three-quarters of Plan Colombia's aid from the United States is composed of funding for the military or police, the eight other objectives of the plan referred to by the Colombian government consist of employment creation, macroeconomic financial strategies, improvement of human rights, promotion of a national conscience, and so on. To say the least, the Colombian government's presentation of Plan Colombia lacks a reasonable sense of proportion. See Presidencia de la República, www.presidencia.gov.co/webpresi/plancolo/plancolo.htm.

130. This information on troop caps is in section 3204(b) of Plan Colombia.

131. Marcella and Schulz, *Colombia's Three Wars*, p. 4.

132. See *El Tiempo*, 16 December 1999.

133. Center for International Policy, CIPONLINE, *Colombia*, 2000, www.ciponline.org/facts.co.htm.

134. Ecuador agreed to a 1999–2009 deal with the United States for the radar site, after Panama refused the United States on this count. See *New York Times*, 31 December 2000. For a discussion of the Brazilian component, see *Expreso* (Lima), 2 May 2000.

135. See *Defense Daily*, 13 March 2000.

136. U.S. General Accounting Office, *Drug Control: Narcotics Threat from Colombia Continues to Grow*, Washington, D.C., June 1999, http://frwebgate. access.gpo.gov/cgi-bin/useftp.cgi?ipaddress=162.140.64.21&filename= ns99136.txt&directory=/diskb/wais/data/gao.

137. As reported in *El Tiempo*, 9 December 2000.

138. See *Dallas Morning News*, 27 February 2000.

139. For an intensive discussion of the nature and effects of glyphosate, see Vargas Meza, *Fumigación y conflicto*, pp. 247–249.

140. Extensive studies indicate that farmers who cultivate coca in this region of southern Colombia (near the FARC's *zona*) receive on average a 293 percent return on their investment. Further, at the beginning of the twenty-first century there was a crisis of overproduction in many of Colombia's legitimate crops, such as coffee, and since coca is very hardy, it is easier to care for and more prolific than some legitimate crops. See, for example, *El Espectador*, 21 May 2000.

141. These complaints were made by numerous Colombian experts during author interviews: Edilberto Imbachi, director, Derechos Humanos, Organización Nacional Indígena de Colombia, Bogotá, 30 May 2000; member of the government peace commission, anonymous interview, Bogotá, 22 May 2000; Ana Teresa Bernal, president, Redepaz, Bogotá, 15 May 2000; Francisco Leal Buitrago, dean, Departamento de Ciencias Sociales, Universidad de los Andes, Bogotá, 15 May 2000; and a retired major- general of the Colombian armed forces, anonymous interview, Bogotá, 17 May 2000.

142. See Rochlin, "Canada, Narcotrafficking, and Streams of Power."

143. For an excellent discussion of the nature of power, and the relation of space to power, see Foucault, "Subject and Power"; and Foucault, "Space, Knowledge, and Power."

144. See Hobbes, *Leviathan*, pp. 161, 185–186, 192, 387–390.

145. For a discussion of the relationship between production systems and systems of warfare, see Toffler and Toffler, *War and Anti-War,* p. 71. With regard to "just in time" warfare, see Bruce D. Berkowitz, "Warfare in the Information Age," *Issues in Science and Technology* 12 (fall 1995): 61.

146. See *El Tiempo,* 25 September 2001 and 2 November 2001.

147. See U.S. Department of Defense, C^4, *Intelligence, Surveillance, and Reconnaissance.*

148. See Sun Tzu, *Art of War,* p. 87.

149. For a good discussion of Jeremy Bentham's concept of the panopticon, with additional enlightening commentary, see Foucault, *Discipline and Punish,* esp. pp. 170–200.

150. Even Colombia's President Pastrana has indicated that in his view the war in Colombia is not winnable. See *New York Times,* 25 February 2001.

151. For a good discussion of the role of fear and uneven growth in relation to warfare, see Thucydides, *History of the Peloponnesian War,* pp. 8, 16, 49.

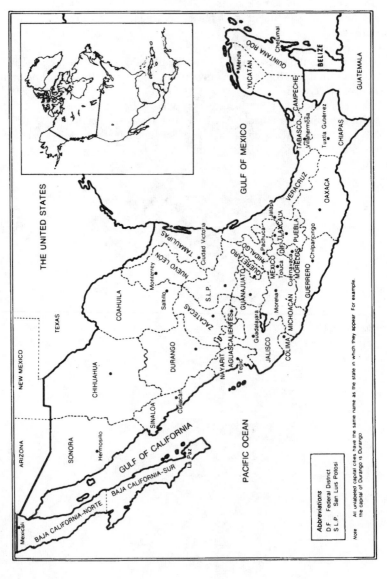

MEXICO

THE UNITED STATES

ARIZONA

NEW MEXICO

TEXAS

SONORA

Hermosillo

CHIHUAHUA

COAHUILA

NUEVO LEON

Monterrey

Saltillo

TAMAULIPAS

Ciudad Victoria

GULF OF CALIFORNIA

SINALOA

Culiacán

DURANGO

ZACATECAS

S.L.P.

La Paz

BAJA CALIFORNIA-NORTE

Mexicali

BAJA CALIFORNIA-SUR

PACIFIC OCEAN

NAYARIT

Tepic

AGUASCALIENTES

Guadalajara

JALISCO

GUANAJUATO

QUERETARO

HIDALGO

Pachuca

Jalapa

VERACRUZ

COLIMA

MICHOACÁN

Morelia

MEXICO

Toluca

D.F.

TLAXCALA

Cuernavaca

MORELOS

PUEBLA

Chilpancingo

GUERRERO

OAXACA

Chetumal

QUINTANA ROO

Mérida

YUCATÁN

CAMPECHE

TABASCO

Villahermosa

Tuxtla Gutiérrez

CHIAPAS

BELIZE

GUATEMALA

GULF OF MEXICO

Abbreviations

D.F.   Federal District
S.L.P. San Luis Potosí

Note   All unlabeled capital cities have the same name as the state in which they appear. For example, the capital of Durango is Durango.

6

Mexico:
The Origins, Ideology,
and Support Base of the EZLN

The Ejército Zapatista de Liberación Nacional (EZLN) bolted onto the international stage on 1 January 1994, the official commencement date of the North American Free Trade Agreement (NAFTA). Relying on the classic tactic of surprise attack, and blessed with considerable communication skills, the Zapatistas initiated a public relations extravaganza. As the planet's premier online guerrilla group, they deftly disseminated many of their official documents and communiqués to a global audience on the Internet. Upon inspection, it is clear that the group's pronouncements are haunted with the heroes and ghosts of Mexican history. The cast of these heroic spirits includes not only Mexicans, such as Emiliano Zapata, Pancho Villa, and Lázaro Cárdenas, but also foreigners such as Karl Marx and Antonio Gramsci. Thus the first part of this chapter is devoted to the historical context of the Zapatistas—stretching from independence in the early 1800s to the advent of neoliberalism in the 1980s. This historical backdrop will provide the context from which to consider the ideology and support base of the Zapatistas, topics that are addressed in the second part of the chapter.

Beginning in the 1880s, Mexico embarked upon a relatively successful transition to modernity. This path was marked by a potent sense of nationalism and common identity, by the dominance of a centralized power and a Leviathan, and by checkered progress toward industrial capitalism. Fundamentally, the Mexican Revolution was nationalist and capitalist—which were the predominant features of Western developed countries. With respect to the world order, during this same era Mexico established strong ties to global capitalism, increasingly dominated by the United States. Beginning in the 1930s under the extraordinary reign of the Partido Revolucionario Institucional (PRI), Mexico implemented

171

a political system based on inclusionary corporatism, in contrast to the highly exclusionary systems present in some other Latin American countries, such as Colombia. Mexico represented the epitome of a strong, centralized, and relatively inclusionary state in the Latin American context. While not being "democratic" in the sense of advanced Western capitalist states, the inclusionary aspect of the Mexican system combined with its workable economy had, until the 1980s, provided the foundation for the modern features of stability and equilibrium. Indeed, no other Latin American country, with the possible exception of Costa Rica, can match Mexico's record in this regard.

There are significant qualifications associated with Mexico's embrace of modernity. This has been evidenced at various points in the twentieth century by the extent of the nation's poverty, the predominance of subsistence agriculture, the lingering of a patchwork of feudal economic and political structures, limited infrastructure, and a rather dependent economic relationship especially with the United States. Further, Mexico has always been an extraordinarily diverse country, with respect to region, ethnicity, and the like. To make generalizations in the Mexican case, then, is not to dismiss the plethora of significant peculiarities that exist within it. But despite those qualifications, perhaps more than any other Latin American country, Mexico has been implementing general political and economic structures that most successfully emulate those present in developed capitalist states. It is also one of the so-called developing countries that for most of the twentieth century fully embraced modernity.

Since the 1970s, Mexico has been struggling to keep pace with another major rupture with respect to both the world order and epistemological structures. The struggle of the EZLN has been reflective of this. At the end of the century the Zapatistas attempted to harness certain features of postmodernism—such as new systems of communication and the advent of new actors in the form of global nongovernmental organizations—to combat the pronounced shift in the world order toward neoliberalism. They have represented a moral conscience that evokes the voices of the forgotten poor, the indigenous, and other excluded groups.

But their preposterous initial declaration of war against the Mexican army, and their intent to topple an economic system that so far has been on the ascendant, suggest that the Zapatistas occasionally have been out of synch with dominant forces present in both Mexico and the world. At the dawn of the twenty-first century, while the group has enjoyed some crucial successes, it has also been saddled with some considerable political and military limitations. This predicament stands in sharp contrast to the context of their hero, Emiliano Zapata, who more or less marched to the rhythm of global politics and consequently succeeded at achieving broad revolutionary goals.

From Liberation to Revolution

Mexico liberated itself from Spanish colonial rule by way of a massive and nationalist revolution.[1] Unlike Colombia and Peru, Mexico did not rely on an outside force to liberate the country. Since the dawn of its independence, Mexico has been characterized by a relatively strong sense of national identity. A crucial historical factor that served to galvanize Mexican nationalism was the loss of nearly half its territory to the United States in 1847. Indeed, it would not be an exaggeration to say that Mexican nationalism has almost always been in relation to the United States, with regard to politics, economics, and culture.

The modern notion of a secular state in Mexico was achieved in the aftermath of a civil war in the 1860s. The conflict involved the presence of French armed forces supporting the Mexican Conservatives, who were engaged in a protracted military contest with the Liberals. Supported by the United States, the Liberals triumphed by 1867. The state became officially secularized, in step with a modern epistemology that suggested that power and knowledge should rely increasingly on science, objectivity, and reason rather than divinity. Despite this official separation of state and church, however, the Catholic Church remained a powerful actor in Mexico.

The termination of the war between the Liberals and Conservatives in 1867 paved the way for Mexico's evolution toward domestic capitalism, and its insertion into the global capitalist economy. This was especially the case after 1880. It was evident, in part, by the construction of a vast network of railways in Mexico, perhaps the paramount symbol of capitalism during this era. While the country had a scant 1,086 kilometers of railway in 1880, this ballooned to 19,205 kilometers by 1910 at the beginning of the Mexican Revolution.[2] Not only was it instrumental for capitalist commerce, but it served to connect politically and culturally diverse parts of the country. The railways provided relatively rapid transportation from the periphery to the nation's capital, which is located at the geographic center of the country. Thus the railways promoted capitalism, nationalism, and centralized power, which represented fundamental characteristics of modernity.

There were other important indicators of Mexico's evolution toward modern capitalism during this period. The country became increasingly urbanized and fortified its infrastructure, through the increasing provision of water and electricity, for example. Much of this infrastructure was concentrated in the nation's capital. Mexico became increasingly integrated into the global capitalist economy during this era. Between 1877 and 1910, for example, exports as a percentage of GNP rose sixfold to 6.1 percent annually while imports increased three and a half times to 4.7 percent annually.[3]

But this evolution from premodernity into the broad outlines of modernity, from colonial feudalism to the capitalism of a developing state, was fraught with profound social and economic inequity. Under what amounted to the dictatorship of Porfirio Díaz during this period, horrific exploitation and inequity were rampant in the country. This was especially true in the countryside, where the hacienda system predominated. Despite progress toward capitalism on many fronts, the hacienda system represented an essentially feudal form of agriculture, complete with sharecropping and what in many cases was tantamount to slave labor. Wealth and political power were concentrated to the extreme through the hacienda system. While about three-quarters of the Mexican population worked in the agricultural sector at the beginning of the revolution in 1910, the overwhelming majority of them worked on haciendas.[4] The intense inequity faced by the majority of Mexico's population represented the rallying point for the revolution of 1910 to 1920.

From a Modern Revolution
to Postmodern Revolutionaries

Since the ghost of Emiliano Zapata figures so strongly in the discourse of the EZLN, the foundations of his ideology and strategy during the revolutionary period are important to understanding the Zapatista movement. Zapata directed what he called a "popular army," the Ejército Libertador del Centro y Sur—the Liberating Army of the Center and South. Based in the state of Morelos, not far from Mexico City, Zapata succeeded in mobilizing the oppressed agricultural population in the southern and central parts of the country. His rallying call of "Land and Liberty" rang true to much of Mexico's population. The centerpiece of Zapata's politics was the Plan de Ayala. It envisioned the nationalization of land controlled by haciendas and other big landowners, and its subsequent redistribution to the campesinos—that is, to the workers on the haciendas as well as other small farmers.[5] While Zapata was not a socialist per se, and while he never overtly proposed the overthrow of capitalism, his enemies, mostly big capital, viewed the essence of the Plan de Ayala to be socialist and anticapitalist.

Prominent features of Zapata's strategy and ideology would later reverberate through the policies of the EZLN. He ordered his troops, for example, to respect completely the property and lives of everyone except the big landowners, insisting that his followers not pillage the communities they entered unless they were enemy territory.[6] Beyond the central issue of land, Zapata was also concerned with the adequate provision of food, education, finance, and security forces for the majority population of campesinos.[7] He insisted that fundamental economic change was mandatory to resolve the crisis in Mexico and emphasized that it was not enough simply to "change the personnel of the government."[8] Strategically, Zapata masterfully used to his benefit Mexico's system of railways—the symbol of capitalism, communication, and centrality—by commandeering them on military adventures.[9] However, the railways at the time stretched only as far south as Oaxaca. Chiapas, the primary domain of the EZLN, was largely off the strategic map.

Zapata celebrated decentralized self-government, a platform that drew considerable popular support. Yet at the same time, this may also have been one of his chief strategic weaknesses. As Adolfo Gilly argues, Zapata may have been blinded by the highlights of decentralized power structures. He failed to consider adequately how to concentrate power in the hands of the state, in contrast to his rivals.[10] The triumphant military occupation of Mexico City by the campesino forces of Zapata and Pancho Villa in December 1914 represented the apex of Zapata's power and strategy during the revolution. But after that time, forces representing small and large capital, rather than the interests of the campesinos, appeared to dominate the political tide. Some suggest that Zapata seemed to be "lethargic" and unfocused after the December 1914 victory, and may even have fallen into a downward spiral of debauchery.[11]

Despite any missteps on the part of Zapata, there is no question as to his iconoclastic position vis-à-vis the Mexican Revolution and the politics that followed. His ideas concerning land reform were reflected in the policies of subsequent generations of Mexican governments, perhaps most notably that of President Lázaro Cárdenas (1934–1940), who implemented the most sweeping land reform in the country's history. The ideas of Zapata are also enshrined in Article 27 of the 1917 Mexican constitution, which established *ejidos* (communal campesino land) and celebrated the right to land. President Carlos Salinas's historic amendment of Article 27 in 1992, which effectively weakened *ejidos* and diluted the notion of the right to land, was one of the key motivating forces behind the actions of the EZLN.

Beyond the role of Zapata, the Mexican Revolution itself is crucially important for understanding the context of the EZLN. Although the idea of redistribution of wealth and land was a significant element of the revolution, it could by no means be considered socialist. It was instead a nationalist revolution, the first major one in Latin America. It was steeped in reformist capitalism, through a model that envisioned a strong role for the state, especially regarding redistribution and even the direction of the economy. But all of this was to occur within a clearly capitalist framework. It also represented a perfect economic fit at the time with the world order as well as with regard to many of the essential elements associated with modernity. The trend was toward a more globalized system of capitalism that featured greater international trade and that was dominated by the United States. Mexico, immediately before and after the revolution, blended into such a system. The Mexican capitalist characteristics that emerged from the revolution—nationalism, reformism, and a strong state—roughly emulated the models that would predominate in advanced capitalist states especially after 1930. In other words, the postrevolutionary politics of Mexico were commensurate with the times.

This nationalist revolution was clearly modern. Revolution itself can spawn nationalism, a sense of common identity, and a myth that can represent a guiding light for subsequent eras. Indeed, the model of the Mexican system that would emerge from the revolution has aptly been termed "revolutionary nationalism." The idea of a political center, rather than a chaotic dispersion of power, represents another essential element of this era. There is no question as to the centrality of Mexico City. Related to this is the modern notion of a strong and centralized government, or Leviathan, that actively promotes political equilibrium and stability. Certainly the Mexican government, from the 1920s to at least 1968, fit the bill in this regard. The ideas of political inclusion and civilian government are other components of the Mexican system during this era that reflected prevailing notions of modernity.

Thus the Mexican Revolution and many of the ideas of Emiliano Zapata generally fit the prevailing world order and epistemological structures of the time. This goes a long way to explaining their success. As we shall see, although the EZLN has summoned the ghost of Zapata, to some extent it has done so in a reactionary way that does not rhyme with some prevailing forces of the period. This is particularly the case with respect to economic issues.

The Rise and Fall of
Revolutionary Nationalism

A key ingredient of the EZLN's initial strength was that the group emerged publicly at a time when revolutionary nationalism was in tatters, and when the hegemony of the PRI had shattered. The EZLN's strategic manipulation of this period of crisis and rupture in Mexican history afforded it a national stature beyond its principal turf of Chiapas. Hence to comprehend the power and appeal of the EZLN, it is necessary to consider the ascendancy and decline of the PRI and of revolutionary nationalism.

The significance of the revolution itself, and of the national solidarity it spawned throughout much of the twentieth century, cannot be underestimated.[12] One institutional reflection of this was the announced formation in 1928 of the Partido Revolucionario, the precursor of the PRI.[13] The party achieved hegemonic status through a unique concoction of inclusionary corporatism that cultivated sustained societal consent, during a period stretching from its inception until at least the late 1960s. The PRI successfully co-opted leading sectors of national Mexican capital, both agricultural and industrial labor, regional political figures, and an assortment of other key political actors. It did so not only by offering leaders of such groups material benefits, but also by providing them with the capacity to distribute such benefits to their constituents. A classic example of this was the system of *charrismo,* whereby the PRI provided labor chiefs with a variety of perks in exchange for ensuring rank and file support for PRI policies and for their vote at election time.[14] A roughly similar system of political co-optation was apparent in other sectors of the Mexican political economy.

The PRI also implemented a significant if uneven program of wealth and land redistribution until about 1982. While the top 10 percent of households held 49 percent of national income in 1950, the figure dropped substantially to 34.4 percent in 1984. The middle 50 percent of households watched their share of national income increase from 47.6 percent in 1963 to 52.8 percent in 1977. The level of extreme poverty dropped from 69.5 percent of the population in 1963, to 34 percent in 1977.[15] That the PRI presided over a more equitable distribution of wealth, especially between the 1960s and early 1980s, fostered a sense of progress among the majority of Mexicans, as many witnessed an improvement in their material well-being. Even for those who did not personally enjoy such improvement, the fact that others did provided a sense of hope.

The PRI also administered significant land reform, but this was often incomplete and sporadic, and never lived up to the promise of the Mexican Revolution. Between 1915 and 1988, about 104 million hectares of land were redistributed, with almost half of this occurring during two *sexenios* of the PRI, the presidencies of Cárdenas (1934–1940, 20.14 million hectares) and Díaz Ordaz (1964–1970, 23.1 million hectares).[16] Not only did this reform progress in fits and starts, but it was also uneven in a regional sense. In Chiapas, for example, the initial effects of the revolution were minimal. By 1930, 1,500 farms of 500 or more acres accounted for about 80 percent of all land in the state, with *ejidos* representing only 3 percent. Significant land reform in the state did not occur until the period 1950–1970, when the number of *ejidatarios* (workers on cooperative agricultural land) doubled from 71,000 in 1950 to 148,000 in 1970. Despite this, land reform in Chiapas has been far from adequate.[17]

The economic policies of the PRI during this era were remarkably successful, and relied principally upon the model of import substitution industrialization (ISI). This involved substantial state intervention in the economy. Through heavy doses of protectionism, the system favored private and national Mexican capital. The underlying premise was that in order for Mexico to catch up to advanced capitalist countries, it would have to do so through a process of industrialization whereby the government would initially protect Mexican industry from foreign competition on what was viewed as an unlevel playing field. Until the 1970s, the ISI approach succeeded with flying colors. Between the mid-1930s and the 1970s, Mexico's average annual growth rate was an extraordinarily healthy 6 percent, considerably higher than any of its Latin American neighbors. Economically, Mexico was the epitome of the successfully strong and active state, a model that witnessed its conception in 1934.[18]

Thus a plethora of features underpinned the PRI's hegemony. Some of these included a revolutionary myth that fostered a common national identity, a resilient system of inclusionary corporatism, land and wealth distribution that benefited the majority population, and strong state intervention that directed the largest and most consistent aggregate economic growth rates in Latin America.[19] But hegemony is never complete. In Mexico, for example, there existed notable flashes of state repression during this era. These included the brutal repression unleashed by Mexican security forces against labor activists in Nuevo León in 1946, against telephone workers in 1958, and against railway workers in 1959. Protesting campesino leaders were the target of government wrath during a number of episodes in the early 1960s.[20] Further, while Mexico embodied many features of modernity, the country remained distinct from the ideal type in obvious ways. For example, its model of corporatism, though relatively inclusionary, was distant from Western democracy. And while industrialization was present in Mexico, there remained considerable remnants of pseudo-feudalism.

But despite those formidable idiosyncrasies, Mexico largely conformed to the broad patterns of modernity. It did so to an extent that exceeded its neighbors in Latin America. Mexican hegemony and modernity went hand in hand. But the tables turned near the end of the century. Beginning in the late 1960s, and definitely by the early 1980s, Mexican hegemony shattered as Western modernity faced its swan song. It was under these circumstances that the EZLN would emerge.

From Stability to Crisis: The PRI and Shattered Hegemony

Cracks in the PRI's hegemony appeared in 1968 with the Mexican army's notorious massacre of protesting students. The decade of the 1960s was infamous in much of the Western world for student activism, and the situation in Mexico mirrored this. Just days before the 1968 Olympic Games in Mexico City, university students rallied in the city's Tlateloco Plaza. The government had been providing increased access to higher education during this era, with one effect being the creation of an educated population who became increasingly critical of government policies and of the unipolar power of the PRI. In what is widely regarded as the most significant instance of military abuse up to this period, the armed forces opened fire upon the unarmed students. The Mexican public was clearly outraged, both by the government's intolerance of public protest and especially by the unnecessarily brutal methods by which the armed forces handled the situation. Rather than hushing social protest, the drama spawned mounting defiance and sparked the emergence of civil society in Mexico.

A twin to that brutal incident was a "dirty war" directed against suspected leftist guerrillas. A major uprising of homegrown Marxist insurgents appeared in the state of Guerrero on 23 September 1968. Over the next fifteen years, a more or less clandestine war—one not openly discussed at the time—was unleashed against the guerrillas and suspected subversives. The grim result was 1,500 suspected guerrillas murdered at the hands of the armed forces, with another 600 "disappeared."[21] As consent waned, the government demonstrated its willingness to unleash substantial coercion in an attempt to maintain general order. This clandestine war was the root of a subsequent rebel group, the Ejército Revolucionario Popular (EPR), and also saw the first appearance of leftist subversives in Chiapas.

The earthquake of 1985, the most significant natural disaster to strike Mexico City in the twentieth century, was a political watershed that sharply accelerated the development of the country's civil society. It occurred when the state apparatus had withered drastically in the wake of the debt crisis that emerged in 1982. Although the government had ordered citizens to remain indoors immediately after the earthquake struck, these commands were ignored as society produced impromptu citizen groups to come to the aid those who were trapped or injured. It was primarily society, and not the state, that successfully dealt with the severe consequences of the earthquake. It represented a clear omen to Mexicans of the vast yet untapped power of civil society. Further, it sparked an unstoppable momentum for the formation of social movements during the 1980s and 1990s. This was especially true in the context of the Mexican debt crisis and the emergence of neoliberalism, as NGOs began to perform roles previously assumed by the state.[22]

The Mexican debt crisis and the consequent advent of neoliberalism spelled the end of the PRI's hegemony. On 13 August 1982, Mexico announced it could no longer make payments on its debt to international creditors. The government had borrowed heavily during the 1970s, with much of the funds siphoned off by corrupt public and private officials. The result was a U.S.-led restructuring of the Mexican economy by the International Monetary Fund, a process that meant the implementation of neoliberal economics in Mexico.[23] Government social spending was cut drastically, state corporations were privatized, and protectionist laws were abandoned to allow for virtually unfettered foreign investment in areas previously dominated by Mexican capital or the Mexican state. This promoted the ascendancy of transnational capital in Mexico, and led to the formation of a faction of Mexican business that would politically represent such interests. Traditional domestic capital—a foundation for the PRI—was placed on the defensive in relation to the rising power of transnational capital. Thus after 1982 the PRI could no longer depend on the undivided loyalty of capital in Mexico. Many probusiness interests defected to the increasingly powerful Partido Acción Nacional (PAN), which eventually won the presidential elections in 2000.

Not only had the PRI lost the undivided support of capital that it had enjoyed since the 1930s, but the carpet was pulled out from the governing party in other realms as well. One of these was Labor. Following the debt crisis, the PRI no longer had available the vast resources required to co-opt Labor leaders and to distribute to the rank and file. This was the case not only in the industrial realm, but also with respect to the agricultural sector, where subsidies and infrastructural support declined precipitously after 1982.

Associated with neoliberal restructuring, and contributing to the demise of the PRI, was a sharp concentration of wealth that virtually undid all progress made on this front between 1950 and the early 1980s. For example, the top 10 percent of the population watched their wealth increase from 32.77 percent of total Mexican GNP in 1984, to 37.93 percent in 1989, to 38.16 percent in 1992, and to 41 percent in 1996. By 1994, when the EZLN emerged, the twenty-four richest Mexican families controlled as much wealth as the 25 million poorest Mexicans (out of a total population of 90 million). While the super-rich grew richer, about one-quarter of Mexico's small and nascent middle class fell back into official levels of poverty. About 57.5 million Mexicans lived under official levels of poverty or extreme poverty by 1994.[24] As wealth became concentrated while impoverishment grew, the Mexican state slashed social welfare programs dramatically, especially during the period 1983–1988. Social spending cascaded 31.5 percent in 1983 alone.[25] Hence the social safety net began to disappear at a time when it was needed the most.

Overall, the major pillars of the PRI's hegemony crumbled after 1982. Capital became fractured, with many former probusiness PRI supporters turning to the PAN. Labor no longer reaped its previous benefits, and consequently could not be co-opted so easily by the government. A reversal of progress toward fairer divisions of wealth, coupled with the slashing of social welfare during Mexico's worst economic crisis since the 1929–1933 Great Depression, meant that the PRI could no longer count on the widespread social consent that is the hallmark of hegemony. High-ranking military officers in Mexico during this period noted a relation between this economic crisis and the proliferation of subversive movements in Mexico. General Mario Acosta Chaparro, in a book he published in 1990, observed that "Russian and Cuban ideological penetration" of Mexico during the 1980s was "without doubt" a result of "the prolongation of an economic crisis without historical parallel in Mexico."[26]

All of this occurred against the backdrop of more obvious corruption and the criminalization of the Mexican political economy. Perhaps the epitome of Mexican electoral corruption is what is widely regarded as the fraudulent election in 1988 of President Carlos Salinas. He claimed, after a week-long delay in the announcement of official election results, to have won with 50.7 percent of electoral support. The PRI's reliance on apparent fraud alienated an already weary support base. It was another symptom of the PRI's loss of hegemony.

Beyond those issues, this era witnessed the parallel ascendancy of narcotrafficking.[27] Located next door to the planet's largest consumer of illicit drugs, Mexico was a natural as a producer of marijuana and opiates and as a conduit for Andean cocaine. The immense fortunes that flowed from this booming industry were an economic windfall for many of Mexico's struggling banks, and also supplied reserves that the government itself could tap into. Further, traffickers provided jobs and even social welfare projects to an economically ravished population. Strategically, narcotrafficking would be utilized by both the U.S. and Mexican governments as a pretext for launching counterinsurgency programs against leftist guerrillas in Mexico and elsewhere in Latin America, under the flimsy guise of the so-called war against drugs. Overall, narcotrafficking complemented the emergence of neoliberalism. The mammoth fortunes associated with it have exacerbated the already rampant corruption of the Mexican state, representing another nail in the coffin of the PRI's hegemony.

The official emergence of the EZLN on 1 January 1994 came against the backdrop of the most significant political and economic crisis to face Mexico since the revolution. The PRI's hegemony and legitimacy were in tatters. Economic malaise predominated, social programs had been slashed, and wealth was concentrated. Crime and corruption were on the ascendant. The solidifying myth of revolutionary nationalism disappeared against what some feared was the false promise to insert Mexico into the first world through membership in NAFTA.

Chiapas and the Emergence of the EZLN

Chiapas is a bastion of diversity. The central valley, in which the capital of Tuxtla Gutiérrez is located, is a relatively rich agricultural center dominated by campesinos. Across the mountains to the west, the Pacific coastal region has among the most fertile agricultural land in the state, and is also a prosperous commercial center for products moving up and down the coastal highway that connects Mexico to Guatemala. Guerrilla warfare and other intense social conflicts have largely been confined to the mountains and jungles of the eastern portion of the state, especially the Cañadas mountains and the Lacandona jungle. This zone of conflict in many ways resembles Guatemala more than Mexico. This is true with regard to the ethnic composition of Chiapas's indigenous population. It is also the case with respect to the historically appalling socioeconomic conditions in the state, which have more in common with poverty-stricken Central America than with the relatively more advanced Mexico. Indeed, Chiapas was a latecomer to Mexico, and remained part of Central America until 1824.

While significant land reform in Mexico generally began during the Cárdenas presidency in the 1930s, such redistribution arrived tardily in Chiapas, since it was not until the period 1950–1970 that any significant reform occurred in the state. During that era, the number of *ejiditarios* (workers on cooperative agricultural land) more than doubled from about 71,000 in 1950 to 148,000 in 1970. About half of all cultivated land was located in *ejidos* by 1970. But this land was often of much lower quality than that possessed by big landowners. In addition, land distribution was highly inequitable.[28] Compounding this problem was the escalation of overcrowding in the region. Chiapas had become a dubious safety valve for a wave of poverty-stricken and often indigenous migrants who were encouraged by the government to settle the area between 1940 and 1970.[29]

There were other important political dimensions associated with the flood of new settlers into Chiapas. Perhaps the most crucial was that these new arrivals did not conform to patterns of social control generally exercised by the PRI. Tens of thousands of such migrants, for example, were evangelical Protestants, who did not fit into the nexus of the cacique system, which connected the traditional Catholic Church, big landowners, and local political bosses. In that case, it was the element of religion that effectively disassociated a significant portion of the population from government control. In other cases, especially in the region of the Lacandona jungle and parts of the Cañadas mountains, the government was virtually absent, leaving the predominantly indigenous population to create their own forms of social and political organization.

This alienation between the government and much of the local population, in what later would become the conflict zone, took a radical turn in the 1970s. Part of this had to do with the context of critical politics that erupted throughout the Western world beginning in the late 1960s. It found expression in Mexico with regard to the 1968 student rebellion as well as the formation during that era of guerrilla groups. With respect to Chiapas, the radical nature of political developments was largely a product of two separate but related phenomena: a movement toward indigenous organization aimed at confronting the roots of their marginalization, and the advent of leftist liberation theology, which defied the conservative and sometimes oppressive politics of the traditional Catholic Church.

Samuel Ruiz, the bishop of the San Cristóbal diocese, converted to liberation theology after attending a 1968 Latin American bishops conference in Medellín, Colombia.[30] His diocese had a geographic reach comprising 80 percent of Chiapas's indigenous population. Since the church played such a fundamental role in the lives of the indigenous people in the state, and often represented their only major contact with the outside world, the shift toward liberation theology is of utmost significance.

What were the primary distinctions that marked these two forms of Catholicism? The traditional Catholic Church, which historically has been aligned with big landowners and which has assumed generally conservative political positions, tended to preach a doctrine of political docility. Quiet acceptance of life's harsh socioeconomic realities might be rewarded by a better life in heaven, according to this framework. Liberation theology, by contrast, argued that the downtrodden indigenous population should struggle vigorously for social justice in this world, rather than being passive victims. Indeed, Bishop Ruiz's sermons have made reference to Thomas Aquinas's concept of a "Just War," and have encouraged peaceful political struggle on the part of the indigenous people. Further, missionaries who promoted the doctrine of liberation theology in the 1970s and 1980s often referred to the plight of the indigenous who had resettled in the Cañadas mountains and in the Lacandona jungle as paralleling the experience of the Exodus.[31]

Hence it is important to appreciate that the religious element represents a key piece of the mosaic in Chiapas's political conflicts. Liberation theology stirred spirited dissent among a significant portion of the indigenous, especially vis-à-vis their social and economic predicament. It encouraged political activism and threatened traditional power networks. Indeed, the radical component of the Catholic Church has been a major supporter of the EZLN. Beyond liberation theology and the Catholic Church, tens of thousands of Protestants resided in the state in the last half of the twentieth century. Representing various denominations under the larger banner of Protestantism, this sizable population remained outside the political nexus of the PRI, big landowners, and traditional sectors of the Catholic Church. They have been a political force unto themselves. Overall, there are strong ties between religion and political conflict in Chiapas, and this remains an important backdrop to explain the emergence of the EZLN.

Alongside the development of political dissent with a religious tone, the indigenous population began to organize in its own right during the early 1970s. Through a major political misstep, the conservative Chiapas government requested Bishop Samuel Ruiz to organize a conference to commemorate the 500th anniversary of the death of Fray Bartolomé de las Casas. Delegations from various indigenous communities attended in abundance, including representatives from the Tzeltal, Tzotziles, Tojolobales, and Choles. The general result of the congress was twofold. First, the indigenous put forth a number of sweeping requests for better political and labor rights, as well as access to land, which they alleged was being encroached upon by large-scale ranchers. This was greeted with considerable alarm on the part of the government and wealthy power brokers. Second, and more important, the congress spawned a number of indigenous organizations that posed substantial challenges to traditional political arrangements. Many such groups became staunch supporters of the EZLN.

Yet another manifestation of radicalization during the late 1960s and 1970s was the influx into Chiapas of relatively small and clandestine subversive movements. Of particular significance was the arrival in about 1972 of the Fuerzas de Liberación Nacional (FLN). In 1974, part of this group was captured by the armed forces in the town of Ocosingo near the time of the indigenous congress noted above.[32] One member of this group who avoided captivity by the armed forces was Flavio César Yañez, who would later become instrumental in the formation of the EZLN.[33] Hence, while the FLN and other groups did not make a big splash in Chiapas during the 1970s, they represented yet another sign of the radicalization of the state that would form the context for the EZLN's emergence in the early 1980s.

Rapid changes were also occurring in the realm of hemispheric affairs during this period. The leftist tone of the 1979 Sandinista Revolution in Nicaragua sparked an immense militarization and counterinsurgency campaign in Central America on the part of the United States, which was unwilling to tolerate what it viewed as another Cuba in the hemisphere. The nightmare scenario for Washington would have been a domino effect whereby leftism spread from Nicaragua to other Central American states and then to Mexico. With regard to its specific effects in Chiapas, it meant the massive militarization of the state on the part of the Mexican armed forces. This was designed to seal the border with Guatemala in order to shield Mexico from a flood of Central American refugees. It was also meant to discourage a new wave of radical guerrillas from influencing Mexico itself.

Residents watched the repressive apparatus of the government grow in the region, at the same time that social and economic assistance went into sharp decline following the debt crisis. For example, agricultural subsidies, which represented a crucial pillar of support for much of the population of Chiapas, declined about 13 percent annually between 1983 and 1988. With the lack of such supports, the overall output of basic crops such as corn and beans fell by a margin of almost 20 percent even though land devoted to their production rose between 10 and 20 percent.[34] With continued migration to the Cañadas and the Selva Lacandona, overcrowding exacerbated existing tensions. State policies of land distribution, for example, did not keep pace with rising demand. This prompted land invasions by campesinos; the invasions numbered 128 in 1983 alone. This, in turn, was met by a murderous campaign on the part of wealthy landowners, with some estimates suggesting that about 800 campesinos died at the hands of paramilitary forces hired by landowners.[35] Moreover, by the mid-1980s about 99 percent of the Selva population had no electricity, potable water, mail, or telephones.[36] Overall, social injustice and the lack of badly needed development programs, against the backdrop of increasing government militarization in the region, served to alienate much of the population.

According to its own documents, the EZLN formed in the Lacandona jungle on 17 November 1983, composed of three meztizos and three indigenous members.[37] One of the meztizos in this founding core of the EZLN, Rafael Guillén, would later become its primary spokesperson and even a revolutionary pop star under the name of Subcomandante Marcos. Guillén, or Marcos, grew up in Tamaulipas, where his family owned a furniture store, and later received honors for his academic work at the Universidad Autónoma de México. As an obviously gifted intellectual, he later found work as a university lecturer. Reminiscing over the formation of the EZLN, Marcos noted that its founding members came from a "tradition of Latin American guerrillas of the 1970s, of vanguard groups, of Marxist-Leninist ideologues, who wanted to struggle for a transformation of the world that would lead to the dictatorship of the proletariat."[38] While this orientation would change considerably in the 1990s, a photo of Marcos in Havana in 1988 hints at the lingering of traditional guerrilla approaches among the EZLN throughout the 1980s.[39] Concerning the arming of this newfound guerrilla group, Marcos cryptically indicated that since 1983 the EZLN began to accumulate its weapons supply "little by little."[40]

After the formation of the Zapatistas in 1983, various phenomena helped to boost their popularity. Among these was the radicalization of what would later become the conflict zone. In particular, the EZLN would find strategic allies in the radical sector of the Catholic Church led by Samuel Ruiz. Indeed, the original Zapatistas assumed biblical names—Marcos, Daniel, Pedro, for example—in a manner that signaled their support for the teachings of liberation theology. In addition, from the outset the Zapatistas were primary promoters of indigenous rights. This paralleled the significant organization among indigenous movements in Chiapas that was already under way. Further, on a broader level the EZLN received more wind in its sails from the withering popularity of the federal and Chiapas governments. Internationally, the Zapatistas in the 1980s benefited from the inspiration of the Sandinistas in Nicaragua.

It was during this time that land issues became the focal point for the larger political struggle in Chiapas. Only 22 percent of the state's cooperative *ejidos* received access to government credit in the period 1985–1989, a proportion that dropped to 16.3 percent in 1990. In addition to the aforementioned difficulties experienced by cultivators of corn and beans, the coffee sector spun into crisis during this period, with a 35 percent fall in productivity between 1989 and 1993. This came amid political difficulties stemming from extreme concentration of land in the coffee sector.[41] Exacerbating the struggle for land was the acceleration of an ecological crisis in what would become the conflict zone. Between 1972 and 1990, a total of 585,000 hectares of land became deforested, some of this by private lumber companies and some by peasants desperate for land to cultivate. Piecemeal government projects created ecological reserves in the Selva, but did not provide sufficient programs that compensated for peasants seeking land. Hence the land reform issue collided with an ecological crisis.

For the Zapatistas, the decade of the 1990s meant the quest of adapting to profound change.[42] The issues of neoliberalism and indigenous rights continued to represent ideological centerpieces for the rebels, and both of these themes found expression in 1992. The EZLN regarded the pitfalls of neoliberalism as the principal global threat facing Mexicans. One manifestation of this was the notorious amendment in 1992 to Article 27 of the constitution, which codified the end of land reform in Mexico, and which permitted the privatization of *ejido* plots. The dream of possessing sufficient land for subsistence seemed further out of reach than ever for many residents of the Chiapas highlands and jungle. During this same year the indigenous population of the state, in commemoration of the 500th anniversary of Columbus's "discovery" of the Americas, riotously demonstrated against abuses to their dignity and rights. Over the course of this politically volatile period, evidence suggests that some indigenous groups in Chiapas were ready to launch an armed struggle, but were persuaded by Marcos that the time was still not ripe for violent action.[43] There were continued rumors of the presence of guerrillas in the mountains of Chiapas throughout 1993.

The EZLN: Ideology and Support Base

The clearest presentation of the EZLN's ideology has been through volumes of official documents released by the group since the eve of the uprising on 1 January 1994. But prior to this, and before the Zapatistas reached the public eye, Subcomandante Marcos authored an important piece in 1992 titled "Chiapas: The Southeast in Two Winds—A Storm and a Prophecy." Here, the message, the messenger, and eventually the medium are worthy of consideration. With regard to content, the work calls attention to the mounting ecological crisis in Chiapas, and to the horrific living standards endured by the indigenous people, who compose the majority of the state's population. The piece underscores, for example, that more than 80 percent of highland residents suffered from malnutrition at the time, and that Chiapas has had the highest mortality rate in the country, with many deaths occurring from curable diseases. For the EZLN, all this came in the context of imperialist exploitation of Chiapas's rich natural resources, such as gas and oil.

The EZLN's ideology, then, has a distinctly environmental tinge as well as an element of sympathy toward Marxism. It is critical of neoliberal economic policies and maldistribution of income.[44] In a sarcastic tone, Marcos writes: "Socialism has died. Long live conformity and reform and the modern world and capitalism and all of the cruelties that are associated with it." The ghost of Zapata is resurrected here to advocate indigenous rights—culturally, politically, and economically. "The oldest of the old in the Indigenous communities," according to Marcos, "say that there once was a man named Zapata who rose up with his people and sang out, 'Land and freedom.' These old campesinos say that Zapata didn't die, that he must return."[45] Marx and Zapata are two of Marcos's friendly ghosts, and populate many of his other works.

Subcomandante Marcos demonstrated his wide intellectual capacity and witty style of writing in this 1992 document. The tone is conversational, engaging, and very literary despite its wide scope. It reads like an engaging magazine article. Marcos speaks to the reader if he is providing a newcomer with an eye-popping informational tour of the state. The lead public relations person for the Zapatistas is no country bumpkin, and with this and other works he has established himself as one of Mexico's leading intellectual and literary figures. His literary sophistication partly underpinned Marcos's pop-star status, and represented an important distinguishing feature for the Zapatistas in attracting the support of urban sophisticates in Mexico City and globally. Another reflection of the EZLN's ingenuity was its use after 1994 of a revolutionary medium for its messages, the frontier of the Internet.

Perhaps the single most important document of the EZLN is its first "Declaration of the Lacandona Jungle," written in late December 1993, just prior to the 1 January 1994 uprising. Beginning with the words "Today we say enough!" the EZLN evoked the ghosts of Zapata and Villa as it attempted to rally its troops for war against the Mexican government. It is crucial to emphasize that the EZLN, in this piece, did indeed issue a declaration of war. It commanded its troops "to advance to the country's capital and to conquer the Mexican armed forces," and issued precise orders concerning the treatment of enemy troops and so on.[46]

That important theme is developed in another document from December 1993, when the EZLN authored the first text of its official magazine, *El Despertador Mexicano*. This inaugural edition was devoted to presenting the EZLN's "Declaration of War" against the Mexican armed forces, and also established a clear blueprint for the Zapatista army during their "advance for national territory."[47] The precision of the orders, which range from a sliding tax scale for private businesses that fall within Zapatista territory to issues concerning human rights among the civilian population, suggests that the EZLN was serious about its military objective. It apparently thought it could conquer key parts of the country.[48] These documents were presented within the context of what the leadership of the EZLN apparently considered would be a protracted military confrontation between the Zapatistas and the Mexican army. Overall, it is important to appreciate that the Zapatistas initially emerged in the cloak of a violent revolutionary struggle. The point is crucial, since the Zapatistas later would attempt reinvent themselves as an essentially peaceful and nonviolent force, but only after the Mexican military demonstrated that it had the capacity to quite easily obliterate the EZLN just days after the so-called war began.

In their first "Declaration of the Lacandona Jungle" the Zapatistas lamented that their declaration of war was a "method of last resort," but that the struggle was a just one for a number of reasons. It is through the EZLN's justification of warfare that its ideology becomes clearer. The Zapatistas criticized the appalling living standards of Chiapas's indigenous population, which they equated with a "war of genocide" on the part of the Mexican state. They complained about the lack of democracy under what they viewed as the illegitimate dictatorship of President Salinas (1988–1994). They argued that the people should reclaim the sovereign power vested in them by Article 39 of the Mexican constitution. The first declaration is also significant since it identifies the eleven central elements of the Zapatista political platform: work, land, shelter, food, health, education, independence, liberty, democracy, justice, and peace.[49]

Their ideological agenda came into closer focus at this time through the EZLN's magazine, *El Despertador Mexicano*. The periodical's first edition demanded fair wages for Mexican workers (by suggesting, for example, that foreign companies pay Mexicans the same wage they pay their nationals). There was a call for agrarian reform to restore the original spirit of Article 27 of the Mexican constitution. The Zapatistas also proposed a "Revolutionary Law of Women," which entailed a feminist platform of equal rights across the board. These included women's right to become revolutionaries and to participate politically in the EZLN and other organizations, to have access to basic health and education services and fair employment, and to control the number of children they have.[50] Indeed, beyond the indigenous population, women represented the single most important target of Zapatista propaganda.

With respect to support base, the first "Declaration of the Lacandona Jungle" was addressed to the "people of Mexico." Although the literature of the EZLN focused especially upon the plight of Chiapas's indigenous population as well as women, the Zapatistas more generally aimed their message at the majority of Mexicans, who were economically marginalized and alienated from the autocratic politics of the PRI. The accompanying document, *El Despertador Mexicano*, was also addressed to *progresistas* (progressives) from other countries.[51] The international dimension of its audience was further cultivated in the coming years. This was principally facilitated when, shortly after this initial declaration, the Zapatistas attempted to widen their reach by posting their documents on the Internet.

Armed conflict between the Mexican armed forces and the Zapatistas terminated on 12 January 1994. During the twelve days of battle, Marcos addressed a letter "To the People of Mexico, to the People and Governments of the World," in which he attempted to clarify the origins, affiliations, and political positions of the EZLN.[52] He denied categorically that the EZLN was influenced by foreign interests, he negated alleged ties between the organization and the Catholic Church, and he pointed out that the Zapatistas were composed overwhelmingly of indigenous Chiapas residents. The letter appeared to be designed in part to manage the anticipated fears of both Mexicans and Americans. It emphasized a "special call to the people and government of North America" to form solidarity with the Zapatistas, and requested that Washington sever its military and economic assistance to the Mexican government.[53] A very similar correspondence from the EZLN was sent on 13 January 1994, "To President Bill Clinton, the Congress and the people of the United States," the day after combat ceased between the Zapatistas and the Mexican army.[54] Hence, virtually from the start, the targeted audience of the Zapatistas has had an important global dimension, with a particular emphasis on the United States.

Within two months after their first public appearance, the Zapatistas vigorously began to assemble a national and international support base among NGOs and social movements. As the painful reality regarding the vast military superiority of the Mexican armed forces vis-à-vis the Zapatistas became apparent, the EZLN urged civil society to develop "other forms of struggle."[55] This amounted to inciting the peaceful efforts of transnational NGO networks that were critical of various facets of Mexican government policy. For example, the Zapatistas addressed a letter to the students of the Universidad Nacional Autónoma de México (UNAM) in Mexico City, attempting to conjure support among its tens of thousands of students.[56] More generally, the EZLN identified sympathetic NGOs as representing a social movement leading the charge for peace and dignity in Chiapas and elsewhere.[57] On 1 February 1994, a couple weeks after the EZLN had been effectively defeated militarily at the hands of the Mexican armed forces, the Zapatistas went to so far as to request that Mexican NGOs form a "belt of peace" to separate the Mexican army from the EZLN so that dialogue could be pursued.[58] The Zapatistas would emerge as heroes nationally and globally among an assortment of NGOs whose interests included indigenous rights, anti-neoliberalism, human rights, and ecological issues.

In an effort to win the support of NGOs and social movements, the EZLN began to refine and disseminate its positions on political, economic, and social issues. In March 1994, for example, the Zapatistas demanded specific indigenous rights including political, economic, and cultural autonomy. They insisted upon new elections in the state of Chiapas, the reform of NAFTA to include better labor rights, and the establishment of new human rights commissions. In vain, the Zapatistas pleaded publicly with the police and military to retreat from their positions in the Chiapas highlands.

Another facet of the EZLN's gift for public relations has been its mastery at using political anniversaries to plug its agenda vis-à-vis the media, NGOs, and the interested public. The anniversary of Zapata's death on 10 April 1994 was used as a platform to promote land rights; the anniversary of the 1968 student massacre on 2 October 1994 was employed to rally scorn at escalating military repression; while the commemoration of Columbus's "discovery" of the Americas set the stage for the EZLN's critique of foreign intervention and domination.[59] With increasing vigor and frequency, the Zapatistas broadcast through the Internet colorful and engaging propaganda with a global reach.

While the popularity of the Zapatistas peaked from 1994 to early 1995, there were some prominent public relations blunders that blemished the EZLN's otherwise stellar record at building a political support base during this period. For example, a tear-jerking letter supposedly written by Zapatista children between six and twelve years old, "To the children of Mexico and the world," looks as if it could have been written by an adult public relations expert. Overall, it comes across as false and highly manipulative.[60] On another occasion, the EZLN provided an ambiguous response when challenged by a popular Mexican feminist who wondered aloud about the Zapatistas' position on abortion, birth control, and related issues in the context of the EZLN's close political relation to the Catholic Church in Chiapas under Bishop Samuel Ruiz.[61]

In what is perhaps one of their most serious political miscalculations, the Zapatistas delivered a severe critique of the center-left Partido de la Revolución Democrática (PRD), led by Cuauhtémoc Cárdenas. The EZLN argued that the party was definitely not the solution to Mexico's profound problems. Marcos suggested that rather than Cárdenas's PRD, what was required was the abandonment of the entire party system. Also necessary, in the view of Marcos, was the creation of a new constitution, the establishment of a transitional government, and a radically revamped political structure that would provide power to the marginalized masses.[62] While Marcos's points are substantial, his criticism of the PRD served to alienate one of the Zapatistas' natural allies. Certainly it did nothing to help the wilting campaign of Cárdenas, who was running for president at the time. Of the three major contenders, Cárdenas would likely have been the most sympathetic toward the Zapatistas.

The relationship between the EZLN and its support base has been one of considerable interaction, whereby the Zapatistas have provided leadership but have accepted and encouraged strong input. One early example of this was an international consultation conducted by the EZLN through the Internet and through the efforts of a variety of NGOs in June 1994. Officially it was designed to seek direction on the future course of the conflict. The central question that was posed was whether or not to reignite violent protest, which was rejected by 96.74 percent of the over 64,000 people who voted. That response was highly predictable, given the military impotence of the Zapatistas. But here the process is more important than the less than surprising outcome. By utilizing such a consultation, the Zapatistas not only developed their democratic base, but also cultivated a bottom-up flow of ideas from their supporters. Further, the EZLN could now claim that its supporters requested that the group halt hostilities, rather than dwelling on the fact that it would be powerless to launch such hostilities in the first place.[63]

The EZLN prolifically produced letters and pronouncements that outlined its ideological positions. By June 1994, with the "Second Declaration of the Lacandona Jungle," much of this assumed a repetitive tone.[64] But toward the end of the year, with Mexico in a political and economic freefall, the messages of the EZLN sounded increasingly engaging and credible. By December 1994–January 1995, the Mexican government was mired in what was arguably its worst crisis since the revolution. The assassination of the PRI's original 1994 presidential candidate, Donaldo Colosio, escalated a political imbroglio that soon helped precipitate the 1994–1995 peso crisis. Chaos within the PRI and unmanageable debt and balance of payments problems, combined with the ever brasher rhetoric of the Zapatistas, led to a speculative run on the Mexican peso that eventually resulted in a nearly U.S.$50 billion rescue package. In January 1995, the Zapatistas issued their "Third Declaration of the Lacandona Jungle," calling on civil society to help topple what looked to the Zapatistas to be a very debilitated government. Their message had not changed much—there was the continued emphasis on developing civil society, forming a transition government, abandoning the party system, and so on.[65] This period of the government's lowest ebb was, conversely, the Zapatistas' high watermark of credibility.

February 1995–August 1996:
The EZLN Loses Military Power

Some have referred to the EZLN as the first postcommunist guerrillas, as information-age guerrillas, as postmodern guerrillas, and the like. What is truly remarkable, though, is that the Zapatistas have the status of a guerrilla group at all. Following the assault by the Mexican military in February 1995, the Zapatista army was sealed into a relatively small enclave and completely neutralized militarily. If the Zapatistas are "post" anything, they are postmilitary guerrillas. Given their military predicament, after February 1995 the Zapatistas concentrated more than ever on winning the sympathy of NGOs and social movements.[66] They found support among those who wished to criticize neoliberalism in general, among those who were scornful of the Mexican government and economy, and among the indigenous population in Chiapas and elsewhere.[67] They attempted to build a support base by harnessing the organized efforts of those who were excluded and powerless within the existing social structures.

A torrent of witty ideas flowed from the EZLN during this period. Among the most important were the group's views on political participation and democracy. For example, in January 1996 the Zapatistas proposed the formation of the Frente Zapatista de Liberación Nacional (FZLN), a political movement representing Zapatista interests.[68] Moreover, in preparation for the San Andrés negotiations with the government, they suggested new and more active forms of political participation such as consultations, referendums, plebiscites, and better access to information and communications.[69] In fact, many of the Zapatistas' own positions at the negotiations had been established through a democratic consultation process with local and global participants. The areas of communication and participation have been a strong suit for the EZLN.

During this period the Zapatistas provided crucial ideological assessments of two relatively new but quite different actors on the Mexican political stage: the PAN and the EPR. Regarding the PAN—the party that dethroned the PRI and assumed the presidency in 2000—the Zapatistas voiced some clear concerns that seemed to presage their assessment of President Vicente Fox. The EZLN wrote that the PAN supported essentially the same economic model as the PRI, and that in relation to this, "the alteration of power is not synonymous with democratic change."[70] Hence the Zapatistas suggested that a PAN victory should not necessarily be viewed as democratic progress in Mexico if it meant the perpetuation of neoliberalism and corrupt authoritarianism.

Brimming with hostility and criticism, the EZLN in August 1996 addressed a letter to the EPR that attempted to distance the Zapatistas from that group. Paradoxically, Marcos essentially suggests in this letter that the EPR is a "bad guerrilla" group. Yet he rejects the dichotomy presented by the government, which portrays the EZLN as relatively good and nonviolent guerrillas, while casting the EPR as malevolent and militaristic subversives.[71] Regardless, Marcos criticizes the EPR for, among other things, wanting to take power militarily in the traditional manner of guerrilla movements. This stands in sharp contrast, he says, to the "new and radical" Zapatistas who wished to gain legitimacy without using arms. This view, though, was hypocritical, given that the Zapatistas had begun as a military guerrilla group and only converted to the peaceful route once the Mexican army had neutralized their military power. The thrust of the message seemed to be a warning from Marcos to the EPR to stay out of Chiapas in what he apparently perceived to be a turf war.[72]

Not surprisingly, many of the EZLN's communications during this period complained of escalating military repression and of the government's alleged alliance with paramilitary security forces. These internationally disseminated documents portrayed the Zapatistas as a local and global symbol of military victimization under neoliberalism through the strategy of low-intensity conflict. The tone of these critiques grew darker from February 1995 to August 1996, when the Zapatistas and the government suspended negotiations on the San Andrés Accords.[73] Near the time of this rupture, the EZLN more vigorously than ever called for the creation of a "network of communication" and of an "intercontinental network of resistance" against Mexican repression and global neoliberalism.[74]

Beyond the shine of the rather sophisticated story line of Zapatista propaganda, a great appeal of this literature is the manner in which the story is told. This is especially the case with respect to the writings of Marcos, who continued to author a variety of works that are engaging, informative, and often persuasive.[75] His creative repertoire features a wide cast of characters. One of these is the popular Durito, a beetle distinguished from the rest of his species by his wide critical familiarity with the perils of neoliberalism. Much of this work has been sprinkled with a dose of humor and self-deprecation, such as when he signed his name "sup-delinquent Marcos."[76] Further, Marcos has not been shy about name-dropping, and when he does he demonstrates a commanding artistic sensibility. For example, his works make note of Shakespeare, Stephen Stills, Miguel de Cervantes and Don Quixote, Jane Fonda and Barbarella, Cyrano de Bergerac, Bertolt Brecht, as well as the usual revolutionary ghosts of Emiliano Zapata, Che Guevara, and Simón Bolívar. Making the depressing and complicated mosaic of war-torn Chiapas seem interesting and changeable has been one of Marcos's principal talents. He put his talents to use during this period when the Zapatistas badly needed it, when the power of public relations would have to compensate for the erosion of military might.

1996–2001:
Ebb and Revival

The San Andrés negotiations between the government and the Zapatistas were suspended in August 1996. This rupture was largely the result of the perception by the EZLN and others that the PRI would not live up to the accords, against the backdrop of heavy militarization of the state. The EZLN also faced severe military challenges. About 30,000 to 40,000 Mexican troops encircled the 3,000-strong Zapatista army, and paramilitary attacks against Zapatista sympathizers were on the rise. The group's analyses during this period were often enlightening. But increasingly its messages came across as repetitive and tired. By early 2000 the Zapatistas would seem out of synch with a good portion of their previous support base, especially regarding the elections of that year. But the tide would turn in favor the EZLN once again, following the group's trek to the nation's capital in early 2001.

On 29 August 1996 the EZLN listed five conditions that would have to be fulfilled for the group to return to the San Andrés negotiations: the liberation by the government of presumed Zapatistas taken captive; the establishment of an interlocutor between the EZLN and the government; the establishment of a verification commission; concrete proposals especially in the area of democracy and justice; and the termination of military repression against the Zapatistas and its supporters.[77] But the government and the Zapatistas were unable to achieve even the minimal consensus necessary to return to negotiations. This suspension of dialogue, which lasted through the close of the century, combined with the military predicament of the EZLN, triggered the onset of a sense of hopelessness in the conflict zone.

Throughout much of 1997 the EZLN continued to author sophisticated critiques of the Mexican political economy. Almost all its documents were posted on the group's website and were addressed to both a local and an international audience. Highlighted themes in their works included the predominance of narcotrafficking and crime in Mexico, as well as many familiar themes regarding neoliberalism and indigenous rights. The pieces written by Marcos cemented his position as one of Mexico's principal intellectual critics and writers.[78] The horrific crescendo of 1997 came in December with the Acteal massacre, in which paramilitaries attacked and killed forty-five innocents in the highlands of Chiapas. The massacre lent credence to the Zapatistas' repeated complaints regarding Mexican military repression and the presence of paramilitary groups that target the left.[79]

While their critiques of the Mexican system remained enlightening, a misinterpretation of the classic Chinese strategist Sun Tzu in one of the Zapatistas' major documents suggests the group's continued weakness in the strategic realm.[80] Marcos, for example, began one of his major works by using the very first sentence from Sun Tzu's *The Art of War:* "Military action is important to the nation—it is the ground of death and life, the path of survival and destruction, so it is imperative to examine it." Marcos used the quote to decry the militaristic aspects of the Mexican state, and particularly to criticize repression directed at the EZLN in Chiapas. Yet a careful reading *The Art of War* clearly suggests that Sun Tzu was arguing that the state refrain from repressing its own people. Sun Tzu suggested instead that the government should follow the Taoist principal of "the Way" and work in harmony with the population to cultivate societal consent.[81] Rather than misassociating Sun Tzu with the PRI, the Zapatistas might have made an heroic ghost of him.

The Zapatistas did not have any significant new fodder for their propaganda machine until the student strike at Mexico City's UNAM in May 1999. Indeed, their communiqués during this period seemed to rehash old but nevertheless important themes.[82] To commemorate the eightieth anniversary of the death of Zapata, for example, the EZLN quoted Zapata's old but pertinent observation that "the rich are getting richer."[83] But a sense of urgency resurfaced in the spring of 1999, when Mexico's first major social disturbance since 1994–1995 appeared in the form of the massive student strike on the huge UNAM campus. The strike, which closed the university for about nine and a half months, began with a clash over the issue of raising tuition from about U.S.2¢ to U.S.$75 per semester and of implementing stiffer entrance requirements. Eight months into the strike, the new rector offered to retract the tuition hikes and to respect other student demands. But the protest continued on a wider platform of anti-neoliberalism.[84] Finally, 2,400 police entered the university and more or less peacefully broke up the strike on 6 February 2000.

The EZLN, through a number of letters and communiqués, identified the leaders of the student strike as Zapatista compatriots. Phrases like "Long live youth and rebels" peppered the EZLN's *comunicados* on this theme.[85] Hence the group attempted to expand its support base by appealing to backers of the UNAM strike. This strategy was not altogether successful, since it appears that although the Mexican public did not want violence to be used against the strikers, as the months wore on they no longer supported the strike's continuation.[86] This, combined with the reserved and remarkably patient response by the Mexican government during this affair, meant that strike leaders and not the state were generally perceived as the problem once the affair had ended. Thus the strike did not boost in any substantial manner the support base of the Zapatistas.

A watershed in the form of a crisis appeared for the Zapatistas with respect to the state and federal elections in the summer of 2000. In June of that year, just prior to the elections, the EZLN declared its lack of support by indicating that "this electoral time is not the time for the Zapatistas." The EZLN found fault with what it viewed as a biased media and with the preponderant resources of the PRI. The group concluded that "no elections under such conditions could be considered fair. . . . For the Zapatistas, democracy is much more than electoral content or an alteration of power. It is also an electoral contest that is clean, equitable, honest and plural."[87] Yet those elections ousted the seven-decade reign of the PRI, both federally and in Chiapas. It indicated to many that the EZLN seriously misjudged the situation.

This episode was crucial. On the one hand, high abstention votes in the conflict zone—at a rate of 50.6 percent in the July 2000 presidential race, and 47.8 percent in the August 2000 race for governor of Chiapas—seem to indicate that many residents took heed of the Zapatistas' view that the electoral process was a farce.[88] On the other hand, and more broadly, both elections demonstrated that effective change could be made through the Mexican electoral system.[89] Further, the election results apparently took the EZLN by surprise, and perhaps launched the group into profound crisis. This is evidenced by the group's long and noticeable silence after the elections. Overall, it is probable that the EZLN lost some of its support base as a result of this situation, since the Zapatistas underestimated the political potential of the ballot box.

Yet there remained severe concerns in the electoral arena, and in Mexico's political system more generally, that could spell problems on the horizon and therefore vilify the Zapatistas. There was certainly a great deal of initial optimism among Mexicans regarding the presidency of Vicente Fox and the ouster of the PRI. But these rising expectations must be met or a severe crisis could be precipitated. That is, if the Fox team and his successors come to be perceived as corrupt like the PRI, if primarily the rich seem to benefit, there could be a serious political backlash by the population. Moreover, even after these successful elections, the problems that came to light in Chimalhuacán in the summer of 2000 demonstrated the lingering corruption associated with the cacique system as well as the crisis of the Mexican corporatist model.[90] Overall, considerable progress was made in 2000 with regard to Mexican democracy, but much remained to be done.

Other factors may have contributed to the erosion of the influence and support base of the EZLN at the turn of the century. Not the least of these was a spending spree on the part of the federal government to win the hearts and minds of the population in and near the conflict zone. Under the presidency of Ernesto Zedillo, the federal government increased social spending in Chiapas at the rate of 5 percent annually in real terms between 1995 and 1999. With regard to education, there was a 31 percent increase in teachers and a 53 percent increase in schools during those years. Health care consultations increased by 65 percent and surgeries by 35 percent. Coordinated poverty-fighting programs such as Progesa were established, and employment was generated by major public works projects such as the construction of highways.[91] Hence, in addition to the repressive features of government policy, of which the Zapatistas complained bitterly, the Mexican state also attempted to redress some of the social problems plaguing residents.

There have been repeated allegations that the fruits of such programs sometimes have been distributed in a manner that denies access to Zapatista supporters, but provides access to supporters of the government or to those who remain neutral.[92] Regardless, it is obvious that the state has attempted to buy the influence of real or potential Zapatista supporters with social programs, at the same time that it has vigorously repressed dissent. But since these social programs have provided actual benefit to the daily lives of its recipients, the plan has been working to a significant extent. The message that the government has been sending to residents of the conflict zone is that they have no real hope with the Zapatistas, but that they can benefit from electoral participation and through government social programs. Ultimately, the strategy has contributed to the slow erosion of the Zapatistas' influence and support base.

By this point the EZLN had suffered two other losses to its support base. The first, and perhaps most serious, was the retirement of Bishop Samuel Ruiz in November 1999. Since the early 1970s the liberation theology Ruiz had promoted helped to mobilize the indigenous communities of Chiapas who later supported the Zapatistas. While Ruiz had no official connection to the EZLN, he was ideologically close to the group and helped construct its support base. Second, during 1999 the Mexican government had engaged in a campaign to expel what it viewed as foreign troublemakers, that is, foreign members of pro-Zapatista NGOs working in Chiapas. This represented an attempt by the government to help neutralize the threat of what it perceived as unfriendly global social networks. To some extent, the attempt may have diminished Zapatista support in this realm.[93] Any effect, however, was of a temporary nature, since the Fox government dismantled much of its predecessor's anti-NGO policy.

The spirits of the Zapatistas and their supporters were lifted considerably in early 2001 with the historic trek of the EZLN from Chiapas to the nation's capital of Mexico City. Huge crowds greeted Zapatista leaders as they bussed their way through southern Mexico—the region of the country with the highest indigenous population and with the worst levels of poverty. Tens of thousands of supporters crammed Mexico City's *zocolo* to welcome the EZLN. Beginning on 24 February 2001, the trek's finale was a historic speech before the Mexican Congress on March 28 by key members of the Zapatista leadership. In terms of support base, the EZLN's public relations tour demonstrated the continued popularity and political relevance of the group, as well as the sustenance of its role as a symbol of indigenous rights and of dignity for the socially marginalized. Indeed, throughout the plethora of pronouncements by the Zapatista leaders, the theme of indigenous rights was dominant. The trip itself was deemed "The March for Indigenous Dignity." Speaking before the Mexican Congress, Comandante David argued that "the hour of the Indian people has arrived."[94]

Overall, the trip brought the EZLN back into the limelight, and provided a boost to its popularity. The episode indicated that the ideology and support base of the EZLN had not changed much since it burst onto the scene in 1994. The Zapatistas were protected by the Mexican army during their entire trip—the same army upon which they had declared war. Thus there were important contrasts between this trek and the historic march to power by Zapata almost a century earlier.

In the late 1990s and into the first year of the twenty-first century the general mood in Mexico was upbeat. This was a result of the ouster of the PRI in the summer of 2000, combined with healthy macroeconomic growth during the late 1990s. Such a positive scenario may have diminished somewhat the popularity and relevance of the EZLN during that era. But the context changed considerably by 2001. Data appeared that demonstrated an undertow of serious social and economic problems. The Mexican Labor Congress showed, for example, that there was a 70 percent decrease in real salaries between 1970 and 2000, with the 1994–2000 period characterized by a serious erosion of purchasing power.[95] Further, while the GDP per capita increased 3.4 percent in the period 1964–1981, it rose only 0.3 percent during the period 1982–2000. Other data suggest intensifying inequity and poverty among Mexicans near the turn of the century. It was estimated that in 2000, only 31 percent of youths ages fifteen to twenty attended any formal school, and that between 30 percent and 50 percent of the active population worked in the informal sector.[96] More than 40 percent of Mexicans survived on less than U.S.$2 per day.[97] While poverty remained significant by any measure, what is remarkable is the huge range of estimates that stretch from 28 percent to 53 percent of the population living in extreme poverty in 2000, compared to 15 percent in 1984 and 16 percent in 1992.[98]

Mexico entered a recession in 2001, with the economy contracting by 0.37 percent that year. Some 80 to 90 percent of its exports were destined for the United States, which had showed signs of a considerable economic slowdown earlier in that year. Rather than the 1.4 million jobs that President Fox had pledged to create, it was estimated that the country actually lost 825,000 jobs between January and August 2001.[99] Against this backdrop, the Fox government admitted in the summer of 2001 that economic inequity in Mexico had reached the worst levels in the country's history, with the top 10 percent of the population controlling 53 percent of the country's wealth.[100] That bad news could be good news for the Zapatistas. The leaders of the EZLN have proven themselves to be masters at riding waves of social discontent, and were poised to do so once again when the opportunity arose.

Conclusion

While much can rightly be made of all that is new with regard to the Zapatistas, it should also be emphasized that they have reflected strong traditional influences and circumstances. For a group that gained notoriety by using words rather than arms, the choice of its name is significant. Emiliano Zapata is, of course, the EZLN's principal ghost.[101] This role demonstrates that, at the dawn of the twenty-first century, the myth of Zapata's struggle for land and liberty during the Mexican Revolution continued to ring true for much of the marginalized population in Chiapas and elsewhere in Mexico. The Zapatistas have focused on some fundamental problems such as widespread inequity and racism that have existed prior to the Mexican Revolution, but that have yet to be resolved. In this sense, the EZLN demonstrates the continuity and longevity of Mexico's internal struggles.

This continuity is also reflected by some of the other ghosts that haunt the Zapatista discourse. There is certainly a presence of Karl Marx in the analysis employed by the EZLN, since much of the group's viewpoint seems to reflect a fresh and rather broad interpretation of the historical materialist framework. That is, economic factors associated with class and production (e.g., neoliberalism, low Mexican wages) are considered in dialectical relation to government structure (e.g., the corrupt authoritarianism of the PRI), ideological forces (e.g., the U.S. vision of NAFTA), security structures (e.g., militarization under NAFTA), ethnic relations, and the like. Zapatista rhetoric also reflects the influence of a roster of post-Marxists. Gramsci's emphasis on the power of ideas and his advocacy of a "war of position" designed to build widespread social resistance at a time when armed struggle is not prudent are prominent in the EZLN's analysis.[102] So, too, is Gramsci's conception of hegemony.

There are other prominent spirits surrounding the Zapatistas. The ghost of Che Guevara is discernible. His tract *Guerrilla Warfare* is especially apparent in some of the EZLN's communiqués authored before and during the group's remarkably short-lived period as actual military guerrillas (1–12 January 1994).[103] In addition, Nicaragua's Sandinistas, which reigned from 1979 to 1990, provided some negative lessons for the Zapatistas. These include the pitfalls associated with a reliance upon a foreign power, and the likely consequence of U.S. intervention to quash any sign of potent leftism in Latin America. But in a highly positive sense, revolutionary Nicaragua in the 1980s demonstrated the importance of NGOs for leftist struggles. Indeed, many of the NGOs dedicated to Latin American affairs in North America and Europe during the 1980s had as their focus Central America and usually Nicaragua. This should be viewed as a precursor for the network of social movements with which the Zapatistas have associated.

Beyond the leftist ghosts that have populated much of the EZLN's ideological platform, the rebel group also heralds much that is new. One way to highlight the unique contribution of the Zapatistas is to compare them to the EPR, a more traditional and rather obscure Mexican rebel group.[104] That outfit, an offshoot of a small guerrilla movement in Guerrero that was the object of a government-led "dirty war" from the late 1960s to the late 1970s, was officially founded in May of 1994. Hence the EPR appeared against the backdrop of a legacy of subversive tendencies in the state of Guerrero that stretched back some thirty or forty years. In the context of a severe economic crisis, tension between peasants and authorities in the state had been escalating for an extended period prior to the June 1995 massacre by government forces of seventeen members of the Organización Campesina de la Sierra del Sur (OCSS), a leftist peasant group. The atrocity, which occurred not far from the popular resort of Acapulco, apparently invigorated the nascent

EPR. The guerrilla group did not surface publicly until the summer of 1996, to commemorate the one-year anniversary of the massacre.

The EPR has attempted to represent the interests of marginalized peasants who feel that armed struggle is their only reasonable hope of achieving fundamental socioeconomic change. The group has remained at large, and has been responsible for flashes of armed attacks in various Mexican states through 2001. It has had no claim or control over specific territory, but may have had a roving presence in as many as eight states. While the EPR is significant to the extent that it was indeed an active guerrilla group in Mexico, it is has not demonstrated a broader importance. Its membership has been unclear and appears to have been quite limited. It has not developed the network of expressed support from NGOs and social movements that the Zapatistas have enjoyed. In addition to a limited support base, its various military attacks have not inflicted particularly significant damage. Hence, due to apparently weak popular support combined with anemic political and military power, at the dawn of the twenty-first century the EPR could not yet be considered a major guerrilla group. But the problems identified by the EPR are indeed significant, and a comparison of the group with the Zapatistas can assist in demonstrating the latter's ingenuity and novelty.

The themes addressed by both rebel groups are remarkably similar. The EPR's "Manifiesto de la Sierra Madre Oriental," for example, offers a litany of critical issues and themes that rhyme with the Zapatistas' agenda. These include the demand for a new constitution and a provisional government, as well as pronounced anti-neoliberalism on number of dimensions. Similarities also entail a call for indigenous autonomy and an emphasis on the necessity of land reform. The evils of paramilitary forces are highlighted. Additional themes include a demand for basic welfare across the board, the abolishment of racism, and praise for revolutionary heroes such as Zapata and Villa.[105] Throughout other documents as well, the EPR mirrors the positions of the EZLN. The EPR, for example, has criticized narcotrafficking and the related corruption of the state, has noted the similarity between Fox and the previous Mexican governments, and has provided moral support for UNAM strikers in their contest against neoliberalism.[106] Overall, the EPR has found fault with many of the same problems identified by the Zapatistas, and in some cases seemed to surpass them.[107]

Given these thematic similarities, what are the relevant distinctions between the two groups? It has already been mentioned that one major difference between them is that the EPR apparently has wished to take power militarily. This difference may flow from the two groups' distinct military predicaments, since the EPR has been militarily at large while the Zapatistas have been strategically contained. Still, the EZLN is ideologically closer to the Gramscian "war of position" than it is to the more traditional guerrilla stance of "taking" power militarily and initiating a dictatorship of the proletariat. Indeed, a close reading of the EPR's literature indicates that the group is influenced ideologically more by classical Marxism than by Gramsci and other post-Marxists. Evidence of this is the EPR's principal reliance on Marxist notions of class struggle and dialectical change, compared to the Zapatistas' broader, looser, and more complex analyses of politics.[108]

Beyond the issue of strategy (see Chapter 7), the biggest differences between the EPR and the Zapatistas are their communication styles and support base. While the *comunicados* of the EPR are clear and to the point, they lack the intellectual spark, analytical vigor, and refined literary style that characterize the works of Subcomandante Marcos. This difference is related to their bases of support. The Zapatistas have fully exploited the intellectual capacities of Marcos to construct a support base that surpasses the indigenous population in Chiapas, and that stretches to big Mexican cities and to the "global village." The EPR, by contrast, has had a much more limited support base and political appeal. Its backers have been principally small pockets of marginalized indigenous peasants in Guerrero and Oaxaca, and to a lesser extent in Veracruz, Hidalgo, Chiapas, and elsewhere. It has not received the stated support of scores of domestic and global NGOs, as have the Zapatistas. The EPR's militaristic tone, its traditional Marxist lenses, and its relatively unsophisticated public relations capacity have limited the group's appeal. While it has possessed some military power that the Zapatistas have lacked, the EPR's political power has been close to nil.

While the Zapatistas represent substantial continuity with the past, a comparison of the EZLN with the more traditional EPR helps reveal prominent areas where the Zapatistas are untraditional. They have been militarily weak, but strong in the realms of communications and constituency-building. Traditional guerrillas, like the EPR in Mexico, the FARC in Colombia, and Sendero Luminoso in Peru, gained clout through military strength. The Zapatistas have gained any influence they possess through intellectual power and an impressive public relations machine.

The EZLN is unique in many other respects. The group has cultivated power through its keen ability to place its collective finger on the pulse of change, domestically and globally. The Zapatistas appeared simultaneously with the emergence of major global ruptures in both material and epistemological realms, and have exploited some of these to their benefit. For example, by January 1994, Mexico was deep into a crisis of authority. The Mexican government under the PRI had lost its hegemony, and relied increasingly upon coercion rather than consent.[109] New under the sun, then, was a crisis of the PRI's authority and of Mexican stability, and the EZLN took considerable advantage of this.

What is also novel, at least in some respects, is what the Zapatistas have set out to achieve since 12 January 1994. Initially the EZLN surely looked as if it wanted to take power when it ordered its troops to march to the Mexican capital and defeat the Mexican military along the way. But it later made necessity into a virtue by claiming it no longer wished to take power but desired instead to contribute to profound structural change aimed at redressing the inequities of neoliberalism and racism. The EZLN has been joined in this general task by many social movements and NGOs. Compared to traditional Latin American guerrilla movements that have aspirations of leading the state, the EZLN instead may have more in common with the aims of transnational social movements. To the extent, for example, that the Zapatistas have represented a localized symbol of defiance against global neoliberalism, they are similar in nature to the massive social protests that have occurred in Seattle and elsewhere. Hence another facet of the EZLN's untraditional power has been its role as a global symbol of indigenous rights and of anti-neoliberalism.

In many ways, the Zapatistas have worked with new forms of power and knowledge. They have been associated with the power of transnational social movements, as well as with the power of propagating words and ideas over the Internet and through other modes of instantaneous global communication. While one should not overestimate the extent to which the Zapatistas have used such technology, it is clear that they indeed have employed it to their benefit. They explored more fully than any other guerrilla group in their generation the spaceless and real-time politics of the Internet. The EZLN has certainly has gotten mileage out of Marcos's odd power of posing as a pseudo-guerrilla pop star, with his most popular venue being cyberspace.

The significance of spirituality among Zapatista supporters also suggests a new approach to knowledge. Rather than relying solely on the empirical or the material, the EZLN has incorporated spiritual knowledge into social struggle. Abandoning the classic Marxist dogma that relegates religion the role of opiate of the people, spirituality and leftist social struggle became intertwined through the movement of liberation theology. This phenomenon made its first widely felt appearance in Central America and in Chiapas in the 1980s, and has underpinned the Zapatistas' endeavors since 1994.

Also new is a fresh roster of political players, a shift appreciated by the Zapatistas. The old list of the state, labor, the military, and political parties has been joined by NGOs and social movements, regional political structures under NAFTA, global economic speculators, and the escalating role of the United States in almost every facet of Mexican society including the military realm. Overall, the players have changed, and so has the game. Some of these players cannot be counted as EZLN allies, such as speculative capital and the government of the United States. Yet the Zapatistas have been keen to spot the emerging importance of social movements and NGOs, and have used this to their advantage.

What factors have contributed to the success of the Zapatistas? With respect to its origins and support base, a key aspect of the EZLN's success has been the political context in the Chiapas conflict zone since about 1970. Tremendous progress at political organization by the indigenous, and on the part of Samuel Ruiz's Catholic Church, which embraced leftist liberation theology, created a near ready-made support base for the Zapatistas. In addition, the EZLN appreciated the virtue of patience, lying in wait for almost eleven years until the group finally felt it could score a great impact by emerging on NAFTA's birthday. Once they appeared, Marcos and the Zapatistas demonstrated enormous skill at political mobilization by using public relations ploys to create and expand a novel network of NGOs and social movements throughout Mexico and globally.

The Zapatistas also owe a considerable portion of their success to their epistemological adventures. They embraced the typical issues addressed by the left—land and wealth redistribution, debt relief, suspicion of foreign and speculative capital, and the like—but surpassed those important themes in a manner that left classical Marxism behind. Beyond the usual and significant leftist preoccupations with class and capital, the EZLN formulated an ideological agenda that featured race and gender at a time when both were politically ascendant globally. Harnessing the new power of identity politics proved to be a strong suit for the Zapatistas. The EZLN explored the new ways of knowing political space and time, and put these to use. Further, no group has more successfully employed the new politics of language than the Zapatistas, from their incorporation of indigenous language rights into their political platform to the fancy and widely disseminated wordplays of Marcos. Overall, the EZLN owes much of its political success to exploring and harnessing new forms of power and knowledge near the turn of the century.

Ironically, despite the group's reputation for harnessing global change, in one important respect the EZLN clearly has struggled against the strong current of world affairs. The Zapatistas have refused to accept transnational capitalism, and hence have represented a reactionary force against an economic model that so far has been on the ascendant. By comparison, the policies of Emiliano Zapata and the ideological corner-stones of the Mexican Revolution were more or less commensurate with the times. Although the redistributionist policies of Zapata were quite revolutionary, these were to occur within a nationalist context of reformist capitalism. Indeed, features such as nationalism, redistributive capitalism, and strong state intervention in the economy were prevalent and accepted features of Western political economy at the time. To a large measure, this symmetry explains why the Mexican Revolution and some of the policies of Zapata were successful. By contrast, perhaps the biggest limiting factor for the EZLN is that the group has marched against the grain of the most dominant economic feature of the world order. Yet the rebels have not been alone in their struggle, and they have attracted supporters precisely due to this issue.

Despite their political limitations, it is clear that the Zapatistas have represented an important phenomenon in Mexican politics and with regard to hemispheric security. Even if they have not presented elaborate and credible alternatives on some fronts, many of the group's stinging criticisms have been quite relevant and have contributed to Mexican political development. The rebels have also been instrumental at strengthening the new power of social movements, transnational NGOs, and identity politics. In this respect, the Zapatista struggle has shown not only that capital is transnational, but also that social movements and NGOs can also work transnationally and fill a political gap left by the debilitation of state structures under the neoliberal arrangement. The EZLN has also demonstrated both the power and the limits of a guerrilla group that has derived its strength from intellectual vigor rather than military might.

Notes

1. See, for example, Gilly, *La revolución interrumpida,* p. 15.

2. Coatsworth, *El impacto económico,* and Gilly, *La revolución interrumpida,* pp. 39–41.

3. See Gilly, *La revolución interrumpida,* p. 46; Rosenzweig, *El desarrollo económico de México.*

4. Frank Tannenbaum, in widely quoted statistics, estimates that almost 57,000 agricultural communities were absorbed by haciendas, with under 13,000 engaged in "free" agriculture. Tannenbaum, *Peace by Revolution,* pp. 192–195.

5. See, for example, Womack, *Zapata y la Revolución Mexicana,* p. 308. Womack provides a detailed account of Emiliano Zapata's origins and his struggles during the revolution.

6. See, for example, ibid., p. 128.

7. See Gilly, *La revolución interrumpida*, p. 316.

8. Quoted in Womack, *Zapata y la Revolución Mexicana*, p. 185.

9. Regarding Zapata's use of the railway system, see Guajardo, "Tecnología y campesinos."

10. This is argued throughout Gilly, *La revolución interrumpida*.

11. See, for example, Womack, *Zapata y la Revolución Mexicana*, p. 336.

12. For an excellent discussion of the meaning of revolutionary nationalism, see Paz, *Labyrinth of Solitude*, esp. pp. 181–182.

13. See Meyer, *Historia de la Revolución Mexicana*, p. 94.

14. See Rochlin, *Redefining Mexican Security*, esp. chap. 2. See also Teichman, *Privatization and Political Change in Mexico*.

15. See Rochlin, *Redefining Mexican Security*, p. 22. See also Martínez, *El perfil de México en 1980*.

16. See Rochlin, *Redefining Mexican Security*, p. 32. See also James Wilkie, ed., *Statistical Abstract of Latin America*, pt. 1 (Los Angeles: UCLA Latin American Center Publications, 1995), p. 53.

17. See Rochlin, *Redefining Mexican Security*, p. 59. See also Benjamin, *A Rich Land, A Poor People*, esp. pp. 15–151 and the book's epilogue.

18. See Meyer, *La Historia de la Revolución Mexicana*, p. 98.

19. See Rochlin, *Redefining Mexican Security*, pp. 4–5.

20. See ibid., pp. 156–157.

21. The thirty-fifth anniversary of this movement was held on 23 September 2000, when surviving guerrilla members recounted their stories, and also gave advice to current guerrilla groups to put down their arms and work within the system. See *La Jornada* (Mexico City), 22 September 2000.

22. See Rochlin, *Redefining Mexican Security*, chap. 5. See also Bartra, "Revolutionary Nationalism and National Security."

23. See Nora Lustig, "Economic Crisis, Adjustment, and Living Standards in Mexico," *World Development*, 18 October 1990.

24. These figures are elaborated upon in Rochlin, *Redefining Mexican Security*, chap. 2, esp. pp. 22–28.

25. For additional figures regarding the slashing of social spending, see ibid., p. 25.

26. General Mario Acosta Chaparro's book is titled *Movimientos subversivos en México*, and was published by the Mexican armed forces. The quote here is taken from the excellent book by Carlos Montemayor, *Chiapas: La rebelión indígena de México*, pp. 71–72. It is also noteworthy that General Acosta Chaparro was arrested and charged in the summer of 2000 under suspicion of high-level direction of narcotrafficking.

27. For a broader discussion of the issue of narcotrafficking, see Rochlin, *Redefining Mexican Security*, chap. 4.

28. For a broader discussion of this theme, see, for example, Benjamin, *A Rich Land, A Poor People*.

29. See, for example, Tello Díaz, *La rebelión de las Cañadas*, p. 44–45.

30. There is a good discussion of this phenomenon in Harvey, *La rebelión de Chiapas*, esp. pp. 89–91.

31. See, for example, Tello Díaz, *La rebelión de las Cañadas,* pp. 47–56, 106.

32. See, for example, Rochlin, *Redefining Mexican Security,* pp. 60–62; and Tello Díaz, *La rebelión de las Cañadas,* pp. 64–68.

33. See Montemayor, *Chiapas,* p. 91.

34. See, for example, Harvey, *La rebelión de Chiapas,* pp. 191–192.

35. For an extended discussion of this, see, for example, Hernández, "Chiapas"; Reyes and López, "Historia de la política agraria en Chiapas"; and Benjamin, *A Rich Land, A Poor People,* p. 241.

36. See Tello Díaz, *La rebelión de las Cañadas,* p. 103.

37. See Ejército Zapatista de Liberación Nacional (EZLN), "Palabras para la celebración del decimoprimer aniversario,"17 November 1994, p. 131.

38. EZLN, Subcomandante Marcos, "Intervención oral del EZLN en palabras de Marcos," 30 July 1996, p. 320, translation by author.

39. See Tello Díaz, *La rebelión de las Cañadas,* p. 118.

40. EZLN, Subcomandante Marcos, "Composición del EZLN y condiciones para el diálogo," p. 74, translation by author.

41. For an excellent and expanded discussion of this, see Harvey, *La rebelión de Chiapas,* pp. 186–190.

42. For an interesting discussion of global context and the new role of the Latin American guerrilla, see EZLN, Subcomandante Marcos, "Intervención oral del EZLN en palabras de Marcos," pp. 319–324.

43. See, for example, Tellos Díaz, *La rebelión de las Cañadas,* p. 207.

44. See EZLN, Subcomandante Marcos, "Chiapas: The Southeast in Two Winds," August 1992.

45. Marcos's "Chiapas: The Southeast in Two Winds—A Storm and a Prophecy" is one of the most important documents from the EZLN, since it portrays the group's position and perspective two years prior to the uprising.

46. The quotes are taken from EZLN, "Declaración de la Selva Lacandona," December 1993 (no specific date), translation by author.

47. EZLN, *El Despertador Mexicano: Órgano Informativo del EZLN* no. 1 (December 1993): 37, translation by author.

48. See ibid., pp. 36–48.

49. See EZLN, "Declaración de la Selva Lacandona."

50. *El Despertador Mexicano,* pp. 42–48, translation by author.

51. Ibid., p. 36, translation by author.

52. EZLN, Subcomandante Marcos, "Composición del EZLN y condiciones para el diálogo," pp. 72–78, translation by author.

53. See ibid., p. 76, translation by author.

54. EZLN, "Ayuda militar de EU a México," p. 85.

55. EZLN, "Otras formas de lucha," p. 103.

56. Letter from Comandancia General del EZLN, "Al consejo estudiantil universitario, Universidad Nacional Autónoma de México," 6 February 1994, pp. 129–130.

57. Letter from Comandancia General del EZLN, "A todos las organizaciones no gubernamentales de México," 20 February 1994, p. 161.

58. Letter from Comandancia General del EZLN, "A todos las organizaciones no gubernamentales de México," 1 February 1994, p. 121.

59. See EZLN, "A las bases del EZLN," 10 April 1994, pp. 213–214; EZLN, "Palabras del EZLN para la manifestación del 26 aniversario," 2 October 1994, pp. 85–87; and EZLN, "En el 502 aniversario del descubrimiento de América," 12 October 1994, pp. 100–104.

60. See Niños Zapatistas, "A los niños de México y el mundo," *EZLN: Documentos y Comunicados 1*, pp. 225–229. An excerpt reads as follows: "We have never known candy, toys, medicine, hospitals, schools, books, milk, meat, vegetables, eggs, and the majority of us don't have sufficient clothes" (p. 226). Translation by author.

61. Subcomandante Marcos, "A Marta Lamas."

62. Subcomandante Marcos, "Discurso del Subcomandante Marcos durante la visita del candidato presidencial," 17 May 1994, pp. 235–239, translation by author.

63. See EZLN, "Resultados de la consulta nacional," 1 June 1994; and EZLN, "Resultado de la consulta," 10 June 1994.

64. EZLN, "Segunda Declaración de la Selva Lacandona," 10 June 1994. In this document, for example, the EZLN summarizes its "First Declaration of the Lacandona Jungle," and reiterates familiar positions on civil society, the composition of the EZLN, the need for a transition government, and so on. Translation by author.

65. See EZLN, "Tercera Declaración de la Selva Lacandona," translation by author.

66. See, for example, Subcomandante Marcos, letter "To the men and women who, through different languages and means, believe in a more humane future and struggle for it today," pp. 283–288, translation by author.

67. On support from critics of neoliberalism, see, for example EZLN, "Primera declaración de la realidad," January 1996 (no specific date).

68. See EZLN, "El diálogo de San Andrés y los derechos y cultural indígena," 15 February 1996.

69. See EZLN, "Propuesta para la Mesa 2 diálogo de San Andrés," 15 February 1996.

70. See EZLN, Subcomandante Marcos, "Ojepse ley otirud," November 1995 (no specific date), p. 113, translation by author.

71. See EZLN, "El EZLN informe sobre su valoración de la situación actual," 29 August 1996.

72. EZLN, Subcomandante Marcos, "A los combatientes y mandos del Ejército Popular Revolucionario," 29 August 1996, translation by author.

73. See EZLN, "El poder judicial, principal sabateador de la paz," 31 May 1996.

74. See EZLN, "Segunda declaración de la Realidad," 3 August 1996, translation by author.

75. The artistic works of Marcos stand in contrast to the more businesslike approach of the correspondence authored by the Comandancia General del EZLN. An example of one of Subcomandante Marcos's most brilliant pieces is "La historia de los espejos," June 1995 (no specific date).

76. See EZLN, Subcomandante Marcos, "La muerta nos visita," 20 February 1995, translation by author.

77. EZLN, "Condiciones del EZLN para regresar a la mesa del diálogo," 29 August 1996, translation by author.

78. See, for example, EZLN, Subcomandante Marcos, "Siete preguntas, a quien corresponda," 1997 (no specific date).

79. Over the next two years, with local and international scrutiny on Mexican human rights, a February 2000 report by the United Nations observed the continuation of such abuses as impunity and illegal repression. But overall, there was general recognition that the human rights situation in Mexico was indeed improving. See *New York Times,* 18 February 2000. Further, of particular concern was the alleged torture and subsequent incarceration of two environmentalists in the state of Guerrero. Rodolfo Montiel, an environmentalist who protested against deforestation in Guerrero and who received the prestigious Goldman environmental prize in a Mexican prison on 6 April 2000, was allegedly tortured by the armed forces and then falsely given a lengthy prison term in August 2000 along with a friend. See Miguel Agustín Pro Juárez Centro de Derechos Humanos, *Quarterly Bulletin* no. 4 (summer 2000). See also *La Jornada,* 29 August 2000.

80. See EZLN, Subcomandante Marcos, "Siete piezas sueltas del recompecabezas mundial," June 1997 (no specific date).

81. Sun Tzu suggests, for example, that "the Way means inducing the people to have the same aim as the leadership, so that they will share death and share life, without fear of danger." See *Art of War,* p. 43. For a further discussion of the central concept of "the Way," see Lao Tzu, *Tao te Ching.*

82. See, for example, EZLN, Subcomandante Marcos, "Tres mesas para la cena de fin de siglo," February 1998 (no specific date), which demonstrates Marcos's wide literary capacity; and EZLN, "V Declaración de la Selva Lacandona," July 1998 (no specific date).

83. EZLN, Subcomandante Marcos, "Comunicado del Comité Clandestino Revolucionario Indígena," 10 April 1998, translation by author.

84. Strikers argued that tuition hikes were part of a wider state agenda of privatizing Mexico's university system and of incorporating neoliberal values into university programs.

85. Letter from Subcomandante Marcos, "Movimiento estudiantil de la UNAM," 22 May 1999, translation by author.

86. This was particularly true given the social memory of the student massacre in 1968.

87. Letter from Subcomandante Marcos, "To the People of Mexico, to the People and Governments of the World," 19 June 2000, www.ezln.org/archive/ezln000619.htm.

88. It is impossible to tell how many people abstained due to Zapatista influence or due to other influences. See Willibadd Sonnleitner, "De la rebelión armada a la alternancia política," *Proceso,* no. 1243 (27 August 2000).

89. Final election results were as follows: For president, Vicente Fox with 43.3 percent, Francisco Labastida of the PRI with 36.8 percent, and Cuauhtémoc Cárdenas at 17 percent. For governor of Chiapas, Pablo Salazar's Alliance Party garnered 52.8 percent of the votes compared to the PRI's 46.7 percent.

90. For a good initial discussion of this, see *La Jornada,* 27 August 2000.

91. On poverty-fighting programs, see Government of Mexico, Presidency of the Republic, "Main Events Relating to the Conflict in Chiapas, 28 February 1998 to 10 December 1999," 24 October 2000.

92. Author interviews with Elizabeth Pólito, professor, Departamento de Sociología, Universidad Nacional Autónoma de Chiapas, and member, Centro de Información y Análisis de Chiapas, San Cristóbal, Chiapas, 31 August 2000; Alma Rosa Rojas, director, Centro para Educación de la Paz, San Cristóbal, Chiapas, 29 August 2000; and Marina Patricia Jiménez Ramírez, director, Centro de Derechos Humanos Fray Bartolomé de las Casas, San Cristóbal, Chiapas, 25 August 2000.

93. Human rights workers such as Mariclaire Acosta publicly decried the expulsion of foreigners from Chiapas during 1999, and noted that it set a dangerous tone at the dawn of the twenty-first century. La Jornada, 7 January 2000.

94. Text published by EZLN, "EZLN to Congress: Words of Comandante David, March 28," chiapas95@eco.utexas.edu.

95. During 1994–2000, a basket of basic shopping items rose 351 percent, while real salary increases amounted to 248 percent. See La Jornada, 5 September 2000.

96. On formal schooling, see La Jornada, 28 August 2000. The Mexican government estimates the presence of about 30 percent of the active labor population in the informal sector. See La Jornada, 26 December 1999. A private specialist in employment studies, Orlando Degado, estimated 52 percent of the active population is involved in the informal sector. See La Jornada, 4 August 2000.

97. See Denise Dresser, "México y Estados Unidos: Pensar distinto," Proceso, no. 1244 (3 September 2000): 52, translation by author.

98. The figure of 28 percent for 2000, and the figures for 1984 and 1992, are from the Grupo Financiero Bancomex-Accival, La Jornada, 13 February 2000. The figure of 53 percent for 2000 is from Julio Boltnivik, who has worked with President Fox's team, Excelsior (Mexico City), 30 August 2000.

99. About 100,000 of the total jobs lost were in the maquiladora sector of northern Mexico. See Excelsior, 22 August 2001; and La Jornada, 22 August 2001. By mid-2002, many began to question the viability of the maquiladora sector as a model of development, since some of these factories shut permanently and moved to locations where products could be made more cheaply, particularly in Asia. See La Jornada, 24 May 2002.

100. Statistics are official government figures. See Excelsior, 13 July 2001.

101. For an analytical discussion of political "ghosts," see Derrida, Specters of Marx.

102. See Antonio Gramsci, Selections from the Prison Notebooks, esp. "State and Civil Society," pp. 206–275, for a discussion of hegemony, war of position, and war of movement.

103. See Guevara, Guerrilla Warfare. His influence is apparent in the EZLN's communiqués in December 1993, for example, in which codes of conduct for soldier behavior were enumerated.

104. The EPR, in contrast to the EZLN, has had a weak public relations arm, and has not enjoyed the network of support from NGOs and social movements that the EZLN has. Members of the EPR, for security reasons, typically

have not been available for interviews. Relatively little is known about this group compared to the Zapatistas, who regularly disseminate a variety of information about themselves and their viewpoints, and who have vast contacts with civil society. For further information regarding the EPR, see Rochlin, *Redefining Mexican Security*, pp. 84–87.

105. See Ejército Revolucionario Popular (EPR), *Manifiesto de la Sierra Madre Oriental*, 7 August 1996, translation by author.

106. See EPR, "Comunicado, sobre Gutiérrez Rebollo," 26 February 1997, translation by author; EPR, "Comunicado Revolucionario," 28 August 2000, translation by author; and EPR, *Insurgente* 4, no. 27 (May–June 2000), translation by author.

107. The EPR, for example, has criticized the anti-abortion proposals of President Fox, and has done so more strongly than the Zapatistas, whose policies on this issue have been limited by the support they derived from the Catholic Church in Chiapas, which has opposed abortion. See EPR, "Comunicado Revolucionario," translation by author. Further, in contrast to the sometimes hostile response by the EZLN toward the EPR, the EPR has shown gracious respect for the Zapatistas on a number of crucial occasions. See, for example, EPR, "Saludo y bienvenida al EZLN a la capital," 12 September 1997.

108. For a discussion of the group's commitment to armed struggle, see EPR, *Insurgente* 4, no. 27 (May–June 2000). For an illustration of the EPR's principal reliance on the Marxian concept of class struggle, see for example, EPR, "Comunicado del EPR," *Expreso Chiapas*, 29 August 2000, p. 6, translation by author. For an illustration of the EPR's celebration of the Marxist dialectic to explain change, see EPR, "Proyecto de pais," 2 December 1996, translation by author.

109. See Rochlin, *Redefining Mexican Security*, chaps. 1–2, 7.

7

The EZLN:
Concepts of Strategy,
Security, and Power

The Zapatistas have confronted classic security themes, but have done so in a manner that often has reflected a new epistemological approach. They have explored fresh dimensions of the relationship between power, knowledge, and truth. To the extent that they have employed a pioneering approach, what may be termed a postmodern perspective, they have been greeted with considerable political success. But the rebels also committed some prominent errors that have severely limited their power, especially when they relied on traditional perspectives that were out of synch with major alterations in the world order. Further, what is crucially significant in this case is the domestic context, especially the generally nonviolent nature of the Mexican system in relation to the Colombian and Peruvian examples. This chapter will explore important elements of that context, with special attention afforded to government strategy.

The EZLN: Essential Strategy

After forming in November of 1983, the Zapatistas undertook their initial objective of constructing a support base. Here the virtue of patience was supreme. It would be eleven years before the six veteran Zapatistas transformed into a 3,000-troop indigenous army that launched the uprising on 1 January 1994. The EZLN's strategy of building a social base of primarily indigenous supporters was assisted by the organizational work already accomplished by the Catholic Church and by an assortment of indigenous groups. Although the Zapatista struggle has been multifaceted, the strong indigenous component of the group had a centuries-long tradition of rebellion throughout Mexico.[1]

A second component of the EZLN's prerebellion stage entailed the contemplation of the great social changes that had been occurring globally and within Mexico, so that an effective strategy could be devised to harness them. The withering of the Soviet Union and the brand of international communism that it represented pointed toward the creation of a rebel movement in Mexico that could not rely on foreign states or superpowers. Hence, what was also required on the part of the Zapatistas was a strategy that appreciated sea changes with respect to political economy, ideology, and the crumbling Cold War alliance system.

The EZLN has acknowledged that it began as a Latin American guerrilla group with the "traditions of the 1970s, as a vanguard group, as Marxist-Leninists ideologically, with the belief that struggle for world transformation would arrive through the dictatorship of the proletariat." But through the 1980s and into the 1990s, the Zapatistas explored the idea of what it meant to be a guerrilla group in a world dominated by the ascendance of transnational capital, of trade blocs, and of preponderant U.S. power.[2] During this lengthy period of reflection, and until the EZLN made its official public appearance, the group considered itself to be a self-defense organization.[3] Hence, this was an era characterized by a predominantly defensive strategy that entailed a process of contemplation, fortification, and prudent timing.

By the end of December 1994 the EZLN decided that it was ready to emerge publicly. The group had constructed a political platform based primarily on four broad themes: indigenous rights, anti-neoliberalism, women's rights, and reconceived democracy. It had assembled a social base of 3,000–4,000 residents of the Chiapas jungle and eastern highlands, most of them indigenous. Although the EZLN was able to accumulate enough weapons to arm its troops—some by local efforts in Chiapas and others purchased in the United States—it was no match for the Mexican army.[4] It is precisely in the area of military matters where the Zapatistas experienced profound difficulties and traumas. Their military strategy for the 1 January 1994 attack consisted of two basic elements. The first concerned a string of components associated with timing. The second dimension involved a long battle-march from the mountains of Chiapas to the nation's capital of Mexico City—a march reminiscent of Emiliano Zapata's almost a century earlier, or perhaps of the Sandinistas' march to Managua during the final stages of the Cold War. Both of the EZLN's strategies rested squarely on traditional pillars.

On the issue of timing, it was with great care and foresight that the Zapatistas selected 1 January 1994 as their launch date. At one level, it involved the classic strategy of surprise attack. Adding to the effect was that the rebels began their march on the morning after the Mexican army's spirited participation in New Year's Eve festivities. The Mexican armed forces obviously were not at all ready for the Zapatistas' alarming appearance. The choice of 1 January 1994 for their debut carried additional symbolic weight, especially in the realms of new political space and fresh political voices. It was the commencement date of NAFTA. Hence the uprising was surely designed to remind the nascent "North American public" (of Canada, the United States, and Mexico) that the terms of NAFTA were not universally appreciated, to say the least. The strategy was tailored to appeal to a transnational network of civil society principally in North America, which could now consider the Chiapas problem more rightly as its own. It was a strategy based on deriving support from global social movements rather than from foreign states. A nosey North American public and global civil society would mean less privacy for the Mexican state, and hence a presumed reluctance simply to exterminate the guerrillas in the traditional manner of a "dirty war" and "disappearances." Overall, 1 January 1994 turned out to be a good day for the Zapatistas.

Judging from their literature, the Zapatistas fully expected to meet military success when they launched their struggle and officially declared war on the Mexican army. Just prior to their commencement, in December 1993, the EZLN published its first magazine, *El Despertador Mexicano,* in which the group outlined its initial strategy:

> In this first edition we present *the Declaration of War we make against the federal army,* and also make known the orders that must be followed by the leaders, officials, and troops of the EZLN *on their advance for national territory.* At the same time, we present *Revolutionary Laws that will be imposed,* with the support of the struggling people, in liberated territories *to guarantee their revolutionary control* and the basis to begin to construct a new homeland.[5]

Thus the Zapatistas essentially began as a violent guerrilla movement, not the famous peaceniks into which they would later evolve. In fact, on more than one occasion the EZLN established the clear strategic goal of achieving the official status of "belligerent force" as recognized by the Law of War in the Geneva Conventions.[6]

Although the Zapatistas would later claim they never wished to "take power," the opposite appears to be the case at the time of their official emergence. In its "Declaración de la Selva Lacandona," published in December 1993, the EZLN issued the following orders to its troops: "First, advance toward the capital of the country to conquer the federal Mexican army, protecting on your advance the freedom of the civilian population and permitting the liberated people to elect, freely and democratically, their own *administrative* authorities."[7] Although the words "freely and democratically" are used, the passage notes that such elections are only for "administrative" authorities. These administrators supposedly would implement the "imposed" revolutionary laws mentioned in the earlier quote from *El Despertador Mexicano*. In fact, that journal specifies the kinds of laws that would be imposed. A very short list of these includes a specified tax scale for capitalist businesses that would fall into Zapatista "territory" (from 0 to 20 percent), a sixteen-point plan for land redistribution, and a variety of reforms such as rent control for urban areas that the EZLN imagined would fall under its control.[8]

Utterly defeated militarily at the end of twelve days of battle, by 12 January 1994 the EZLN was no longer talking about military strategy. The new objective of not taking power was expressed only after it became entirely clear to the Zapatista leadership that they vastly lacked the capacity to take the power they initially wanted. The EZLN began very much as a traditional but militarily misguided guerrilla group. Its plans of marching to the capital, of defeating the Mexican army, of accumulating vast urban and rural territory upon which it would impose revolutionary laws, all suggested an extraordinarily poor grasp of strategic affairs, and a basic misunderstanding regarding social prospects for revolution in Mexico. By November 1994, the EZLN admitted that it had "committed many errors," including mistakes related to the group's military limitations.[9] More fundamentally, Subcomandante Marcos would later suggest that the initial military operation of the EZLN was an immense mistake, largely because it clung to the politics of the past. In January 2001, seven years after the EZLN's initial uprising, Marcos reflected that "the EZLN was prepared for January 1, but not for January 2. . . . The First Declaration . . . was constructed with the criteria of political-military organizations and movements of national liberation from the 1970s."[10]

But the astonishingly rapid and decisive military failure suffered by the Zapatistas precipitated a fertile period of rethinking, one that would yield sometimes brilliant policies. As traditional combat ensued during the first twelve days of January 1994, the EZLN began to appreciate that any power or influence it would wield would not be in the military realm. Instead, the Zapatistas eventually would derive significant political power from their unique style of organization. Beyond its contingent of primarily indigenous supporters in Chiapas, the EZLN almost instantly began to cultivate support from a network of Mexican as well as foreign NGOs and social movements. In a strategic sense, its reliance on those social forces proved to be at least as important as its local support base. Beyond this, the EZLN established the fresh goal of representing a predominantly political force utilizing "new forms of struggle."[11] The group worked hard to exploit this strategy in a trajectory stretching from January 1994 into the twenty-first century. The Zapatistas would rely on the newfangled power of symbols and words that promoted indigenous rights and that criticized neoliberalism, among other themes. While the EZLN's peak of power in this regard was probably 1994–1995, it remained a significant force after that time.

Other strategies employed by the Zapatistas were tailored to specific eras. For example, between their military failure in January 1994 until their dramatic containment by the Mexican army on 9 February 1995, the EZLN worked diligently to take advantage of the economic and political crisis facing the country. They accomplished this largely through successful propaganda efforts and by serving as catalysts for the formation of critical social movements. For this task the Zapatistas had much material with which to work. The national context featured high-level political assassination, rampant corruption, escalating evidence of crime and narcotrafficking, as well as profound economic calamity. Perhaps the height of the EZLN's manipulation of this volatile scenario was the group's false claim in December 1994 that it had broken free from the grip of the Mexican armed forces and had taken more territory—an episode that contributed to the Mexican peso crisis and subsequently to the world's largest financial bailout package at the time.[12] Hence the EZLN's strategy was to project a clear and solid Zapatista voice against the backdrop of chaos in Mexico. But the rebels helped trigger events that led the Mexican government to perceive that it had no other choice but to isolate physically the EZLN in a manner that it hoped would diminish the group's overall power.

The Mexican army's complete military encirclement of the EZLN on 5 February 1995, which effectively sealed the group into a relatively small piece of territory, naturally prompted yet another switch in strategy for the Zapatistas. Placed on the defensive by the Zedillo government in its feverish attempt to restore order in the country, the EZLN shifted its strategy to one of sheer survival through an increased reliance on its network of supportive NGOs and social movements. The two essential pillars of Zapatista strategy at this time were, first, bolstering links with civil society, and second, attempts at negotiating with the government in the realm of indigenous rights. But the suspension of dialogue with the government in 1996, coupled with the ascent of right-wing paramilitary forces in Chiapas characterized by the late 1997 massacre at Acteal, pushed the EZLN into increasing isolation.

During the last three years of the century, and still struggling for survival, the EZLN attempted to maintain what appeared to be its fading level of support from civil society. Given their military predicament and the rather hostile aura of President Zedillo, the Zapatistas rightly harbored little hope for meaningful negotiations with the government. A central institution established for conflict resolution, the National Commission for Intermediacy (CONAI), was disassembled during this period. As it turned out, the rebels embarked on a dreary waiting game that would last until the end of 2000. Beyond their initial military miscalculations, perhaps the most serious political mistake committed by the Zapatistas was their failure to see the potential for positive democratic prospects from the summer 2000 elections. In this sense, the rebels seemed to lose touch with the major current of Mexican politics. This represented a significant misstep for a guerrilla group that built much of its reputation on an uncanny tendency for having its finger on the pulse of political change. In its endeavor to recover from that immense error, by the fall of 2000 the EZLN had shifted its strategy once again.

In November of that year the group woke up to the prospects of a relatively good relationship with the incoming government, the first non-PRI administration since the revolution. The EZLN altered its previous strategy by breaking its months-long silence, and by attempting to reestablish dialogue with the newly elected government of Vicente Fox. True to their renowned style, the rebels did so with great fanfare. The Zapatistas conducted two press conferences, the first just two days prior to the inauguration of the Fox government, and the second the day after.[13]

A series of events led to the EZLN's remarkable bus tour from Chiapas to Mexico City in winter 2001. It represented the group's most politically important episode since being sealed into a small enclave by the Mexican military some six years earlier. Given that the Zapatistas appeared ready to talk, President Fox held out an olive branch to the rebels almost immediately after he assumed office. After a protracted negotiation period, the government gave in to most of the EZLN's demands. The most significant of these concerned the withdrawal of troops in a total of seven positions from "Zapatista communities," which was partially met by the government.[14] Another request included the official recognition of the agreements established on indigenous rights in the San Andrés Accords that were suspended in 1996. The Fox team responded by reigniting consideration of these accords in the Mexican Congress. The EZLN also demanded the release of many Zapatistas taken prisoner by the government, and this too was conceded by the Fox administration. A similar list of requests was publicly presented by the EZLN in early December 2000 to incoming Chiapas governor Pablo Salazar.[15] Once these demands were met, the stage was set for the tour and for dialogue between the rebels and the state.

From the perspective of the EZLN, the situation was strategically complicated and represented a gamble. The "March for Indigenous Dignity" thrust the group back into the limelight, and garnered them the opportunity to generate the public support necessary to sustain their political relevance. In what amounted to a public relations extravaganza, they were provided with a loud political voice throughout their trek, with the finale being the privilege of making a series of speeches before the Mexican Congress. There were also contextual elements in their favor. Southern Mexico, which had been ravaged by an agricultural crisis in the wake of NAFTA and which was home to the majority of the country's indigenous population, was a particularly hospitable locale to conduct the tour.[16] Further, the severe downturn that had struck the Mexican economy beginning in 2001 meant that the EZLN would be able to use this as ammunition against the otherwise popular government of Vicente Fox.

But there were also risks for the EZLN. Having been given a national podium to present their views, the Zapatistas had to rest on the political power of their ideas and would have a harder time convincing the public that that they were victims of government oppression. They stood to lose any popularity they had gained from being perceived as martyrs. Second, there was some humiliation for the EZLN associated with being protected during their tour by the Mexican army, against which the Zapatistas had declared war in 1994. Finally, they had to take the risk that Vincente Fox could emerge as the big political winner of the episode, given his apparently magnanimous gestures.

In the end, both the Zapatistas and Vicente Fox emerged as winners. The huge and sympathetic crowds the EZLN attracted during the tour represented a clear demonstration of the group's continued political relevance. Further, the media attention generated by the episode provided a needed boost to the group's flagging popularity. All this was accomplished with little that was new in terms of ideology or policy. The various speeches along the way were standard fare for the EZLN. Indigenous rights was the main theme of the march, and Marcos reiterated in Mexico City that the group did not wish to take power, as if the Zapatistas somehow had the capacity to do so.[17]

The rebels were able to seize the political benefits of the tour, and then they launched a political salvo against the government when the EZLN broke off negotiations on 30 April 2001. Afterward the Mexican Congress began a process that culminated in July with the ratification of an indigenous rights law that fell far short of the San Andrés Accords of 1996. The accords were regarded by the Zapatistas as a crucial agreement they had established with the government in the key area of indigenous rights. During their historic speeches at the Mexican Congress, the Zapatista comandantes urged the Congress to approve the essence of the San Andrés Accords. The law that actually passed provided far less autonomy to the country's 10 million indigenous people than the 1996 accords would have done. The Mexican states with the largest indigenous populations categorically voted against the law. Thus the nonindigenous majority had refused to provide the indigenous minority with the autonomy they wanted to obtain through the ballot box. The Zapatistas seized on this and suggested that the Mexican government was incapable of granting the indigenous population the dignity they deserved. The Zapatistas' gamble turned out to be a strategic success. They boosted their popularity and reclaimed their role as a key representative of indigenous rights.

A final point concerns what promises to be an important strategic consideration well into the twenty-first century. The Zapatistas have voiced their strategic opposition to Plan Puebla-Panama, a potential free trade zone comprising southern Mexico and the Central American states. Beyond being touted by President Fox as the key to development in southern Mexico in the wake of post-NAFTA agricultural disaster in the region, the concept is supported by the World Bank, the International Monetary Fund, and the Interamerican Development Bank.[18] For Mexico, the plan involves mammoth projects in sectors such as forestry, hydro-electricity, petroleum, and tourism. It also entails the construction of major highways, airports, sea ports, and perhaps a super-railway stretching from the coast of Oaxaca to Veracruz, which could rival the Panama Canal. A central motive behind Plan Puebla-Panama appears to be the government's attempt to win additional investment in Mexico to compensate for the loss of investment in the *maquiladora* sector, which is located predominantly in the north of the country. Two hundred thousand of just over 1 million jobs were lost in that sector in 2001, and ninety-seven such factories shut their doors in that year, and further closures are expected. This is because the *maquilas,* with average wages of about U.S.$2–$3 per hour including benefits, have had difficulty competing with rivals in El Salvador ($1.59/hour), the Dominican Republic ($1.53/hour),

Indonesia ($1.19/hour), and China (43¢/hour).[19] Hence, Plan Puebla-Panama will include an industrial component with cheaper wages than the *maquiladora* sector, drawing on surplus labor from Mexico's south as well as from Central America.

Key political issues associated with the plan include threats to biodiversity as well as incursions into land where the indigenous population currently resides.[20] Debates concerning implications of the apparent failure of the *maquiladora* sector are also relevant to the logic of development underpinning Plan Puebla-Panama. The strategic implications of this project are immense. The Zapatistas, having proven themselves strategic masters regarding the implications of new spaces of production, as they have already demonstrated with regard to NAFTA, are likely to focus much of their strategy on the plan in coming years. The EZLN already has voiced its official opposition to what it views as a neoliberal and exploitative scheme that is bad for the environment and for the indigenous population.

Analytical Context

Let us apply the classic strategic themes to the Zapatista case, beginning with the related notions of good government and the important power associated with societal consent. This concept was central for a wide spectrum of thinkers, including Thucydides, Ibn Khaldun, and Machiavelli, and Gramsci in the twentieth century. This represents an important piece of the Mexican mosaic to the extent that the PRI's hegemony had been eroding since at least the mid-1980s. A decade later, social consent for the government sank to an all-time low. Under such circumstances, the Zapatistas' strategy was to bolster their own power by adroitly exploiting the wilting social consent for the government. The strategy worked, particularly during the government's 1994–1995 crisis. Even though the Mexican state recovered its legitimacy among the majority of the country with the election of the Fox administration, the political disaster of the 2001 indigenous rights law substantially eroded indigenous consent for the government. The Zapatistas strategically took advantage of this.

Timing represents a classic and multifaceted security issue. Certainly the EZLN very much appreciated the value of timing. Indicative of this was the group's remarkable demonstration of patience for eleven years prior to its official appearance on the carefully chosen date of 1 January 1994. Also demonstrative of their appreciation of timing was the

Zapatistas' noteworthy silence for several months between the elections of summer 2000 and the imminent inauguration of the new state and federal governments at the end of the year. While the EZLN generally has demonstrated a good grasp of timing, there have been some notable miscues. The most prominent of these concerned the ill-timed launching of the rebels' initial military attack in 1994, and the group's failure to appreciate sea changes in electoral politics that toppled the PRI in the summer of 2000. Timing naturally has been a favorite topic for classic strategists. For example, this is a central aspect of "the Way," which represents the theoretical foundation for both Sun Tzu I and Sun Tzu II. As we observed in Chapter 1, both thinkers refer to "seasons," "climate," and "weather" to denote shifting temporal environments in relation to strategy and security. Knowing when to act is key, particularly during eras of dramatic change.

There are other temporal dimensions of strategy that are relevant to the struggle of the EZLN. One such issue concerns the dual elements of duration and speed in relation to victory or defeat, and how the role of chance and Clausewitzean fog can influence these. As we observed when we visited the literature of the Zapatistas, the group's initial strategy entailed a militarily triumphant march to the nation's capital in 1994 coupled with their radical transformation of the country's political economy. As it turned out, the EZLN was forced to cope with a drastically different pace and space of warfare than it initially predicted. For the Zapatistas, rather than a steady and protracted military confrontation or a momentous thrust to the halls of power, fog and chance surprised them with a slow-motion war that featured their military containment. In response, the EZLN's strategy was designed to resist what Clausewitz might describe as the government's policy of "using the duration of the war to bring about a gradual exhaustion of his [the enemy's] physical and moral resistance."[21]

Paradoxically, the EZLN and its supporters harnessed the nearly instantaneous communication of the Internet to fight a laggard and protracted low-intensity war. The EZLN typically has relied upon a network of its supporters to disseminate its news and views over the Internet. The Zapatistas' strategy has been to deploy information in a manner that approximated global surveillance over the actions of its enemy, the Mexican government. Beyond this, a noteworthy episode of this "real-time" combat has been the use of so-called floodnet software by a group of Zapatista supporters to bombard targeted Mexican government offices with up to 600,000 "hits" per minute, thereby inundating their computer systems.[22] Hence the temporal element of what Paul Virilio and Sylvere Lotringer have termed the "information explosion" is key.[23] Like inundating "hits" and informational surveillance of critical events, the instantaneous and simultaneous dissemination of information can generate power.[24] As Subcomandante Marcos has observed, it has been the strategy of the Zapatistas to generate images and information that the Mexican government "cannot control from Mexico, because the information is simultaneously on all sides."[25] For such a strategy to be successful, speed is of the essence. As Sun Tzu observed, "The condition of a military force is that its essential factor is speed, taking advantage of others' failure to catch up, going by routes they do not expect, attacking where they are not on guard."[26]

While the theme of time itself appears to be universal in the classics of security, what has changed over the centuries is how time is known, or the epistemological approach to time. The world known by the Zapatistas is not one of interrupted and slow-motion wars such as those witnessed millennia ago by Thucydides, whereby, for example, the belligerents would halt combat for several months in order to harvest crops. The time of warfare faced by the Zapatistas is continuous and virtually simultaneous, although the duration of the war itself has been protracted. It has been the EZLN's appreciation of this new episteme of time that has largely been responsible for its sustaining of power. The Zapatistas have striven to be masters of timing and of real-time information wars. To the extent that they have relied on the near instantaneous time of the Internet, they have appreciated that, in Virilio and Lotringer's words, "the peak of speed is the extermination of space."[27] Space is compressed and borders can disappear when information is transmitted at speeds that provide virtually simultaneous surveillance.

Thus, our discussion of temporal politics has delivered us to the realm of space. The politics of space is a topic addressed by all the strategic masters and remains a crucial issue in security studies. Before we consider the effects of new spaces such as cyberspace, NAFTA, and so on, let us examine the relevance of traditional space vis-à-vis Zapatista strategy. To begin, the group's desire to march to the capital of Mexico City through a protracted civil war is an approach to space akin to that of Emiliano Zapata at the beginning of the twentieth century. Also quite traditional in the context of Latin American guerrilla movements is that the Zapatistas launched their movement in the geographical space of a poor, isolated, and rural area. The fact that the EZLN found itself backed into a small enclave by the country's armed forces is also quite traditional, in the sense that the rebels have endured the spatial effects of the classic strategy of containment. More generally, most of the traditional features of Zapatista strategy were limited to the first twelve days of military combat with the government.

Since 12 January 1994, their approach to space generally has been quite novel and has incorporated a fresh epistemological perspective. Space has been known differently by the Zapatistas on a number of levels. With the formation of NAFTA, the crucial space of production has changed, and with it a new political and strategic space has emerged. A politics of "North America" has been in the making, with the Zapatistas distinguished as veteran political participants. Given the EZLN's shrewd strategic manipulation of NAFTA, the group stood poised to seize upon the new production space entailed in Plan Puebla-Panama. While the plan is far from fruition, the proposed free trade zone between southern Mexico and the Central American states would raise important strategic concerns. Certainly the EZLN and its indigenous sympathizers throughout southern Mexico possess the potential to impose important obstacles to the plan. This represents a highly likely strategy for the rebels in the twenty-first century, given the EZLN's stated opposition to the proposed free trade zone and its record of appreciating the benefits of new strategic space.

The EZLN has been on the frontiers of other new political spaces as well. The global propensity toward ethnic identities and new political spaces to represent them has been consistent with Zapatista policy. Indeed, indigenous autonomy has been one of the group's key demands. This assumed special relevance when the Mexican Congress ratified an indigenous rights law in 2001 that fell far short of the economic, political, and cultural autonomy demanded by many indigenous communities. Such autonomy was enshrined in the 1996 San Andrés Accords between the government and the Zapatistas. This important clash highlights the traditional space of the nation-state that was central to those who opposed indigenous autonomy on the grounds that it would Balkanize the country, versus the postmodern space of identity politics advocated by the Zapatistas and by their indigenous supporters. On other dimensions, the new space of the biosphere and of ecological politics has been central to Zapatista objectives. Further, while Emiliano Zapata attempted to employ the spatially revolutionary technology of the railway on his ride to victory, the EZLN has endeavored to surf the politics of cyberspace and the global media. These and other changes meant that space could be known in new ways, and the mastery of such alterations could yield beneficial strategic results.

In terms of the classic strategic theme of organization, what is strikingly original about the Zapatistas has been *who* they have organized and *how* they have organized them to achieve various strategic objectives. The analogy of the network is appropriate here with respect to both the EZLN's distinct style of organization and also that of the Internet itself.[28] Given its preponderant indigenous membership and the strong presence of women, the composition of the Zapatistas is noteworthy but not entirely unique.[29] Rather, other components of their support base have distinguished the rebels. Through a national and foreign network, the Zapatistas have enjoyed support not from nation-states as might have been the case during the Soviet era, but from NGOs and individuals all over the globe, especially in North America. The EZLN was successful at organizing constituents with wide-ranging political identities involving gender, indigenous rights, anti-neoliberalism, sexuality, ecology, and the like. Indeed, this global network of multifaceted transnational support is truly unique. Examples include the linkage between Chiapas-based NGOs such as the umbrella group CONPAZ, a plethora of Mexican human rights NGOs such as Mexico City's Comisión Mexicana de Defensa y Promoción de los Derechos Humanos, international NGOs such as Global Exchange (based in California), and the Internet news group Chiapas95 (based in Austin, Texas).[30] Despite its support for the Zapatistas, it is important to emphasize that this network should not be considered a monolith, given the prominent political distinctions among the organizations.[31] But the Internet has been a primary tool utilized for organizing this support base. Numerous NGOs throughout Mexico have emphasized that the Internet has helped render political organization and education both inexpensive and fast.[32]

While guns are a primary tool of traditional war, the Internet has been the essential tool of netwar. As one U.S. defense specialist put it, a netwar "refers to an emerging mode of conflict (and crime) at societal levels, involving measures short of traditional war, in which the protagonists use network forms of organization and related doctrines, strategies, and technologies attuned to the information age."[33] Rather than targeting the enemy and its army with death and destruction, the EZLN targets the human mind through the dissemination of information and images designed to promote political support and to provide surveillance aimed at neutralizing state violence.[34] The Zapatistas as knowledge warriors conform to Jean Braulliard's interesting observation, "first safe sex, now safe war."[35]

Thus the Zapatistas have been empowered by their use of the written word and pictorial images. Perhaps the Internet has rendered language politically more important than ever. Marcos's gift for prose helped the EZLN achieve a global audience for its messages and provided a pool of potential supporters waiting to be organized. His beautiful writing style, the raw availability of his provocative and well-chosen words in numerous translations on the EZLN's website, and the group's consistent demand for indigenous language rights have been among the features harnessed by the Zapatistas in testimony to the power of language. It is this fresh epistemological approach to language in relation to power that distinguishes the EZLN from traditional guerrillas. Virilio also suggested decades ago that real-time speed combined with compressed space would essentially make the entire world into a cinema.[36] To the extent that this has been the case, Marcos's pop star looks and charm have been a perfect vehicle for Zapatista power. His image has been splashed across the planet on a plethora of magazines and newspapers, especially during 1994 and 1995.

Beyond the conceptual issues associated with the EZLN's talent for organizing a support base beyond the bounds of the Chiapas highlands, some open questions linger regarding the formal organization of the EZLN itself. Prominent is whether or not there exists some national or even international directorate for the group. Based on what is known from the EZLN's literature, there is a General Command and a series of Clandestine Indigenous Revolutionary Committees, with the Zapatista army at the service of these bodies. Each organizational component has established ties to the grass roots of local Chiapas communities, which has permitted opportunities for a democratic flow between them. While this is significant, it is not particularly new. This grassroots connection has been a classic feature of Latin American guerrilla movements. Che Guevara, for example, urged guerrillas to engage in "intensive popular work" and consultation to cultivate decisive strategic support.[37] Further, the EZLN, like other guerrilla groups, has created a related political front, the Frente Zapatista de Liberación Nacional. The FZLN has disseminated information over the Internet and has been partially responsible for organizing supportive NGOs.[38]

With respect to traditional combat, the EZLN's organization seemed altogether inappropriate during the first several days of January 1994. One example of this was its reliance on huge and vulnerable units comprising many hundreds of combatants. This bulky structure exceeded the organizational recommendations of even traditional guerrilla strategists such as Che Guevara, who warned against using more than 100 troops for large columns under the most favorable conditions. As the January 1994 assault by the Mexican armed forces progressed, the EZLN eventually shifted to Guevara's old-fashioned guerrilla fighting units of eight to ten troops.[39] But by this time the restructuring was far too late. Finally and perhaps most importantly, the Zapatistas broke the cardinal rule, expressed here by Guevara, that "the fundamental principle is that no battle, combat, or skirmish is to be fought unless it will be won."[40] The organization of the EZLN as a combat force lost its significance after its military defeat just days after the war began.

Hence there exists the natural correlation that to the limited extent that the Zapatistas actually fought a traditional guerrilla war, their view of military organization was also traditional (though ill conceived). In the main, however, a key source of the EZLN's power has been its ability to organize a novel support base, principally through appreciating the security dimensions located on the epistemological frontiers of time and space. Although the EZLN's epistemological approach to organization and power may be novel, the theme of organization itself remains classic.

This leads us to the intersection between the strategic issues of time, space, and organization. One is struck by the frequency with which both Sun Tzu and Sun Tzu II refer to water in relation to political power. Flowing water is an analogy of the synergy that occurs among speed, space, and mass (organization). Through an image of the momentum of water carving away boulders, we observe the astonishing power of a formless mass of water in relation to speed and space. The speed of the water is what gives it power, as does its formless organization and related ability to adapt to whatever comes in its constantly changing path. Yet this path is a distinct and precise one. As Sun Tzu notes, "When the speed of rushing water reaches the point where it can move boulders, this is the force of momentum. When the speed of a hawk is such that it can strike and kill, this is precision. So it is with skillful warriors—their force is swift, their precision is close."[41] This analogy of water—or the synergy among temporal, spatial, and organizational principals of strategy—has found expression in the EZLN's most successful strategic endeavors.

Finally, a brief comparison of the Zapatistas with the EPR suggests that the concept of "era" may not be as important as epistemology when analyzing guerrilla movements. While the EPR has operated during the same relative time frame as the EZLN, its approach to warfare has been highly traditional. The EPR has organized itself into combat units employing traditional guerrilla violence and has relied heavily on Che Guevara's hit-and-run tactics.[42] Beyond attacking police units and the like, the group bombed a series of prominent banks in 2001. It has been highly secretive and has demonstrated a nomadic tendency rather than a penchant for staked territory.

In terms of objectives, strategy, and organization, the EPR is nearly indistinguishable from Mexican guerrilla groups in Guerrero of the 1970s, from which it is derived. The EPR has stated that it wished to "take power," and has recited old-fashioned Marxist-Leninist dogma. It has constructed a traditional support base consisting almost exclusively of marginalized peasants. Although it established a website and has communicated through the Internet, it has failed to cultivate the relatively widespread national and global support base enjoyed by the Zapatistas. Mexico's Procuraduría General de la República (PGR) has claimed to have established links during the 1990s between the EPR and Peru's highly traditional duo of guerrilla groups, Sendero Luminoso and the MRTA.[43] Overall, the EPR has approached guerrilla warfare through the lens of a traditional episteme—complete with its Marxist-Leninist dogma, its traditional support base, and its traditional strategy and tactics. It has not demonstrated any new epistemological approaches to time, space, organization, political identity, strategy, and goals such as have characterized the Zapatista struggle. Hence, when analyzing guerrilla groups, epistemological approach can be more important than era.

Government Strategy

The broad features of the Mexican government's strategy are well known and not terribly complicated. At first, the government seemed to have no strategy or system of intelligence at all with regard to the Zapatistas. It was caught totally off guard by the EZLN uprising on 1 January 1994. But within a day, the Mexican army mobilized and proceeded to confront the guerrillas. After twelve days and about 150 casualties, the rebel group was completely overpowered by the army and direct violent combat between the two sides ceased.

The government's woes in Chiapas were related to a web of other crises in the mid-1990s. Not the least of these was the economic calamity of December 1994–January 1995. Although the speculative run on the peso had multiple roots, an important contributing factor was the false but widely advertised claim on the part of the Zapatistas that the group had broken out of army encirclement and seized additional territory. This proverbial last straw led foreign investors and speculators to push the panic button, withdrawing billions of dollars within days. In this context of a speculative financial crisis and a tarnished public image for the nascent NAFTA, the government was compelled to win back the confidence of foreign investors. The Mexican government had to demonstrate that it was indeed in control, despite mounting chaos in the country.

A major component of the government's response was the massive 9 February 1995 offensive against the Zapatistas. It represented a desperate though ultimately successful government endeavor to save face and reassert control. Through this operation EZLN safehouses across the country were raided and some leaders of the group were arrested, and the government revealed during a television extravaganza the "true identities" of the Zapatista leaders, including Marcos. This government offensive relied heavily on intelligence operations. Indeed, since 1994 the state has relied on a network of clandestine *grupos de inteligencia,* whose job has been to spy on the Zapatistas and other subversive groups.[44]

But despite this clever use of intelligence services, there were also blunders during this period. Just as the EZLN initiated its struggle with a throwback to the Cold War era, so too did elements of government policy during the February 1995 offensive. As Subcomandante Marcos would later comment, "To our good fortune, the government applied the same policies [to the Zapatistas] as they did to the classic guerrilla: accusations of foreign control, foreign funding," and the like.[45] Those unsubstantiated government allegations quickly drifted into oblivion. Throughout the rest of the decade and into the twenty-first century, the Zedillo administration's central and simple strategy was to contain the EZLN within a limited space, to isolate the rebels, and to do so in a protracted way that would promote fatigue and disgust among Zapatista members and supporters.

Militarily the government relied on a strategy of low-intensity conflict. Among other things, this entailed the military occupation of specific communities suspected of supporting the Zapatistas, combined with a generally heavy military presence throughout the conflict region. During this period, an estimated 30,000 to 40,000 Mexican army troops occupied the conflict zone in Chiapas, representing between 15 percent and 30 percent of the total Mexican armed forces.[46] Twinning this strategy was the implementation of a variety of quickly assembled government social programs aimed at winning the hearts and minds of the local population.

Alongside this strategy of low-intensity conflict, a plethora of right-wing paramilitary groups proliferated that attacked or harassed Zapatista supporters and NGOs. The Academia Mexicana de Derechos Humanos presented evidence that at least ten paramilitary groups existed in Chiapas by 2000, with the largest and most powerful of these being Desarrollo, Paz, y Justicia, which began in 1995; Los Chinchulines, which originated in 1996; and the Movimiento Indígena Revolucionario Antizapatistas, which formed in 1997.[47] Some reliable estimates suggest paramilitary forces have murdered hundreds of indigenous people in Chiapas since 1995—many times more than the official casualty rate of the EZLN's first twelve days of military combat. Further, over 20,000 people were documented to have been displaced by the paramilitaries during the period 1995–2000.[48]

In some publicized episodes, such as the Acteal massacre, clear links between the paramilitaries and high levels of the local Mexican army were established.[49] The central government has been accused for years of turning a blind eye toward paramilitaries, and for embracing a system of judicial impunity that strengthens the paramilitary forces and other abusers of human rights.[50] Although the paramilitaries and the Mexican government have had the parallel interest of diminishing the power of the Zapatistas and their supporters, there has never been clear evidence that the federal government or national army directorate has supported or directed such groups. In fact, in November of 2000 the federal government sent 1,000 troops to Chiapas in what appears to have been an unsuccessful attempt to eradicate the paramilitaries, though it may have weakened them. Within this atmosphere of conflict, at the dawn of a twenty-first century at least 10,000 indigenous people had been displaced by warfare in Chiapas.

With respect to political strategy, the federal government engaged in dialogue with the Zapatistas until the autumn of 1996, when the so-called peace negotiations associated with the San Andrés Accords terminated in utter failure. The government demonstrated no inclination toward enacting the policies entailed in the accords with respect to indigenous autonomy. Thus between 1996 and 2000 the Zedillo administration avoided meaningful negotiations with the EZLN. At the same time, the government provided a substantial increase of social programs in the conflict zone, especially with regard to health, education, and employment. The idea was to wrestle the population's sympathy away from the EZLN and toward the state. The government's strategy seemed to be based on the premise that the protracted political and physical isolation of the Zapatistas, in tandem with a greater provision of social assistance and a more orderly economic and political scenario nationally, would mean that the EZLN would slowly fade into oblivion.

The government embarked on a totally refashioned policy with the election in 2000 of President Vicente Fox. The country's new leader, a former chief executive officer with Coca-Cola who was blessed with considerable political charisma, presented himself as a bold and shrewd negotiator. Rather than isolating the EZLN and hoping that the group would simply fade out of memory, Fox openly engaged the rebels and provided them with the political voice they had been seeking. The president's national security adviser, Adolfo Aguilar Zinser, seemed particularly sympathetic to the rebels. In December 2000 he observed that "it is the Zapatistas and their supporters who have been threatened, who have lost the most people since 1994. . . . War was not declared against us but against a regime that is now over and done with. We have come to make peace."[51]

In a spirited effort to reestablish negotiations with the EZLN, the Fox government gave in to Zapatista demands for troop withdrawals as well as the release of EZLN members held prisoner. Beyond facilitating speeches by Zapatista comandantes at the Mexican Congress in 2001, the president urged members of Congress to support the indigenous rights law that mirrored the San Andrés Accords. On that point, Fox faltered badly—the majority of members of the Mexican Congress, even from the president's own party, did not support the autonomy the indigenous people had demanded. While the president appeared genuinely interested in establishing a lasting peace with the rebels, he did not possess the political influence necessary to convince a majority of Mexicans that an unadulterated indigenous rights law was good for the country as a whole. Overall, rather than playing the role of enemy to the Zapatistas, Fox delivered them from isolation and possibly from imminent oblivion. Unlike Zedillo, Fox did not seem to be afraid of the ELZN's message or of the public support it could generate. Despite some missteps, in general he skillfully engaged in what has been a classic of Mexican political strategy, the fine art of co-optation.

At the same time, in contrast to the policies the Zapatistas were advocating, the president touted Plan Puebla-Panama as the key to resolving the severe economic malaise in southern Mexico. He insisted that a new free trade zone for the region would balance the negative effects that had been spawned by NAFTA in the country's agricultural sector. Because NAFTA had been a success in general, according to President Fox, especially with regard to the provision of jobs in the north and center of the country, a roughly similar formula could work for the troubled south.[52] Overall, the president appeared highly confident in his own views and policies, so much so that he was willing to meet the EZLN head on. He gambled correctly that this would boost his own already strong popularity. He also was riding on the premise that although the Zapatistas would be capable of regenerating some political support once they emerged from isolation, their popular appeal was relatively limited within the larger Mexican framework.

Coupled with the strategy of engagement vis-à-vis the Zapatistas, the Fox government demonized the EPR, and the rebel group that remained militarily at large. With the EZLN militarily contained, the government could afford to negotiate with the group on terms largely defined by the state. But the EPR and its offshoots were different. They embraced a modern and traditional epistemology, and launched a commensurate brand of guerrilla tactics, such as the bombing of banks and police installations. The strategy of the Fox government focused on the deployment of intelligence operations to dismantle the group. Further, the government was unwilling to afford the EPR with any political legitimacy. As the rebels with military power, the EPR was portrayed by the government as the "bad" guerrilla group, while the militarily toothless EZLN represented the "good."

Analytical Context of Government Strategy

The political ebb for the Mexican government occurred during the period between 1988, when apparently fraudulent elections catapulted Carlos Salinas to power, and 1995, after which stability slowly returned to the country. This period was marked with what bordered on political and economic chaos. As Lao Tzu observed, "In government it is order that matters."[53] Further, the classic themes of good government, the power of consent, and basic economic and political justice represent essential strategic concepts identified by Thucydides, Sun Tzu I and Sun Tzu II, Ibn Khaldun, Machiavelli, Hobbes, and others. Yet it was on precisely those crucial issues that the Mexican government failed to deliver. It looked increasingly corrupt and illegitimate, societal consent plummeted as economic crisis loomed and social programs were cut, while crime and narcotrafficking escalated. Periods of great change are notoriously difficult to manage, as the Mexican government found out when it attempted to cope with the huge transformations emanating from globalization and from NAFTA. Nevertheless, classic themes of good government and leadership cannot prudently be neglected.[54] When they were, it essentially set the stage for the appearance and power of the Zapatistas.

Conversely, as the government steered toward better leadership and slowly cultivated more popular support, the Zapatistas' power faced mounting challenges. The relatively clean elections federally and in Chiapas during 2000 can be viewed as nothing other than a clear credit to the Zedillo administration. So, too, was the provision during the late 1990s of substantial increases of social welfare to Chiapas. Further, the Mexican government bolstered its intelligence capacity, as was demonstrated in the strategically successful raid against the EZLN in February 1995.[55] The government has also employed intelligence operations to curtail the EPR and has infiltrated with spies remote indigenous communities in Oaxaca and elsewhere to flush out the group's supporters.[56] As demonstrated by the writings of Sun Tzu, a key component of classic strategy is to foresee and arrest security problems before they emerge, through the use of intelligence and other devices.[57] While the Mexican government initially failed to take heed of classic security themes, it successfully recovered lost ground as the 1990s progressed.

Many other elements of government policy were related to classic strategic issues. The tactic of military encirclement is a venerated one, as is the classic strategy of surprise attack.[58] Both were employed by the government in the February 1995 offensive. The subsequent government policy of divide and conquer vis-à-vis the community of Zapatista supporters, and of exhausting them and the EZLN in a protracted struggle, are also popular themes in the classic strategic literature. Examples of this included the funneling of government funds to strategically placed communities in an effort to pry them from the influence of the Zapatistas. With regard to the strategy of divide and conquer, numerous NGOs engaged in the Chiapas struggle, for example, have reported infighting among themselves in relation to accepting state funds and participating in government programs.[59] Certainly the Clausewitzean tactic of exhaustion proved to be a reliable one for the government as it engaged in years of empty dialogue vis-à-vis the EZLN during the late 1990s.

The government has adopted fresh epistemological approaches to a host of classic security themes. The first of these concerns changes in the general political constellation that have arrived with NAFTA. Until the implementation of the free trade agreement, the Mexican government was more or less able to operate under the private umbrella of the national-security state. The government generally addressed Mexican problems as it pleased, with scant consideration for foreign political actors. The height of this was the 1968 student massacre by government forces in Mexico City, despite the presence of the Olympic Games in the country. But since the implementation of NAFTA, the situation has transformed. Many politically powerful eyes have set their gaze on Mexico. This surveillance has included careful scrutiny by an assortment of critical NGOs, which have had the capacity to disseminate instantly what they view as unacceptable aspects of Mexican security policy. North American NGOs in particular have viewed NAFTA not only as an economic space, but as a political one that provides them with some clout vis-à-vis Mexican affairs. Here we confront issues surrounding the emergence of new strategic space.

The Mexican government in 1999 deported foreign members of NGOs, such as Global Exchange, in an attempt to better control the delicate situation in Chiapas. But other foreigners are likely to move in, and regional and global NGOs will likely continue to monitor Mexican policies. The space of national privacy associated with an earlier epistemological era vanished with the emergence of NAFTA. That is, the Mexican government previously considered security threats largely in terms of the maintenance of internal order, with local subversives as the chief enemy.[60] But it has been compelled to know strategic threats in new forms, ranging from the infowar deployed by transnational NGOs to the whims of global speculative capital.

At least as important as the attention Mexico has received from foreign NGOs has been the changing position of the United States vis-à-vis Mexican security. This, too, is illustrative of the changing spatial relations of security. Although a book by the present author has been devoted to this topic, a number of summary points can be made here.[61] First, during NAFTA negotiations in the early 1990s, both the Mexican and U.S. governments seemed to turn a blind eye to even the possibility of Mexican security problems in terms of guerrilla movements or other subversive forces. This was based on what turned out to be the incorrect premise that because Mexico had been stable since the revolution, this stability naturally would continue into the indefinite future. But when the Zapatistas appeared, alarm bells rang, and U.S. influence over Mexican security issues went into overdrive.

A U.S.-influenced restructuring of the Mexican military occurred. This paralleled broader military influence over other sectors such as communication, transportation, and even local policing duties, among other changes.[62] U.S. military assistance to the Mexican government escalated, especially after the two countries formed their first formal military pact in 1996. The United States has provided military training to Mexican soldiers and officers through institutions such as the School of the Americas, where Mexicans made up about a third of total students in 1997 and about a fourth in 1998. About U.S.$20 million in agreements were established in 2000 for U.S. military sales to Mexico (including equipment, training, and services).[63] In that context, during 2000 the CIA estimated that the Mexican government itself devoted about U.S.$4 billion to military expenditures.[64] Overall, while it may be an exaggeration to suggest that U.S. military influence on Mexico has been as profound as its economic influence under NAFTA, there is no question that since the establishment of this trade agreement Washington exercises far greater strategic influence over Mexican affairs than ever before.

While some U.S. military assistance to Mexico was apparently devoted to containing the guerrillas in southern Mexico, there was an attempt to conceal this by claiming that such aid was provided to combat narcotrafficking in the country. This was largely a result of the sensitive topic in Mexico of creeping U.S. strategic influence over Mexican territory, as well as the potentially dangerous public relations issue in the United States of rampant guerrilla movements within the borders of its new trade partner.[65] All of this meant that the U.S. strategic shadow over Mexican national space would occur partially under the guise of the so-called war against drugs.

For example, a 1996 report by the U.S. General Accounting Office acknowledged that several helicopters provided by the United States to Mexico to fight narcotrafficking were actually used to transport Mexican military personnel in 1994 during the beginning of the Chiapas conflict.[66] Between 1996 and 1999, the U.S. government granted Mexico about $100 million to fight drug trafficking, which included military training as well as equipment such as planes and radar.[67] More specifically, during that period the Pentagon devoted dozens of military helicopters to Mexico allegedly for combating airborne shipments of illicit drugs. Yet it is known that traffickers almost never used air routes in Mexico during this time frame, and instead preferred to ship by marine containers. Not one jetload of cocaine or other drugs was detected by this operation for the first three years after its implementation in 1996.[68] Given the utter failure demonstrated by that record, the possibility arises that these helicopters might actually have been used for other purposes, perhaps to combat subversives, as was the case in the example noted from 1994. Related to this, in July 1999 the U.S. General Accounting Office heavily criticized the policies of the U.S. Drug Enforcement Agency in Mexico, citing highly ineffective work and poor fiscal accountability.[69]

Overall, U.S. military influence over Mexico naturally has increased since NAFTA. The trade agreement altered the spatial dimensions of North American security. This has been a result of two general factors. First, when production moves from a national basis to a regional one, national security transforms to regional security. Second, Mexico's cascade into near chaos between 1994 and 1995, which featured the emergence of guerrilla groups such as the Zapatistas, meant that Washington felt compelled to ensure that order would return to Mexico. There is much new in this regard. Spatially, the nation-state remains, but has given way to new political spaces that are regional, such as NAFTA, and others that are localized and autonomous, such as the land claimed by the indigenous in Chiapas and elsewhere.[70] All of this altered the manner in which the Mexican government could deal, even in its own national space, with strategic issues such as the Zapatistas. This new epistemological approach to space and borders set the stage for the EZLN's struggle with the Mexican government.

Shifts in temporal relations have also been reflected in government strategy. Time and its relation to security represents a prominent theme in the strategic literature. In general, the Mexican government's attitude toward time has been changing dramatically. There is no clearer or more profound example of this than the recent downsizing for government employees of their lunch break, from the previous two- to three-hour lunch to the one-hour U.S.-style version.[71] Family and business relations have been altered by this revision of the government's official view of time. In the case of business, for example, the previous long lunch period permitted an opportunity to close a deal with an important client, and then return to work for a few hours to get the paperwork in order. For family life, lunch was the main meal of the day and a leisurely time for the family to socialize. This shift is more significant than it might at first appear. It represents a common symbol that Mexico would now march to the beat of the U.S. approach to time, to the pace of transnational capital and real-time communication.

Partially due to the Zapatista rebellion, the Mexican government learned the hard way how remarkably little time it would take for stock market investors to withdraw almost U.S.$50 billion, as they did over the Christmas–New Year's holiday of 1994–1995. The wrath of global speculators was particularly harsh on Mexico. It was a result of the instantaneous information available globally that depicted a crisis in the realms of balance of payments and debt against the backdrop of mounting political turmoil. The reaction time for the government shrank to near nothing. Foreign investors could press a computer button to retract billions of dollars of investment in nanoseconds. This meant that the Mexican government was forced to contend with the alarming acceleration of strategic time.

While the changes occurring within the realms of time and of space are significant enough in their own right, it is the synergy between temporal and spatial changes that has contributed to what security specialists have deemed the revolution in military affairs.[72] With regard to

Mexico in particular, the clearest manifestations of this revolution have been the advent of netwar, or information war, as well as the implementation of the doctrine of low-intensity conflict. With respect to netwar, there were two general groups that concerned the U.S. and Mexican governments. First, there were outfits such as Chiapas95, an Internet news distribution service that has provided quick and often critical information regarding the activities of the Mexican government in Chiapas. Common themes included information regarding human rights abuses, paramilitary activity, military abuse, and government fraud. The broader notion is that an Internet group such as Chiapas95 represented a network of support for the Zapatistas. The government's response was interesting. It created its own websites, which contained increasingly more information on Chiapas and other relevant themes.[73] The idea was to provide information and perspectives other than those disseminated by the Zapatistas and their supporters. More generally, as David Ronfeldt and his colleagues have keenly observed, "It takes networks to fight networks. Governments that would defend against netwar will, increasingly, have to adopt organizational designs and strategies like those of their adversaries."[74] Overall the government's strategy of infowar may be in some sense considered clever, but it was altogether reactionary and unoriginal. It was the Zapatistas, not the government, who defined the terrain of cyberspace as a site of warfare.

An additional component of the Mexican government's strategy was directed at the second perceived threat, that of pro-Zapatista NGOs located in Mexico, especially in Chiapas. The Zedillo administration attempted to co-opt a variety of NGOs, usually through the provision of funding or access to an assortment of government programs.[75] Hence the government's strategy has involved the co-optation of hostile or potentially hostile Mexican NGOs in an effort to encourage them to work within the political system, rather than supporting subversive tendencies in the country. No government in the world has a better historical record of political co-optation than Mexico. The state's strategy of netwar involved the provision of information on its own websites, combined with a strategy of breaking a hostile network by winning over as many NGOs as possible through co-optation.[76]

Paralleling this, especially between 1995 and 2000, the government implemented a strategy of low-intensity conflict. In contrast to the carpet bombing and traditional carnage associated with other sorts of war, this strategy is all about subduing the enemy with relative subtlety. It is used when the enemy cannot be demonized, in contrast to the cases of

Iraq's Saddam Hussein and Serbia's Slobodan Milosevic. That is, the Zapatistas did not make good media enemies, given their relatively reasonable demands, their reticence to engage in violence or terrorism, and their proven capacity to manipulate the media, making themselves virtual guerrilla pop stars. If the Mexican government had chosen to launch a traditional war against the Zapatistas, seeking to exterminate them, the widespread bad publicity generated from such an endeavor likely would have sparked additional popular uprisings and thus even more woes for the state.

The strategy of low-intensity conflict is designed not to eliminate enemies quickly, but to contain them in the short run and neutralize them through exhaustion in the long run. Containment is a classic strategy. Despite the strategic opportunities for the Zapatistas in the new space of the Internet, traditional space remains as important as ever. As Marcos observed in 2001, physical isolation remained the central political problem for the Zapatistas.[77] Further, the temporal aspect is also significant, since low-intensity conflict entails a protracted struggle. This long, slow-motion war is meant to create fatigue and disgust among belligerents, and to instill in the general population a sense of the guerrillas' irrelevance.

At the same time, the strategy of low-intensity conflict entails the state's key attempt to wrestle the guerrillas' local support base away from them through a variety of tactics. These include the sudden provision of generous government programs to lure the target population away from the guerrillas, such as the Mexican government's new array of social welfare policies for Chiapas's conflict zone. In more severe cases, when social programs alone are insufficient to achieve the desired result, the military literally occupies communities suspected of guerrilla sympathy. In July 1995, for example, tens of thousands of government troops stormed the conflict zone, especially in the municipalities of Ocosingo, Altamirano, and Las Margaritas. In the heartland of Zapatista support in the Lacandona jungle, there was an extraordinary ratio of one soldier for every three residents.[78]

Beyond this, the formation and activity of paramilitary forces seems to have worked in parallel with government objectives of weakening and intimidating the left. It may be considered a general feature of low-intensity conflict. While there has been no evidence that the federal government has trained or directed the paramilitaries, what is absolutely clear is that the government has not been nearly as energetic in its attempts to contain and neutralize the paramilitaries as it has been vis-à-vis the EZLN and the EPR. Further, there has indeed been clear evidence that municipal and state authorities in Mexico have worked closely with the paramilitaries.[79]

The government's strategy has been successful in many ways. Although it got off to a poor start, and made a number of blunders along the way, overall the Mexican government has succeeded at containing and managing the Zapatistas. Zedillo's strategy of isolating the EZLN while simultaneously providing more aid to the conflict region served to diminish the political influence of the Zapatistas. President Fox's bold strategy of providing a political voice to the Zapatistas, and of thrusting them into the public limelight, demonstrated considerable political skill and enormous confidence. The episode showed that while the rebels represented an important political force and wielded a credible political platform, there was no longer any reason for the government to isolate or mute them. Beyond garnering domestic popularity from his dealings with the EZLN, cleaning up the mess in Chiapas was viewed as representing an important first step for the Fox administration's clear endeavor to assert itself globally through membership in UN peace forces and other programs of the UN Security Council.[80]

Despite those successes, important problems loom on the horizon. The recession since 2001 threatened to neutralize President Fox's campaign promise of more jobs. Threats of additional economic destabilization emanating from the potential for an Argentine debt default remained worrisome early in the twenty-first century, despite the IMF's provision to Mexico of a special cushion should a crisis materialize.[81] The onset of severe economic problems could clearly bolster rebel support, as it did in 1994–1995. Indeed, Mexico's secretary of national defense recognized in August 2001 that increasing inequity and poverty contributed to the proliferation of guerrilla groups in during the 1990s and into the twenty-first century. He argued that "the solution is not military, but it is a problem of social development, of improving the economic and social conditions in zones where manifestations of guerrilla activity has surged."[82] That worthy goal would be more difficult to achieve in an atmosphere of economic contraction. Beyond this, while Fox's Plan Puebla-Panama has received some support on a strictly economic level, it is fraught with enormous strategic implications that could be exploited by the EZLN and other rebels. Finally, Mexican democracy failed the indigenous population of southern Mexico, who demanded more autonomy as enshrined in the San Andrés Accords. The diluted indigenous rights law ratified by the Mexican Congress in 2001 is likely to alienate further a considerable portion of the country's indigenous population, and may push them into the camp of the EZLN and other rebels. Thus the conflict between the Zapatistas and the government appears to be far from over.

There have been many new and important twists within the realm of security as reflected in the Zapatista experience, but the themes outlined by the classic strategists remain as relevant as ever. Examples include the significance of good leadership, the cultivation of societal consent, the government's duty of procuring order and stability, and the role of temporal and spatial strategic elements. It is the fresh epistemological approach to those classic themes that has been crucially important for success. Beyond the significance of fresh epistemological interpretations of classic themes, does the Zapatista experience suggest anything fundamentally new in the realms of strategy and warfare? Here we confront the profound debate concerning the role of death in warfare. With respect to the classics, certainly death and destruction were prominent features of war, as evidenced by the writings of Thucydides, Machiavelli, Hobbes, and others. It was Clausewitz, in his monumental tract *On War,* who argued for the necessary connection between war and political murder. "War is a clash between major interests, which is resolved by bloodshed—that is the only way it differs from other conflicts."[83] Yet other classic strategists with equal clout would disagree with that assessment of warfare. In *The Art of War,* Sun Tzu notes, for example, that "those who render others' armies helpless without fighting are the best of all."[84]

One question, then, is whether the government's struggle with the Zapatistas can be considered a war at all. If it is considered a war, then from the perspective of most classical strategists, with the exception of Sun Tzu I and Sun Tzu II, the Mexican case may indeed herald something new, and that is the lack or diminishment of political murder. Alvin and Heidi Toffler coined the term *demassification* to argue that murder and widespread destruction are no longer necessary features of warfare. "Mass destruction will no doubt be with us for as long as we can foresee. . . . But demassified destruction, custom-tailored to minimize collateral damage, will increasingly dominate the zones of battle, exactly paralleling changes in the civilian economy."[85] Hence the argument is not that war will no longer entail political murder and mass destruction, but that there increasingly will be cases of warfare where those elements are not prominent, as with the Zapatistas in Mexico. One still needs to make a clear distinction between wars that rely heavily on political murder, such as those in Colombia, and wars that do not, as in the Mexican case. While any war involves an attempt to subdue the enemy, the use of political murder to obtain that objective represents a fundamental point of distinction.

Conclusion

What is the significance of the experience of the EZLN vis-à-vis conceptions of power, strategy, and security? Once the Zapatistas were confronted with their immense military failure literally the day after they declared war on the Mexican government on 1 Janauary 1994—an error that was rooted in their clumsy employment of a rather traditional perspective—a desperate but highly fertile period of reflection ensued. The result was a fresh epistemological approach to power, security, and strategy. It proved successful in many ways, though it also met considerable limits. The biggest success of the Zapatistas, according to Subcomandante Marcos, has been the creation of some degree of hope among the marginalized indigenous population of Chiapas. "The fundamental change has been for the good; there's hope. There was not any before 1994."[86] Beyond this, with respect to the Zapatistas' relation to security and warfare, perhaps the most important thing about the EZLN is that it is still around years after its military defeat. More specifically, the Zapatistas have demonstrated the deterrent power of real-time infowar, reflecting what Bentham, and later Foucault, called the panopticon.

In what ways have "systems of thought" ruptured and transformed in relation to the realm of security?[87] With regard to the new episteme of space and time, for example, the Zapatistas have established a global reach through real-time Internet communication, despite their physical isolation in Chiapas. They took strategic advantage of the shrinkage of space and time in a pioneering manner, which has represented an important basis of their power. Further, much of that communication has been launched not by the ELZN directly, but by a network of supportive NGOs at the local, national, regional, and global levels. In that sense, new ways of knowing time and space have precipitated new forms of political organization. Rather than the traditional guerrillas of the Cold War, who where reliant on foreign states, the EZLN has been reliant on a novel organization of local and foreign NGOs. The Zapatistas successfully exploited in a strategic sense the new space of NAFTA. How can we conceive of space and time in a pioneering way that harnesses great and sudden change on a number of fronts and use this to our strategic benefit? That was the problem the EZLN addressed with some considerable success.

Beyond time, space, and organization, the Zapatistas also explored new forms of power associated with words and language. In the world of real-time communication, the written word is more important than ever. The power of the word has been celebrated by Subcomandante Marcos, whose gift for both fictional and nonfictional prose is extraordinary. Not only have these words had a global reach through the new vehicle of the Internet, but they were not filtered by the traditional global media. The EZLN's harnessing of the availability and rapidity of those unfiltered words helped place the Zapatistas on the epistemological frontiers of strategy and power.

An important dimension of epistemology concerns how one knows the truth—that is, there is a relationship between knowledge, political power, and what is common regarded as the truth.[88] During a previous era, it was more or less easy for countries such as the United States and Mexico to manipulate the truth by controlling the kinds of information publicly available, especially through the traditional media. Often the only thing the public at large knew about the "enemy" was what they read or heard in the elite media, and that counted as the truth. The ability effectively to control what the public knew to be the truth translated into enormous political power. But that monopoly on information, that filter of knowledge and of truth, evaporated during the information revolution associated with the Internet. The American and global public have known about the Zapatistas based on information that the Zapatistas themselves have disseminated. Beyond this, the incorporation of spirituality as a means of determining truth has been an essential element of liberation theology, and this has had a strong influence on many EZLN supporters. Hence an important dimension of this epistemological shift has been the appearance of a new configuration of knowledge, political power, and truth. This aspect of the Zapatista experience represents among the most significant elements of the epistemological shift that has occurred within the realms of strategy, security, and warfare.

With regard to the related theme of language, there is much that is both new and traditional vis-à-vis the politics of the EZLN. For example, the official language of Spanish has been an old and huge barrier for the indigenous of Chiapas. The inability of many of the indigenous in that state to speak Spanish has meant they have been essentially shut out from the justice system, since they may be unable to communicate cases of abuse to authorities or may be presented by authorities with documents they are unable to read.[89] If that is a traditional problem, what is new is the Zapatistas' demand for a recognition of the relation between the power of language and the power of the state. The Zapatistas know language is power, and this is expressed in their demands for an official status for indigenous languages, among other elements of their platform.

Another feature of this new epistemological approach to security and power concerns the political identities of the EZLN's targeted support base. While its local supporters predominantly have been Mayan Indians, the political platform of the Zapatistas has been aimed at women, anti-neoliberals, environmental groups, gays and lesbians, and the like. This reflects an attempt to organize an umbrella group of the marginalized in a manner that provides them with a newfound voice and power. The EZLN has stood as a symbol for a broad conglomerate of the dispossessed, whose collective interests and spatial locations have exceeded the capacity of traditional national parties. Hence, rather than the mobilization of cadres of campesino guerrilla fighters cultivated during the Cold War by Che Guevara and others, the Zapatistas have attempted to obtain power from organizing newly emerging political identities based on ethnicity as well as social and economic marginalization. With their finger on the pulse of change, the Zapatistas successfully experimented with "knowing" and then organizing political identity in new ways.

The Zapatistas have also prompted security specialists to reexamine the nature of war. Classic security strategists such as Clausewitz defined war by its relationship to widespread bloodshed and violence. Yet real-time surveillance and an information war have served to limit "war casualties" to the first twelve days of the Zapatistas' struggle, with no direct combat after that. We are familiar with Clausewitz's contention that "war is simply a continuation of political intercourse, with the addition of other means."[90] But perhaps more relevant to the case of the EZLN is the converse postulate that politics itself "is a war continued by other means."[91]

Does the case of the Zapatistas suggest that the use of information and surveillance—a twenty-first century panopticon—can be deployed universally as a deterrent to the bloodshed associated with traditional war? Does it mean, in other words, that "demassification" or wars without much death and violence are the wave of the future? The answer is that the Zapatista experience represents an exceptional case, and so the convention of war as murder and mayhem will likely persist. Although this theme will be more fully explored in the concluding chapter, a question that can be posed here concerns why information, networking, and surveillance have stopped or reduced political murder in Mexico, while those same features have not halted the rampant carnage characteristic of Colombia's brutal civil war. The Mexican case demonstrates that for information, networking, and surveillance to be a deterrent to bloodshed, there must be present a developed civil society in tandem with state political structures that are relatively centralized, legitimate, accountable, and militarily powerful. There must also be a national or regional culture that deplores political violence. Even Mexico's most traditional and violent guerrillas, the EPR, have not come close to resorting to the degree of carnage unleashed by Sendero Luminoso and the FARC. Mexico's relative stability and its generally successful transformation from modernity to postmodernity have set the stage for a kinder and gentler treatment of the Zapatistas than might otherwise have been the case.

Ironically, it is Mexico's membership in the neoliberal trade bloc of NAFTA—the ultimate symbol of politico-economic postmodernity that the Zapatistas love to hate—that has been one of the most important factors in preventing the rebels from being militarily exterminated. If the walls of national privacy had not been torn down, if a transnational civil society among NAFTA members had not emerged, the EZLN would likely have met the same fate as the 1,500 guerrillas murdered at the hands of the Mexican state in the 1970s. Regional politics and regional security under NAFTA have been nothing less than a godsend for the EZLN. Further, perhaps we have here an updated version of the old inside/outside duality, whereby the United States and Canada are now willing to consider Mexico "inside" as a result of NAFTA, but it remains a dog-eat-dog world for outsiders such as Colombia.[92]

Notes

1. See Carlos Montemayor, in his editorial in *La Jornada* (Mexico City), 29 September 2000.

2. EZLN, Subcomandante Marcos, "Intervención oral del EZLN," 30 July 1996, p. 320, translation by author.

3. Se Tello Díaz, *La rebelión de las Cañadas,* p. 105, translation by author.

4. Ibid., p. 174.

5. See EZLN, *El Despertador Mexicano: Órgano Informativo del EZLN* no. 1 (December 1993): 37, translation and italics by author.

6. See EZLN, "Declaración de la Selva Lacandona," December 1993 (no specific date). See also EZLN, Subcomandante Marcos, "Composición del EZLN y condiciones para el diálogo," 6 January 1994, p. 75, translation by author.

7. See EZLN, "Declaración de la Selva Lacandona," translation and italics by author.

8. See EZLN, *El Despertador Mexicano,* pp. 36–48, translation by author.

9. EZLN, "Palabras para la celebración del 10th aniversario de la formación del Ejército Zapatista de Liberación Nacional," 17 November 1994, p. 136, translation by author.

10. Subcomandante Marcos, interview with *La Jornada,* 8 January 2001, translation by author.

11. EZLN, "Tercera declaración de la Selva Lacandona," 2 January 1995 (no specific date), translation by author.

12. EZLN, "Saluda a los insurgentes y milicianos," 1 January 1995, p. 194.

13. See EZLN, "Obra en dos actos, sobre la clase política, que no termina," published in *La Jornada,* 30 November 2000; and EZLN, "Comunicado de Comité Clandestino Revolucionario Indígena–Comandancia General del EZLN," published in *La Jornada,* 2 December 2000.

14. By January 2001 the government retracted troops from three military installations, as well as from the municipality of Palenque.

15. EZLN, "Tres comunicados del EZLN," 8 December 2000, published in *La Jornada,* 11 December 2000.

16. There was a 45 percent drop in corn prices in Mexico between 1998 and 2001, leaving many Mexican farmers unable to compete with U.S. agribusiness, which can produce corn and other crops cheaper than Mexicans. Sugar cane and coffee crops were also in crisis at this time. See *New York Times,* 22 July 2001.

17. See *La Jornada,* 12 March 2001.

18. For a good discussion of Plan Puebla-Panama, see, for example *La Jornada,* 28 May 2001 and 16 June 2001.

19. See *New York Times,* 26 December 2001.

20. For a good discussion of preliminary issues surrounding Plan Puebla-Panama, see *La Jornada,* 26 August 2001.

21. See Clausewitz, *War,* p. 93.

22. "Special Report: The Communications Revolution/Languages of Technology," *Time,* 11 October 2000, www.pathfinder.com/time/magazine/articles/ 0,3266,32558,00.html.

23. See Virilio and Lotringer, *Pure War,* p. 177.

24. On the theme of simultaneity, see, for example, Dearth and Williamson, "Information Age/Information War," p. 23.

25. This quote from Marcos is from a 1996 interview with Yvon LeBot, and reprinted in Ronfeldt et al., *Zapatista Social Netwar in Mexico,* p. 70.

26. See Sun Tzu, *Àrt of War,* pp. 152–153.

27. See Virilio and Lotringer, *Pure War,* p. 77.

28. See Brian Kahin, "Thinking About Information Infrastructure," in Stuart Schwartzstein and William Owens, eds., *The Information Revolution and National Security: Dimensions and Directions* (Washington, D.C.: Center for Strategic and International Studies, 1996), p. 10.

29. The membership of Peru's Sendero Luminoso also had a strong contingent of women and indigenous people.

30. CONPAZ is now defunct.

31. In my interviews throughout Chiapas, many groups were supportive of the Zapatistas, but have had differences between themselves over issues such as the best way to approach the state, their faith in elections, and so on. Virtually all the groups I interviewed throughout Mexico indicated that the Internet made organization and education cheaper and faster than ever before imaginable, and

was helpful in this regard. Author interviews with Marina Patricia Jiménez Ramírez, director, Centro de Derechos Humanos Fray Bartolomé de las Casas, San Cristóbal de las Casas, Chiapas, 25 August 2000; Alma Rosa Rojas, Centro para Educación de la Paz, San Cristóbal de las Casas, Chiapas, 29 August 2000; Gustavo Castro Soto, Centro de Investigaciones Económicos y Políticos de Acción Comunitaria, San Cristóbal de las Casas, Chiapas, 29 August 2000; and various members of the Comité de Derechos Humanos Fray Pedro Lorenzo de la Nada, Ocosingo, Chiapas, 15 September 2000. Further, Judith Alder Hellman wrote a provocative article that provided a critique of some Zapatista supporters, including Internet newsgroups such as Chiapas95 as well as a variety of NGOs. Their sometimes varying ideological agendas are discussed, as well as political contests among them. See Judith Alder Hellman, "Real and Virtual Chiapas," www.yorku.ca/org/socreg/hellman.txt (originally printed in Leo Panitch and C. Leys, eds., *Necessary and Unnecessary Utopias—Socialist Register* [New York: Monthly Review Press, 1999]). This sparked a spirited and critical response to Hellman's work. See, for example, the piece authored by the lead organizer of Chiapas95, Harry Cleaver, "The Virtual and Real Chiapas Support Network: A Review and Critique of Judith Alder Hellman's 'Real and Virtual Chiapas: Magic Realism and the Left,'" *Socialist Register 2000*, www.eco. utexas.edu/faculty/Cleaver/anti-hellman.html.

32. For a short list of these groups, see previous endnote.

33. Ronfeldt et al., *Zapatista Social Netwar in Mexico*, p. 9.

34. On targeting the human mind, see Stein, "Information Warfare," pp. 175–176.

35. On the idea of knowledge warriors, see Toffler and Toffler, *War and Anti-War*, p. 141. Braulliard quoted in James Der Derian, "Global Swarming, Virtual Security, and Bosnia," in Stuart Schwartzstein and William Owens, eds., *Information Revolution and National Security* (Washington, D.C.: Center for Strategic and International Studies), p. 183.

36. Virilio, *Speed and Politics*, p. 85.

37. Guevara, *Guerrilla Warfare*, p. 16.

38. See the Zapatista website, www.ezln.org.

39. Guevara, *Guerrilla Warfare*, pp. 54–55. For more on the organization of the Zapatistas, see Ronfeldt et al., *Zapatista Social Netwar in Mexico*, esp. p. 47; and Steven Wager and Donald Schulz, "The Zapatista Revolt and Its Implications for Civil-Military Relations and the Future of Mexico," in Schulz and Williams, *Mexico Faces the Twenty-First Century*, p. 170–171.

40. Guevara, *Guerrilla Warfare*, p. 12.

41. Sun Tzu, *Art of War*, p. 96.

42. Guevara, *Guerrilla Warfare*, p. 13.

43. *Expreso* (Lima), 28 August 2001.

44. This fact was not officially revealed until 2001. See *La Jornada*, 12 July 2001.

45. Subcomandante Marcos, interview with *La Jornada*, 8 January 2001, translation by author.

46. For a good discussion of a variety of aspects of the Mexican army's presence in Chiapas and estimates of the number of Mexican troops in the region, see

Centro de Investigaciones Económicos y Políticas de Acción Comunitaria (CIEPAC), *Siempre cerca, siempre lejos,* esp. pp. 126–135. The Mexican government has suggested that only 17,000 to 25,000 troops have been in the area, with social critics suggesting twice that amount.

47. Other groups include Máscara Roja, Alianza San Bartolomé de los Llanos, Los Quintos, Los Puñales, Los Tomates, Los Plátinos, and Los Chentes. For the report on the paramilitaries by the Academia Mexicana de Derechos Humanos, see *La Jornada,* 1 June 2000. For other discussions of the paramilitaries, see, for example, various editions of *Proceso* since 1996, including no. 1017 (29 April 1996), no. 1019 (13 May 1996), no. 1104 (29 December 1997), no. 1105 (5 January 1998), no. 1108 (26 January 1998), and no. 1171 (12 April 1999). See also CIEPAC, *Siempre cerca, siempre lejos,* esp. pp. 137–155.

48. See "Exterminio en Chiapas," *Proceso,* no. 1104 (28 December 1997): 6–17; and *La Jornada,* 31 December 1997. Some sources place the number of those murdered by the paramilitaries at about 1,500 between 1995 and 1997. See also CIEPAC, *Siempre cerca, siempre lejos,* chap. 10.

49. Retired General Julio César Santiago Díaz was sentenced in the spring of 2000 to eight years in prison for his role in the Acteal massacre. See *La Jornada,* 18 May 2000.

50. Reacting to an Amnesty International report that criticized torture and impunity in Mexico, the director of the Centro de Estudios de Derechos Públicos at ITAM indicated that "Mexican legislation favors torture and the same law is conducive to impunity." See *La Jornada,* 9 October 2000. Further, peasants I interviewed in Ocosingo, Chiapas, pointed to the continued and strong presence of paramilitaries in the area. They indicated that many who have been harassed by paramilitary forces do not report these incidents due to intimidation or language barriers, or because of a presumption of collusion between authorities and the paramilitaries. These interviews were conducted in September 2000, and participants wished to remain anonymous for security reasons.

51. Quoted in *El Universal* (Mexico City), 14 December 2000, translation by author.

52. For an excellent and detailed discussion of the variety of effects of NAFTA on the Mexican economy during the period 1994–2000, see Gobierno de México, Senado de la República, *Análisis de los efectos del Tratado de Libre Comerico de América del Norte en la economía mexicana,* vols. 1–2.

53. Lao Tzu, *Tao te Ching,* p. 12.

54. The theme of good leadership is common in the classic literature. In his discussion of the necessity of a Leviathan, for example, Hobbes notes that there must be good laws, good punishments, and a just social contract. See Hobbes, *Leviathan,* pp. 387–390, 192. Similar views are expressed by Ibn Khaldun (see, for example, Issawi, *Arab Philosophy of History,* pp. 57, 100–101).

55. See Rochlin, *Redefining Mexican Security,* esp. chap. 3. Further, it was reported in early 2001 that the Mexican government used crude but effective methods of intelligence, such as paying local Indians up to 900 pesos for each piece of information that it considered important vis-à-vis the Zapatistas. See *Reforma* (Mexico City), 15 January 2001.

56. On the topic of the history of the Mexican intelligence system, see the interview with security expert Sergio Aguayo in *Proceso,* no. 1242 (20 August 2000). On the use of intelligence against the EPR, see, for example, *La Jornada,* 25 October 1999.

57. See, for example, Sun Tzu, *Art of War,* pp. 2, 3, 82, 116–117.

58. For example, Sun Tzu mentions encirclement in *The Art of War,* p. 13, and surprise as well, p. 94. Sun Tzu II also mentions the strategic value of encirclement in *The Lost Art of War,* p. 13. Clausewitz mentions the importance of surprise in *On War,* p. 198, as well as the importance of exhausting the enemy, p. 93.

59. Author interviews with members of the Comité de Derechos Humanos Fray Pedro Lorenzo de la Nada, Ocosingo, Chiapas, 15 September 2000; Jorge Angulo Barrero, professor, Centro de Estudios Indígenas, Universidad Nacional Autónoma de Chiapas (UNAM), San Cristóbal de las Casas, Chiapas, 1 September 2000; Otto Shuman, professor and linguist, UNAM, San Cristóbal de las Casas, Chiapas, 1 September 2000; and Elizabeth Pólito, professor, Departamento de Sociología, UNAM, and Centro de Información y Análisis, San Cristóbal de las Casas, 31 August 2000.

60. See Rochlin, *Redefining Mexican Security.*

61. Ibid.

62. Ibid., p. 169.

63. Latin America Working Group, "Mexico," 1999, www.ciponline.org/facts.mx.htm.

64. U.S. Central Intelligence Agency, *World Fact Book 2000,* "Mexico," www.cia.gov/cia/publications/factbook/geos/mx.html.

65. Even high-placed officials in Mexico, such as military generals, have been uneasy about admitting the increasing depth of U.S. influence over Mexican strategic affairs. Author interview with Diputado General Alfredo Ochao Toledo, president, Comisión para Seguridad Nacional, Mexico City, 12 July 2001.

66. *La Jornada,* 13 June 1996.

67. See U.S. General Accounting Office, "Update on US-Mexican Counternarcotics Activities," 4 March 1999, www.access.gpo.gov/cgi-bin/getdoc.cgi?dbnames=gao&docid=f:ns99098.txt.

68. See *New York Times,* 23 December 1998.

69. See *La Jornada,* 23 July 1999.

70. The broad topic of Mexico's role in North American regional security is addressed in Rochlin, *Redefining Mexican Security.*

71. See *New York Times,* 17 October 1999.

72. See Mackubin Thomas Owens, "Technology, the RMA, and Future War."

73. See, for example, the website of the Mexican federal government, executive branch, http://world.presidencia.gob.mx/index.htm.

74. See Ronfeldt et al., *Zapatista Social Netwar in Mexico,* p. 17.

75. My interviews suggest that attempts by the government to co-opt NGOs and to make things difficult for those that do not cooperate existed throughout the late 1990s. Author interviews with Onécimo Hidalgo, CONPAZ,

San Cristóbal de las Casas, Chiapas, 5 June 1996. More recently, author interviews with Gustavo Castro Soto, Centro de Investigaciones Ecónomicos y Políticas de Acción Comunitaria, San Cristóbal de las Casas, Chiapas, 4 September 2000; Otto Shuman, linguist, Universidad Nacional Autónoma de México, San Cristóbal de las Casas, Chiapas, 1 September 2000; and Elizabeth Pólito, Centro de Información y Análisis de Chiapas, San Cristóbal de las Casas, 31 August 2000.

76. The systematic harassment of NGOs and their members is not restricted to Chiapas. Shortly after I interviewed Hilda Navarrete Gorján, director of the human rights group in Guerrero, Comisión la Voz de los Sin Voz, her office was stormed by eighty members of the armed forces, who harassed her through the night. Whether this was in retaliation for her speaking to a foreign researcher such as myself or for other reasons, it is clear that NGOs in Mexico are sometimes the target of government wrath.

77. Subcomandante Marcos, interview with *La Jornada*, 8 January 2001.

78. See Rochlin, *Redefining Mexican Security*, pp. 81–82.

79. This has already been observed in relation to the Acteal massacre in late 1997. Beyond that incident, at least seventeen paramilitary groups were reported to be operating in the region of Loxicha, Oaxaca. The federal Mexican Senate in January 2001 was presented with evidence that paramilitary forces worked closely with local military installations and municipal governments to target suspected members of the EPR. These paramilitary groups were paid between 200 and 500 pesos for each suspected member of the guerrilla group they identified, and they sometimes even accompanied the military to the homes of suspected guerrilla members. *Excelsior* (Mexico City), 18 January 2001.

80. Mexico's foreign minister, Jorge G. Castañeda, indicated that the Fox government's goal of playing a larger role in the peace programs of the United Nations could be advanced by a resolution to the Chiapas conflict. *La Jornada*, 4 January 2001.

81. The IMF has provided the Mexican government with a contingency fund of U.S.$17–$20 billion to ward off the potential for a repeat of the 1994–1995 peso crisis, given potential problems in Argentina surrounding a potential default. See *La Jornada*, 9 May 2001.

82. Quote by Ricardo Clemente Vega García, secretary of national defense, *La Jornada*, 28 August 2001, translation by author.

83. Clausewitz, *On War*, p. 149. He also observed that "war is thus an act of force to compel our enemy to do our will. . . . Kind-hearted people might of course think there was some ingenious way to disarm or defeat an enemy without too much bloodshed, and might imagine this is the true goal of the art of war. Pleasant as it sounds, it is a fallacy that must be exposed: war is such a dangerous business that the mistakes that come from kindness are the very worst" (p. 75).

84. Sun Tzu, *Art of War*, p. 67.

85. Toffler and Toffler, *War and Anti-War*, p. 72.

86. Subcomandante Marcos, interview with *La Jornada*, 8 January 2001. Translation by author.

87. See Foucault, "Will to Knowledge," p. 11.

88. For an excellent discussion of this point, see Foucault, "Truth and Juridical Forms."

89. Author interview with three indigenous campesinos at the Comité de Derechos Humanos Fray Pedro Lorenzo de la Nada, Ocosingo, Chiapas, 15 September 2000.

90. Clausewitz, *War,* p. 605.

91. Foucault, "Two Lectures," p. 90.

92. See Walker, *Inside/Outside.*

8

Conclusion

The rebel groups under consideration here, as well as government forces reacting to them, enjoyed success and suffered failure largely in accordance with how well they interpreted classic security themes within a shifting epistemological context. These enduring themes include space, time, intelligence/espionage, coercion, consent, good government, and the perils of severe economic inequity. A consideration of the classic strategic texts can be especially enlightening during periods of great change, since they can provide a point of reference from which to consider what is old and what is new. The adherence to a particular system of thought matters more than epoch regarding the interpretation of those classic strategic themes, since rebel groups operating in the same time frame have adopted wildly different strategies with distinct epistemological bases.

Peru and Sendero Luminoso

Sendero Luminoso, although it officially originated in 1980, reached its peak of power precisely during the fall of the Soviet Union and of international communism. The rebels helped the Bush administration (1988–1992) in its task of creating a new enemy to replace the Soviet bogeyman, a phenomenon that was subsumed under the Andean drug war of 1989–1992. Interestingly, the experience of Sendero Luminoso hinted at important elements that would become associated with postmodern guerrillas. These include the issue of ethnicity with regard to Sendero's indigenous membership, the group's role in the transnational business of narcotrafficking to ensure the ultimate goal of financial self-sufficiency, and its vigorous protest vis-à-vis neoliberalism. Yet despite the presence of those important components, Sendero was decidedly modern epistemologically. For example, rather than embracing identity politics and related social movements that were spawned on the basis of ethnicity, SL reduced the indigenous struggle to one of class. The Sendero experience demonstrates the importance of epistemological interpretation, since it put a modern spin on issues that would be approached much differently by postmodern guerrillas.

In terms of strategic success, Sendero proved most adept at managing the classic themes of organization and, to a lesser extent, leadership. SL's scheme of organizing and recruiting through the state education system was brilliant in that it took advantage of an existing organizational structure and manipulated it to serve revolutionary designs. Eager students arrived at school to learn about the world, and did so through the modern and neo-Maoist lens of "Gonzalo Thought." There is no doubt that this strategy helped boost the group's ranks to over 23,000 rebels. Also related to the strategic feature of organization was Sendero's cell structure, which afforded the rebels with considerable security vis-à-vis the state. The group's hierarchical framework meant that commands were transmitted and carried out smoothly among the lower ranks, who were expected to take orders dutifully.

Yet despite the highly workable features of Sendero Luminoso's organizational design, it also hosted serious flaws. One of the reasons for the failure of the Velasco government's vast land reform policy was that it was carried out in a top-down, authoritarian fashion that did not allow for grassroots power or even input. The same could be said of Sendero, despite the fact that the rebels themselves criticized the Velasco regime for its lack of provision of autonomous power to indigenous communities. This was not the only hypocritical feature of Sendero's policies, as we observed in Chapters 2 and 3.

The classic theme of leadership represented another mixed blessing for Sendero Luminoso. Abimael Guzmán was indeed revered by his followers, who were encouraged to worship him as a godlike figure. Although he has not received much credit outside of Peru as an ideological luminary, devotees referred to Guzmán as the fourth sword of Marxism. He was charismatic, and he quashed any kernel of dissent that he perceived could threaten the effectiveness of the organization. Coupled with the positive features of Sendero's leadership, there were also important blemishes. Not the least of these was that the organization could not function without Guzmán and was not at all prepared to continue the group's struggle in his absence. It turned out to be Sendero's single biggest vulnerability, since the group fell apart almost immediately after Abimael Guzmán was captured.

Another major strategic error of Sendero Luminoso was its failure to cultivate a significant measure of consent, and its concomitant reliance on the most brutal expressions of violence and terrorism. While classic strategists emphasized the strategic imperative of political consent and support, SL's near unifocus on horrific carnage meant unfavorable strategic consequences. Even if SL had succeeded in its objective of "taking" Lima and then Peru, the absence of substantial consent would have meant that it would always have had to impose its rule through force and most likely would have faced protracted and escalating resistance. Further, Sendero relied so heavily on violence that it drastically reduced prospects for social consent by repulsing potential members or supporters. The overwhelming popularity of rondas, the state-supported autonomous defense groups, demonstrated the limited nature of consent enjoyed by Sendero even in the countryside, which represented its most favorable terrain. Ultimately, the rebels' extraordinary reliance on violence created a legacy whereby Peruvians generally associate the memory of SL with unabashed carnage rather than with any positive achievements.

A strategically troublesome area for Sendero Luminoso had to do with the concepts of space and time. The group clashed with some of its supporters in an epistemological sense with regard to these important themes. For example, the rebels' attempt to strangle the cities by preventing indigenous contact with them interfered with centuries of indigenous commerce with urban centers, as well as connections established between the Andean indigenous highlands and the urban giant of Lima. SL also collided with the indigenous view of time, especially regarding what the population viewed as cycles of family life and of agriculture. Further, we saw that the Inca tradition viewed major change as occurring through a reversal of position, in contrast to Sendero's view of progress that was based on linear time and dialectical contradiction.

Overall, Sendero Luminoso was a failure in terms of achieving its ultimate goal of taking power over the state. More importantly, from the perspective of the Peruvian population, it is hard to say that the Sendero experience benefited society in any way. The rebels' successes were limited to their victory in a series of military battles and their ability to evoke utter terror on the part of the Peruvian population and even the state. While its victories in those battles were impressive in a military sense, Sendero indeed lost the war. What is perhaps so remarkable about the group is the scarcity of praise it has received in published material, or even in the community of Ayacucho, where the group germinated and enjoyed its deepest support. Because of their widespread use of violence and terrorism, the rebels actually poisoned social situations. Further, their participation in transnational crime weakened their ideological credibility, debasing the prospects for longevity of Sendero's professed ideals.

Not only were the rebels epistemologically out of tune with their indigenous supporters, but they also missed the beat of basic global changes. SL embraced a staunchly communist and isolationist ideology when both were increasingly out of synch with global developments. They insisted on the modern notion of one absolute truth, as defined by the deified Abimael Guzmán. They failed to appreciate the growing importance of identity politics and of autonomous power, even though both these features were readily apparent in the group's support base. Sendero also neglected to cultivate outside support and viewed with notorious contempt and suspicion various NGOs that heralded a new form of transnational democracy. Rather than focusing on a fresh wave of political relations that would entail generating consensual power through ideas and information wars, Sendero retained its penchant for terror, alienating would-be supporters on the left.

For its part, the government of Alberto Fujimori, with help from Washington, reversed a ten-year record of strategic failure on the part of the state by acting on ideas developed during the previous García administration regarding the employment of intelligence operations to obliterate Sendero. Given its pyramid structure, SL represented a perfect target for such a strategy. Perhaps this strategic endeavor foreshadowed an increasing tendency by the U.S. and Latin American governments toward intelligence- and information-based warfare, which were later used to greater degrees in the cases of Mexico and Colombia. Yet intelligence operations by themselves are insufficient to ward off future prospects of subversion. While Sendero neglected to develop ideas regarding indigenous identity politics and related autonomous power, and also failed as a credible critic of neoliberal policies due to its own hypocrisy, it is likely that these issues will take flight once again through a different political constellation. At the beginning of the twenty-first century, Peru faces persistent problems regarding racism, an inequitable division of wealth, widespread indigenous impoverishment, overcentralized power in Lima, and the absence of political hegemony, among other problems. Especially important vis-à-vis the prospects for subversive tendencies has been a persistent lack of hope, especially among the indigenous population of the highlands. This enduring and potentially dangerous mood haunts many of the novels of Peru's greatest author, José María Arguedas. For example, in *The Fox from Up Above and the Fox from Down Below,* he writes:

> Now the pelican's a buzzard in reverse. The buzzards used to swallow all the nasty garbage; nowadays the cocho hangs around waitin', like

a bad thief, ashamed of himself, in the markets of all the ports; it's worse in Lima. From the rooftops, standin' up there in rows, cold, or hangin' around, givin' their last gasp, they stare down at the ground, ya hear? They're getting old. They're dyin' by the thousands; they smell bad. The fishermen feel sorry for them. They're like Incas changed into hopeless beggars, ya know what I mean?[1]

Hence, it is not unlikely that another rebel group will take hold of these historic problems if significant progress is not made toward resolving them.

Colombia, the FARC, and the ELN

The FARC has given the Latin American left its biggest black eye since Sendero Luminoso and has mimicked many of that group's worst errors. Not the least of these has been a strategy of horrific violence reflective of an utter lack of respect for human life. When criticized by the global NGO Human Rights Watch (HRW) in the summer of 2001 for its use of indiscriminate violence and an assortment of other human rights violations, the FARC responded that the HRW was simply an ultra-right-wing agent of U.S. intervention in Colombia.[2] While great debates have taken place since the end of the Cold War aimed at redefining the left, an essential and unarguable feature that unites these diverse perspectives has been a clear commitment to human compassion and social justice. Yet a group such as the FARC that has employed a strategy involving the routine the murder of innocent lives is not at all compatible with these essential ideals of the left. In fact, especially since the mid-1990s the FARC has transformed into a formidable criminal-military machine with a feeble ideological basis, and with little political legitimacy or credibility.

Related to the group's emphasis on violence has been its failure to cultivate any significant measure of consent outside its former coca-growing *zona*. The FARC's political arm received just 4 percent of national support in 2001.[3] Its political and ideological platform has been weak, to say the least, and this stands in contrast to its equally violent compatriots, Sendero Luminoso. Any power enjoyed by the group has had to do with force and the related influence derived from narco-dollars, which in turn only served to minimize the rebels' political legitimacy. Given the dreadful experience of the Union Patriótica in the late 1980s and early 1990s, whereby a portion of the FARC indeed attempted to participate in legitimate politics but saw its candidates and supporters systematically assassinated, the rebels seemed to have abandoned altogether any emphasis on the power of ideas. This has proved to be a grave strategic error. It is clear that the ideological and political development of the FARC could have reduced the group's exaggerated dependence on force, and rendered it a more legitimate actor that could conceivably help lead the country out of its historical shackles of chaos and warfare.

Most remarkable about the group's leadership, though, has been their "stop-at-nothing" attitude. Shortly after the tables began to turn against the FARC when the United States implemented Plan Colombia and when the strength of paramilitary forces escalated, the FARC did the unthinkable and joined forces in 2001 with their guerrilla rivals the ELN. Similarly, having faced mounting military resistance by enemy forces to its traditional dominance over rural areas, the FARC in 2001 threatened to take the war to Colombia's cities. This threat is crucial, since prior to this point warfare had been conducted overwhelmingly in rural areas. Although the group has attracted scant support in the country's urban centers, where over 70 percent of the population resides, the FARC's threat of urban terror signifies an unswerving and strategically misguided commitment to wield military might as the principal source of the group's power. Further, this strategy has backfired badly by pushing the Colombian electorate in 2002 to support the hawkish policies of newly elected president Alvaro Uribe Vélez.

Although the FARC failed to heed crucial strategic lessons regarding the balance of consent and force, it has made sound decisions on other fronts. It has shown good organizational skills with regard to recruitment, security, and location of forces. Its 17,000 troops have been dispersed throughout the country, therefore staving off the prospects of any centralized attack against the rebels. Further, its leaders, although well known, have not cultivated a cult of leadership. The FARC, then, has not been vulnerable to a strategy of decapitation as was effective against Sendero Luminoso. The group's leadership has also demonstrated some limited diplomatic success, such as winning the ear of the European Parliament by appreciating its resentment toward unfettered U.S. power in the Americas.

The FARC has met mixed success vis-à-vis the classic strategic themes of time and space. It has successfully manipulated the premodern approach to space prevalent in the country by convincing the dithering government to provide the group with its own city-state of sorts in its *zona* between November 1998 and February 2002. It has also claimed a stake in an assortment of key strategic regions throughout Colombia—

areas that are vital in both an economic and a military sense. With regard to the classic theme of temporal politics, the group's timing has been stellar throughout the 1990s, when it took advantage of a power vacuum in the country. Further, the FARC apparently has been successful at tuning in to the quick pace of the global economy with its busy role in narcotrafficking and arms trading. Yet the group has failed with regard to the new features of time and space associated with the Internet. This is because that medium is most helpful to groups that have developed a sophisticated ideological platform from which to generate local and global consent. Lacking the power of ideas, the FARC's website has been technologically sophisticated but ideologically empty.

Overall, the FARC's triumphs have been almost exclusively military in nature. It has grown more in the 1990s than in the three previous decades together, and it represents the largest and most militarily powerful Latin American guerrilla group to enter the twenty-first century. It certainly has been one of the major actors of Colombia's protracted civil war. Perhaps the FARC's crowning jewel was the *zona* over which it temporarily presided. But while the FARC may have won many battles, it is far from clear that it will win the war.

There is no evidence to suggest that the FARC has contributed to improving the lives of Colombians or that it has helped advance important social issues. This constitutes the group's most outstanding failure. At the end of the day, the FARC stands as one of the major contributors to the carnage and chaos that has plagued Colombia. Because the rebels have not generated any significant political consent, they stand little chance of emerging as a major political actor in the country. Having chosen the route of military force and terror to take power over the country—and having degraded their struggle through a dependence on crime, indiscriminate violence, and the widespread use of children as soldiers—they are not likely to survive politically in the event that their military star falls prey to Plan Colombia. In *One Hundred Years of Solitude,* a work that tells the political history of Colombia perhaps better than any political science textbook, the noted artist Gabriel García Márquez offers the following pertinent statement: "What worries me . . . is that out of so much hatred for the military, out of fighting them so much and thinking about them so much, you've ended up as bad as they are. And no ideal in life is worth that much baseness."[4]

A slightly likelier prospect for conflict resolution concerns the ELN, unless it permanently joins forces with the FARC. Although it has been a full participant in Colombia's civil war, the group's troop size of 4,000 to 5,000 has rendered it militarily weaker than either the FARC or the paramilitaries. Further, the ELN has attempted to achieve political legitimacy by avoiding political murder in many cases. It also claims to have shunned a role in crimes such as narcotrafficking, although this is disputed. All of this makes this group a likelier candidate for meaningful negotiation than the FARC.

But most factors seem to mitigate against that possibility. First, although the ELN has attempted to embrace the strategic lesson of garnering social consent for its cause, the group has failed at this endeavor. Second, its attack on the country's power grids succeeded at attracting political attention without committing murder, but it earned the group a reputation as terrorists. Third, its "taxes" on transnational businesses largely have been viewed as extortion, and its "retention" of various individuals has been seen as kidnapping. Thus the ELN has been socially branded as a criminal and terrorist organization. Further, the group has attempted to manipulate the feudal sense of space in the country by pleading for its own *zona,* with this representing the crux for any peace agreement with the government. But it seemed clear by 2001 that neither the Colombian government nor the U.S. government was prepared for that eventuality. Overall, the ELN has shown itself to be a kinder and weaker version of the FARC. Although the ELN had the right idea when it attempted to avoid murder and carnage to the extent committed by the FARC, ultimately it has failed to cultivate the consent necessary to render it a major political actor.

Colombia is a landscape without heroes or apparent "good guys." The Colombian state has done one of the poorest jobs of governance in the Americas for almost two centuries, as was observed in Chapters 4 and 5. A recent example of the government's sheer strategic ineptitude occurred when the Pastrana administration granted the FARC its *zona* in 1998, but had to invade four years later to get it back. Further, if the government had succeeded in doing its essential job of protecting UP members in the late 1980s and 1990s, instead of acquiescing to paramilitary power, it might actually have succeeded in promoting conflict resolution when it was still early enough to save tens of thousands of lives. Overall, not only has the Colombian government failed to comprehend any subtle epistemological changes in classic strategic lessons, it seems to have lacked even a basic grasp on most matters of strategy and good government.

Despite deep recession and escalating civil warfare, the Colombian government in 2000 sponsored a major exhibit by the renowned painter Pablo Picasso. Tours of this remarkable collection of art in Bogotá featured a narrative by the museum guide that touched upon Picasso's

"Blue Period," whereby he lapsed into profound sadness while being surrounded by the misery of poverty. Subsequently the painter moved toward his more abstract work, which featured fractured images meant to convey the chaos and disconnectedness that the artist perceived during protracted European warfare. This story of Picasso's work seems close to the basic plot of Colombia's political imbroglio, especially his concept of fragmentation.

Epistemologically, Colombia represents a crazy quilt of sorts. No single epistemological approach has been dominant. Colombia, moreover, never went through a clear transition from premodern to modern systems of thought. The government itself neglected to assist in such a project. For instance, it failed to bring the country through any semblance of modernity—lacking a strong and legitimate central state, lacking anything near a monopoly on the use of arms, and lacking any sense of social justice or the vision necessary to bring the country in line with the legitimate global economy. Remarkably, the state's premodern absence in huge portions of the country has contributed to Colombia's ambience as a collection of warring city-states rather than a nation-state with a common identity. It was this feudal disposition toward space that led the government in 1998 to cede the FARC its *zona,* a piece of jungle the *políticos* could not see from Bogotá. Gabriel García Márquez keenly observes this general idea of epistemological fracture throughout his masterful work, as he does, for instance, when he alludes to the fantasies of one of his characters who sought "to obtain scientific proof of the existence of God."[5] The absence of a predominant episteme has been keenly noticed by Colombians, and represents an essential factor in the nature of the country's warfare.

Indeed, the lack of preeminence of any one system of thought is the most remarkable feature of the Colombia imbroglio. It helps explain the chaos present in the country, and also points to the enormity of the project of reaching some semblance of peace and order. It is hard to imagine any short- to medium-term solution that would be definitive. At minimum, two or three generations would be required to construct a state apparatus that stresses social justice, and that is present throughout the country. Further, a common political identity would need to be fostered, as would some semblance of a national conception of political space—perhaps with a postmodern twist featuring a newfangled federation for Colombia. An entrenched culture of violence, which historically has been accepted as a legitimate means of settling political disputes, would have to be erased and a Leviathan-like conflict resolution mechanism put in its place. How do you build a country where there is none, especially when the notion of "country" itself represents a quickly moving target? It is a question that will take generations of Colombians to answer.

From the perspective of the United States, Colombia has emerged as a laboratory to deal with Latin American guerrillas who display considerable military might, have lucrative links to crime, and have a penchant for terror. Since the FARC cannot be eliminated solely through a relatively simple intelligence operation—as could Sendero Luminoso through the capture of its leader—it represents the most significant challenge faced by the United States in Latin America in quite some time. Washington has attempted to meet this challenge by reconceiving warfare in some fundamental respects. The use of neo-mercenaries is quite remarkable in this regard and represents the ultimate sign of the privatization of war. While it may prove to be efficient in the manner described in Chapter 5, it is also fraught with considerable worries, not the least of which concerns the issue of accountability in warfare. Also noteworthy is the deployment of a satellite surveillance system that envelopes the country. The United States has been dabbling with the panopticon to win the war against the FARC, and hence has been experimenting with the new terrain of time, space, communication, and intelligence to diminish the rebels' power. This technology is complemented by hugely funded paramilitary ground forces who share the identical objective of obliterating the FARC, but who claim not to be directed or supported by Washington. In many ways, one can be wowed by the new epistemological approach pursued by the United States on those issues. But the enormous strategic weakness here is that the United States has not demonstrated the least concern regarding the forces that spawned dissent and civil warfare in the first place and is treating only the symptoms of the problem.

Mexico and the Zapatistas

The Zapatistas embraced a modern epistemology beginning with their formation during the early 1980s until they were defeated by the Mexican military on 12 January 1994—just twelve days after they initiated the war. Their initial discourse featured traditional guerrilla violence, praise for a vanguard party of sorts, a commitment to relive Zapata's revolutionary march to the country's capital, and a traditional Marxist ideological bent. Remarkably, the EZLN succeeded at converting what could have been a disaster into a checkered victory by defining a new epistemological approach to leftist struggle.

The rebels vastly redefined the meaning of political space. In lieu of a traditional guerrilla march to conquer Mexico City, for example, the Zapatistas cast their net to both a national and global audience by posting their thoughtful pronouncements on the Internet. While Nicaragua's Sandinistas and other rebel groups previously succeeded at attracting support from international NGOs, the Internet added a new dimension by allowing for instant communication and discussion among Zapatista supporters. As we saw in Chapters 6 and 7, this led to a refashioning of what counted as political truth, with the state and big media losing their monopoly in this important arena. Armed with vital information and analysis, EZLN cheerleaders could lend support from personal computers dispersed around the world. Beyond the loyalty of individual supporters, the EZLN emerged as heroes leading the charge for a variety of social movements engaged in struggles involving anti-neoliberalism, indigenous rights, and women's rights. While the Internet helped disseminate the EZLN's messages, that instrument itself would not have been useful without the intellectual capacity to harness it in creative ways. We saw, for example, that the Internet has been of little service to the FARC due to that group's lack of political development. Generally, the Zapatistas charted a fresh epistemological approach to strategic themes concerning political space, time, organization, and truth.

Many of the EZLN's accomplishments have stemmed from a solid understanding of the classic strategic theme of good leadership. As a gifted writer, Marcos has added the dimension of art to the Zapatistas' political struggle. He has mastered the technique of presenting complicated political issues in an accessible and often entertaining package, and has been the EZLN's central attraction for global media attention. Yet as the all-indigenous Zapatista comandantes are fond of noting publicly—as Comandante Esther did when she spoke before the Mexican Congress in 2001—the pale-skinned Marcos is only a subcomandante. The point is that while Marcos makes an excellent public relations specialist, any credit for the generally good leadership of the EZLN must be spread widely.

In contrast to Sendero Luminoso and Colombian rebel groups, the Zapatistas have demonstrated a clear understanding regarding the nature of power that can be derived from consent. Given their lack of military capacity and their confinement by the Mexican armed forces, the group has had to rely on generating considerable social consent from ideas they developed on a number of themes. Further, this societal consent has helped shield the Zapatistas from potential strikes on the part of the armed forces. It has enabled the Zapatistas, in conjunction with other social movements, to define social issues within Mexico and globally.

In this regard, the EZLN has been most successful at advancing indigenous issues and at attracting government aid to Chiapas. Neither theme, however, has been a total success for the Zapatistas. The amendment proposed in 2001 to the Mexican constitution regarding indigenous rights has fallen far short of the 1996 San Andrés Accords, and was not endorsed by Mexican states with the highest proportion of indigenous residents. On the issue of aid to Chiapas, many pro-Zapatista communities ironically have refused to accept assistance and have viewed such acceptance as a sellout to the government. Despite these problems, overall the Zapatistas have been successful at advancing important social issues and at being a catalyst for positive political action. Most importantly, the EZLN has instilled a sense of hope among the dispossessed.

The glaring weakness of the EZLN has been its almost complete lack of understanding regarding military affairs, as evidenced by the group's ill-fated military foray in January 1994. Until 2001, they represented "caged guerrillas" to the extent that they were completely surrounded and neutralized militarily by the Mexican armed forces. Because of their lack of military power, it is hard to call them guerrillas at all, despite the adornment by Marcos and others with guns and traditional guerrilla garb. Indeed, the highly publicized caravan by the Zapatistas to Mexico City in the winter of 2001 saw the rebels protected along the way by the Mexican armed forces—evidence of an extraordinary relationship between the military and these supposed guerrillas. A Mexican general observed that "we have the best guerrillas in the world," a tongue-in-cheek reference to the Zapatistas' military toothlessness.[6] With or without military might, it seems entirely fair to deem the Zapatistas as the best guerrillas in Latin America, given their highly positive contributions particularly in the area of indigenous rights.

For its part, the Mexican government has done a generally stellar job at managing the ELZN. It was suggested that historically Mexico made a successful transition from premodernity to modernity. The government embodied a Leviathan, it was relatively inclusive and secular, it fostered clearly defined social progress, and it fomented a strong sense of nation state and patriotism. Since the mid-1990s it has made a bid for postmodernity. This has been expressed, for example, through membership in NAFTA, through a plan for enhanced representation in globalized arenas such as the UN Security Council, and especially with regard to the nontraditional manner in which it has dealt with the Zapatistas. The government generally has not relied on indiscriminate force or widespread human rights abuses, as it did during the 1970s in Guerrero and elsewhere, and as other governments have done vis-à-vis their respective rebel movements, as exemplified by the cases of Colombia and Peru. The Mexican government's strategy of containment has been effective. Following their decisive February 1995 offensive, the Zedillo team all but ignored the EZLN and apparently hoped it would fade into oblivion, which the group narrowly avoided. The Fox administration has been aggressive in a positive manner in terms of providing an enhanced national voice to the Zapatistas. Demonstrative of this was the government's active cooperation in the EZLN caravan during 2001, as well as provisions it made for the Zapatistas to address the Mexican Congress at that time. It proved to be a brilliant strategy on the part of the government, and may contribute to prospects of peace and conflict resolution.

Regarding the classic security themes, then, the government has shown generally good leadership since the fall of President Salinas. It has begun to appreciate significant alterations in the cast of political actors, such as social movements, NGOs, and the like. It has made visible efforts to muster social consent and has minimized the use of force. The government has shown a penchant for appreciating new forms of strategic struggle through the increased use of intelligence, computers, surveillance devices, and netwar—in short, it has increasingly relied on C⁴ISR. It has therefore adapted to new ways of knowing time and space. On the issue of spatial politics, the embrace of regional production through NAFTA has meant a newfangled regional security. But this has remained a touchy issue, particularly with the older generation of Mexican military leaders, who for most of their careers have viewed the United States as more of a threat than a regional partner.[7] As Carlos Fuentes observed in *The Old Gringo*, "They're right when they say this isn't a border. It's a scar."[8] An effort is underway to heal that scar, though it remains unclear as to whether it will be effective. Overall, the Mexican government has been a strategic success. It has appreciated continuity as well as important transformations with regard to the classic themes of space, time, leadership, intelligence, and consent versus coercion.

But the picture is not a completely rosy one. The Fox government has admitted to the widespread problems facing the country while blaming them all on the seven-decade reign of the PRI. But these problems will be difficult to resolve. Most alarming are statistics released in the summer of 2001 that reveal the worst division of wealth in the country's history, a process that has shrunk the middle class and made poverty even worse for millions.[9] Such inequity can breed subversion, as various episodes in Mexican history have demonstrated. Also worrisome is the potential failure of the *maquilladora* sector to remain globally competitive in terms of wages, and the subsequent proposal of Plan Puebla-Panama to create lower paying jobs.[10] Rather than real development, this could lend credence to the "race to the bottom" scenario and hence stimulate the creation of subversive movements.

Further, while the government has done a generally good job vis-à-vis Chiapas, its record is substantially worse in the state of Guerrero, which by the late 1990s has been home to the highest levels of political violence in the country. Oaxaca has found itself in a similar predicament. Activity by the EPR rebels has been reported in both states, and the government has been aggressive in its battle to subdue them in an effort to avoid the international embarrassment it perceived when the Zapatistas emerged on NAFTA's birthday. But as we saw in Chapter 7, the government's anti-EPR strategy has come at the price of relatively high levels of human rights abuses on the part of the state.[11] With the unifocus of relevant NGOs on Chiapas, the harsh floodlight of public opinion has not yet illuminated the worthy cases of Oaxaca and Guerrero. Related to this, another worrisome issue concerns the 2001 constitutional amendment regarding indigenous rights, which was vehemently opposed by all of the Mexican states with large indigenous populations. While it is a reflection of the complexities of democratic structures, it is regrettable that it came at the time it did. For many indigenous communities, particularly in the south of the country, the case represented one of their first meaningful encounters with newly emerging democratic structures. If political structures are viewed as a sham by substantial numbers of the indigenous, who already constitute the poorest and most disenfranchised of Mexicans, subversive tendencies are likely to escalate.

Rebels, Classic Security Themes, and Systems of Thought

Strategic themes identified in the classic texts of Thucydides, Sun Tzu I and Sun Tzu II, Machiavelli, Hobbes, and others are as relevant as ever, and are clearly related to the successes and failures of the guerrilla movements considered here. These seemingly timeless issues include spatial and temporal politics, intelligence/espionage, leadership, organization, good government, the duality of consent/coercion, and the perils of exaggerated inequity. Throughout the drama of human history, these have been pressed through various epistemological filters. Three such filters have been considered here—premodern, modern, and postmodern systems of thought. The ability to consider classic strategic themes within appropriate epistemological frameworks is key to dealing effectively with conflict.

With regard to the world order, Latin American guerrilla movements in the twenty-first century must grapple with a context that is both post-Soviet and post–September 11. The fall of the Soviet Union, and of the Havana-Moscow nexus, has meant that Latin American guerrillas require independent sources of financing. In both the Colombian and Peruvian cases, the rebels turned to narcotrafficking and other crime as a lucrative source of funding. In all the case studies considered here, independent financing has meant a freer political hand and is one expression among many of the privatized nature of warfare at the dawn of the twenty-first century.

The post-Soviet strategic environment is also marked by the revolution in military affairs. A chief manifestation of this is the elimination of previous barriers associated with space and time. The advent of real-time surveillance, for example, has rocked the world of intelligence/espionage, as evidenced by many of the features of Plan Colombia. Further, communications technology has fundamentally altered the nature of subversive organization, especially through the ability to appeal to a global audience. This is related to the ascendance of new political actors, such as transnational social movements, that have been key supporters for rebels such as Mexico's EZLN. A related breakthrough is the Internet, which has been skillfully employed as a powerful weapon by the Zapatistas—guerrillas who are politically developed enough to offer intelligent content online. It has helped the rebels break the government's former monopoly on what counts as political truth. Thus the RMA has meant new ways of knowing strategic time and space, espionage, guerrilla organization, intelligence, and even "truth" itself.

The terrorist attack on New York's World Trade Center has further redefined the global security environment. While Peru's Sendero Luminoso and Colombia's FARC relied on terrorism long before the Trade Center attack, that pivotal event has introduced a new political context. On the one hand, it clearer than ever that terrorist attacks represent a relatively inexpensive method to garner extraordinary levels of public attention and to generate popular fear. This translates into potential political clout in the eyes of guerrilla groups such as the FARC, which initiated a fresh campaign of terror in 2002. But on the other hand, the nomenclature of "terrorist" has replaced "communist" as the convenient Thucydidean pretext for Washington to obliterate its enemies in an atmosphere of muted public criticism.[12]

Beyond security issues, economic features of the world order have greatly affected the environment in which Latin American guerrillas have charted their strategic course. A unipolar world has meant little choice for Latin American countries with regard to models of economic development. In the cases of Peru, Colombia, and Mexico, neoliberal economic structures were imposed by the IMF in a fashion that has fanned the flames of social discontent by slashing already anemic social programs. Rising economic inequity, especially in Mexico and Colombia, has also played into the strategic hand of leftist guerrillas in those countries. Chronic debt crises, calamitous currency speculation, and global overproduction have debilitated each of the governments under consideration, and Latin American guerrillas naturally have taken advantage of this.

The sometimes hazardous atmosphere associated with the global political economy has made the cardinal strategic objective of good government hard to achieve. The classic goal defined by Machiavelli of benefiting the many rather than the few is difficult to realize during times of social welfare cuts and the worsening maldistribution of wealth.[13] Thus a strong state entails not only a Hobbesian Leviathan that monopolizes the use of force, but also a positive presence in terms of agencies that promote human development. A significant contributing factor to Latin American guerrilla warfare has been illegitimate state structures and the political interests they represent. Sage strategic advice is offered by Sun Tzu, who suggests that "those who render others' armies helpless without fighting are the best of all."[14] To accomplish that, it is necessary to resolve the profound social inequity and political exclusion that underpins the formation of guerrilla movements in the first place.

Notes

1. Arguedas, *The Fox from Up Above and the Fox from Down Below,* p. 100.

2. *El Tiempo* (Bogotá), 22 July 2001.

3. Colombia Objectiva, www.geocities.com/capitolhill/lobby/6882/index/htm.

4. García Márquez, *One Hundred Years of Solitude,* p. 154.

5. Ibid., p. 58.

6. Author interview with Diputado General Alfredo Ochoa Toledo, president, Comisión de Seguridad Nacional, Mexico City, 12 July 2001.

7. See Rochlin, *Redefining Mexican Security.*

8. Fuentes, *The Old Gringo,* p. 185.

9. The Fox team is fully aware of this threat. Author interviews with Raul Benitez, Consejero Adjunto de Planeacion y Estudios Estrategios, and José Luis Valdez, Consejero Adjunto del Agenda de Riesgo, both from the Consejeria Presidencial de Seguridad Nacional, Mexico City, 12 July 2001.

10. For a discussion of this, see *New York Times,* 26 December 2001.

11. For a discussion of abuses of human rights by the state in Guerrero, see *La Jornada* (Mexico City), 30 July 2001.

12. War between Athens and Sparta began with Sparta's insistence that Athens "drive out the curse of the goddess." This represented for Thucydides the universal tendency to create pretext for war. See Thucydides, *History of the Peloponnesian War,* p. 69.

13. Machiavelli, *Prince,* p. 86.

14. Sun Tzu, *Art of War,* p. 67.

Acronyms and Abbreviations

APRA	Alianza Popular Revolucionaria Americana
AUC	Autodefensas Unidas de Colombia
C⁴ISR	command, control, communications, computers, intelligence, surveillance, and reconnaissance
CGSB	Coordinadora Guerrillera Simón Bolívar
CIA	Central Intelligence Agency
CNG	Coordinadora Nacional Guerrillera
CONAI	National Commission for Intermediacy
DINCOTE	Dirección Nacional Contra el Terrorismo
ELN	Ejército de Liberación Nacional
EPL	Ejército Popular de Liberación
EPR	Ejército Revolucionario Popular
EU	European Union
EZLN	Ejército Zapatista de Liberación Nacional
FARC	Fuerzas Armadas Revolucionarias de Colombia
FLN	Fuerzas de Liberación Nacional
FZLN	Frente Zapatista de Liberación Nacional
GDP	gross domestic product
GEIN	Grupo Especial de Inteligencia Nacional
GNP	gross national product
HRW	Human Rights Watch
IEPRI	Instituto de Estudios Políticos y Relaciones Internacionales
IMF	International Monetary Fund
IRA	Irish Republican Army
ISI	import substitution industrialization
ISR	intelligence, surveillance, and reconnaissance
MAS	Muerte a Secuestradores (Death to Kidnappers)

MIR	Movimiento de Izquierda Revolucionario
MPRI	Military Professional Resources Inc.
MRTA	Movimiento Revolucionario Túpac Amaru
NAFTA	North American Free Trade Agreement
NGO	nongovernmental organization
OCSS	Organización Campesina de la Sierra del Sur
PAN	Partido Acción Nacional
PGR	Procuraduría General de la República
PRD	Partido de la Revolución Democrática
PRI	Partido Revolucionario Institucional
QL	Quintín Lame
RMA	revolution in military affairs
SIN	Servicio de Inteligencia Nacional
SL	Sendero Luminoso
SSHRC	Social Sciences and Humanities Research Council
TNC	transnational corporation
UN	United Nations
UNAM	Universidad Nacional Autónoma de México
UP	Union Patriótica

Bibliography

Álvarez, Victor. "Notas sobre la constitución del estado en Colombia." In Freddy Salazar, ed., *El estado y la fuerza*. Bucaramanga: Universidad Industrial de Santander, 1999, pp. 121–176.

Arguedas, José María. *The Fox from Up Above and the Fox from Down Below*. Pittsburgh: University of Pittsburgh Press, 2000.

———. *Los Rios Profundos*. Lima: Editorial Horizonte, 1993.

Arquilla, John. "Strategic Implications of Information Dominance." *Strategic Review* 22, no. 3 (summer 1994): 24–30.

Arquilla, John, and David Ronfeldt. "Cyberwar Is Coming!" *Comparative Strategy* 12, no. 2 (1993): 141–165.

Autodefensas Unidas de Colombia (AUC). Carlos Castaño. "Carta abierta a Andrés Pastrana Arango, presidente de la república." 17 February 2001. www.colombialibre.org/cartas/Pastrana_17.htm.

———. Carlos Castaño. "Entrevista del Comandante Castaño a RCN radio." 18 February 2001. www.colombialibre.org/reportajes/rcnradio.htm.

———. "Entrevista a los comandantes de las ACCU: Santander Lozada y César Marín." 9–10 September 1998. www.colombialibre.org/santa.htm.

———. "Nucleo de paramillo acuerdo." 26 July 1998. www.colombialibre. en/param.htm.

———. "Political-Military Nature of the Movement." May 1998 (no specific date). www.colombialibre.org/en/estatuto.htm .

———. "Reportaje del Comandante Castaño al periodico *Notitarde*." 23 December 2000. www.colombialibre.org/reportajes/notitarde.htm.

Bartra, Roger. "Revolutionary Nationalism and National Security." In Sergio Aguayo Quezada and Bruce Bagley, eds., *Mexico: In Search of Security*. New Brunswick, N.J.: Transaction, 1993, pp. 143–174.

Baudrillard, Jean. *The Illusion of the End*. Stanford, Calif.: Stanford University Press, 1992.

Benjamin, Thomas. *A Rich Land, A Poor People: Politics and Society in Modern Chiapas*. Albuquerque: University of New Mexico Press, 1989.

Blasier, Cole. "Social Revolution: Origins in Mexico, Bolivia, and Cuba." *Latin American Research Review* 2, no. 3 (summer 1967): 28–64.

Blondet, M. *La situación de la mujer en el Perú, 1980–1994*. Lima: Instituto de Estudios Peruanos, 1994.

Booth, John, and Thomas Walker. *Understanding Central America*. Boulder: Westview, 1993.

Brown, Michael. "The Revolution in Military Affairs: The Information Dimension." In Alan Campen, ed., *Cyberwar: Security, Strategy, and Conflict in the Information Age*. Fairfax: Armed Forces Communications and Electronics Association, 1996, pp. 31–52.

Burt, Jo Marie. "Sendero Luminoso y la 'batalla decisiva' en las barriades de Lima: El caso de Villa el Salvador." In Steve Stern, ed., *Los Senderos Insólitos del Perú*. Lima: Instituto de Estudios Peruanos, 1997, pp. 263–300.

Camacho Guizado, Alvaro, and Francisco Leal Buitrago, eds. *Armar la paz es desarmar la guerra*. Bogotá: Tercer Mundo, 1999.

Cameron, Maxwell, and Philip Mauceri, eds. *The Peruvian Labyrinth: Polity, Society, Economy*. University Park: Pennsylvania State University Press, 1997.

Campen, Alan, Douglas Dearth, and Thomas Gooden, eds. *Cyberwar: Security, Strategy, and Conflict in the Information Age*. Fairfax, Va.: Armed Forces Communications and Electronics Association, 1996.

Castañeda, Jorge. *Utopia Unarmed: The Latin American Left After the Cold War*. New York: Vintage, 1994.

Centro de Investigaciones Económicos y Políticas de Acción Comunitaria (CIEPAC). *Siempre cerca, siempre lejos: Las fuerzas armadas en México*. México D.F.: CIEPAC, 2000.

Chernick, Marc. "La negociación de un paz entre múltiples formas." In Francisco Leal Buitrago, ed., *Los laberintos de la guerra: Utopías e incertidumbres sobre la paz*. Bogotá: Tercer Mundo, 1999, pp. 3–58.

Clausewitz, Carl von. *On War*. Princeton: Princeton University Press, 1989.

Coatsworth, John H. *El impacto económico de los ferrocarriles en el porfiriato*. México D.F.: Ediciones Era, 1984.

Collier, Ruth B., and David Collier. *Shaping the Political Arena*. Princeton: Princeton University Press, 1991.

Coral Cordero, Isabel. "Las mujeres en la guerra: Impacto y respuestas." In Steve Stern, ed., *Los Senderos Insólitos del Perú*. Lima: Instituto de Estudios Peruanos, 1997, pp. 337–363.

Cotler, Julio. *Estado y nación en el Perú*. Lima: Instituto ed Estudios Peruanos, 1992.

Cox, Robert. *Production, Power, and World Order*. New York: Columbia University Press, 1987.

de la Cadena, Marisol. "Las mujeres son mas indias: Etnicidad y género en un comunidad del Cusco." *Revista Andina* 9, no. 1 (1991): 7–29.

Dearth, Douglas, and Charles Williamson. "Information Age/Information War." In Alan Campen, ed., *Cyberwar: Security, Strategy, and Conflict in the Information Age*. Fairfax, Va.: Armed Forces Communications and Electronics Association, 1966, pp. 13–30.

Deas, Malcolm, and Fernando Gaitán Daza. *Dos ensayos especulativos sobre la violencia en Colombia*. Bogotá: Tercer Mundo, 1985.

Degregori, Carlos Ivan. "Cosechando tempestades: Las rondas campesinas y la derrota de Sendero Luminoso en Ayacucho." In Steve Stern, ed., *Los Senderos Insólitos del Perú*. Lima: Instituto de Estudios Peruanos, 1997, pp. 133–160.

del Pino, Ponciano. "Familia, cultura y 'revolución': Vida, cotidiana en Sendero Luminoso." In Steve Stern, ed., *Los Senderos Insólitos del Perú*. Lima: Instituto de Estudios Peruanos, 1997, pp. 161–192.

Der Derian, James. "Interview with Paul Virilio: Speed Pollution." *Wired*, May 1996. www.wired.com/archive/4.05/virilio_pr.html.

Derrida, Jacques. *Specters of Marx: The State of the Debt, the Work of Mourning, and the New International*. New York: Routledge, 1994.

Dix, Robert. "The Varieties of Revolution." *Comparative Politics* 15, no. 3 (April 1983): 282–294.

dos Santos, Theodore. "The Structure of Dependence." *American Economic Review* 60, no. 2 (1970): 231–237.

Ejército de Liberación Nacional (ELN). "A rechazar el Plan Colombia." 9 December 2000, caobo23@geneva-link.ch.

———. "Comunicado del ELN: Visita no grata." 28 August 2000. caobo23@ geneva-link.ch.

———. *Correo del Magdalena: Órgano Informativo del ELN*, no. 113 (21 September 1999). caobo23@geneva-link.ch.

———. *Correo del Magdalena: Órgano Informativo del ELN*, no. 122 (15 May 2000). caobo23@geneva-link.ch.

———. "Entrevista con Nicolás Rodríguez y Antonio García: Carocol de Colombia." 1 January 2000. caobo23@geneva-link.ch.

———. "Pastrana le incumple a la paz." 20 July 2000. caobo23@geneva-link.ch.

———. "Por un Gran Acuerdo Nacional." *Correo del Magdalena: Órgano Informativo del ELN* no. 115 (18 October 1999). caobo23@geneva-link.ch.

———. "Posición del ELN sobre la privatización de ISA-ISAGEN." March 2000. Pamphlet.

———. "Venemos contra la paz." 20 May 2000. caobo23@geneva-link.ch.

Ejército Peruano. *Guerra no convencional: Contrasubversion*. Lima: Ejército Peruano, 9 August 1989.

Ejército Revolucionario Popular (EPR). "Comunicado revolucionario, posición política ante el nuevo gobierno de V. Fox." 28 August 2000. www.pengo.it/ pdpr-epr/comunicados/c_280800.htm .

———. "Comunicado, sobre Gutiérrez Rebollo, confirma que el poder del narcotrafico esta en el propio estado." 26 February 1997. www.pengo.it/pdpr-epr/comunicados/c_280800.htm .

———. *Insurgente* 4, no. 27 (May–June 2000).

———. "Manifiesto de la Sierra Madre Oriental: Programa político." 7 August 1996. www.pengo.it/pdpr-epr/manif_smo.htm.

———. "Proyecto del pais." 2 December 1996. www.pengo.it/pdpr-epr/proyecto.htm.

———. "Saludo y bienvenida al EZLN a la capital." 12 September 1997. www.pengo.it/pdpr-epr/comunicados/c_120997.htm.

Ejército Zapatista de Liberación Nacional (EZLN). "A las bases del EZLN." 10 April 1994. *EZLN: Documentos y Comunicados 1*, pp. 213–214.

———. "A los niños de México y el mundo." 30 April 1994. *EZLN: Documentos y Comunicados 1*, pp. 225–229.

———. "A todos las organizaciones no gubernamentales de México." 1 February 1994. *EZLN: Documentos y Comunicados 1*, p. 121.

———. "A todos las organizaciones no gubernamentales de México." 20 February 1994. *EZLN: Documentos y Comunicados 1*, p. 161.

———. "Al Consejo Estudiantil Universitario, Universidad Nacional Autónoma de México." 6 February 1994. *EZLN: Documentos y Comunicados 1*, pp. 129–130.

———. "Ayuda militar de EU a México." 13 January 1994. *EZLN: Documentos y Comunicados 1*, pp. 85–86.

———. "Condiciones del EZLN para regresar a la mesa del diálogo." 29 August 1996. www.ezln.org/condiciones.htm.

———. "Declaración de la Selva Lacandona." December 1993 (no specific date). www.ezln.org/primera-lacandona.htm.

———. *Documentos y Comunicados 1*. México D.F.: Ediciones Era, 1998.

———. *Documentos y Comunicados 2*. México D.F.: Ediciones Era, 1998.

———. *Documentos y Comunicados 3*. México D.F.: Ediciones Era, 1998.

———. *El Despertador Mexicano: Órgano Informativo del EZLN* (1 December 1993). *EZLN: Documentos y Comunicados 1*, pp. 36–48.

———. "El diálogo de San Andrés y los derechos y cultural indígena." 15 February 1996. *EZLN: Documentos y Comunicados 3*, pp. 145–153.

———. "El EZLN informe sobre su valoración de la situación actual." 29 August 1996. *EZLN: Documentos y Comunicados 3*, pp. 360–366.

———. "El poder judicial, principal sabateador de la paz." 31 May 1996. *EZLN: Documentos y Comunicados 3*, pp. 249–250.

———. "En el 502 aniversario del descubrimiento de América." 12 October 1994. *EZLN: Documentos y Comunicados 2*, pp. 100–104.

———. "La historia de los espejos." June 1995 (no specific date). www.ezln.org/espejos.htm.

———. "La muerta nos visita." 20 February 1995. *Documentos y Comunicados 2*, pp. 233–237.

———. "Obra en dos actos, sobre la clase política, que no termina." Published in *La Jornada*, 2 December 2000.

———. "Otras formas de lucha." 20 January 1994. *EZLN: Documentos y Comunicados 1*, pp. 102–103.

———. "Palabras del EZLN para la manifestación del 26 aniversario del 2 de Octubre de 1968 en el Zócolo de la cuidad de México." 2 October 1994. *EZLN: Documentos y Comunicados 2*, pp. 85–87.

———. "Palabras para la celebración del decimoprimer aniversario de la formación del Ejército Zapatista de Liberación Nacional." 17 November 1994. *EZLN: Documentos y Comunicados 2*, pp. 131–138.

———. "Primera declaración de la realidad." January 1996 (no specific date). www.ezln.org/primera-realidad.htm.

———. "Propuesta para la Mesa 2 diálogo de San Andrés." 15 February 1996. *EZLN: Documentos y Comunicados 3*, pp. 161–167.

———. "Resultado de la consulta." 10 June 1994. *EZLN: Documentos y Comunicados 1*, pp. 257–259.

———. "Resultados de la consulta nacional." 1 June 1994. *EZLN: Documentos y Comunicados 1*, pp. 249–251.

———. "Saluda a los insurgentes y milicianos que rompieron el cerco." 1 January 1995. *Documentos y Comunicados 2*, p. 194–195.

———. "Segunda declaración de la Selva Lacandona." 10 June 1994. www.ezln.org/archive/segunda-lacandona.html.

———. "Segunda declaración de la realidad." 3 August 1996. www.ezln.org/segunda-realidad.htm.

———. "Siete piezas sueltas del recompecabezas mundial." June 1997 (no specific date). www.ezln.org/archive/piezas.htm.

———. Subcomandante Marcos. "A los combatientes y mandos del Ejército Popular Revolucionario." 29 August 1996. *EZLN: Documentos y Comunicados 3*, pp. 366–369.

———. Subcomandante Marcos. "A Marta Lamas." 5 May 1994. *EZLN: Documentos y Comunicados 1*, pp. 232–234.

———. Subcomandante Marcos. "Chiapas: The Southeast in Two Winds—A Storm and a Prophecy." August 1992. Translated into English by the EZLN. www.ezln.org.

———. Subcomandante Marcos. "Composición del EZLN y condiciones para el diálogo." 6 January 1994. *EZLN: Documentos y Comunicados 1*, pp. 72–76.

———. Subcomandante Marcos. "Comunicado del Comité Clandestino Revolucionario Indígena." 10 April 1998.

———. Subcomandante Marcos. "Discurso de Subcomandante Marcos durante la visita del candidato presidencial del PRD, Cuauhtémoc Cárdenas." 17 May 1994, pp. 235–239.

———. Subcomandante Marcos. "Intervención oral del EZLN en palabras de Marcos para las 4 mesas de trabajo del tema de política." 30 July 1996. *EZLN: Documentos y Comunicados 3*, pp. 319–324.

———. Subcomandante Marcos. "Movimiento estudiantil de la UNAM." 22 Mayo 1999. www.ezln.org/archive/ezln990522.htm.

———. Subcomandante Marcos. "Ojepse ley otirud." November 1995 (no specific date). *EZLN: Documentos y Comunicados 3*, pp. 108–123.

———. Subcomandante Marcos. "Siete preguntas, a quien corresponda: Imágens del neoliberalismo en el México." 1997 (no specific date). *EZLN: Documentos y Comunicados 3*, pp. 427–449.

———. Subcomandante Marcos. "Tres mesas para la cena de fin de siglo." February 1998 (no specific date). www.ezln.org/news/ezln980226-sp.html.

———. "Tercera declaración de la Selva Lacandona." 2 January 1995. www.ezln.org/tercera-lacandona.htm.

———. "Tres comunicados del EZLN." Published in *La Jornada*, 11 December 2000.

————. "V declaración de la Selva Lacandona." July 1998 (no specific date). www.ezln.org/archive/-quinta-lacandona.html.

Ferris, John, and Michael Handel. "Clausewitz, Intelligence, Uncertainty, and the Art of Command in Military Operations." *Intelligence and National Security* 10, no. 1 (January 1995): 1–58.

Foucault, Michel. *The Archaeology of Knowledge and the Discourse on Language.* New York: Tavistock, 1972.

————. *Discipline and Punish: The Birth of the Prison.* New York: Vintage, 1977.

————. *The Order of Things: An Archaeology of the Human Sciences.* New York: Vintage, 1970.

————. *Power/Knowledge: Selected Interviews and Other Writings, 1972–1977.* Edited by Colin Gordon. New York: Pantheon, 1980.

————. "Space, Knowledge, and Power." In James Faubion, ed., *Power: Essential Works of Foucault, 1954–1984.* New York: Free Press, 2000, pp. 349–364.

————. "The Subject and Power." In James Faubion, ed., *Power: Essential Works of Foucault, 1954–1984.* New York: Free Press, 2000, pp. 326–348.

————. "Truth and Juridical Forms." In James Faubion, ed., *Power: Essential Works of Foucault, 1954–1984,* vol. 3. New York: Free Press, 2000, pp. 1–89.

————. "Two Lectures." In Colin Gordon, ed. *Power/Knowledge: Selected Interviews and Other Writings.* New York: Pantheon, 1980, pp. 78–108.

————. "The Will to Knowledge." In Paul Rabinow, ed. *Ethics: Subjectivity and Truth—Essential Works of Foucault,* vol. 1. New York: New Press, 1997, pp. 11–16.

Fuentes, Carlos. *The Old Gringo.* New York: Noonday, 1985.

Fuerzas Armadas Revolucionarias de Colombia (FARC). "A la comunidad internacional: Conflicto interno y narcotrafico." April 1998 (no specific date). www.burn.ucsd.edu~farc-ep/comunicados.

————. "Acuerdos de la Uribe: Estado mayor de las FARC-EP." 28 May 1994. www.burn.ucsd.edu~farc-ep/comunicados.

————. "Carta pública al pueblo y a los sectores progresistas de Norteamerica." April 1998 (no specific date). www.burn.ucsd.edu~farc-ep/comunicados.

————. "Clinton Go Home." 23 August 2000. www.farc-ep.org/comunicados/2000/clinton.html.

————. "Comunica a la comunidad internacional: Codena profanación de cadaveres." 19 February 1998. www.burn.ucsd.edu~farc-ep/comunicados.

————. "Comunicado." 2 May 1997. www.burn.ucsd.edu~farc-ep/comunicados.

————. "Comunicado." 10 July 2000. www.farc-ep.org/comunicados/2000/jul1100.html.

————. "Comunicado a la opinion pública." 10 September 1998. www.burn.ucsd.edu~farc-ep/comunicados.

————. "Comunicado a la opinion pública nacional y internacional." 28 September 1997. www.burn.ucsd.edu~farc-ep/comunicados.

———. "Comunicado de prensa." 8 June 1997. www.burn.ucsd.edu~farc-ep/ comunicados.

———. "Comunicado pública a extranjeros y colombianos."12 July 1998. www.burn.ucsd.edu~farc-ep/comunicados.

———. "Comunicado público." 12 November 2000. www.farc-ep.org/comunicados/ 2000/nov1200.html.

———. "Contra la intervención, Unidad Patriótica y Latinamericana." 1998 (no specific date). www.burn.ucsd.edu~farc-ep/comunicados.

———. "Denuncia pública." 5 August 1997. www.burn.ucsd.edu~farc-ep/ comunicados.

———. "El bloque sur de las FARC-EP informa a la opinion pública." 17 October 1997. www.burn.ucsd.edu~farc-ep/comunicados.

———. "El Gobierno Samper es el culpable." 6 August 1998. www.burn.ucsd. edu~farc-ep/comunicados.

———. "La estrategia política del libertador en las guerras de la independencia." May 1997 (no specific date). www.farc-ep.org/mbnc/libertador.html.

———. "Las FARC-EP llaman al pueblo colombiano no votar y empazar la construcción de un verdadero poder popular." 8 October 1997. www.ucsd. burn.edu~farc-ep/comunicados.

———. "Ley 02: Sobre la tributación." March 2000. www.farc-ep.org.

———. "Manifesto de Movimiento Bolivariano por la Nueva Colombia." 25 March 2000. www.farc-ep.org.

———. Manuel Marulanda Vélez. "Texto completo del discurso pronunciado por el comandante en jefe de las FARC-EP Manuel Marulanda Vélez." 27 May 1994. www.burn.ucsd.edu~farc-ep/comunicados.

———. "Mensaje de Año Nuevo." 26 December 2000. www.farc-ep.org/ comunicados/2000/dic2000.html.

———. "Octava conferencia nacional de las FARC-EP: Programa agrario de los guerrilleros de las FARC-EP." 2 April 1993. www.burn.uscd.edu~farc-ep/comunicados.

———. "Octava conferencia nacional de las FARC-EP: 30 años de lucha por la paz, democracia, y soberanía." April 1993 (no specific date). www.burn. ucsd.edu~farc-ep/comunicados.

———. "Plataforma para un gobierno de reconstrucción y reconciliación nacional." 3 April 1993. www.farc-ep.org/mbnc/plataforma/html.

———. "34th aniversario de las FARC-EP, comisión internacional." 27 May 1998. www.burn.ucsd.edu~farc-ep/comunicados.

———. "36 años por la paz y la soberanía nacional." 20 May 2000. www.farc-ep.org/nuestra_historia/36_aniversario_de_las_farc-ep.html .

Gamarra, Jefrey. "Estado, modernidad y sociedad regional: Ayacucho 1920–1940." *Revista Apuntes* no. 31 (1992): 103–114.

García Márquez, Gabriel. *One Hundred Years of Solitude.* New York: Avon, 1970.

Gill, Stephen, ed. *Gramsci, Historical Materialism, and International Relations.* Cambridge: Cambridge University Press, 1993.

Gilly, Adolfo. *La revolución interrumpida.* México D.F.: Ediciones Era, 1994.

Gleick, James. *Chaos: Making a New Science.* New York: Penguin, 1988.

Gobierno de Colombia. Departamento Nacional de Planeación. *El gasto militar: Desarrollo teórico y comparativo internacional—Informe 2: Justicia y seguridad.* Bogotá: Departamento Nacional de Planeación, 2000.

Gobierno de México. Senado de la República. *Análisis de los efectos del Tratado de Libre Comerico de América del Norte en la economía mexicana: Una visión sectorial a cinco años de distancia.* México D.F.: Senado de la República, 2000.

González Prada, Manuel. *Horas de luchas.* Lima: Editorial Universo, 1974.

Goodwin, Jeff, and Theda Skocpol. "Explaining Revolutions in the Contemporary Third World." *Politics and Society* 17, no. 4 (September 1989): 489–509.

Gorriti Ellenbogen, Gustavo. *Sendero: Historia en al guerra milenaria en el Peru.* Lima: Editorial Apoyo, 1990.

Government of Mexico. Presidency of the Republic. "Main Events Relating to the Conflict in Chiapas, 28 February 1998 to December 1999." 24 October 2000. www.world.presidencia.gob.mx/chiapas/documents/events/htm.

Gramsci, Antonio. *Selections from the Prison Notebooks.* New York: International Publishers, 1971.

Guajardo, Guillermo. "Tecnología y campesinos en la Revolución Mexicana." *Mexican Studies* 15, no. 2 (summer 1999): 291–322.

Guevara, Che. *Guerrilla Warfare.* Lincoln: University of Nebraska Press, 1961.

Gunder Frank, Andre. *Latin America: Underdevelopment or Revolution.* New York: Monthly Review, 1969.

Gurr, Ted Robert. *Why Men Rebel.* Princeton: Princeton University Press, 1970.

Guzmán, Abimael. *Historic Speech from the Dungeons of the Enemy: Speech from the Tiger Cage.* 24 September 1992. www.blythe.org/perupcp/docs_en/speechf.htm.

Hall, Ninal, ed. *Exploring Chaos: A Guide to the New Science of Disorder.* New York: Norton, 1994.

Harvey, David. *The Condition of Postmodernity.* Cambridge: Blackwell, 1989.

Harvey, Neil. *La rebelión de Chiapas: La lucha por la tierra y la democracia.* México D.F.: Ediciones Era, 2000.

Hernández, Luis, "Chiapas: Reestructuración y cambio." *El Cotidiano* no. 61 (March–April 1994).

Hobbes, Thomas. *Leviathan.* New York: Penguin, 1982.

Hunefeldt, Christine. "The Rural Landscape and Changing Political Awareness: Enterprises, Agrarian Producers, and Peasant Communities, 1969–1994." In Maxwell Cameron and Philip Mauceri, eds., *The Peruvian Labyrinth: Polity, Society, Economy.* University Park: Pennsylvania State University Press, 1997, pp. 107–133.

Huntington, Samuel. "The Clash of Civilizations?" *Foreign Affairs* 72, no. 3 (summer 1993): 22–49.

Issawi, Charles. *An Arab Philosophy of History: Selections from the Prolegomena of Ibn Khaldun of Tunis (1332–1406).* Princeton: Darwin Press, 1987.

Jaramamillo Uribe, Jaime. "Nación y región en los orígenes del estado nacional en Colombia." In *Travesías por la Historia*. Bogotá: Biblioteca Familiar Presidencia de la República, 1997, pp. 118–122.

Jiménez Bacca, Benedicto. *Inicio, desarrollo, y ocaso del terrorismo en el Perú*. Lima: Imprenta Sanki, 2000.

Kaplan, Robert. "The Coming Anarchy." *Atlantic Monthly*, February 1994, pp. 44–76.

———. *The Ends of the Earth: A Journey at the Dawn of the Twenty-First Century*. New York: Random House, 1996.

Kiel, Douglas. *Chaos Theory in the Social Sciences*. Detroit: University of Michigan Press, 1997.

Kirk, Robin. *Grabado en pierda: Las mujeres de Sendero Luminoso*. Lima: Instituto de Estudios Peruanos, 1993.

Kline, Harvey. *Colombia: Democracy under Assault*. Boulder: Westview Press, 1995.

Lao Tzu. *Tao te Ching*. New York: Penguin, 1963.

Leal Buitrago, Francisco. "Las utopías de la paz." In Francisco Leal Buitrago, ed., *Los laberintos de la guerra: Utopías e incertidumbres sobre la paz*. Bogotá: Tercer Mundo, 1999, pp. 109–170.

Machiavelli, Niccolo. *The Discourses*. New York: Penguin, 1970.

———. *The Prince*. New York: Mentor, 1980.

Manrique, Nelson. "La guerra en la region central." In Steve Stern, ed., *Los Senderos Insólitos del Perú*. Lima: Instituto de Estudios Peruanos, 1997, pp. 193–222.

Mao Tse-tung. *On Guerrilla Warfare*. 1937, reprinted from original by Maoist Documentation Project. www.maoismorg/msw/vol16/mswv6-2g.htm.

Marcella, Gabriel, and Donald Schulz. *Colombia's Three Wars: U.S. Strategy at the Crossroads*. Carlisle, Pa.: U.S. Army War College, Strategic Studies Institute, 1999.

Mariátegui, José Carlos. *Siete ensayos de interpretacion de la realidad Peruana*. Lima: Empresa Editorial Amauta, 1998.

Masterson, Daniel. "In the Shining Path of Mariátegui." *Journal of Third World Studies* 11, no. 1 (spring 1994): 154–177.

Martínez, Ifigenia. *El perfil de México en 1980*. México D.F.: Siglo XXI, 1980.

Mauceri, Philip. "Military Politics and Counter-Insurgency in Peru." *Journal of Interamerican Studies and World Affairs* 33, no. 4 (winter 1991): 83–109.

McClintock, Cynthia. *Revolutionary Movements in Latin America: El Salvador's FMLN and Peru's Shining Path*. Washington, D.C.: U.S. Institute of Peace, 1998.

Meyer, Lorenzo. *Historia de la Revolución Mexicana: 1928–1934*. México D.F.: El Colegio de México, 1995.

Montemayor, Carlos. *Chiapas: La rebelión indígena de México*. México D.F.: Editorial Joaquín Mortiz, 1998.

Moore, Barrington. *Social Origins of Dictatorship and Democracy: Lord and Peasant in the Making of the Modern World*. Boston: Beacon Press, 1966.

Morgenthau, Hans. *Politics Among Nations: The Struggle for Power and Peace*. New York: Knopf, 1960.

Movimiento Revolucionario Túpac Amaru (MRTA). "Comunicado del MRTA sobre la situación actual en Perú." January 2001 (no specific date). www. nadir.org/nadir/initiativ/mrta/ener2001.html.
———. "Comunicado 1." 17 December 1996. www.voz-rebelde.de/com1esp.htm.
———. "The Goal of the Revolutionary Strategy of the MRTA Is the Seizure of Power and the Building of Socialism." No date. http://burn.ucsd.edu/~ats/mrta/history.htm.
———. "La historia del Movimiento Revolucionario Túpac Amaru." 9 June 1990. www.nadir.org/nadir/initiative/mrta/historiamrta.htm.
———. "Las resoluciones de 1 Marzo 1982, acerca la lucha armada." 1 March 1982. www.nadir/org/nadir/initiativ/mrta/marzo1.htm.
———. "Mensaje a la nación." 19 April 2000. www.nadir.org/initiativ/mrta/mensajecer-e.htm.
———. "Neoliberalism and Globalization." No date. http://burn.ucsd.edu/~ats/mrta/neo-lib.htm.
———. "Nota de prensa." 13 March 2001. www.nadir.org/nadir/initiativ/mrta/mrtaex2.htm.
Orquist, Paul. *Violence, Conflict, and Politics in Colombia.* New York: Academic Press, 1980.
Owens, Mackubin Thomas. "Technology, the RMA, and Future War." *Strategic Review* 26, no. 2 (spring 1998): 63–70.
Owens, R. J. *Peru.* London: Oxford University Press, 1963.
Paz, Octavio. *The Labyrinth of Solitude.* New York: Grove Press, 1985.
Pearce, Jenny. *Colombia: Inside the Labyrinth.* London: Latin American Bureau.
Pécaut, Daniel. "Presente, pasado, y futuro de la violencia en Colombia." *Desarrollo Económico* 36, no. 144 (January–March 1997): 891–930.
Peñarada, Ricardo. "De rebeldes a cuidadanos: El caso del Movimiento Arado Quintín Lame." In Ricardo Peñaranda and Javier Guerrero, eds., *De las armas a la política.* Bogotá: Tercer Mundo, 1999, pp. 75–132.
Peñarada, Ricardo, and Javier Guerrero, eds. *De las armas a la política.* Bogotá: Tercer Mundo, 1999.
Pérez Martínez, Manuel. "Ejército de Liberación Nacional: El ELN que y he vivido." In Carlos Medina Gallego, *ELN: Una historia contada a dos voces.* Bogotá: Rodríguez Quito Editores, 1996, pp. 169–242.
Pizarro Leongómez, Eduardo. *Insurgencia sin revolución: La guerrilla en Colombia en una perspectiva comarada.* Bogotá: Tercer Mundo, 1996.
———. *Las FARC (1949–1966): De la autodefensa a la combinación de todas formas de lucha.* Bogotá: Tercer Mundo, 1991.
Ramírez Tobón, William. "Violencia, guerra civil, contrato social." In *Colombia: Cambio de siglo—Balances y perspectivas.* Bogotá: Planeta, 2000, pp. 21–68.
Rangel Suárez, Alfredo. *Colombia: Guerra en el fin de siglo.* Bogotá: Tercer Mundo, 1998.
Reyes, Eugenia, and Alvaro F. López. "Historia de la política agraria en Chiapas." *El Cotidiano* no. 62 (May–June 1994).
Reyna, Carlos, and Eduardo Toche. *La inseguridad en el Perú: Indices y interpretaciones para los '90.* Lima: DESCO, 1999.

Richani, Nazih. *Systems of Violence: The Political Economy of War and Peace in Colombia.* New York: State University of New York Press, 2002.

Roberts, Kenneth, and Moises Arce. "Neoliberalism and Lower-Class Voting Behavior in Peru." *Comparative Political Studies* 31, no. 2 (April 1998): 217–247.

Rochlin, James. "Canada, Narcotrafficking, and Streams of Power." *Canadian Foreign Policy* 7, no. 1 (fall 1999): 109–146.

———. *Discovering the Americas: The Evolution of Canadian Foreign Policy Towards Latin America.* Vancouver: UBC Press, 1994.

———. *Redefining Mexican Security: Society, State, and Region Under NAFTA.* Boulder: Lynne Rienner, 1997.

Rodríguez Bautista, Nicolás. "Ejército de Liberación Nacional: Una historia de vida." In Carlos Medina Gallego, ed., *ELN: Una historia contada a dos voces.* Bogotá: Rodríguez Quito Editores, 1996, pp. 27—168.

Romero, Mauricio. "Élites regionales, identidades, y paramilitares en el Sinú." In Ricardo Peñarada and Javier Guerrero, eds., *De las armas a la Política.* Bogotá: Tercer Mundo, 1999, pp. 175–218.

Ronfeldt, David, John Arquilla, Graham Fuller, and Melissa Fuller. *The Zapatista Social Netwar in Mexico.* Washington, D.C.: RAND, 1998.

Rosenzweig, Fernando. *El desarrollo económico de México, 1800–1910.* Toluca: El Colegio Mexiquense, 1989.

Ruelle, David. *Chance and Chaos.* Princeton: Princeton University Press, 1993.

Sarmiento Anzola, Libardo. "Debacle del Estado Social" In Luis Restrepo Moreno, ed., *Síntesis 2000: Anuario social, político y económico de Colombia.* Bogotá: Instituto de Estudios Políticos y Relaciónes Internacionales, Universidad Nacional de Colombia, 2000, pp. 27–39.

Schulz, Donald, and Edward Williams, eds. *Mexico Faces the Twenty-First Century.* Westport: Praeger, 1995.

Sendero Luminoso. "Construir la conquista del poder." 1991 (no specific date). www.blythe.org/peru-pcp/docs_sp/iipleno.htm.

———. "Contra la dictadura genocida." March 1995 (no specific date). www. bythe.org/peru-pcp/docs_sp/contrala.htm.

———. "Desarrollar la guerra de guerrillas sirviendo la revolución mundial." 1981 (no specific date). www.blythe.org/peru-pcp/docs_sp/desarrolla.htm.

———. "Desarrollemos la creciente protesta popular." September 1979 (no specific date). www.blythe.org/peru-pcp/docs_sp/protesta.htm.

———. "Documentos fundamentales y programa." 1998 (no specific date). www.blythe.org/peru-pcp/docs_sp/docfund.htm.

———. "En conmemoracion del 40 aniversario de la Revolución China." 30 September 1989. www.blythe.org/peru-pcp/docs_sp/40ani-sp.htm.

———. "Entrevista al Presidente Gonzalo." July 1988 (no specific date). www.blythe.org/peru-pcp/docs_sp/entrevis.htm.

———. "Historic Speech from the Dungeons of the Enemy: Speech from the Tiger Cage." Abimael Guzmán. 24 September 1992. www.blythe.org/peru-pcp/docs_en/speechf.htm.

————. "Instructions." June 1994 (no specific date). www.bythe.org/peru-pcp/docs_en.instuct.htm.

————. "Las citas del Presidente Mao." No date. www.bythe.org/peru-pcp/docs_sp/m-citas.htm.

————. "Línea internacional del PCP." No date. www.blythe.org/peru-pcp/docs_sp/linint.htm.

————. "Línea masas." No date. www.bythe.org/peru-pcp/docs_sp/linmasa.htm.

————. "Línea militar." 1988 (no specific date). www.blythe.org/peru-pcp/docs_sp/linmil.htm.

————. "No votar: Sino generalizar la guerra de guerrillas para conquistar al poder." February 1985 (no specific date). www.blythe.org/peru-pcp/docs_sp/votar.htm.

————. "Para entender Mariátegui." 1969 (no specific date). www.blythe.org/peru-pcp/docs_sp/mariat2.htm.

————. "Plan of Strategic Development." 1990 (no specific date). www.blythe.org/peru-pcp/docs_en/elec4.htm.

————. "Por la nueva bandera." 28 March 1980. www.bythe.org/peru-pcp/docs—sp/lanb.htm.

————. "Preparar la ofensiva estrategica traves de construir la conquista del poder." January 1995 (no specific date). www.bythe.org/peru-cpc/docs_sp/ofensiva.htm.

————. "Retomemos a Mariátegui y reconstituyamos su partido." October 1975 (no specific date). www.blythe.org/peru-pcp/docs_sp/mariat2.htm.

————. "Sobre la campaña de rectificación con elecciones no, guerra popular, si!" August 1991 (no specific date). www.blythe.org/peru-pcp/docs_sp.rect/htm.

————. "Sobre la construcción del partido." August 1976 (no specific date) www.bythe.org/peru-pcp/docs_sp/partido.htm.

————. "Sobre la dos colinas." 1991 (no specific date). www.bythe.org/peru-pcp/docs_sp/partido.htm.

————. "Somos los iniciadores." 19 April 1980. www.blythe.org/peru-pcp/docs_sp/iniciad.htm.

————. "III pleno del Comité Central." March 1992 (no specific date). www.bythe.org/peru-pcp/docs_sp/third-p.htm.

————. "Unir al puelbo conta la dictaduria fascista." February 1998 (no specific date). www.bythe.org/peru-pcp/docs_sp/unir-p.htm.

Skocpol, Theda. *States and Revolutions*. New York: Cambridge University Press, 1979.

Starn, Orin. "Sendero inesperados: Las rondas campesinas de la Sierra Sur Central." In Steve Stern, ed., *Los senderos insólitos del Perú*. Lima: Instituto de Estudios Peruanos, 1997, pp. 223–256.

Stein, George. "Information Warfare." In Alan Campen, ed., *Cyberwar: Security, Strategy, and Conflict in the Information Age*. Fairfax, Va.: Armed Forces Communications and Electronics Association, 1966, pp. 175–184.

Stepan, Alfred. *The State and Society: Peru in Comparative Perspective*. Princeton: Princeton University Press, 1978.

Stern, Steve, ed. *Los Sendero insólitos del Perú*. Lima: Instituto de Estudios Peruanos, 1997.

Sun Tzu. *The Art of War*. Boston: Shambhala, 1988.

Sun Tzu II. *The Lost Art of War*. San Francisco: HarperCollins, 1996.

Szafranski, Richard. "A Theory of Information Warfare: Preparing for 2020." *Airpower Journal* 9, no. 1 (spring 1995): 56–65.

Tannenbaum, Frank. *Peace by Revolution*. New York: Columbia University Press, 1933.

Tapia, Carlos. *Las fuerzas armadas y Sendero Luminoso: Dos estrategias y un final*. Lima: Instituto de Estudios Peruanos, 1997.

Teichman, Judith. *Privatization and Political Change in Mexico*. Pittsburgh: University of Pittsburgh Press, 1995.

Tello Díaz, Carlos. *La rebelión de las Cañadas*. México D.F.: Cal y Arena, 1999.

Tilly, Charles. "War Making and State Making as Organized Crime." In Peter Evans, ed., *Bringing the State Back In*. Cambridge: Cambridge University Press, 1985.

Toffler, Alvin, and Heidi Toffler. *War and Anti-War: Survival at the Dawn of the Twenty-First Century*. New York: Little, Brown, 1993.

Thucydides. *A History of the Peloponnesian War: A Comprehensive Guide to the Peloponnesian War*. Edited by Robert Strassler. New York: Free Press, 1996.

U.S. Department of Defense. *C^4, Intelligence, Surveillance, and Reconnaissance* (Washington, D.C.: U.S. Department of Defense, 1996). www.dtic.mil/execsec/adr96/chapt_27.html.

Vanden, Harry. *National Marxism in Latin America: José Carlos Mariátegui's Thought and Politics*. Boulder: Lynne Rienner, 1986.

Vargas Llosa, Mario. *The Storyteller*. New York: Penguin, 1990.

Vargas Meza, Ricardo. *Fumigación y conflicto: Políticas antidrogas y delegitimación del Estado en Colombia*. Bogotá: Tercer Mundo, 1999.

Vásquez, G. L. "Peruvian Radicalism and the Sendero Luminoso." *Journal of Political and Military Sociology* 21, no. 2 (winter 1993): 197–217.

Virilio, Paul. *Speed and Politics*. New York: Semiotexte, 1977.

Virilio, Paul, and Sylvere Lotringer. *Pure War*. New York: Semiotexte, 1997.

Walker, R. B. J. *Inside/Outside: International Relations as Political Theory*. New York: Cambridge University Press, 1993.

Wickham-Crowley, Timothy. *Guerrillas and Revolutions in Latin America*. Princeton: Princeton University Press, 1992.

Wise, Carol. "State Policy and Social Conflict in Peru." In Maxwell Cameron and Philip Mauceri, eds., *The Peruvian Labyrinth: Polity, Society, Economy*. University Park: Pennsylvania State University Press, 1997, pp. 70–103.

Weber, Max. *Economía y sociedad*. Vol. 2. México D.F.: Fondo de Cultura Económica, 1977.

Womack, John. *Zapata y la Revolución Mexicana*. México D.F.: Siglo Veintiuno Editores, 1999.

World Bank. *Distribution of Income and Consumption*. 2001. www.worldbank.org/data/wdi2001/pdfs/tab2_8.pdf.

Wright, Ronald. *Stolen Continents: The New World Through Indian Eyes Since 1492*. New York: Viking, 1992.

Wriston, Walter. "The Twilight of Sovereignty." *Fletcher Forum* (summer 1993): 117–130.

Zuluaga Nieto, Jaime. "De guerrillas a movimientos políticos," In Ricardo Peñarada and Javier Guerrero, eds., *De las armas a la política*. Bogotá: Tercer Mundo, 1999, pp. 1–74.

Index

About the Book

During the swan song of the Soviet Union and the immediate aftermath of the Cold War, many insurgent groups that had been dependent on Moscow or Havana quickly faded into political oblivion. But some existing groups, as well as emerging ones, flourished within a new and uncharted political constellation. This comparative study probes the origins and effects of Latin America's most potent insurgent movements—in Peru, Colombia, and Mexico—some of which are thriving now in large part by exploiting the revolution in military affairs.

Rochlin considers the intriguing question of what makes a successful revolutionary movement at the start of the twenty-first century. Addressing the commonalities and distinctions among four subversive groups, he focuses on domestic and international context, support base, ideology, strategy, and prospects for power. Rochlin also explores the roots, metamorphoses, and prognoses of the conflicts. His in-depth discussion of these powerful rebel groups emphasizes the ways in which they are successfully rethinking the meaning of politics, revolutionary activity, and strategy in a new era.

James F. Rochlin is professor of political science at Okanagan University College in Canada. He is the author of *Redefining Mexican Security: Society, State, and Region Under NAFTA* (1997) and *Discovering the Americas: The Evolution of Canadian Foreign Policy Towards Latin America* (1994).